Acknowledgments

Believe it or not, this book was born on a bench in the Moscone Center in San Francisco. Bob Elliott, the acquisition editor for this book, struck up a conversation with me after a talk I gave at the Software Development West Conference. Bob and I shared the same vision of a book that not only defines high-level intranet and client/server concepts, but provides real-world experience in employing those concepts to build real systems, with real budgets, using real technology and tools. In other words, a book that tells it like it is. I would also like to thank Brian Calandra, Bob's assistant, for patiently gathering up the content, and for being there to answer questions.

Others who deserve a mention here include my wife, who did a lot of the busy work, and was patient with me as my weekends turned into marathon writing sessions. Chris VanBuren, my agent, for working this deal. Maurice Frank, the editor of *DBMS* Magazine, who provided the content for the vendor list that appears in Appendix A, and who was forgiving as a few of my column deadlines slipped. Spanky the wonder retriever, who kept my feet warm as I typed away at this book in my cold basement. Finally I would like to thank AT&T Solutions for sharing the vision of this book with me.

To my lovely wife Celeste, and the Panda.
Thanks for everything.

Contents

Reader's Guide to the Book

The writer, Washington Irving, once said, *"There is a certain relief in change . . ."*

Those words were never truer as today's organizations speed away from the simplistic world of centralized "big iron" information technology to the open but complex environment of client/server computing. The prize is innovative client/server systems that are smaller, cheaper, faster, and more productive for end-users.

Client/server, at its core, provides the ultimate freedom of mix-and-match software components at the client, server, and all points in between. There is, however, a price we must pay for such freedom, and that price is added complexity. Client/server developers must understand the basic as well as the advanced concepts of client/server computing to maximize its benefit. This is no easy task. In this book, I'll provide you with the majority of the information you'll need to become a more successful client/server developer or architect. Read on, and let me show you the way.

The Revolution

The revolution that is client/server application development changes the way we approach systems development. Rather than integrate applications and data on large centralized processors, we now take the 'divide and conquer' approach to meet our information technology requirements.

The signs of the times are all around us. Mini- and mainframe computers, once a stable entity in business application development, are now large, costly monstrosities that are only useful for processing legacy applications (or heating a room). Today we don't buy newer and faster central processors to support a larger user load, we learn to scale through distribution. We lubricate that distribution with hundreds of new wonder tools and middleware layers that handle the complexities of diverse operating systems, GUIs, and networks for us.

As we move toward the end of the 1990s, the client/server revolution is more important than ever. Today client/server developers take on enterprise class systems with thousands of users. Client/server developers also continue to leverage the power of the Internet and intranets to further extend the power of client/server development technology to the World Wide Web.

Reinventing Application Development

As we move toward client/server application development, we reinvent application development and application developers in the process. Structured development techniques refined in the '80s are now being replaced by the more efficient object-oriented development paradigm. Where once we learned how to implement network protocol-level APIs into applications, we now rely on higher-level middleware layers that handle network and operating system differences for us. The new line of visual development environments allows developers to paint applications rather than program them, and that relegates the raw code in text editors to the history books.

The requirements of client/server created a whole new type of developer. Where once COBOL was a valued skill, C++, Delphi, and PowerBuilder now take the spotlight in Sunday's want ads. Database administration requires specialized skills in a particular database technology such as Oracle, Sybase, or Informix—no two are alike. Moreover, the emphasis on application design and development in the world of client/server begins with the architecture. The application is no longer the single point of failure.

Client/server developers must also live in a world of constant change and technology du jour. In just the past few years, client/server development moved from the simple two-tier model (client applications communicating with a single database server), to the more complex but scaleable three-tier and multitier client/server architectures, using many distributed processors and intelligent middleware layers. As the approach to client/server architectures changes so rapidly, so do the tools. Keeping up with an industry such as this is a job in and of itself. Reading this book is a step in the right direction.

The Second Revolution

There is a second client/server revolution underway. The revolution is the World Wide Web, and the client/server-ready "mini Webs" that operate within corporate firewalls known as intranets. *I think this is the single most significant change in the way we are building client/server systems, and it's important that client/server developers learn how to leverage the power of Web-enabled technology.*

The intranet allows developers to do what we've been doing with client/server for years, but now we can use popular off-the-shelf Web technology. In many respects, the Web is just a new platform that client/server developers need to support.

The allure of the intranet is its ability to integrate client/server applications from within a Web browser. End-users simply link to a Web server to invoke a client/server application, rather than load a complex array of protocol stacks, interpreters, and middleware layers for each application that often don't work and play well with others. In addition, the intranet is naturally multi-platform. Build an application for the Web, and it runs everywhere by default. This architecture also brings client/server back into centralized control, and best of all it's cheaper to deploy and support than client/server for large organizations.

New innovations such as Sun's Java, Microsoft's ActiveX, and native Web server APIs make dynamic application development for the Web (in both its Internet and intranet incarnations) a reality. An array of tools that support these technologies is already available to client/server developers.

Clearly, the intranet and client/server development are joined at the hip. Most client/server tools are migrating quickly to the Web-enabled world, including the industry leaders such as Powersoft's PowerBuilder, Borland's Delphi, and Microsoft's Visual Basic. This trend will continue, and it's why the proper use of the intranet as enabling technology and a platform is a consistent theme throughout this book.

Why I Wrote This Book

I wrote this book after searching for a book like it. There are books that cover enabling technologies of client/server, but none provide information about how to make those technologies work together to build real-life client/server applications. I could find books on application development, but many focused on a particular tool (e.g., PowerBuilder, Delphi, C++), and none covered architecture or enabling technology in enough detail.

This book provides information that you won't find in any other client/server book. Rather than present client/server concepts, terms, and technology in a hodgepodge of conceptual information, this book provides relevant technical information, and shows the reader how to use the information to build a sound system architecture and a solid client/server application. The book is full of practical application examples of this technology, and presents case studies where applicable.

For the past seven years, I've been writing about client/server technology for major technical magazines. In that time, I worked with over a hundred client/server vendors, wrote dozens of client/server tool and technology reviews, spoke at many conferences, and at the same time, built an array of client/server applications as a developer, architect, project manager, and now as a consultant. Sometimes things went right. Sometimes things went wrong. I would like to share those experiences with you.

What This Book Covers

This book teaches the reader how to build a client/server system from its foundation, using an easy-to-follow, step-by-step procedure. The book not only teaches you how to use the technology correctly, but presents practical information such as how to estimate project costs, pick the most cost-effective software and hardware solution, as well as what to do when things go wrong.

Client/server is an ongoing revolution of new technology and new approaches to build and downsize business systems. Despite the hype, many system designers and developers find that developing client/server systems that meet their business requirements and fall within budget is a daunting task. In many organizations, failed client/server design and development efforts outnumber successes.

Within these pages, we will take the mystery out of client/server design and development by revealing secret tactics that top client/server architects use when they design and build client/server systems. The book, which is written in easy-to-understand layman's language, describes how the reader can apply state-of-the art tools and techniques to solve real-life business problems, with illustrations wherever possible to help you understand complex points.

Who Should Read This Book

The reader I had in mind as I wrote this book is an experienced client/server developer or architect—someone who already knows the basics. These readers will discover new ideas and strategies within these pages and learn new ways to deploy this technology. Those of you who are less technical (e.g., information technology managers) should also find this book a useful guide to the fast-growing client/server world.

Experienced client/server developers will find that this book provides all the missing details that pertain to construction of client/server architecture beyond the bounds of application development environments, such as server sizing, multitier client/server architectures, and infrastructure design. In addition, the book covers the many client/server tools that are available today, which should be especially useful to developers who are looking for better ways to build and manage client/server applications.

Client/server architects will find that the step-by-step design information will guide them through the successful design and deployment of client/server systems. The "Finding the Right Tools" section is invaluable for those who must select critical development tools required to build client/server applications.

Finally, traditional client/server developers will find detailed information in this book about how to move to the intranet. I'll not only provide an overview of enabling technologies such as ActiveX, Java, CGI, NSAPI, and ISAPI, but I'll tell you what tools work best for intranet development today.

How This Book Is Organized

The book contains five sections; *Client/Server Building Blocks, Designing Client/Server Solutions, Finding the Right Tools, Creating the Right Client/Server Architecture,* and *Implementing the Solutions.*

Client/Server Building Blocks (Chapters 1 through 3) cover the basic elements common to all client/server architectures, including the roles of the client, server, and network. After reading this section, you'll be ready to tackle the more advanced techniques and tools covered in the rest of this book—where you'll put the concepts you've learned in this section into practice. (Experienced client/server developers can safely choose to skim or skip these chapters.) *Designing Client/Server Solutions* (Chapters 4 through 7) describes the elements of good client/server system design—from architecture to application. Chapters 4 and 5 introduce database and middleware technologies and tools. In addition, I cover two-tier, three-tier, and multitier architectures and related development models. Chapters 6 and 7 describe the key technologies and tools for designing and building object-oriented client/server systems.

The *Finding the Right Tools* section (Chapters 8 through 15) provides detailed information on a variety of client/server development tools, and shows how to select the right tool for your client/server project. Each chapter tackles a category of tools, explaining the advantages and tradeoffs of each, and uses available products as examples. This section covers such areas as repository-driven development, programming languages, database connectivity, and specific middleware tools. By the end of this section, you'll be able to identify the right tool for the job at hand as well as evaluate its strengths and limitations.

Creating the Right Client/Server Architecture (Chapters 16 through 20) covers the complex world of three-tier and multitier architectures that allow you to scale applications to the enterprise. I cover the latest in distributed objects, TP monitors, application-partitioning, and the tools that support these technologies. I'll let you in on the secrets of creating a client/server architecture that's right for your project.

For example, I'll explore database funneling and show how to use TP monitors as a middle-tier solution for application transaction processing. In addition, I'll show how to get the most from using distributed objects, including the use of CORBA-compliant object request brokers (ORBs) such as SOM/DSOM, as well as the inner workings of Microsoft's Component Object Model (COM) and how it fits into the Distributed Component Object Mocel (DCOM). Finally, this section covers the new breed of application partitioning tools such as Forte and Dynasty, that provide process distribution capabilities with drag-and-drop simplicity. When finished with this section, you'll have a working knowledge of advanced client/server architectures, enabling technologies, and tools.

Implementing the Solution (Chapters 21 through 24) shows the client/server developer how to tie all the pieces together to create the final system, as well as how to test the system to assure reliability and performance. I'll also show you how you can bring client/server applications to your company's intranet. The book wraps things up with a discussion of the future of client/server development and where to place your bets in the near future.

Aside from standard text and figures, you will find additional helpful sources of information in the book. For example, when I begin discussion of intranet issues related to the main discussion of client/server development, you'll see this:

The Intranet

The intranet is the concept of using Web-enabled technology within organizations.

In addition, from time to time in the chapters, I'll provide tips and recommendations using this format:

Recommedation [sic]

When using ODBC, make sure you test the performance and efficiency of your database drivers. Poorly written ODBC drivers often cause performance problems for two-tier client/server computing.

When I have information that I think you'll find useful, you'll see:

Information

There has been a movement afoot to retrofit existing relational databases to handle objects, as well as the migration to intranets. These hybrid databases are known as universal databases.

Finally, when relevant, I'll provide you with short case studies to support the concepts discussed in the chapters. They'll look like this:

The ABC Warehouse Management System

The ABC company needed a computer system to manage inventory in their warehouse . . .

At the end of the book, I'll provide a list of references where you can obtain additional information on the topics covered.

Enjoy my book,

David S. Linthicum

I

Client/Server
Building Blocks

Driving
Forces

What drives client/server computing is the fundamental belief that personal computers (PCs) connected to small servers provide the best price/performance. In other words, we can do more with less, and thus bring computing power that was once out of reach to those who need it.

As an example, I've built countless systems for small businesses that simply could not afford mainframe time, or minicomputers to automate their critical activities. For them, client/server is a liberating process that allows them to leverage their existing equipment and interfaces, and provides them with the processing power they need to keep up with their larger competitors.

Large businesses find that the client/server paradigm offers more "bang for the buck" than their existing centralized systems. Most of the Fortune 500 are moving quickly to smaller distributed systems, which they can adapt more precisely to their processing and user requirements.

Client/server uses many smaller systems. Client/server applications, if built right, can provide the processing power of larger systems by distributing the processing load among PCs and servers. Each component of a client/server system takes on a portion of the processing load, and constantly coordinates with other related processes on the same network, sometimes across the Internet. Using client/server and other distributed-processing paradigms, the idea is to increase processing capacity through process distribution, rather than increasing the size of the central processor.

The Intranet Movement

The intranet movement is an extension of traditional client/server development, which provides many of the same benefits as well as several new ones.

The intranet movement grew out of the popularity and hype that surrounds the Internet and the Web. As developers learned how to deploy Web applications for use by many strangers, a few learned how to leverage the same technology for internal Web-based applications. Web technology is easy to use, widely available, inherently multi-platform, and the most attractive feature is that it's inexpensive. Developers are just beginning to understand the potential of the intranet as a new application development platform, but in just a few months, we've gone very far.

The Future of Intranets

The future of the intranet is bright. A study from Zona Research, Inc., states that the intranet will enjoy more growth by the year 2000 than commercial applications deployed over the Internet. And that means Web technology will find a larger market share within the firewalls. Zona asserts that corporate users are better able to leverage the power of Web technology, and have the most to gain from its internal use as a multi-platform information dissemination and application deployment vehicle. Other research organizations agree with Zona. IDC contends that the future demand for intranet applications will be five times that of traditional Internet applications by the year 2001.

What technical capabilities make the intranet the new client/server platform of choice? There are many.

First, intranet architecture allows end-users to run applications inside the familiar environment of the Web browser. The hyperlinking point-and-click interface for the Web provides users with an intuitive way to navigate through applications and locate the information they need using a common look-and-feel. This means that users don't have to use multiple interfaces, and the learning curve is virtually nonexistent.

Moreover, application integration happens inside the Web browsers, and not within the native operating systems of the clients. Web browsers provide common access to all internal resources and applications, as well as external Internet-based resources. Therefore, we can not only run Web-based applications within the organization, but also applications that exist on remote Web sites.

Using enabling technologies such as Sun's Java and Microsoft's ActiveX, users can download and invoke sophisticated dynamic applications simply by clicking on an icon. These dynamic applications have the capability to link back to external resources such as real-time information, database servers, or queues through standard connectivity application programming interfaces (APIs) such as the forthcoming Java Database Connectivity (JDBC).

With new Web browsers such as Microsoft's Explorer, which is free for the asking, users have the ability to run intranet applications built for use with Java or ActiveX. Netscape supports Java, along with many other types of applications, through its open plug-in interface. This interface allows nonstandard Web-enabled applications to execute inside their Navigator browser.

Another significant advantage is the Web-based technology's ability to run on a hodgepodge of operating systems and processors, to support the same communications standards and infrastructure, as well as the interface. The intranet uses "open" standards such as TCP/IP, HTTP, HTML, CGI, and Java. Organizations are not locked into proprietary middleware layers that come at a price, such as message-oriented middleware (MOM) or DCE.

However, the intranet is still not for every application. The file-oriented characteristics of the intranet can cause performance problems in high-volume transaction-oriented applications. As many as two hundred users may request the same HTML file at the same time, or invoke the same CGI process. Of course, we can solve some of these performance problems with tricks like higher-end multi-processing Web servers. Java and ActiveX use a "download once, run many times" (DORMAT) procedure that will disconnect the user from the performance limitations of the Web server. Unfortunately, true mission-critical applications that use Java or ActiveX are slow to appear. Those who use the intranet for "must run" applications should proceed with caution.

Benefits of Client/Server

There are several reasons why so many continue to migrate toward client/ server. They include speed of development, the allure of the GUI, and empowerment of the end-user.

Client/server development and rapid application development (RAD) are joined at the hip. Popular client/server development tools including Powersoft's PowerBuilder, Borland's Delphi, and Microsoft's Visual Basic provide developers with the ability to create applications much more quickly than when using traditional programming languages and compilers. Developers can build simple applications in a single day as the end-user looks on. Application generators, well-populated object libraries, and interface painters are the technologies that drive RAD.

These tools allow developers to paint applications by selecting prebuilt GUI controls from palettes, and integrating the controls to create the final application. Developers define the behavior of the application by setting properties and other repository attributes. If any code is required, it's usually an easy-to-use fourth-generation language (4GL), or a script.

The GUI movement, set in full motion by the popularity of Windows, drives the client/server movement as well. Client/server applications, by their nature, leverage the ease of use and consistency that most users seek in applications. Today, non-GUI applications are almost impossible to deliver to end-users. Users are more comfortable and productive with applications that look similar and work together with other productivity applications such as word processors, spreadsheets, and Web browsers.

Finally, there is a human aspect to client/server development in that client/server is an empowering technology. In the world of client/server applications, data exists on smaller, more accessible systems. In past years, data was locked inside large, intimidating machines, and thus information was difficult to obtain for specific purposes. Today, users can move vital information from client/server applications directly into spreadsheets or other analytical tools for whatever need they may have. Client/server opens up a whole new data-accessible world for the end-user.

What's Client/Server?

The term "client/server" is such an overused buzz-word that it's difficult for developers to understand what it really means in terms of application development. For the purposes of this book, let's use the universal definition of client/server and put architectures aside for now. By the way, this is only intro-ductory information about client/server for those who may be unfamiliar with or just starting to use the technology, or for those of you who may want to refresh your knowledge of the basics. We'll go into greater detail in subsequent chapters.

Client/server is not a way of using tools or a database, it's a computing model that's been in use for some time. Client/server in its simplest form allows developers to split the processing load between two logical processes: the client and the server. Although both the client and the server may exist on the same physical computer (e.g., local database servers that run native to Windows and come with many client/server development tools), most of the client/server sys-tems run the client process on one computer and the server process on another. A network connection between the client and the server allows the client and the server to exchange information as required by the application (see Figure 1-1). Each process functions independently from the other, performing specialized tasks for the application.

Okay, now that we know basically what a client and a server are, what do they look like? Usually, a client is a desktop computer running some sort of front-end software. Front-end software is any software that can send a request to the server (e.g., a database server) and process the information as it returns from the server. The server receives and processes a request on behalf of the client, returning only the information the client requests, or performing a par-ticular operation.

To make this a bit clearer, let's look at an example of a typical client/server system, say a front-end application built using PowerBuilder for the client's ap-plication and Oracle as the database server. Through the use of middleware (discussed later in this chapter), the PowerBuilder application knows how to communicate with the Oracle server. The client PowerBuilder application sends a database request to the Oracle database server in the form of an SQL (struc-tured query language) statement that translates the request into a dialect the Ora-

Figure 1-1 *Basic client/server architecture.*

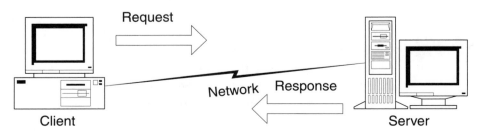

cle database server can understand. The Oracle database server sends only the requested data back to the client, processing the database request independent of client processing. This cooperative relationship between the client and the server, in this case, a PowerBuilder application and an Oracle database server, allows the system to maximize performance by sharing the processing load.

Components of Client/Server

As you can see from this explanation of client/server, there are three basic components of client/server: the front-end software, middleware, and the server software. Front-end software includes any application development tool such as PowerBuilder, Delphi, or Visual Basic, as well as reporting tools, spreadsheets, or even word processors (e.g., Microsoft Word connected to a database server using ODBC). Front-end software can assemble and send requests to servers, and then receive and process the information on behalf of the user.

Using our PowerBuilder application as the example again, the application accepts information from the user, such as information the application may need to search a database for a particular customer name. Using that information, the front-end application assembles a database request and submits it to the remote database server for processing. After processing the request, which usually takes just a few seconds, the database server returns only the requested information to the front-end application. The front-end application processes the information, displaying it for the user in a proper and attractive format (see Figure 1-2).

Front-end application development tools (PowerBuilder, Delphi, Visual Basic, etc.) dominate the client/server development market. These tools facilitate RAD, which, simply put, allows developers to create user interfaces by painting screens using prebuilt GUI controls. The utilization of the object-oriented development model as well as the ability to "snap in" custom controls (e.g., OpenDoc, ActiveX, and Java applets) allow developers to reuse existing code. These tools also provide business graphic capabilities and limited report generators. Of course, these tools also provide built-in database connections to popular databases such as Oracle, Sybase, or Informix.

Reporting tools are functionally equivalent to front-end application development tools in that they provide built-in database connectivity, as well as the ability to send requests to the database and process the returning information. However, reporting tools are more for creating ad hoc reports and graphs than they are for creating applications (although developers can incorporate

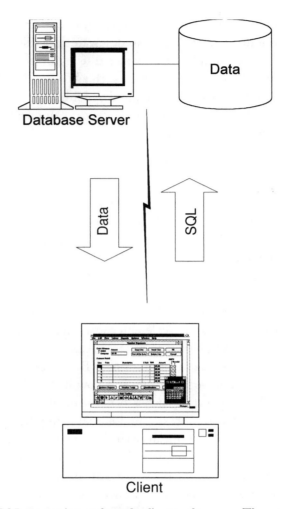

Figure 1-2 *An SQL request is sent from the client to the server. The server responds with only the information requested. The front-end application formats the information for presentation to the end-user.*

reports using reporting tools inside front-end applications). For you managers out there, these reporting tools mean easy access to corporate information using a new type of Decision Support System (DSS) technology known as on-line analytical processing (OLAP), discussed later in this book.

Middleware is a common communications mechanism that exists between the client and the server to provide navigation through the GUI, operating systems, network, and native database layers. Many call middleware the "/" in client/server. For the purposes of this book, it's the software that resides between the front-end application and the server. There are many flavors of middleware, including middleware that exists only for database access, such as ODBC; middleware managed using object request brokers (ORBs); middleware that handles security, such as DCE (distributed computing environment); intelligent middleware; and synchronous and asynchronous general purpose middleware layers for many types of applications such as RPCs and message-oriented middleware.

Complex Client/Server

Traditional client/server systems use two-tier architectures, since there is only a client and a server. There are other more complex architectures, such as three-tier and multi-tier (sometimes called *n*-tier). These new models provide better scalability and performance, but do so at the price of complexity and development costs.

The two-tier client/server systems are easy to conceive and build. However, they can't readily scale enterprise-level applications. The problem is that database servers, without assistance, can't support thousands of simultaneous clients. Each client can take from 64 KB to over 2 MB of memory, depending on the database server software, and how it's configured to handle client connections. When supporting such a load, the database server's operating system runs out of memory and processor resources, forcing the operating system to thrash.

Thrashing means that the operating system does not have enough physical memory to support the number of connected clients. The crashing of the system is usually the end result of such torture. To support large processing loads without crashing the servers, client/server developers employ three-tier or multi-tier client/server architectures. With three-tier architectures, the developer places another tier, or application server, between the client and the database server (see Figure 1-3). The application server handles most of the application processing, such as business logic processing and database integrity processing. The client only handles the interface processing, and the database server only handles the database processing. Application servers usually run TP monitor software, such as Tuxedo or Encina, or they can run distributed objects such as ORBs. Each technology has its strengths and weaknesses, which we'll look at in greater detail later.

The biggest benefit that developers derive from the use of a center-tier application server is its ability to funnel database requests. In other words, the application server can service thousands of clients using only a handful of data-

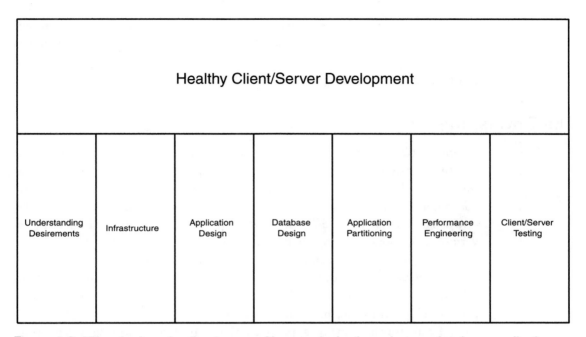

Figure 1-3 *Using the three-tier client/server architecture, the developer places another tier, or application server, between the client and the database server.*

base connections. With this model, the developers have more elbow room as to the number of clients they can support. However, developers must build three-tier client/server applications using a variety of programming languages and specialized tools. Thus development costs increase and the complexity level goes up.

The multi-tier client/server architecture works very much like the three-tier client/server architecture, although you may use as many application servers and processes as you need. The large majority of multi-tier client/server systems are built using application-partitioning tools (such as Forte or Dynasty) or through the use of distributed-object technology. These tools provide the developer with the ability to define logical objects on a single workstation, and then distribute the objects for execution on any number of servers. Developers can repartition multi-tiered applications at any time to enhance performance, or better organize the application processing.

Also, like three-tiered client/server, the multi-tiered client/server architecture can funnel database requests and provide transaction processing capabilities to support enterprise-level applications. In addition, since the partitioning is a dynamic process, developers may change partitioning schemes at any time to provide the best performance. Traditional client/server and three-tier client/server require that you commit to the application partitioning design before you write the code to support it, since many of the partitions are written in different languages.

The Downsizing Movement

There are two major forces that drive client/server; the downsizing movement and the upsizing movement. The downsizing movement refers to the process of moving applications from larger and more expensive mini- and mainframe computer systems to the more economical client/server platform. At its core, downsizing splits applications into two or more partitions that can execute on various processors (e.g., the client and the server).

What drives downsizing in most organizations is cost. Client/server systems are cheaper to build, deploy, and maintain—that is, if they are done right. Client/server can beat any mainframe application in hardware and software cost, development time, and user satisfaction.

There are three major approaches to downsizing: rehosting, wrappering, and new application development. Rehosting is the process of migrating a centralized mainframe application (e.g., an inventory control system) by partitioning it at least between the client and the server, and by porting it to a client/server system. The goal is to use as much of the existing code as possible on the new client/server platform. Usually, this also means re-engineering the application, providing enhancements to the base application as well as the interface.

Often it's cheaper to perform a complete rewrite of the system. In most of the rehosting projects I've been associated with, developers are just prolonging the inevitable.

Wrappering is more sophisticated than rehosting. Wrappering means that developers encapsulate portions of an existing application inside objects, and distribute those objects on various processors. Wrappering is a by-product of the object development process. It not only provides developers with a means to organize an application as autonomous, reusable units of work, but also allows them to mix and match which object resides on which processor to support the dynamic application partitioning model (discussed later in this book). Many tools such as Forté's Forté and Dynasty's Dynasty provide developers with wrappering mechanisms.

Like rehosting, there are down sides to retaining the legacy code to support client/server applications. Developers often have to rewrite large portions of the code using another language (e.g., C++) to support wrappering, and there is a point where rewriting the application using a true client/server language or tool makes better sense. Both rehosting and wrappering exist to a large extent because they are easily sold to management, who often wince at the thought of trashing code that cost them millions of dollars to develop just a few years ago.

Downsizing by developing entirely new applications with client/server is usually the best way to get to client/server. While you can reuse the code for application design purposes, and existing design documents as a base for the new applications, most of the application is created from scratch. This provides the greatest degree of flexibility for the developers since they are not constrained by having to remain true to the legacy code. New application development is generally the most cost-effective approach to client/server development (although you need to consider the specific needs of your particular application, of course), especially considering the cost of years of application maintenance, and the flexibility to easily move to new technologies (e.g., tool upgrades) as they become available. Moreover, new development provides a better opportunity for the architects, designers, and developers to meet the exact requirements of the end-users.

The Intranet Is Economical

Cost is the real reason for migration to the intranet. The intranet, and applications that run on it, are significantly less expensive for organizations to deploy. Browsers don't require much horsepower to get them running. If users can run a browser and support a network connection, they are intranet-ready. Training costs go down as well. Intranet applications offer the same look and feel. Deployment costs are virtually nonexistent since users simply link to an internal Web server to invoke an application or view information. No need to visit the workstation to load software and middleware. Typical deployment costs using the intranet can be as low as $100 per user, which includes support. Traditional client/server applications require many visits to the workstation, and with licensing fees, the cost to deploy most client/server systems can be as much as $3000 per user.

The integration issues are where traditional client/server fell down hard. Application deployment in an organization that supports multiple client/server applications is no easy task. Throw in the typical hodgepodge of platforms, and things get even more difficult. Middleware layers often don't work and play well with others. Multiple protocol stacks are usually in the mix, and today's client/server tools expect to find a Pentium 100 or better at the client to make the application at all usable. The intranet promises to put client/server back in control. The complex mass of proprietary technology that makes up the client/server application development and deployment environments, also makes client/server the most frustrating platform to deploy applications.

The intranet exploits the least common denominator approach, using the Web browser as the single point of integration that removes both developers and users from the complexity of the underlying operating system, network, and GUI. To add an application, the user simply enters the appropriate internal universal resource locator (URL), and the new application appears in front of the user in a few seconds. Java applets and ActiveX components also download as needed from the internal Web server. Bug fixes and new feature deployment happen centrally by updating content (HTML, CGI, Java applets, ActiveX components, etc.) on the internal central Web server.

The intranet can also handle multiple data types. The Web is not limited to text and graphics, and data is handled the same way by the cross-platform browser technology. Data can be video, sounds, Java applets, or any other type of object with content.

Remote access is a natural for the intranet. Road warriors will find that linking their laptops and running intranet applications remotely is functionally the same as surfing the Internet. The software and hardware that links remote PCs to the Internet may be leveraged on the intranet as well. In addition, the central characteristics of the intranet make updating content a simple matter of updating a single file.

Finally, intranet development is quick and easy. Client/server vendors have shifted their focus to the Internet and intranet, and tools and technology that deploy applications to the Web continue to hit the market fast and furious. PowerSoft, Microsoft, Borland, and Symantec have all announced intranet strategies, and some already offer products (such as Symantec's Café and Borland's JBuilder) that include rapid Java-based application development (RJAD).

The Upsizing Movement

In contrast to downsizing, upsizing is the process of upgrading single-user applications that live on PCs to multi-user client/server applications. In the

'80s, many organizations, understanding the power of the PC, chose to build applications for the PC. Tools such as dBase III and IV, as well as Clipper and Rbase 5000, drove such applications.

The limitation of single-user applications was their inability to share data with others. Thus, many of these single-user systems began to provide information sharing capabilities by using shared file servers that allow such applications to share database files. While this was a step in the right direction, there were performance, scalability, and database integrity issues with what I call a shared-database-file architecture. The performance and scalability problems result from the fact that the application must download the entire file across the network (usually in small chunks) to perform such operations as a search of the database for a customer name. The database engine resides with the application, and not with the data, as is the case using the client/server model.

Client/server computing is a natural upgrade path for such applications for many reasons. First of all, many of these applications were built with tools such as Microsoft's FoxPro, Borland's dBase IV, and Borland's Paradox that now support both Windows and client/server. Thus it's just a matter of making a few modifications to the single-user system, and migrating the database to your database server of choice. Microsoft's FoxPro, for example, has a subsystem called the "Upsizing Wizard" to walk you through just such a task.

Second, in many instances, the only additional hardware required is a server and database server software. Sometimes the database server can reside on existing file servers such as Oracle and Sybase for Novell Netware.

Finally, the existence of data in a centralized server means that the information is accessible by other applications, including reporting tools and on-line analytical processing (OLAP) tools. Therefore, the information no longer lives in isolation, nor does the application's users.

 ## Is Moving to the Intranet Upsizing or Downsizing?

Are applications that move to an intranet considered upsizing or downsizing? If an application moves from a large centralized system to the intranet, then we can safely say that we are downsizing that application. If we move an existing single-user/single-machine application to the intranet, then we are upsizing. However, if we move an existing client/server application to the intranet, we are "netsizing," or Web-enabling that application.

Should You Care About Client/Server Application Design?

Let's change gears. Now that we understand the basics of client/server, we can begin to discuss the concept of the client/server design process, its importance for application developers, and set the stage for the rest of book.

You'll find throughout this book that I stress the importance of design and architecture. This does not mean that I suggest we practice "analysis paralysis" (spending so much time on analysis and design that the real work is neglected), only that we learn to think things through before we throw a tremendous amount of resources into tools and technology to build a system. I've seen too many projects fail due to bad tool selection, lack of a sound architecture, or general lack of vision, all problems that came about due to lack of a proper client/server system design. In other words, not one failed project sweated through the details beforehand.

Although we'll get into client/server system design in greater detail later in this book, let's briefly discuss some of the basic design activities that should take place to assure a healthy client/server system (see Figure 1-3). They include:

1. Understanding the end-users' "desirements"
2. Planning the infrastructure
3. Application design
4. Database design
5. Application partitioning
6. Performance engineering
7. Client/server testing

UNDERSTANDING "DESIREMENTS"

The first step when building a client/server system is to understand the requirements of the end-user. I refer to the user requirements as 'desirements,' since it's not only the business requirements they consider, but the functionality that they desire the system to have upon delivery. In other words, desirements is the process of defining their expectations, and mapping those expectations into real technical solutions. The issue here is not the difficulty in determining the desirements, but the fact that neglecting desirements will lead to a failed client/server development project no matter how well you build the system (see Chapter 7).

INFRASTRUCTURE DESIGN

If you've ever sat in a traffic jam, or got an "all circuits busy" announcement when making a phone call, you've experienced poor infrastructure. If the infrastructure is poor for your client/server system, your users will experience similar frustration.

Most developers consider infrastructure a network that carries information from the client to the server, and back again. However, infrastructure also includes the size and speed of the processors, systems to track and resolve bugs, and available support, to name only a few additional items. Planning the proper infrastructure for your client/server system assures its success. (See Chapter 3.)

APPLICATION DESIGN

Although we live in a world where RAD plays a larger rule than the now antiquated structured analysis and design methodologies, designers and developers still need to think through the proper design of an application. Today this entails object-oriented analysis and design, and computer-aided software engineering (CASE) technology, in conjunction with functional prototypes. Developers need to put enough effort into design that the application uses the object-oriented model correctly, making maximum use of reusable code and streamlining application maintenance. (See Chapter 7.)

DATABASE DESIGN

Most client/server systems use some sort of database to store information. Designers and developers need to work through this process as well, making sure relational databases are normalized, and that object-oriented databases mesh seamlessly with the application objects. Moreover, designers and developers need to structure databases so they provide optimal performance. (I'll cover database design in Chapter 4 of this book.)

PARTITIONING POWER

At some point in the client/server application development life cycle, the developer or architect needs to determine which parts of an application will execute where. This is the process of partitioning an application between the client, the server, and sometimes to application servers. The idea is to spread the load as evenly as possible to maximize the performance of your system. However, this is done without the aid of real performance information, thus developers are forced into using performance models, hoping that no costly adjustments will need to be made after deployment. (See Chapters 16 and 20.)

PERFORMANCE ENGINEERING

Along the same lines as application partitioning, designers and developers need to consider how the client/server system will perform when deployed. Generally speaking, the performance of any client/server system is defined by its slowest component. Thus, a faulty middleware layer will detract from any performance gains you may realize from a new souped-up server. Client/server uses the throughput model to measure performance, and predicting overall system performance during the design process is a difficult task. (See Chapter 16, 20, and 22.)

Testing Considerations

Finally, developers and designers need to consider how to test the system to assure its success after deployment. You need to test all the major components of a client/server system, including interface, middleware, network, and database components by themselves. Then, test all the components working together (integration testing). Regression testing and object testing are also in the mix, as well as performance testing, and finally, user acceptance testing. (See Chapter 21.)

Right Tool for the Job

In the mix of client/server development, developers have some important decisions to make beyond design—decisions such as which tool or tools to build the system in, and which development model to use. In many projects that I've been involved with, these are emotional not technical decisions. This is where projects begin to take on weight. Like taking on too much weight in a boat, too many bad decisions can sink a project.

For example, I've seen many a tool selection decision made because the MIS director's son uses it at college, or the vendor came into the company and did a very impressive RAD demonstration (usually by just assembling objects already predefined within the tool). By not using a technical tool selection process, the project risks using the wrong tool for the job. Since many projects can spend millions of dollars in direct labor cost associated with building the client/server application with a particular tool, this decision is not trivial. Thus I've dedicated a good portion of this book to this process.

Selecting the right client/server development tool for a development project is a daunting task. There are hundreds of tools to select from, each with its own strengths and weaknesses. The tools are dynamic, and tools change technical capabilities (e.g., the addition of application partitioning capabilities, or intranet-enabled tools) often. Each tool differs in features, and it's difficult to depend on marketing information to provide all the answers you need. Developers need to employ the proper guidelines to select development tools.

The key to selecting the right tool is to understand the application's requirements. Developers need to go from the application requirements to the tool, and never from the tool to the application requirements. The best way to do this is to list the features and functions the tool should have to be successful. For instance, your application may require connection to real-time market information for a finance application, or utilization of laser scanners for retail client/server applications. Of course, you need to consider many other mitigating factors as well.

Each application carries its own set of criteria, but there are some general issues that you need to address when selecting a tool. These issues include object-oriented development, database connectivity, component integration, cross-platform support, and high-end technical capabilities such as three-tier and *n*-tier support. We'll discuss these issues in greater detail later in the book.

Why So Many Projects Fail

There is a trend in the world of client/server in that one out of every two client/server projects fails to deploy applications to the users who need them. This is disturbing to me, since most of these project failures could have been avoided, and the money saved if they had just added a few more processes in the design and development of their client/server system. The end result is wasted money, developers fired, and end-users without the applications they really need.

Typically, I've found that projects fail for one, sometimes two of the following reasons:

1. Unrealistic expectations of the technology
2. Bad metrics for estimating the cost of the project
3. Significant unexpected cost overruns
4. Using the wrong set of tools for the application requirements
5. Lack of a good application design
6. Inability to obtain user buy-in
7. Lack of proper infrastructure
8. Lack of the correct skill sets
9. Neglecting the database
10. Political reasons

These are, of course, not the only reasons projects fail, but they are the top ten. The key here is to understand these issues so you may avoid them in current or future projects. Reading this book is a step in the right direction.

Now that we've briefly seen some of the issues that face those of us who take on client/server development, it's time to dive into the detail.

2

Client/Server
Fundamentals

Okay, I know this is a review for you client/server superstars. Yet it's important for advanced, intermediate, and novice client/server developers to have a clear understanding of the fundamentals of client/server. Using this information as a base of knowledge, I'll move to the advanced client/server development concepts that subsequent chapters will cover. For those of you who are "too cool for school," it's okay with me if you skip to more challenging subject matter. However, it's also cool to review. You may learn something new.

And in the Beginning

In the beginning IBM created the PC. It had potential, but not processing power. Early PCs were relegated to menial tasks such as word processing, spreadsheets, and Ms. Pac Man. Early PC-based application development languages included 8086 assembler, BASIC, and a new language called C. The first IBM PC cost more than $5000 and came with only 64 KB of RAM, a 360 KB floppy, and no hard drive.

As PC-based technology advanced in the '80s, so did the PC's processing power and acceptance into the mainstream computing marketplace. However, most PCs were still isolated devices that performed menial functions, but with more muscle, better monitors, and larger disks. It was during this period that PC-based database systems became the solution of choice for low-powered database applications. Products such as Paradox, dBase III+, and R:Base 5000 ruled the PC-based database application development market. These products provided advanced relational database capabilities as well as powerful fourth-generation programming languages (4GL) to create applications. These tools were the beginning of the client/server revolution, as they whetted users' appetites for access to enterprise data from the familiar environment of the PC.

Network Revolution

As the PC population grew, so did the networking movement. Using networking products from Novell, 3Comm, and Microsoft, organizations were soon able to share data encapsulated in files on local area networks (LANs). LANs allow users to share files, E-mail, and data as if the information was local to the client (see Figure 2-1). Networking was nothing new, but its use to link together

Figure 2-1 *Networks allow clients to share files.*

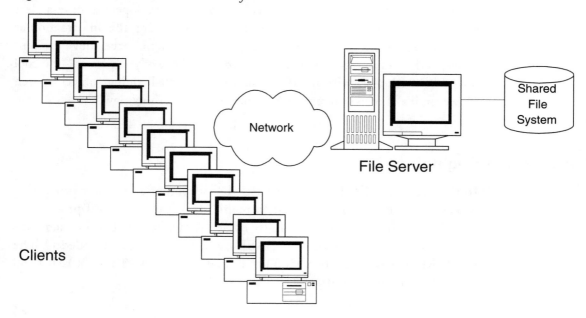

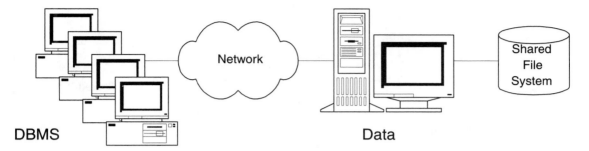

DBMS   Data

Figure 2-2 *File-oriented database applications.*

smaller PCs was. Moreover, the cost of networking devices dropped sharply over the years as competition increased along with technical capabilities. Seemingly overnight, PCs found themselves connected to some sort of network.

Single-user DBMSs (such as the ones mentioned above) soon found that LANs offered a new way to share database information by allowing several users to access database files at the same time. These types of databases are file-oriented databases.

Unlike single-user file-oriented DBMSs, these multi-user versions could provide concurrency control, or the ability for a DBMS to control simultaneous access to tables and records, making sure not to damage the data with a concurrent write-access (see Figure 2-2). However, this architecture has severe limitations.

Hitting the Wall

We found a way to leverage the power of the PC for information processing through the use of file-oriented DBMSs, as well as the ability to share data among users, but there are limitations to the file-oriented architecture. These limitations include security, performance, and scalability.

Performance is a problem when using a file-oriented database due to the fact that almost all the database processing must occur at the client using a local database engine. The file server only serves up the file, never performing independent database processing on behalf of the client. For instance, when searching a large customer database for a particular customer record, the file-oriented database must download the entire database file one chunk at a time to find a single record (see Figure 2-3). This highly inefficient method of processing centralized database requests leads to performance problems as many users hit the database file at the same time.

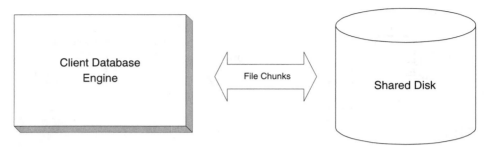

Figure 2-3 *File-oriented databases have to load and unload data files across the network.*

Moreover, since the database engines that reside on the client are rudimentary, there are usually no additional protection features such as roll-back, roll-forward recovery, or logging. This means that developers have no way to automatically back out of a transaction when an error occurs. We will learn more about the benefits of using a database server in Chapter 5.

Hand-in-hand with performance issues is the file-oriented architecture's ability to scale. As the number of users approaches fifty (from my experience), many file servers simply can't serve all the client requests for file information. Thus, response time becomes so bad that users can't stand it, or worse, the concurrency control mechanism breaks down and damages the file(s), resulting in lost data.

When to Use a File-Oriented Architecture

Despite the problems, file-oriented database application development is alive and well, and provides an inexpensive alternative to client/server. Unlike client/server development tools, there is no need to purchase a database server.

Many popular multi-user file-oriented DBMSs still exist today, such as Visual dBase and Paradox from Borland, and FoxPro and Access from Microsoft. However, all these tools also provide client/server capabilities, or the option to link to a remote database server.

You should consider the file-oriented DBMS architecture if your application's requirements do not include:

- Need for highly granular security (row level, column level, etc.)
- Need for on-line transaction processing (OLTP) capabilities

- Need for advanced concurrency control
- Need for logging
- Need for high-speed application processing
- Need to support more than fifty users now or in the future
- Need to support automated recovery operations
- Need to push the application processing load to a shared processor (e.g., application server or database server)
- Need to put a client/server system development project on your résumé for a quick job change

Since this is a client/server book, it would be fitting to state that the file-oriented DBMS architecture has no place in modern systems development. However, as developers we must learn to provide solutions that offer the best value. File-oriented architecture is still a good fit for small workgroup applications—applications that don't require full-blown database servers for database processing.

Security may also be a problem in the context of the prevailing file-oriented architecture. File-oriented DBMSs can't provide the granular security features of their larger host-based counterparts. For instance, file-oriented DBMSs have no way to protect data beyond the rudimentary security provided by the network operating system. Many modern systems require that DBMSs protect rows and columns, as well as tables and databases.

What's a Client?

Let's begin our discussion of the components of client/server computing with the client. The client in the client/server model can be any sort of device that communicates over a network with a server. This means that a client can be a PC, a Unix workstation, a laptop, a Macintosh, or even a cellular phone or personal digital assistant (PDA) (see Figure 2-4). Sometimes a client is simply a process running on the same machine as the server process.

Typically, clients are IBM-compatible PCs or Macintosh computers connected to servers via a network. Using the pure client/server model, the client works on a request/response model. This means that the client sends a request to a server (e.g., SQL), and expects a response from the server (e.g., response set).

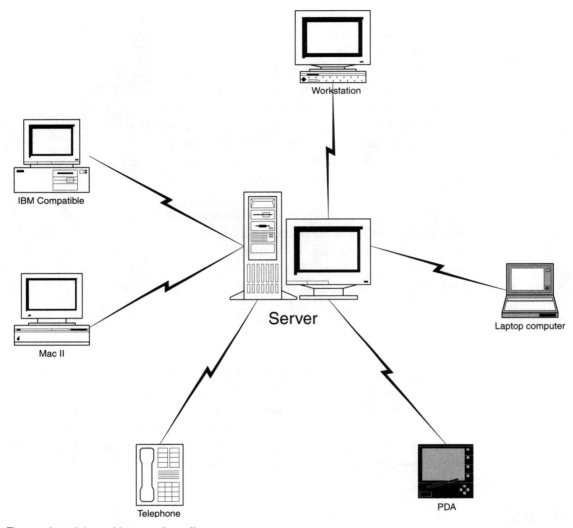

Figure 2-4 *Many things can be a client.*

The client/server developer can look at a client as a collection of layers, including:

- Processor
- Application
- GUI
- Operating system
- Middleware
- Network

THE PROCESSOR

When using a client/server architecture, you split the application processing load between the client and the server. The *processor* allows the client to perform its share of the application processing activity. All layers interact with the processor in one form or another. The type and speed of the processor you use is dependent on your client platform of choice. PC uses Intel processors such as 486 and Pentium processors, where Macintosh platforms use Motorola or PowerPC processors.

THE APPLICATION

The *application* is the software that the user interacts with, which provides all required business functions such as gathering data, data processing, calculations, and printing. The application can reside at the client or the server, but with the client/server model it usually resides at both. For instance, consider an application written in PowerBuilder using an Oracle database server running remotely. PowerBuilder allows the developer to create objects that run on the client, gathering user input and processing the information, requesting data as required from the Oracle database server.

The developer can also create objects that run on the server, using the stored procedures and trigger mechanisms that most relational DBMSs provide (covered in detail in Chapter 5). Stored procedures and triggers, simply put, are small procedural programs that exist and execute on the database server. Developers may use stored procedures and triggers as a way to place some of the application processing load on the server using the traditional two-tier client/server model.

This only covers application distribution (application partitioning) capabilities in the two-tier client/server environment. There are many other ways to distribute the load using the three-tier and multi-tier client/server architectures. We'll look at those in more detail in later chapters.

GRAPHICAL UNIVERSAL INTERFACE

The *GUI* is software that provides a graphical interface to any number of operating systems or application services. Examples of GUIs are Windows 95, Windows NT, and Motif, and Mac OS. For developers, the GUI provides a set of APIs that developers can exploit when using development tools to create GUI objects for the users, objects such as list boxes, menus, buttons, drop-down boxes, and animation.

For example, Windows 95 and Windows NT provide the Win32 API that gives developers a mechanism to make the GUI dance to the tune of the application. In most cases, the developers don't deal with the API directly. Instead they deal with development tools (Visual Basic, PowerBuilder, Borland C++, etc.) that know how to deal with the native GUI API on behalf of the developer.

Web Browsers: Graphical Universal Interface Inside of Graphical Universal Interfaces

In the context of the intranet, the browser functions as a GUI for the user via native interfaces such as Java, CGI, NSAPI, or ISAPI. However, the browser also functions within native GUIs such as Windows 95, Windows NT, or Motif.

The ability of the browser to work with so many GUIs is what makes the Web application naturally multi-platform. Therefore you can write a Web application once, and deploy it without modification on any platform that supports a Web browser.

OPERATING SYSTEM

The *operating system* is important to client/server developers due to the services provided to both the client and the server. In many cases, I've seen client/server applications carefully designed, developed, and deployed, only to be dragged down by a client or server operating system that just couldn't cut the mustard. Don't let this happen to you.

Today, advanced operating systems provide several basic services for clients and servers, including:

- Memory management
- Threading
- Process management
- Interprocess communications (IPC)
- Input/output services

The memory management subsystem assures that the application will have enough memory to process the client or server application, and protect the application from other processes running concurrently in the same physical memory. The memory system allows for the loading of very large applications or objects into memory. If there is not enough physical memory for the application, the operating system should know how to swap portions of the application to disk without affecting performance dramatically.

Threading provides the developer with the ability to take a "divide and conquer" approach to application development. Applications can launch small, lightweight processes known as threads. These threads span out from the main process, concurrently processing a portion of an application. For example, developers may place a lengthy database query in its own thread, freeing up the main process to continue interacting with the user. Servers depend on threading, due to the nature of the heavy processing load. Many database servers, for example, allocate a single thread for each client connection.

Threading is only possible on multi-threading operating systems such as OS/2, Unix, Windows NT, and even Windows 95. Threading is becoming relevant for the client/server developer with the popularity of Windows 95 and Windows NT on desktops. Most advanced 32-bit development environments, including Visual Basic, Delphi, Visual C++, and PowerBuilder, can exploit threading.

With the popularity of multi-tasking operating systems, there comes the need for process management. Process management means that the operating system can perform such functions as task protection, task pre-emption, task priority, and semaphores.

Task protection assures that all the processes running on the client won't interfere with other processing running on the same machine. For example, you don't want your personal information manager (PIM) to bring down your client/server application.

Task pre-emption, on the other hand, is the operating system's ability to pre-empt a process in a multi-tasking environment for another process to gain access to processor resources. Thus, one application cannot monopolize processor time. The significance of Windows 95 is its ability to provide true pre-emptive multi-tasking capabilities. Windows 3.11 had few protections for tasks that saturated the processors, not allowing others to obtain processor time.

Task priority means that the operating system can process tasks using their priority to schedule processor time. Semaphores provide the operating system with a means of synchronizing access to shared resources among many concurrently running processes.

IPC means that the operating system provides a mechanism that allows processes to communicate with one another. Therefore developers can launch many different tasks that execute simultaneously in their own address space and can communicate using an IPC. For example, an OLE automation allows developers to establish IPC between a container process and a server process. Although the container and the server are different programs (e.g., Microsoft

Excel and a Delphi client/server application) that communicate through Microsoft's Lightweight Remote Procedure Call Mechanism (LRPC) from application to application.

Finally, operating systems must provide a means to move information into and out of the operating system and thus the application. This means that the operating system must provide access to information residing on disk, in memory, or through a keyboard or a mouse. In addition, the operating system must allow applications to access printer, network, and monitor services.

THE OPERATING SYSTEM RACE

In the world of client/server development there are five major operating systems: Windows 95 and Mac OS for clients, and Windows NT, OS/2, and Unix for both clients and servers.

The market share for each operating system is always a disputed topic. However, IDC reports that Windows 3.11 and DOS reside on 49.2 percent of the clients, Windows 95 on 29.2 percent, Windows NT on 0.07 percent, Macintosh on 7.0 percent, OS/2 on 6.4 percent, and 7.5 percent on something else (1995 statistics). It's safe to say that by now Windows 95 has eaten its way deeper into the market shares of the other operating systems.

Windows 95. Windows 95, despite some problems after its initial release, is the operating system that brought the majority to 32-bit development, and brought more power to the client. Windows 95 is not the first operating system to provide advanced capabilities such as 32-bit pre-emptive multi-tasking. However, it's the popularity of Windows 95 and its role as a successor to Windows 3.11 that pushed Windows 95 into the limelight.

Today, most PCs ship with Windows 95 pre-installed, and most client/server development environments support the advanced native capabilities of Windows 95. Most client/server developers will find that Windows 95 is the client of choice in most organizations. Windows 95 is Intel-only since many of its subsystems are written in processor-dependent assembly language for performance reasons.

Windows NT. Windows NT in its version 4 incarnation looks almost identical to Windows 95, and it's difficult for most casual users to tell the differences. Behind the scenes, NT is a very different beast.

First of all, Windows NT is written entirely in portable C. Thus Microsoft can offer NT on a number of platforms including Intel, PowerPC, Alpha, and MIPS, supporting both single- and multi-processing systems. Using pure C means that Windows 95 will run a few cycles faster than NT, but the performance differences are not notable. Also missing from Windows NT are power management features (needed to manage battery power on laptop computers), and support for plug-and-play devices.

Windows NT comes in both a server and a workstation version. The client workstation version provides basic operating system features (such as the ones listed above), as well as a transactional file system and network support using TCP/IP, NetBEUI, IPX/SPX, PPP, and AppleTalk. NT Workstation also provides C2 level security and support for the component object model (COM) and the distributed component object model (DCOM). The server version comes with everything the client does, but adds file and print services, as well as a built-in Internet server, disk mirroring and stripping services, and support for multi-processing.

Windows NT for the Intel runs almost all Win32- and Win16-based software for Windows 3.11 and Windows 95. Windows NT on other processors requires special versions of such software for each processor. For instance, you must run the PowerPC version of Word for Windows on the PowerPC version of NT. This can cause confusion. With its version 4, Windows NT now offers an Intel processor emulation feature which allows non-Intel versions of Windows NT to run off-the-shelf Intel versions. This, of course, is at the cost of performance.

Where Is Microsoft Going?

Now that Windows 95 and Windows NT look pretty much alike, many Microsoft operating system consumers are asking the question: Where is Microsoft headed? Although I can't do the Vulcan mind meld with Bill Gates, it's pretty clear that Windows 95 and Windows NT are merging into a single operating system—an operating system that supports both client and the server.

Windows 95 was Microsoft's bridge to bring Windows 3.11 Win16 applications to the waiting 32-bit arms of Windows 95. Now that most Windows developers and software vendors support or will support Win32, they support Windows NT by default. For example, 32-bit client/server applications that run on Windows 95 run as native applications on Windows NT as well. This makes the operating systems (Windows 95 and Windows NT) interchangeable.

Once the majority of applications support both Windows 95 and Windows NT, there is not much reason to support two operating systems. Therefore, it's a safe bet that we'll see only one "super OS" from Microsoft in years to come.

OS/2. OS/2 is the tragic story of the operating system world. Although advanced for its time, it failed to capture the hearts and minds of developers and users. OS/2 was the first operating system for the Intel to offer advanced operating system features such as pre-emptive multi-tasking, an advanced GUI, and a flat memory model. However, this came at the cost of advanced hardware. Early OS/2 required 8 to 16 MB of RAM and a large hard drive, premiums in the days when such configurations were rare and costly.

OS/2 was originally a joint venture of Microsoft and IBM, and was hailed as the replacement for DOS. However, IBM and Microsoft had a falling out and IBM received custody of OS/2, while Microsoft advanced its Windows product. As Paul Harvey would say, "Now you know the rest of the story."

Today, OS/2 is a well-tested, solid operating system with an advanced GUI that can support clients as well as servers. OS/2 supports multi-processing on the server side. However, many client/server tools, as well as applications, have chosen to support Windows instead of OS/2. That may leave OS/2 low on the list of operating systems for your next client/server project.

Unix. Unix is a workhorse operating system that runs on almost all processors, including Intel, PowerPC, and RISC. Unix is the operating system of choice for servers; however, Unix workstations also work as clients.

Unix is the oldest of the operating systems presented here, with over twenty years of experience under its belt. Most Unix operating systems provide advanced features such as multi-tasking, threading, built-in network support, and support for multiple users. It's truly an operating system that runs everywhere, and provides maximum flexibility.

Like Baskin Robbins, Unix comes in dozens of flavors, or proprietary ports, hybrids of the original Unix kernel. These versions of the Unix operating system use strange names such as Irix, AIX, DG/UX, HP/UX, and Solaris. All provide the same basic Unix features, but also provide their own proprietary features and processor support. Solaris, for instance, uses its own GUI and supports Intel in Sun's own line of CISC-based Unix workstations and servers. AIX is an IBM product, and only supports IBM's RS/6000 line of RISC-based Unix workstations and servers.

Macintosh. The Macintosh operating system (Mac OS) was one of the first working GUIs to make a splash in the personal computer marketplace. Macintosh PCs make excellent clients, but like OS/2 and Unix, Mac has not drawn the major client/server tool vendors into its camp. For instance, while you can get PowerBuilder for the Mac, you can't get Delphi. Moreover, the Mac OS does not make a very good server platform since it does not scale well, and only supports limited threading.

Apple has been losing market share lately due to its inability to keep up with the price/performance of the PC world, as well as Apple's unwillingness to license its architecture to third-party vendors. However, there are 10 to 15 million very dedicated Macintosh users out there, many of whom require support for client/server applications. Things could change for Apple when it ships its new advanced operating system (code name Copland). Copland will supposedly bring Apple back as a competitor.

MIDDLEWARE

Middleware (covered in greater detail in Chapter 3), simply put, provides developers with an easy way to get at external resources. External resources may include a database server, a queue, a 3270 terminal, or access to real-time information.

Although not as sexy as RAD tools and speedy database servers, advances in middleware technology have led to today's client/server revolution. Rather than write down to the native operating system and network level, developers can simply program to a well-defined standard middleware API, or have their development tool traverse the API for them. The API, in turn, passes the request down to a middleware service layer which can translate the request into the appropriate native operating system and network calls.

There are several types of middleware including database-oriented, RPCs, message-oriented middleware, transaction processing (TP) monitors, object request brokers (ORBs), and now hypertext transfer protocol for the Internet and intranets.

NETWORK

The network portion of the client/server model provides a transport mechanism from the client to the server and back again. Networks are really a collection of network interface cards (NICs), hubs, routers, and wires tied together to form a group of interconnected computers. The Internet is an example of a network—the largest network in the world.

Most client/server systems depend on the network to transmit requests from the client to the server, as well as return response sets back to the client in real time. Thus a healthy network is a foundation of successful client/server development.

PROTOCOLS

Network protocols such as TCP/IP, IPX/SPX, NetBIOS, and SNA provide a regimented method to transmit information across a network. Generally speaking, most protocols work with client/server as long as everyone communicates using the same protocol. For example, if my client only runs IPX/SPX, there is no way to link into a server running TCP/IP. However, my server that runs TCP/IP may also be configured to run IPX/SPX. This allows the server to talk to clients running TCP/IP or IPX/SPX.

Although there are places for all protocols, TCP/IP seems to be the network protocol of choice for the world of client/server. Also, TCP/IP is the native protocol for the Internet and almost all intranets.

LOCAL AREA NETWORKS

LANs (local area networks) are just small independent networks that serve a group of collocated users. For example, a single LAN may serve several dozen users in the human resources department.

WIDE AREA NETWORKS

WANs (wide area networks) are a collection of LANs and network users that are geographically disbursed. For example, an entire corporation with several offices in several cities across the country will use a WAN to link all the users together.

INTERNET

The Internet is an example of the largest WAN in the world. The Internet is really a large collection of computers all networked together to serve a common purpose. No one really owns the Internet. However, its popularity in recent years has propelled its importance as a global information resource. The appearance of Web technology has made the Internet easy to use and navigate, and has led the way to the next revolution of client/server development.

INTRANET

The intranet, as the name implies, is an offshoot of the Internet. Basically, it means the use of Web technology (browsers, Web servers, HTTP, HTML, and Java) for information decimation and application deployment within organizations.

What's a Server?

Moving from the client to the network to middleware, it's now time to explore the concept of a server. Taking a bird's-eye view, a server is any machine or process that provides a service to another process. Typically, servers are computers that exist on a network configured to provide a particular resource, such as files, data, Web, or application processing services. In the world of client/server, servers come in four basic forms: file servers, application servers, database servers, and Web servers.

File servers provide files to clients as needed. Clients access files on file servers as if they were stored on the local disk. Examples of file server software (network operating systems) include Novell's Netware and Microsoft's Windows NT Server. As you may remember from earlier in this chapter, developers use file server software to share database information, as well as word-processing documents and E-mail.

Application servers are specialized computers that exist on a network and perform all sorts of application processing services. Typically, these computers run transaction-processing (TP) monitors, distributed objects, or custom-built processing services. Clients may invoke these application services through APIs. Application servers allow developers to place common application services in a central location and remove the application processing load from the client. Application servers also provide a mechanism to support the three-tier client/server architecture.

Database servers are computers that exist on a network and provide database processing services upon request from the client. For instance, a client may send a database request in the form of SQL. The database server processes the database request on behalf of the client, sending only the requested information back to the front-end application.

Database servers run DBMS software such as Oracle, Informix, and Sybase (see Figure 2-5).

Figure 2-5 *Database Server.*

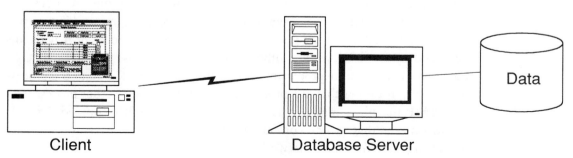

Client   Database Server

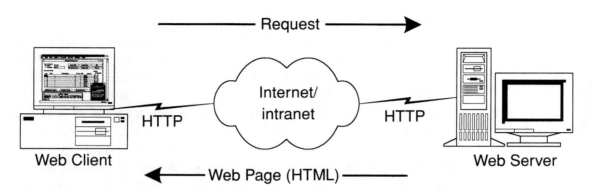

Figure 2-6 *Web Server.*

Web servers are computers that exist on the Internet or intranets that provide HTML documents, or graphics, video, or even database services upon request from a client running a Web browser. The Web browser links to the Web server using the TCP/IP network protocol and HTTP requesting content (HTML document, graphics, video, etc.) The Web server sends the content to the browser that presents the content to the user (see Figure 2-6). Web servers run Web server software such as Netscape's Enterprise Server or Microsoft's Internet Information Server.

PROCESSOR POWER

Unlike clients, servers require heavy-duty processors or multi-processing capabilities. The type and number of processors your server requires depend on the type of system you're trying to build, as well as the number of clients you want to support. For instance, while Sybase running on a single-processor PC can support up to fifty clients, you'll need more processor horsepower to support more than fifty.

The trend today is not only to provide faster processors, but multi-processor capabilities as well. There are two types of multi-processing architectures: asymmetric and symmetric. Asymmetric multi-processing means that certain tasks are allocated to specific processors. For example, one processor may handle input and output (I/O), while another is in charge of database processing. In contrast, symmetrical multi-processing (SMP) divides the work among the processors equally, meaning that any processor can do the work of other processors.

SMP machines may run as loosely coupled or tightly coupled. Loosely coupled means that several computers with one or more processors can share processing time through a network connection. Tightly coupled SMP means that all processors exist inside the same physical machine.

Recently there has been a shift away from using the asymmetric multi-processing architecture to SMP. Database servers such as Oracle, Sybase, and Informix have special SMP versions that divide single queries up for parallel execution on all available processors. The result is a dramatic increase in performance (see Figure 2-7). Most advanced 32-bit operating systems such as Netware, OS/2, Windows NT, and Unix support SMP.

DATABASE MANAGEMENT SYSTEMS AND SERVERS

As previously mentioned, database management systems (DBMSs) such as Oracle, Sybase, and Informix typically run on a machine with an advanced 32-bit operating system such as Windows NT, Unix, or OS/2. Database servers do nothing all day but listen for SQL requests over the network from clients. The database server receives the request and processes the request on behalf of the client. If the client requests information, the database server returns only the data that the client requests: the result set (see Figure 2-8). This is a more effi-

Figure 2-7 *Parallel Query Execution.*

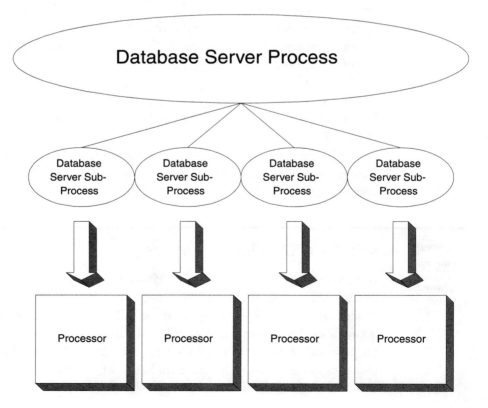

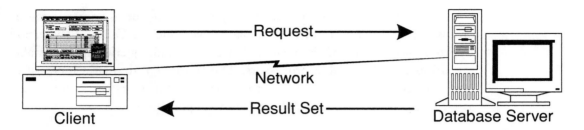

Figure 2-8 *DMBSs provide a request/response architecture.*

cient process than passing all the database records back to the client, as happens when using file-oriented DBMSs. Also, this does not require as much network bandwidth.

The strength of the client/server architecture is that the database server software runs on its own machine. Thus the client offloads most database processing to the server, freeing the client to continue interacting with the user.

Database servers are heavyweight processes that require a lot from an operating system and server hardware. Most DBMSs require a threading operating system which allows the DBMS to keep each client connection and database engine in its own thread. This provides faster execution and better use of multi-processing servers.

Database servers also require a tremendous amount of memory. As clients connect to a database server, each needs a certain amount of memory. A database server that supports one hundred or more clients can easily require more than 128 KB.

Finally, database servers are I/O-bound, meaning they place a heavy burden on disk drives. Thus, host operating systems and hardware need an I/O system that's ready for heavy use.

What's A Database Server?

A database server is actually a DBMS that resides on its own specialized machine. The DBMS, host operating system, and server hardware that resides on a network make up what we call a database server. However, in many cases, developers refer to the DBMS itself as a database server. For the purposes of this book, we'll use the term database server to mean some entity that can process database requests on behalf of the client.

What Now?

Now that we've covered the basics of client/server computing, it's time to move down into the process and technology of building client/server applications. It's important to remember that client/server is really a complex architecture, and not an application development mechanism.

Unlike the days when developers built large COBOL applications on large computers that they might never see using databases they did not build or maintain, client/server developers must wear many hats. These hats include those of a system architect, network technician, database designer, database administrator, and now Web and intranet technology expert.

Although we are beginning to once again specialize in specific portions of client/server development (front-end developer, database developer, etc.), the technology continues to change directions as quickly as the fashion industry. Thus the most effective client/server designers and developers are the ones who can become "jacks of all trades." It's a challenging position to take, but it's the only way that makes sense for now. The client/server industry shows no signs of slowing down.

3

The Pipe and
Middleware

Have you ever waited in traffic or received an "all circuits busy" message when you try to make a phone call? These are simple examples of a poor infrastructure. In my experience, most organizations view infrastructure as a "nice to have," not a "must have." This is a mistake. A poor infrastructure is a surefire way to kill your client/server or intranet system before it has a chance to live.

In the world of client/server and intranet development, a good infrastructure means that all the underlying technology supports the client/server developer, as well as the deployed application. This includes the network (the pipe), middleware, hardware, and the humans who must solve the inevitable problems one runs into when developing and deploying a client/server system. In this chapter let's talk about middleware and networking, and how they make or break a client/server application.

Infrastructures should be an important issue with client/server developers, not because they are usually the ones responsible for creating and maintaining infrastructure, but because they are ultimately responsible for the success or failure of their client/server application. Therefore, I'm covering the topic of infrastructures from the client/server developer's perspective, leaving out most of the grisly details. Briefly I'll discuss networking, but most of this chapter covers the plumbing and wiring that holds client/server applications together—middleware.

Neglecting the Plumbing

Client/server systems only perform as well as their slowest component. The network is critical to the success of client/server since it's the plumbing that ties together the clients and the servers. Slow networks and middleware layers mean poorly performing client/server systems, mad users, and henpecked developers.

In about half the systems I've worked with over the years, the speed and stability of the network is an afterthought. For instance, an old client of mine absolutely refused to upgrade an old 8-bit PC network on migrating an OLTP application from the mainframe to client/server. Despite my pleading, the budget took only development and server hardware into account, with none left over to upgrade the network. The result was a very well-designed application and database (if I do say so myself), severely limited by the pipe between the clients and the server. Naturally, performance and network downtime were constant problems, and lost productivity far exceeded the cost of the new network which eventually had to be purchased. Sometimes people won't listen.

As a rule of thumb, when you consider building and deploying a client/server system, someone needs to look at the network at the same time. The process is just a matter of considering the load that the new client/server system will place on the network, the existing network's ability to handle the load, and adding 20 percent for expansion (e.g., the emergence of the intranet). Network designers and managers can do this using network design tools, simulation tools—or better yet, through a functional prototype. That, however, is the topic of another book. Let's address the fundamentals.

Network Fundamentals

Networking concepts change so quickly that keeping up to date with current concepts and terminology is difficult for most of us, especially developers. We saw that recently in the explosion of the intranet as a new layer of Web technology on top of existing corporate networks. Other technologies such as ATM (asynchronous transfer mode) continue to emerge. Let's quickly uncover some basic jargon pertaining to network components and how they relate to client/server.

We divide network components into two categories: the physical link and communications software. The physical link is the hardware that provides the physical connection between the computer systems (see Figure 3-1). The communications software uses the physical link to move data over some sort of network such as TCP/IP, HTTP, or middleware. Middleware, simply put, is another layer of software (an API really) that sits between the application or the resource server and the network (see Figure 3-2). Middleware is the glue that holds client/server applications together.

Figure 3-1 *The physical link and communications software.*

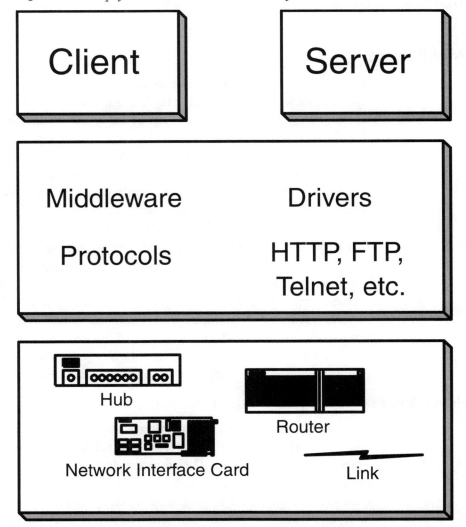

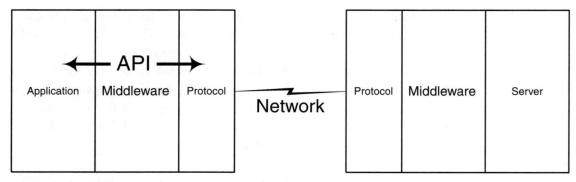

Figure 3-2 *Middleware.*

Middleware

Although I'll cover middleware here as part of infrastructure issues, I'll touch upon middleware throughout the book. Also, there are a few chapters dedicated to specific types of middleware such as TP monitors and distributed objects. This is because middleware is related to so many concepts of client/server. For example, TP monitors and object request brokers, while considered middleware, provide another location for client/server application processing and thus provide a way to create three- and multi-tiered client/server systems. The intranet is another new architecture that's tied together with Web-based middleware. There are many new middleware products and Web-enabled databases that tie your data automatically to public or private Web servers.

Let's cover the basics here. As mentioned in Chapter 2, middleware gives developers an easy way to get at external resources using a common set of application services such as an API. External resources may include a database server, a queue, a 3270 terminal, or access to real-time information (e.g., a real-time stock market feed). In the world of client/server, we usually associate middleware as a means of connecting clients to servers without having to negotiate through many operating systems, network, and resource server layers.

HIDING BEHIND AN APPLICATION PROGRAMMING INTERFACE

In the early days of client/server development developers had to employ protocols (such as NetBIOS directly) to access information or processing services that existed on other computers. Therefore, developers had to commit to a particular protocol and thus limit compatibility with other platforms and networks. For instance, I created a peer-to-peer client/server system using NetBIOS that had to undergo a complete rewrite when it moved to a TCP/IP-ONLY based network.

Middleware expands your options since changes to the underlying network, GUI, and operating system are hidden from the developer and the application.

The networking components of middleware function like a protocol converter. The client/server developer uses an application programming interface (API) to dispatch a message. The network services translate the message into the appropriate protocol (e.g., TCP/IP, HTTP, NetBIOS) where it's transmitted to another computer. The resolution of protocol differences happens in the background, away from the client and server portions of the application. Using this model, you can conceivably swap network protocols every day, without the users ever knowing, and without making any changes to the applications if the API does not change (see Figure 3-3).

Besides protocol translation services, middleware is also responsible for translating data on the fly between one system and another. For example, data residing on mainframes is very different from data residing on Unix systems, and data residing on Windows. This happens in the background too.

In my opinion, it was the arrival of advanced middleware layers that really allowed client/server and distributed application development to take off. Not only did they tie clients to database servers for two-tier client/server, but they can tie many different systems together to form virtual systems. These virtual systems give users the ability to access a multitude of distributed resources through a single log-in or API (see Figure 3-4). What's more, the interest in middleware continues. Microsoft, for instance, is extending its interest in middleware beyond ODBC to message-oriented middleware (e.g., Project Falcon) and TP monitors (e.g., Transaction Server). This trend will continue.

Figure 3-3 *Resolution of protocol differences.*

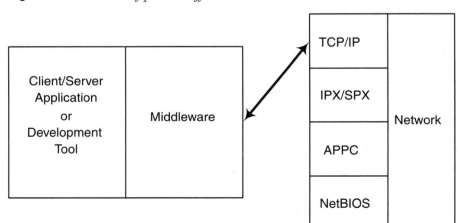

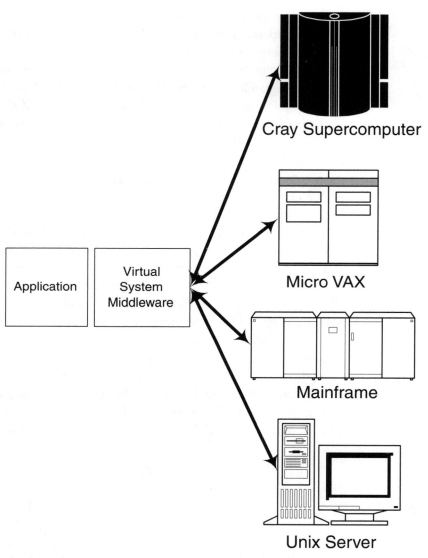

Figure 3-4 *Middleware forms a virtual system.*

CLASSIFYING MIDDLEWARE

Trying to classify middleware is like trying to categorize species of water insects. There are just too many of them, and they move much too fast. The easiest way to look at types of middleware is to divide middleware products into one of two categories: primitive and database-oriented middleware.

Primitive middleware does not mean that the middleware lacks advanced functionality, only that the middleware is designed to perform a variety of roles beside accessing data. Primitive middleware is the middleware layer that's able to tie together many different systems to create a single logical system. I call this a virtual system, and it makes sense to call primitive middleware virtual system middleware. For example, using virtual system middleware, I can access hundreds of computers and resource servers (application servers, database servers, knowledge servers, etc.) through a single application. The application can get at all these resources through the magical API of the primitive middleware layers. In other words, this is the plumbing and wiring of distributed computing.

Primitive middleware products include remote procedure calls (RPCs), message-oriented middleware (MOM), object request brokers (ORBs), the distributed computing environment (DCE), TP monitors, and mainframe access middleware such as APPC, APPN, and CPI-C. These powerful middleware products give developers the ability to customize client/server applications, while remaining network- and platform-independent. They also facilitate communications through a known platform-independent API found on each platform that makes up the client/server system.

Database-oriented middleware, in contrast, refers to middleware built specifically for database access. Database-oriented middleware may use a primitive middleware layer, such as RPCs or messaging, to move information to and from a database. Microsoft's Open Database Connectivity (ODBC) is a good example of widely used database-oriented middleware as is IBI's EDA/SQL, but there are many other products (explained later in this chapter).

REMOTE PROCEDURE CALLS

Remote procedure calls (RPCs) are really just a method of communicating with a remote computer where the developer invokes a remote procedure on the server by making a simple function call on the client. RPCs hide the intricacies of the network and operating systems using this mechanism that's very familiar to the developer. The client process that calls the remote function has to suspend itself until the procedure is complete. This means that RPCs are synchronous in nature, or block the process from continuing until the function returns.

Although RPCs are easy to use and understand, they can be something of a problem when you try to incorporate them into modern client/server computing. First, stopping an application from processing during a remote call can slow down the performance of an application. That makes the application dependent upon the remote servers being up and running. Second, the architecture of an RPC requires a high-speed network since there is a tremendous amount of network communication between the client and the server when using RPCs. Therefore, RPCs are only a good fit on high-speed networks. RPCs were the base middleware layers (although we did not call them RPC middleware then) of early client/server systems. RPCs run many database-oriented middleware layers, as well as network operating systems such as Sun's Network File System (NFS) and the Open Software Foundation's DCE (discussed next).

DISTRIBUTED COMPUTING ENVIRONMENT

DCE (the distributed computing environment) is a complex but effective middleware solution. Developed by the Open Software Foundation (OSF), DCE makes many diverse computers work as a single virtual system—the ultimate in distributed client/server computing. However, the heart of DCE is a classic RPC mechanism. Therefore all the limitations of RPCs, including blocking and the need for a high-speed network, are inherent in DCE as well. I've found DCE to suffer from chronic performance problems that are difficult to work around, and use a tremendous amount of resources (see sidebar).

Despite the limitations, DCE is a key infrastructure component in many large organizations. Developers can use DCE as a middleware layer that spans every system in the company, tying together many systems, applications, and users. What I really like about DCE is its ability to provide a comprehensive multi-vendor network operating system solution. Typically, DCE was the only middleware layer that I could use to solve such problems. I can't imagine building large distributed client/server systems without having DCE as a potential solution. Competitors to DCE include message-oriented middleware products which can operate asynchronously (discussed next).

Distributed Computing Environment: The Heavyweight Middleware

Despite the success of DCE (distributed computing environment) as a reliable middleware layer, DCE remains a solution for larger systems due to the amount of resources DCE requires on smaller systems (such as PCS) to provide acceptable performance. Typical DCE PC installations require at least 16 MB of memory for a typical client/server application. Therefore, we often kick DCE off the list of potential middleware solutions due to the cost of upgrading existing PCS.

If DCE is in the running as a middleware layer for your client/server development environment, you need to consider the amount of processors and memory resources required on the client. Those who attempt to use DCE on substandard PCS will find that users won't accept the performance. This is where middleware causes—not solves—a problem.

At the heart of DCE's client/server servers is its RPC. The RPC lets developers reach across platforms to access many types of application services including database, distributed objects, and TP monitor access. DCE can also provide a sophisticated naming service, a type of synchronization service, a distributed file system, and built-in network security. Client/server developers will find that DCE is available on most platforms including IBM's VMS, VMS, Ultrix, OS/1, ACE, HP/ux, and AIX, as well as PC operating systems such as DOS, Windows 3.11, Windows NT, Windows 95, and OS/2.

MESSAGE-ORIENTED MIDDLEWARE

If you don't have the bandwidth to support RPCs, and if you can't depend on a server always being up and running, you may find that message-oriented middleware (MOM) may be a better fit for your client/server application. Like RPCs, MOM provides a standard API across hardware and operating system platforms and networks (see Figure 3-5). MOM can also guarantee that messages reach their destination, even when destinations are not available at the moment.

MOM uses one of two models: process-to-process messages and message queuing. The process-to-process model requires that both the sending and receiving process be active to exchange messages. The queuing model stores messages in a queue, so only one process can be active. The use of the queuing

Figure 3-5 *Message-Oriented Middleware.*

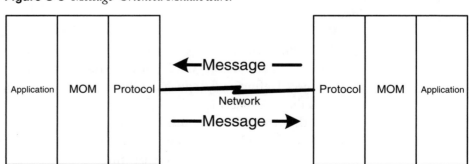

model makes sense when communicating between computers that aren't always up and running, over networks that are undependable, or when there is a lack of bandwidth.

The basic difference between MOM and RPCs is that MOM is asynchronous. This means that MOM is nonblocking, or does not block the application from processing when invoking the middleware API. RPCs block processing until the procedure call returns. MOM message functions can return immediately although actual completion of the request may not have occurred. Thus the application can continue processing, with assurances that the application will know when the request is complete. This model is most useful for transaction-oriented applications that need to traverse many platforms. Unlike DCE, the platform doesn't necessarily have to be up and running for an application to request services. The request sits in a queue, and when the server comes back on line, the request is processed. This makes MOM a better fit for the Internet, since there is not much bandwidth and many servers on the Internet may not always be up and running.

There is a tradeoff when using MOM, as MOM does not perform as well as RPCs. Some client/server developers can coax better performance out of MOM applications by exploiting the parallel-processing aspects of messaging, since messaging applications can submit several concurrent requests.

OBJECT REQUEST BROKERS

An ORB (object request broker), simply put, is an engine that can communicate with other local or remote objects using a common interface and line protocol such as TCP/IP. ORBs can make requests to other ORBs, as well as process responses. The beauty of ORBs is that all this happens behind the scenes, hidden from the user and the client/server application. The idea is to guarantee portability and interoperability of all application objects, even objects that exist on various connected computers. OMG's CORBA defines how these objects interface with each other, and we discus ORBs in detail in Chapter 19.

We define ORB interfaces via an Interface Definition Language (IDL). The IDL defines the interface between one object and the next. Microsoft's Component Object Model (COM) uses a similar mechanism, known as the ODL (Object Definition Language). Object services are basically just a group of services that use object interfaces. They provide a base set of services encapsulated within the ORBs. In other words, object services augment the base functionality of the ORB. This mechanism will enable ORBs to provide functions such as security, transaction management, and exchanging data.

Common facilities are a collection of services that relate more to clients than to the server. Component document facilities (such as those offered by OpenDoc) are a good example of common facilities. Common facilities are optional, but object services are mandated for CORBA. Application objects, as their name implies, are objects that exist in support of a particular application. Developers define these objects using the IDL so that they can communicate with other CORBA-compliant ORBs.

ORBs are valuable as middleware because they are naturally multi-platform. Therefore ORBs can reside on any number of computer systems, facilitating communications through the common interface of the ORB. This is also known as an "information bus," since the ORBs facilitate communication in the same way a bus facilitates communications between components inside a computer system.

Despite the architecture of ORBs, they have not set the middleware world on fire. However, as ORBs become more popular for general purpose client/server programming, that could change. They should be a consideration for those of you looking at DCE or MOM, as they provide the same base services.

With the interest in the intranet, developers are now looking to distributed objects to deploy dynamic applications to the intranet. IIOP (Internet Inter-ORB Protocol), the common communication mechanism between ORBs, is potentially the protocol that will replace HTTP in the future. HTTP was never designed for client/server application development, and developers can deploy applications by working around its limitations. IIOP, in contrast, was designed from the ground up for distributed application development. IIOP could mean that everyone running a browser is also hosting an ORB. Netscape is putting its weight behind IIOP (see Chapter 19 for more details).

TRANSACTION-PROCESSING MONITORS

TP monitors are industrial-strength middleware products that provide many features that make large-scale client/server transaction-oriented development possible. The use of TP monitors on a few of my past projects has made me a believer in the power of building a client/server system around TP monitors. TP monitors are still the only way to go for high-volume, high-use client/server systems. I've dedicated Chapter 18 to the discussion of TP monitors and their use for client/server development.

A holdover from the mainframe world, TP monitors allow developers to make client/server scale to an enterprise level system (a thousand client/server users or more) through a superior architectural solution.

TP monitors manage transactions on behalf of the client, can route transactions across many diversified systems, provide load balancing and thread control. Developers can even assign execution priorities to transactions to better manage performance, or launch transactions on a predetermined schedule.

To call TP monitors a middleware layer does not do TP monitors justice. They are really an operating environment where a large portion of the application code executes. In fact, we call TP monitors that run on their own server "application servers," since most of the application logic and processing resides on that server. The use of an application server is the fundamental difference between two-tier and three-tier client/server computing (see Figure 3-6). TP monitors provide an independent location for business processing. The client acts only as an interface to the TP monitor, invoking functions. The TP monitor, in turn, can access the database on behalf of the client. Usually TP monitors run on their own server, but they can share the same machine with a database server. I, however, would not recommend this.

The most significant feature of a TP monitor is its ability to multiplex and manage transactions to remove the one-client-to-one-connection restriction of traditional two-tier client/server development. The TP monitor can only use a few connections to a database server to manage hundreds of clients. We also know this as database funneling. This means that by using a TP monitor, developers can create client/server systems that handle many more clients than the database server could comfortably handle. If the number of clients increases, the TP monitor simply kicks off new share connections to the database server.

TP monitors also protect a client/server application from potential disasters since TP monitors can reroute transactions around server and network failures. In addition, if a transaction fails, TP monitors can recover from the failure and never leave the system in an unstable state. TP monitors can use all types of connections middleware including RPCs and MOM, and can communicate with database servers using native database middleware or even ODBC.

APPLICATION PROGRAM-TO-PROGRAM CONNECTIONS, APPLICATION PROGRAM-TO-PROGRAM NETWORKS, AND COMMON PROGRAMMING INTERFACE FOR COMMUNICATIONS

Although client/server system development usually entails using smaller systems (never program anything bigger than you are, I say), there is still a need to access information and processing services on mainframes. This also provides an easy transition to pure client/server since developers can move to client/server in a phased approach. For example, it does not usually make sense to suddenly turn off a large mission-critical DB2 application running on a mainframe. Instead the developer can use the mainframe as a database server (albeit

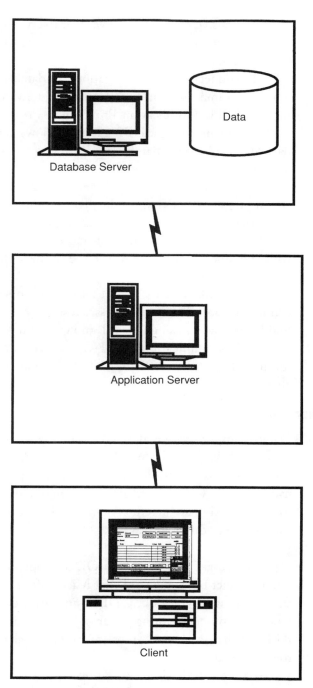

Figure 3-6 *Using an application server for three-tier computing.*

a very expensive one). This allows client/server applications to access data that resides on the mainframe in the same way they access data on traditional database servers.

To connect a client workstation to a database that resides on a mainframe, developers must rely on specialized middleware layers and protocols. These include APPC (Application Program-to-Program Connections), LU6.2, and CPI-C. For instance, a DB2 gateway allows standard clients to access DB2 data that resides on a mainframe. APPC provides interprocess communications between PCS and mainframes.

APPC is based on LU6.2, and LU6.2 uses small programs called transaction programs (TPs) to conduct conversations with each other using connection-oriented session services. This program allows a middleware service (e.g., APPC), to create a session when more than one LU connects to another. As with any other middleware server, the connection has to be active for a conversation to take place.

APPC, like NetBIOS, uses a common control block structure to facilitate communications between processes residing on each computer. APPC is a true middleware layer, using an API known as the Common Programming Interface for Communications (CPI-C) for access to the underlying middleware services. Like other APIs, CPI-C hides the complexity of APPC from the client/server developers that use it.

DATABASE MIDDLEWARE

Database middleware is all the software that connects some application to some database. Like primitive middleware layers, database middleware allows developers to access the resources of another computer, this case a database server, using a single well-defined API. Although database middleware is a bit easier to understand in architecture, many products make up this market, and they do things in very different ways.

Open Database Connectivity. ODBC (open database connectivity) is really not a product but a standard that Microsoft created several years ago just after the Windows revolution. ODBC simplifies database access from Windows (and a few other operating systems) by allowing the developer to make a single API call that works with most relational databases, and few that don't follow the relational model.

To me ODBC is a translation layer. Like all middleware layers, ODBC provides a well-defined API. When using the API, ODBC can determine which database the application would like to communicate with and load the

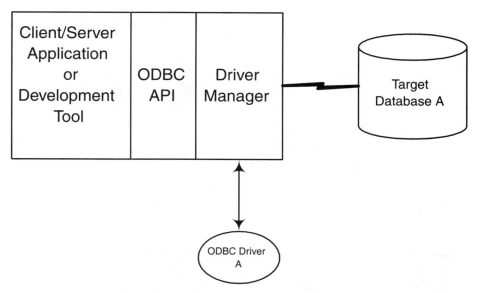

Figure 3-7 *The driver manager.*

appropriate ODBC driver. A driver manager manages the process of loading and unloading drivers for the developer and application (see Figure 3-7). This means that a client/server application using ODBC is database-independent. However, if there are any database-specific calls (such as passing SQL directly through to the database, or invoking a number of stored procedures and triggers), the application is no longer database-independent. It may make sense not to use ODBC, but move to a native database layer.

ODBC is now in a 32-bit version of Windows 95 and Windows NT, and most relational databases have ODBC drivers available. You can buy the drivers from the database vendors, or better yet through third-party ODBC driver vendors such as Intersolv or Visigenic. While ODBC is free, the drivers are not. Most popular client/server tool vendors provide database access features using ODBC. In fact it's the only way Microsoft's Visual Basic can talk to a database.

There is much debate out there about the use of ODBC. I've sat in on debate after debate about ODBC's ability to provide performance, access database features, and provide a stable application deployment platform. Here's my take on things. While ODBC had a rough start, and did not provide the performance that developers were looking for, the ODBC of today (generally speaking, since performance is driver-dependent) provides high performance database access. I've seen a few tests where ODBC has even outperformed the native middleware layer. What's more, version 2 of ODBC can access most of the native database features, such as access-stored procedures and triggers, tracking transaction, and recovering from errors—albeit without the same degree of control as when using middleware that's native to a particular database.

The bottom line is, ODBC is good enough for most two-tier client/server applications. You should consider using ODBC if you operate in a multi-database environment and need to access several databases from the same application, or if your database is likely to change during the life cycle of the application (such as scaling to a larger user load). Using ODBC will enable your application to move from database to database quickly. You may want to avoid ODBC if you're married to a particular database server and things aren't likely to change—if you need to build many proprietary database functions into your application.

Java Database Connectivity:
Open Database Connectivity

While ODBC gives developers a database-independent API for most Windows-base client/server systems, Javasoft is creating a similar specification for most Java development environments. JDBC (Java database connectivity) allows Java developers to access data residing on remote relational databases using standard Java classes.

JDBC is finding its way into most Java development environments such as Symantic's Visual Café Pro, Borland's JBuilder, and many others. Like ODBC, JDBC provides database-independent database access. A JDBC driver manager loads and unloads the appropriate drivers (Java classes residing on a Web server) to link any number of databases to a Java application or applet (see Figure 3-8). Most major relational database vendors such as Oracle, Sybase, and Informix already have JDBC drivers. Or developers can link to any ODBC accessible database using an ODBC bridge. See Chapter 23 for additional discussion on JDBC.

Integrated Database Application Programming Interface. During the rise of ODBC, Borland created its own database-independent API called IDAPI (Integrated Database Application Programming Interface). IDAPI goes beyond ODBC by providing a networked interface that enables the driver to reside on a remote computer allowing many clients to access the same set of drivers. ODBC vendors are doing this trick today as well.

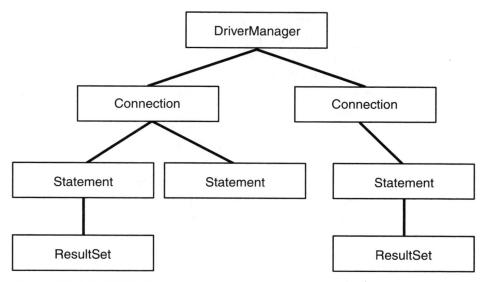

Figure 3-8 *The JDBC driver manager.*

While IDAPI began as an alternative to ODBC, Borland has since given up the battle and you'll find IDAPI today inside the Borland Database Engine (BDE). Borland includes the BDE with most of their development products including Delphi, dBASE, and Paradox. BDE can manage links to local database files as well as remote database server connections and can link to databases using native drivers or ODBC.

Going Native. Besides ODBC and other database translation interfaces, there are many native database middleware products. These are APIs provided by your database vendor or a third party with access to a particular database. While often these were older C and C++ libraries, most client/server development tools ship native database middleware with their products. For example, PowerBuilder and Delphi provide native database drivers providing access to most major database products.

The advantage to using native database middleware over ODBC is the ability to provide high-performance database access, and the ability to access features native to a specific database. However, using native database middleware locks into that middleware vendor since your client/server application uses calls specific to the database.

Structured Query Language Gateways. Structured query language (SQL) gateways are magical APIs that provide access to most databases residing on many different types of platforms using a single API set. They are like virtual system middleware products, but are just for database processing. For example, using an ODBC interface and an SQL gateway, I can access data residing in a DB2 on a mainframe, Oracle running on a minicomputer, and Sybase running on a Unix server. The developer simply makes an API call, and the SQL gateway does all the work for you.

SQL gateways translate the SQL calls into a standard format known as the Format and Protocol (FAP). FAP is the common connection between the client and the server, and is the common link between very different databases and platforms. The gateway can translate the API call directly into FAP, moving the request to the target database translating the request so that the target database and platform can react.

There are a few gateways on the market such as Information Builders, Inc. Enterprise Data Access/SQL (EDA/SQL, and standards such as IBM's distributed relational data access (DRDA) and ISO/SAG's remote data access (RDA). It's important that the developer knows they are available, and what each can do.

Enterprise Data Access/Structured Query Language. EDA/SQL is my favorite SQL gateway for many reasons. First, it works with most database servers and platforms. Thus it can bridge many enterprises where there are dozens of servers running on dozens of different platforms that need to be accessed from a single application. Second, it uses ODBC as the excess mechanism, and not some proprietary API. Thus, I can get to EDA/SQL connected databases using any number of client/server development tools. Finally, IBI has been around for a while and does not jump from product to product. It is in the middleware business, not the database business. Thus, I have confidence in its support of me, and not a product.

EDA/SQL can access more than fifty relational and nonrelational database servers, and can access all these databases using ODBC. There are several EDA/SQL components including the API/SQL, EDA/Extenders, EDA/Link, EDA/Server, and EDA/Data Drivers. API/SQL provides the call level interface (ODBC) allowing the developer to access the EDA/SQL resources. EDA/Extenders are really redirectors of SQL calls, which route the request across the network. EDA/Link provides the network connections by supporting more than twelve communication protocols, and EDA/Server resides on the target database processing the requests on behalf of the client. Finally, the EDA/Data Drivers, like ODBC drivers, provide access to more than fifty different target databases.

Remote Data Access. RDA (remote data access) is a standard, not a product, giving developers a standard way of accessing data. RDA uses OSI, and supports dynamic SQL. RDA also allows the client to be connected to more than one database server at the same time, and does not support typical transaction-related services. I always thought RDA was a good standard, but due to lack of vendor support and RDA's inability to snap into popular client/server development environments, it's no longer relevant for client/server development. For now, avoid it.

Distributed Relational Data Access. DRDA is an IBM database connectivity standard, and has many database heavyweights behind it such as Sybase, Oracle, IBI, and Informix. Like other database gateways DRDA is trying to provide easy database connectivity between any number of databases operating in multi-platform environments.

DRDA defines database transactions as remote requests, remote units of work, distributed units of work, and distributed requests. A remote request means that one SQL request is sent to one database. A remote unit of work means that many SQL commands are sent to one database. A distributed unit of work means that many SQL commands are sent to many databases. However, each command is sent to one database. Finally, a distributed request means that many SQL commands are sent to many databases and each command can execute on several databases.

While DRDA is a well-defined standard, the fact that DRDA requires that databases comply with standard SQL syntax makes DRDA a long shot for many organizations where many systems run many databases at different stages of maturity. Thus, it does not have much value as glue. I like DRDA because it's not a product, but a standard. However, IBM has come up with many standards in the past that just did not grow legs. I'm afraid that DRDA will be one of them.

Creating the Pipe

While most of this book is concerned with the development and deployment of database applications, it's important not to lose sight of what's in the middle. Clearly we are moving slowly toward an environment where standards will rule the day, and developers don't have to worry about network, operating system, and database interoperability. Today, however, integration in an infrastructure is a problem that needs solving and no one but the client/server developer is going to solve it.

What you need to take to heart is the fact that you need to study your available infrastructure solutions before you have to build a system. You need to understand what's in the technological bag of tricks today, so you can pull them out at the right time to solve specific problems.

In the next few years, as application partitioning and multi-tiered client/server development takes on a greater number of client/server development projects, the use of middleware will become more important. Not only is the middleware connecting client to server, but middleware glues entire applications together, linking objects to objects, interface to interface. What's more, the interest in the intranet may be more of an interest in finally finding a common middleware layer than in a new application development platform.

Designing Client/Server Solutions

Database Design
and Development
for Client/Server

The ability to store and process data is the real value of computers. Client/ server computing leverages the power of databases, which are at the heart of most client/server systems.

We've stored the same sort of data for applications for years now, but the way we store information evolves almost constantly. For example, in just the last fifteen years we've moved from flat-file, ISAM (Indexed Sequential Access Method), and partitioned data sets, to hierarchical databases, then relational, and now object-oriented and multi-dimensional databases. Although the data that we store in databases remains largely the same (text and numbers), the models and database engines that manage the data are in a constant state of flux. The trick is to figure out what works, what's hype, and what's going to go away. Certainly no easy task.

The Heart of Client/Server

Databases, in the form of DBMSs and database servers (databases residing on remote servers) are the heart of any client/server application. The database not only acts as a central location for the storage of data, but protects the data from outside forces that would violate business or integrity rules. Today's database systems, through stored procedures and triggers, can share the application processing load, and store binary information such as audio and video data as well.

We live in the days of a universal server concept, or a database server that's all things to all applications. For instance, version 7 of Oracle can not only serve up data, but can act like an object-oriented database for tight integration with object-oriented development environments. Or it can act like a multi-dimensional database for use in data warehousing applications, or even a relational database. Oracle can even send and receive information to and from Web browsers using HTML directly.

Like everything client/server, database technology continues to move forward very quickly, and client/server developers must keep pace with the changes. In the next couple of chapters, I'll provide you with basic and advanced information you'll need to work effectively with client/server database technology.

Database Concepts

Databases are nothing more than a large collection of data. To manage this data, we need to employ database management systems (DBMSs). DBMSs are specialized software programs that store, retrieve, and manipulate data. In the client/server world, database servers run DBMSs to manage the data remotely, away from the client. Examples of DBMSs for database servers include Oracle, Sybase, or Informix.

All DBMSs employ some sort of model. A model defines how the data is logically organized in the DBMS, independent from the way data is physically stored on disk. Although several different DBMS models emerged over the last decade, the three that are most relevant to client/server are the object-oriented model, the relational model, and the multi-dimensional model.

RELATIONAL DATABASES

It's no secret that relational databases rule the world of client/server. Although many of my associates have argued the "why" of this, I believe that the simplicity of the relational model is the most compelling reason for its popularity. We seem to think in the relational model already. Also, we still use databases mostly as a storage mechanism for data, versus a location for application processing. Relational databases meet that need nicely.

What are the other contributing factors? Relational database technology is available, we understand it, and relational databases provide the least amount of risk for client/server systems. Using nonrelational products (e.g., object-oriented and multi-dimensional databases) adds risk to client/server development projects due to the lack of support from the mainstream client/server development market.

This could change in the near future. For example, many relational database vendors such as Oracle, Sybase, and Informix provide universal databases that can pretend to be object-oriented, multi-dimensional, and Web-ready (intranet as well), and store binary information such as video.

Being All Things to All Data—Universal Databases

There is a movement afoot to retrofit existing relational databases to handle objects and migration to intranets. These hybrid databases, known as universal databases, can be all things to all data. The big players in the universal database market include Oracle, Informix, and Sybase.

In mid-1996, Oracle announced the introduction of its universal database. Oracle's Universal Server integrates the existing Oracle database server with several special purpose servers that include text, video, message, spatial data, and HTML, using an object-oriented or relational model.

Informix takes a different architectural approach. To support objects, Informix bought an object-oriented database company, Illustra. Informix is building the Illustra database into Informix's existing relational database technology. The version of Informix's first attempt at a universal server is due out in early 1997.

Rather than build object-oriented capabilities into its existing relational engine, Sybase looks to support objects through a partnering relationship with Persistence Software, Inc. Persistence provides a middleware solution that can map relational databases (such as Sybase's SQL Server) into objects on the fly. By simply layering a product on top of an existing relational database engine, Sybase will handle objects before other database vendors.

Relational databases organize data in two-dimensional tables, and nothing but tables, tied together using common attributes (known as keys). Each table has rows and columns (see Figure 4-1).

Rows contain an instance of the data. For example, my address would be a row in a customer table in the database of my local power company (see Figure 4-2). Therefore, each row represents a record.

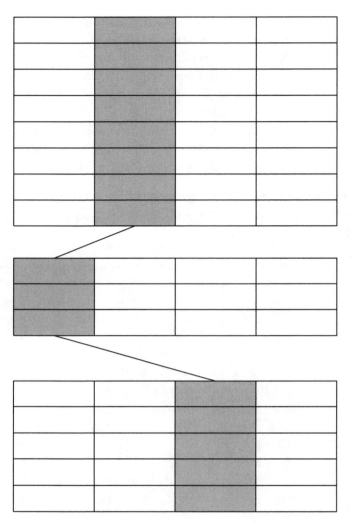

Figure 4-1 *Keys tie Tables Together.*

Columns are really a named placeholder for data that defines the type of data the column is set up to contain. For example, the columns for the customer table may include Cust_Number, Cust_First_Name, Cust_Last_Name, Cust_Address, Cust_City, Cust_Zip, and Cust_Birth_Day. While some columns may be set up to accept both text and numeric data, the Cust_Birth_Day would be set up to accept only date formatted information (e.g., 09/17/62), and the Cust_Number column would accept only numeric data.

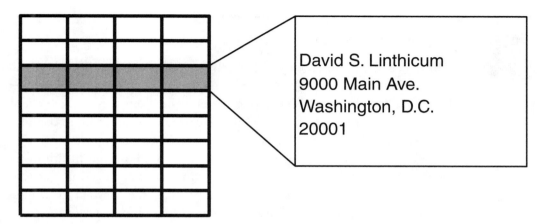

David S. Linthicum
9000 Main Ave.
Washington, D.C.
20001

Figure 4-2 *Rows contain data.*

Keys are columns common to two or more tables. Keys link rows together to form groupings of data. Consider the previous example. While the customer table tracks information about power customers, there may be a billing table to track billing information. The columns in the billing table may include Cust_Number, Billing_Month, and Billing_Amount. As you can see, the Cust_Number column is common to both the customer and the billing tables, and acts as a key to link the databases together. While I may only have one row in the customer table, I have many rows in the billing table.

It's the job of client/server applications to use the features of relational databases to present data to the end-users. For example, if we built an application for the power company database example in Figure 4-2, we would create a series of screens and menus that allow the end-user to update, delete, view, or create reports for the customer and billing tables.

This was a simple example. Most applications that you'll work with use complex databases. For instance, most relational database-driven client/server applications I've worked with contain as many as a hundred active tables that represent a variety of information. The challenge for the client/server developer is to design a proper database for the application, as well as design the application itself. Later I'll discuss the important concept of database design.

We'll discuss some more of the technical details of relational database technology in the next chapter, including stored procedures, triggers, and other advanced features of modern relational databases. I'll review features of particular databases as well.

Separating Roles

While I've played the role of both database designer and database administrator (known as the DBA), as well as application designer and developer, I see a clear trend toward separating the tasks between two or more client/server professionals. As the world of client/server becomes more complex, I can see why this is a good idea.

The DBA concerns herself or himself with the overall health of the database. This includes a sound design, performance engineering, data dictionary maintenance, user administration, backups, the constant installation of bug fixes and patches, and interaction with application developers.

Clearly, the DBA's position is a full-time job. While some developers can pull double duty, in many situations the database gets neglected and so does half the client/server application. The DBA's role becomes even more important when considering large multi-tiered distributed applications that support a large user base, or when there are many different applications that use the same database.

I recommend that developers work on the front-end, and DBAs work on the back-end. Things will go much smoother, and the project will have a better chance of success.

OBJECT-ORIENTED DATABASES

The object-oriented database model is a relatively new concept. Just a few years ago, object-oriented databases were thought to be a challenge to the dominance of the relational model. Although object-oriented databases are more prominent today, they have not overthrown Sybase, Oracle, Informix, and Computer Associates. However, they did have some effect. Most relational vendors offer object-oriented database capabilities within existing relational database technology—the universal database (see Sidebar). What's more, the interest in the Web is renewing interest in object-oriented databases for content and Web-aware data storage.

Although it is still a "relational world," many OO DBMSs are making inroads into organizations that find the object-oriented database model a better fit for certain applications. OO DBMSs meet the information storage requirements for mission-critical systems that have complex information storage needs. Examples are applications that require storage of complex data such as a repository, or applications that use binary data such as audio, video, and images.

For example, Computer Associates' Jasmine multi-media and Web development tool uses an object-oriented database to store multi-media content. In many instances, developers use object-oriented database technology since it's tightly integrated with traditional object-oriented development technology (such as C++ and Smalltalk). Today, however, we have the middleware required to make relational databases appear as object-oriented, not to mention universal servers.

Those who have experience with object-oriented programming languages (such as C++ or Smalltalk) already understand how objects contain both data and the methods to access that data. OO DBMSs are nothing more than systems that use this model as the basis for storing information, and therefore support the object-oriented concepts of encapsulation and inheritance (explained in detail in Chapter 6).

Data management illustrates the fundamental differences between traditional relational database technology and object-oriented databases. In traditional relation databases, developers separate the methods (programs that act upon the data) and the data. In contrast, object-oriented databases combine data and methods together.

Figure 4-3 depicts the basic idea behind an object-oriented database. The data resides (is encapsulated) inside the object. Surrounding the data are a series of methods, or small structured programs that control access to the data. Developers define the methods programmatically, and embed the methods inside the object-oriented database, functionally equivalent to stored procedures and triggers. To access the data, a program (e.g., a program that resides on the client) dispatches a message to the method. The message instructs the method to carry out an operation (e.g., delete) (see Figure 4-4).

OO DBMS vendors contend that OO DBMSs can process complex structures better since all objects contained in an OO DBMS are addressable

Figure 4-3 *OO Database.*

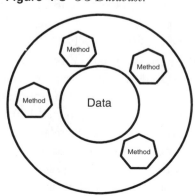

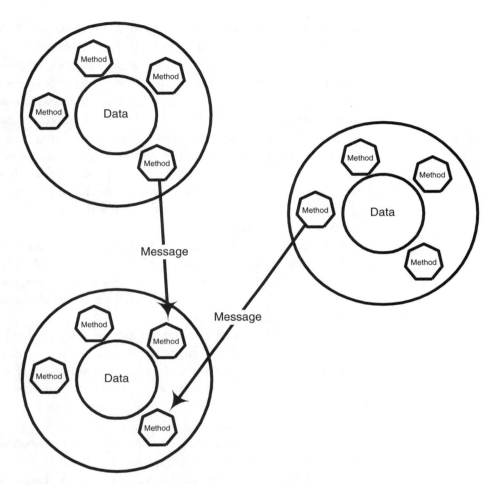

Figure 4-4 *Messages provide communication between objects.*

by a unique global object identifier. This concept enables quick lookup of individual objects since data is stored with the methods used to access the data (encapsulated). Only OO DBMSs that store data and methods together can obtain this type of enhanced performance.

The popularity of object-oriented programming languages and related object-oriented tools leads to a real need for database systems that support the object-oriented model. Using OO DBMSs, programmers no longer have to shift from object-oriented to relational and back again. Everything in an application can be considered an object. All objects, either persistent or run-time, are treated the same in the eyes of the object-oriented application. This single paradigm approach simplifies object-oriented development.

The tradeoff is the cost of using a nonstandard database. Most OO DBMSs don't enjoy wide development tool support, and therefore in many cases you'll have to learn C++ or Smalltalk in order for OO DBMSs to be of any value. With the advent of Universal servers and sophisticated wrappering mechanisms, the need for traditional OO DBMSs could easily subside. Most OO DBMS vendors are very small companies, and don't have the R&D budgets of the big three relational database vendors. Once again, the big guys beat the little guys, no matter how good the product.

Turning Tables into Objects

Just a few years ago, the press and developers were enamored with the new object-oriented database model. Many even predicted its ultimate dominance in the database market. Object-oriented databases seem to be a better fit for object-oriented development tools, and they can better handle complex data structures and the storage of binary content like images, video, and audio.

The object-oriented database revolution has yet to materialize. Relational databases are still the dominant technology, and part of almost all client/server development projects. Object databases have yet to grow legs.

The need to use object-oriented technology to create the front-end application, and the need to use relational technology on the back-end results in model mixing. Model mixing means that client/server developers must use relational databases directly from their object-oriented development environments. This is usually a process of dropping back to nonobject-oriented procedural programming from API access. This has the effect of circumventing the real benefit of object-oriented development (covered later in this book).

There are solutions to the problem of model mixing. These new methods let developers communicate with relational databases as emulated persistent objects. This is accomplished by adding object-to-relational translation and mapping layers between the object-oriented development environment and the relational database.

Data Mixing

The heart of the problem is the basic architectural differences between relational and object-oriented databases. The relational model is a two-dimensional representation of data, decoupled from the application logic. Object databases allow developers to create a highly complex multi-dimensional grouping of data and binary information where the object and data exist together.

If relational databases are state-of-the-art in database technology, developers need to understand how to mix the best of relational database technology with the best of object-oriented development environments. As this book is being printed, we are still wrestling with the best way to do this.

LEARNING FROM SMALLTALK

The best of examples of mixing relational and object-oriented technology can be seen in the strides that Smalltalk tool vendors such as Parcplace-Digitalk and IBM made with integrating relational databases directly in their development environments. Smalltalk is a pure object-oriented development environment. Therefore, everything from variables to data must be represented as an object.

Access to relational databases (e.g., Sybase, Oracle, Informix) can only occur using object-to-relational mapping mechanisms, and through "relational wrappers."

Object-to-relational mapping mechanisms let developers remap (link) the properties of an object or set of objects to the properties of a relational database. This remapping process allows the relational database to appear as a persistent object or objects, native to the Smalltalk development environment. For instance, one table maps to one object type, and one record maps to one object.

Relational wrapper is a layer that sits between the objects and the database. The relational wrapper watches for changes in the contents of an object, and generates the SQL to make the appropriate changes in the attached relational database. The relational wrapper can also detect changes in the relational database, and automatically alter the contents of the connected object. Developers simply process the database as an object within the application. The data translation is transparent.

OTHER SOLUTIONS

You can apply the Smalltalk object-to-relational concept to other development environments as well. Many products access relational databases as objects. Some of the best solutions I've seen include Persistence from Persistence Software, Inc., and DBTools.h++ from Rouge Wave Software, Inc.

Persistence, from Persistence Software, Inc., provides an object-to-relational solution through middleware. The Persistence middleware layer restructures relational data as a set of common objects that reside on a virtual object server (analogous to application servers).

There are two major components to Persistence: a development tool and an object server. The development tool automates the object-to-relational mapping. The object server manages the object data integrity and the system optimization mechanism.

DBTools.h++ provides a set of C++ classes that lets C++ developers access relational databases through C++ objects. DBTools.h++ transforms rows and columns of relational databases into C++ objects that are easily manipulated inside the C++ application.

Object-oriented database servers are available for client/server development. However, few specialized client/server tools (e.g., PowerBuilder, Delphi, and Visual Basic) support the features of object-oriented databases directly. If you're sold on object-oriented technology, you're better off using traditional object-oriented languages such as C++ or Smalltalk.

Smalltalk (covered in Chapter 12), for example, is a pure object-oriented tool where everything exists as an object, including the database. Relational databases must be "wrapped," so they will appear as an object inside the Smalltalk environment. Object-oriented databases that already support the pure object-oriented model don't have to be wrapped. They also provide better performance since there is no need to translate relational data to objects, and back again.

MULTI-DIMENSIONAL DATABASES

It's funny how computer technology is like the fashion industry. What's out this year may be in next year, and what was in several years ago may come back someday. That's true of multi-dimensional databases.

I first saw multi-dimensional database technology when I worked at Boeing Computer Services in the mid-'80s. The multi-dimensional database was attached to Boeing's EIS (Executive Information System), a mainframe-based 4GL development environment. This was one of the first 4GLs I worked on.

After using traditional database technology such as hierarchical, network, and relational, I was amazed at how well the multi-dimensional database model fit into systems that had to support decision support system (DSS) facilities. DSS capacities mean the ability for users to sort through the data by "slicing and dicing" their way through the logical data structure which represents a cube, to generate meaningful information in support of management decisions.

Multi-dimensional databases went through an evolution over the years, and are now repackaged as databases that support on-line analytical processing (OLAP) or data mining, all wrapped up in a relatively new concept known as data warehousing. Data warehousing is the current focus of many MIS directors who seek a means to turn thousands of gigabytes of company data into meaningful information for those who need it. Multi-dimensional databases are a tool to make this a reality.

Multi-dimensional databases manipulate data as if it resided in a giant cube. Each side of the cube represents a dimension of the multi-dimensional database (see Figure 4-5). For example, one side of the cube can contain sales, on the other side you'll find customers, and the next, sales districts. Inside the cube you'll find all the intersections of the dimensions that allow the end-users to examine every possible combination of the data by "slicing and dicing" their way through the cube with an OLAP tool. For our purposes, OLAP and multi-dimensional databases are joined at the hip.

There are basically two ways that OLAP products store data for multi-dimensional analysis. The first is a true multi-dimensional database server such as Arbor Software's Easbase. Here the data is actually stored as a multi-dimensional array, also known as a "real cube." Another more convenient way to employ OLAP is to maintain the data in relational databases, but map that data so it appears as multi-dimensional data stored to the OLAP tool and end-user. This is known as a "virtual cube," where the illusion exists at the metadata layer (see Figure 4-6).

Figure 4-5 *Multi–dimensional database.*

Northeast

Western	Southern			
		20	34	12	Memory Chips
		3	45	100	Processors
		25	45	78	Hard Drives

1995   1996   1997

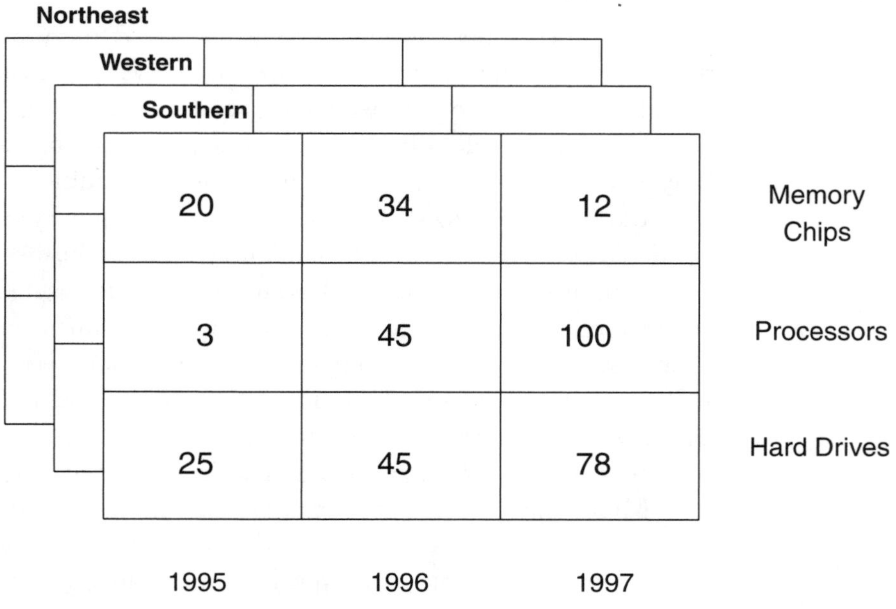

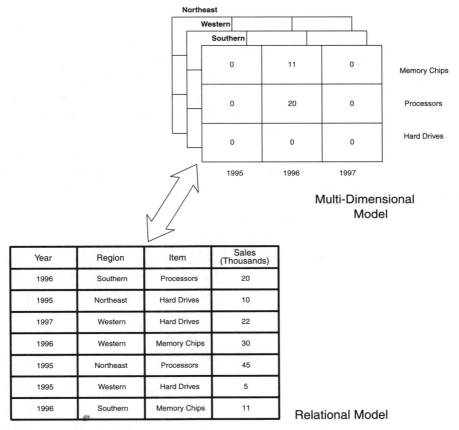

Multi-Dimensional
Model

Year	Region	Item	Sales (Thousands)
1996	Southern	Processors	20
1995	Northeast	Hard Drives	10
1997	Western	Hard Drives	22
1996	Western	Memory Chips	30
1995	Northeast	Processors	45
1995	Western	Hard Drives	5
1996	Southern	Memory Chips	11

Relational Model

Figure 4-6 *Virtual cube.*

What Are On-Line Analytical Processing Tools?

On-line analytical processing (OLAP) tools give end-users the power to examine, analyze, and summarize corporate data with just a few clicks of the mouse. A new entry into the client/server arsenal of tools, OLAP provides a natural way to look at data. OLAP also provides decision makers with the power to finally get information out of the database servers that they really need, and avoids the hassle of using traditional query languages and tools. Thus, OLAP significantly cuts the time it takes to serve up information, it does not require complicated development, and is quickly becoming the favorite pastime of information-hungry executives. I'll cover OLAP and reporting tools in more detail in Chapter 14.

Although there is no clear definition of OLAP, most OLAP products provide point-and-click access to multi-dimensional data from PCs connected to traditional database servers or proprietary multi-dimensional databases. Some OLAP tools, such as BrioQuery for Windows from Brio Technology, Inc., Prodea Beacon from Prodea, and PowerPlay from Cognos Corp., provide just the OLAP client side to both relational and multi-dimensional databases. Other OLAP products, such as Easbase Analysis Server from Arbor Software Corp., offer just the multi-dimensional server side. However, a few OLAP products (such as LightShip Server from Pilot Software, Inc.) provide both the multi-dimensional database server as well as the client.

Reporting tools (close relatives of OLAP tools) also let end-users extract information out of the database. However, reporting tools require that the end-user have a rudimentary knowledge of the database to create database queries, form relations, and format those queries into meaningful reports and graphs. Although reporting tools can get at the same information as OLAP tools, they work best in the hands of developers, not end-users.

The power of multi-dimensional database and OLAP is that this technology provides a multi-dimensional view of the database that closely resembles the way the end-user understands the business. OLAP offers a natural "drill down" interface that allows users to move through layer upon layer of the data abstractions until they find the information they need. Once found, the user can print or graph the data, as well as import it into documents or spreadsheets.

For instance, an executive seeking sales information by various categories for an upcoming board meeting can click on the sales dimension, and then on other dimensions beneath it such as sales by product, sales by industry, sales by salesperson, and so on. Upon selecting one of these "subdimensions," the executive can search further by selecting additional dimensions until he or she finds the required information. The executive need not understand the structure of the database, relational database technology, or even know exactly what to look for; the OLAP tool will be a guide for the process.

The selling point of OLAP and multi-dimensional databases is flexibility. By clicking on the data itself, end-users can combine data in any order for any reason. OLAP tools place no limitations on what the end-user can do with the data. What's more, end-users can display data at any level of aggregation, and end-users can retrieve results over several time periods.

Database Design

Now that we know the basics of three popular database models, let's turn our attention to what it takes to transform user requirements into a database for a client/server system. This is known as database design, or the process of creating a logical database model from requirements, then mapping the logical database design to a physical database.

Although a detailed discussion of requirements gathering for a database design is beyond the scope of this book, database analysts, DBAs, and developers need to understand how to derive requirements by gathering information from users. Usually this is a process of user interviews, gathering relevant items such as invoices, ledgers, and other reports, or holding joint application design (JAD) sessions. No matter what technique you use, the end result should be a clear understanding of the business functions, the data, and the expectations of the end-users. Fail to do this, and the system is a failure—even if it's well-built. Take my word on this.

You can break database design into two basic stages: logical database design (sometimes called conceptual database design) and physical database design. Each has its place in the client/server system development life cycle.

LOGICAL DATABASE DESIGN

Logical design is the process of creating an architecture for a database that's independent of a physical database model, development tool, and a particular DBMS (Oracle, Sybase, Informix, etc.). This is a useful way to approach a project, since developers can make an objective database solution decision, moving from the high-level requirements to the implementation details. The logical data model is an integrated view of business data throughout the application domain, or data pertinent to the client/server application under construction.

Entity-Relationship Diagram. The heart of the logical database design is the entity-relationship diagram (ERD). An ERD is a graphical representation of data entities, attributes, and relationships between entities (see Figure 4-7).

An entity is a person, place, object, or concept that may attract data. For instance, entities found in a car dealer client/server database application might include cars, salespeople, and a sales transaction. Attributes are characteristics of entities, or particular data elements. For instance, attributes of the car entity might include vehicle identification number, color, make, and model year. Relationships on ERDs demonstrate how each entity is related to other entities. For instance, the relationship between the salespeople entity and cars is that sales-people sell cars (see Figure 4-8).

ERDs use special symbols (notation). The notation varies between data modeling methodologies. However, they all provide some way to represent entities, attributes, and relationships. I prefer IDEF1X (used by ERwin)-type data models and fully attributed data models. You can also model data using Bachman, Chen, or Information Engineering (IE) notation. Although methodologists may disagree, when creating a logical database, the notation you use really doesn't make that big a difference. Use what works for you, or your organization.

There are many tools to automate the logical database modeling process. Known as CASE (computer-aided software engineering tools) these products not only provide an easy way to create logical database models, they can also build logical database models into physical database models, and create the physical schema on the target database through standard middleware. I'll talk about some of my favorite data-modeling CASE tools later.

Figure 4-7 *ERD.*

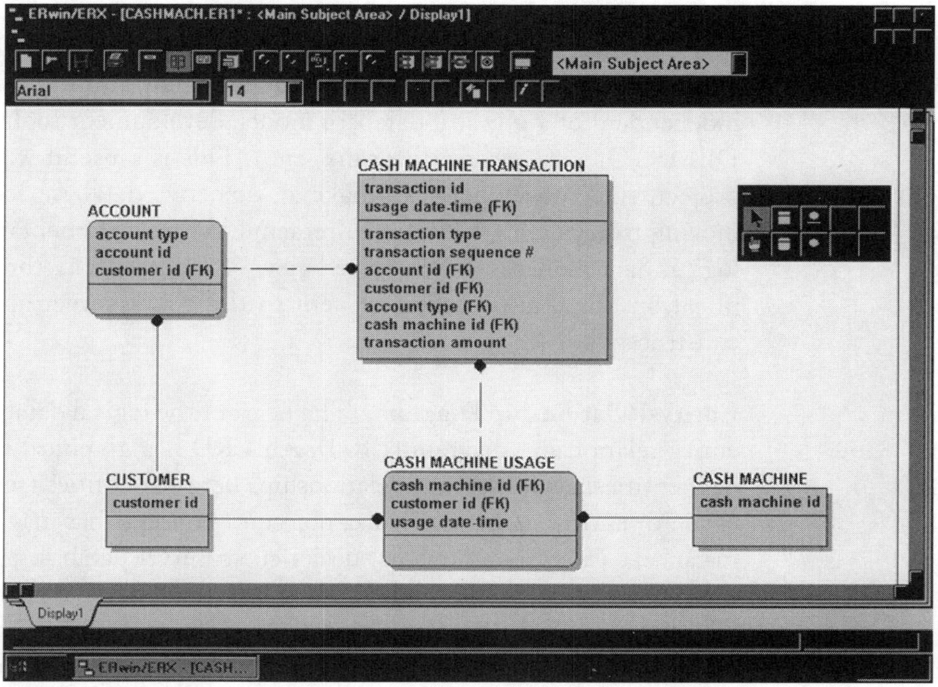

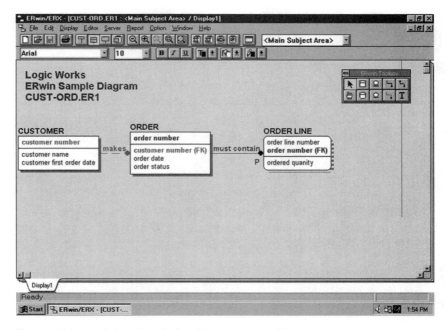

Figure 4-8 *Defining the relationship between entities.*

Data Volume and Response Time. Other issues that DBA and developers must deal with when they design the client/server database are the amount of data that the users intend to pump in and out of the database on a hourly, daily, weekly, and monthly basis. For instance, in our car dealership example, it's not likely that the salespeople will sell more than a dozen or so cars a day. The handful of users want reasonable response time from the database (e.g., two seconds to retrieve, update, and delete information). Thus the database designer can figure the amount of data that the database needs to retain—in this case only twelve new records a day (average). A single-processing PC-based relational database server would work nicely.

In contrast, other databases may require the processing of significantly more data. For instance, a catalog mail order house that I worked with received 1200 to 2000 orders a day. What's more, the hundred or so users who were on the phone with customers needed a one-second response time or better when retrieving information for customers. Therefore, the database I designed for them and the architecture they selected needed to support that high level of data. A multi-processing high-end relational database server fit the bill. A rather expensive bill, but in the long run, the system saved the business millions of dollars.

Avoiding Zealots Through Logical Design

Some developers, DBAs, and development teams may be bound to a particular database by emotional rather than technical and rational reasons. For example, some DBAs love Sybase, while others love Informix, and they would not dare consider another relational database, or a database that uses another model (e.g., object-oriented or multi-dimensional). I call these folks database zealots.

This is not to say that database zealots are always wrong. Only that they usually fail to consider other databases that may be better solutions to solve the problem at hand. In many cases, database zealots have a point in using the same databases as much as possible in an organization, which reduces support costs.

Logical database design is a good way to make your point with database zealots, since it naturally moves from the high-level requirements down to the implementation details. Developers and DBAs can use this information to make an objective decision about the correct database technology to meet the requirements.

You'll find that even the most stubborn zealot will willingly switch to other products and database models if you demonstrate that circumstances exist to warrant the switch. In other instances you'll even prove that the database they love is a good fit for the project. The trick is to keep everyone objective and select the best database solution.

Normalization. Before your logical database design is complete, you need to normalize the model. Normalization is the process of decomposing complex data structures into simple relations using a series of dependency rules. Normalization means that we reduce the amount of redundant data that will exist in the database. It's a good idea to do this in both the logical and physical database design.

There are several rules for normalization called the first, second, third, fourth, and fifth normal forms. Each is a test of the state of a database to determine its level of normalization. I think the experts have overcomplicated this process, but I'll try to make it as clear as possible.

First normal form (1NF) means that the database is in a state in which the intersection of each row and column contains only automic (meaning single) values.

Second normal form (2NF) means that the relation is in 1NF, and each non-key attribute is functionally dependent on the primary key. The primary key is the unique column that creates the link to other tables, such as the customer number in the previous power company example, or your Social Security number in many credit reporting systems.

Third normal form (3NF) is a relation that's in 2NF, and there are no nonkey attributes (columns) that are functionally dependent on another nonkey attribute. In many databases I've dealt with, we stop at 3NF since it's fully normalized for all practical purposes.

DATA DICTIONARIES AND REPOSITORIES

Another helpful activity while you create your logical database model is to create a data dictionary. A data dictionary is a repository of all metadata (data about data) for an organization. It's helpful to track data elements as you identify them, making sure that each has a place in your logical and physical database design (see Figure 4-9).

Data dictionaries also help capture business rules and constraints that must be dealt with in the design of the database. For example, it's important to note that a stock price can never be less than zero, or that a customer number has to be entered along with customer information. Most CASE tools and client/server development tools provide facilities to collect data inside a data dictionary. Some tools can reverse-engineer existing databases to create a data dictionary automatically.

Figure 4-9 *Data Dictionary.*

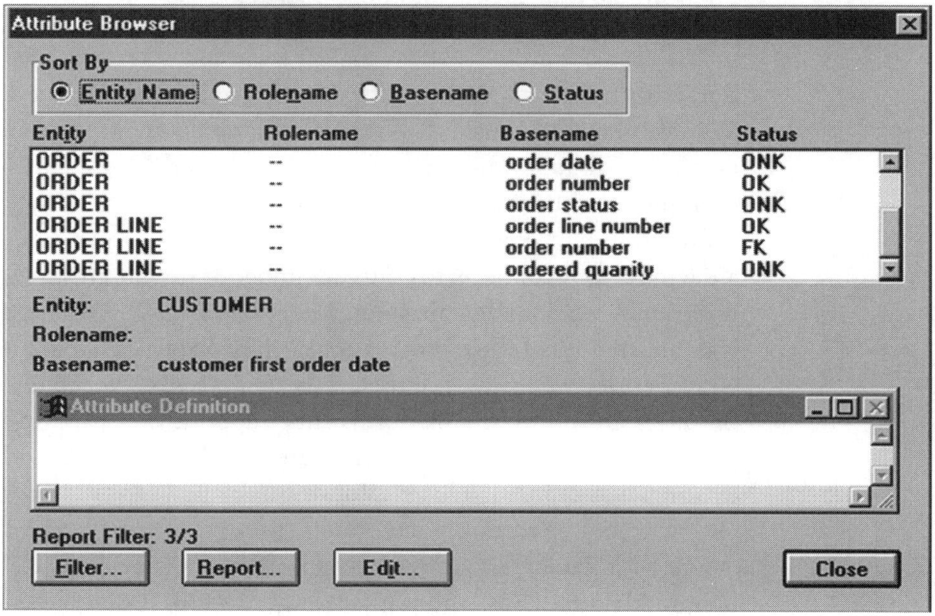

PHYSICAL DATABASE DESIGN

Okay, now that you understand the problems your system needs to solve (business requirements) and you have a completed logical data model, it's time to create a physical database design. The physical database design means mapping the logical database design to both a available database model (e.g., relational, object-oriented, or multi-dimensional) and a physical database structure for the model you select. For example, the physical database design is concerned with selecting and implementing file organization and access methods, as well as figuring out how to index the database.

The physical database design process is the last step in the database design process. However, it's the step in database development where I see the most errors occur. The physical database design process must be performed carefully since the physical database affects performance, integrity, security, and a number of issues that affect the base application and end-users.

The input for the physical database design includes the ERDs you created in the logical database design process, as well as the data dictionary, business rules, and other user processing requirements. The DBA needs to perform several steps that include selection of a database model, mapping the logical database design to a physical database schema, and performance engineering activities. The DBA may even select the proper middleware for the database and partition the data across several databases. It's no easy task, and there is no one formula that DBAs and developers can use to ensure that they made the right physical database design decisions.

Selecting a Model. When selecting the right database model for your database, you need to consider all the information you gathered such as number of users, data volume, and type of data, as well as the logical database design. For example, if you need to store a lot of complex information, including binary information, an object-oriented database may be a good fit. But if you need a database that connects to a large number of development and OLAP tools, a traditional relational database may be a better fit. If you need to provide data warehousing capabilities, then a multi-dimensional database may be best.

Besides the features of the database models, you need to consider available products, including the platforms they support. Don't forget the cost of those products when all things are considered, and their ability to integrate in your existing environment. This is a lot to think about.

I recommend that when going through this process you create a matrix where your database requirements go down one side, and your candidate database models go across the top (see Figure 4-10). Using a ranking system, you

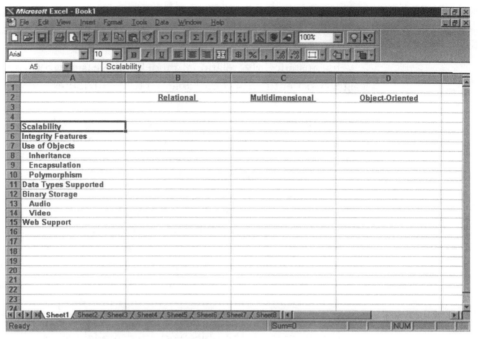

Figure 4-10 *Database Requirements Matrix.*

can see which database model meets your requirements. From there you can use the same matrix to select a particular database product that uses the model. We'll talk more about specific database products in the next chapter.

Start with Relational Solutions

With the high cost of nonrelational database support, and considering that they don't work and play well with standard tools, DBAs and developers should always consider the relational model first. If there is a good reason not to use the relational model, only then should developers and DBAs consider other alternatives.

The fact is, 98 percent of the client/server projects use relational databases because they are readily available and the easiest to support. Although they are not always the right solution, by considering the relational model first, then looking for reasons not to use it, you'll save yourself steps in the long run.

Mapping the Physical from the Logical.   After selecting a model, you need to map your logical database design to your physical design. This depends on the model you select.

For instance, the relational model is the easiest to map from your logical design. Most entities become tables, and the attributes become columns. Database designers can create primary and secondary keys to link the tables together. In addition, the database needs to be normalized again for efficiency, usually by splitting some tables in two, and combining others. Sometimes, the physical database must be denormalized from the logical design to provide better database performance. Fully normalized databases are often just too slow due to the fact that the databases must update so many tables and indexes.

Also, when mapping the logical database design to the relational model, DBAs and developers should create an indexing scheme that allows the database to rapidly search the tables. The DBA needs to address the database configuration as well, including hash tables, bucket sizes, database partitions, and other features that directly affect database performance. You'll have to consult the administration documentation for your particular database. They are all a bit different.

If you move to the object-oriented model, you need to map the ERD into an object diagram. The object diagram depicts the object-oriented structure of the database, taking the best advantage of inheritance features in object-oriented databases. Remember, you can always leave the data in a relational database and use a middleware or wrapping solution (see previous description of this technique) to make a relational database appear as object-oriented.

You can map to multi-dimensional databases in one of two ways. First, you can purchase a true multi-dimensional database and map the entities and attributes into a multi-dimensional depiction of the data. Or, you can maintain the data in a relational database and use an OLAP tool to make a relational database emulate a true multi-dimensional database. The tradeoff is performance. True multi-dimensional databases tend to perform better.

USING COMPUTER-AIDED SOFTWARE ENGINEERING

CASE (Computer-aided software engineering) is a big help to client/server developers because it takes you through the entire software development life cycle, supporting both the physical and logical design of the database. CASE supports the initial requirements gathering, data dictionary development, structured or object-oriented process design, database design, and most important, database schema generation. I'll cover CASE in detail in Chapter 15.

Front-end development tools don't support formal analysis and design, or database design methodologies (although some have design facilities). The front-end development tool vendors teamed up with CASE vendors to fill this void. Let's examine a few of my favorite CASE tools—ones that work well for logical and physical database design.

System Architect. System Architect is a Windows-based upper CASE tool supporting the majority of structured and object-oriented analysis and design methods (see Chapter 7 for a description of the methods) and data modeling methods. System Architect uses a top-down approach to software design, allowing developers to mix and match methods (see Figure 4-11).

Considering database design and deployment, System Architect uses a schema generator allowing database designers to move logical and physical database designs directly into physical database schemas. System Architect supports Oracle 7, DB2, Rdb, Informix, Ingres SQL, Sybase, AS/400, SQL Server, Paradox, Progress, dBase III, and XDB. The schema generator is also able to create referential integrity features in a database such as the generation of triggers.

Figure 4-11 *System Architect CASE Tool.*

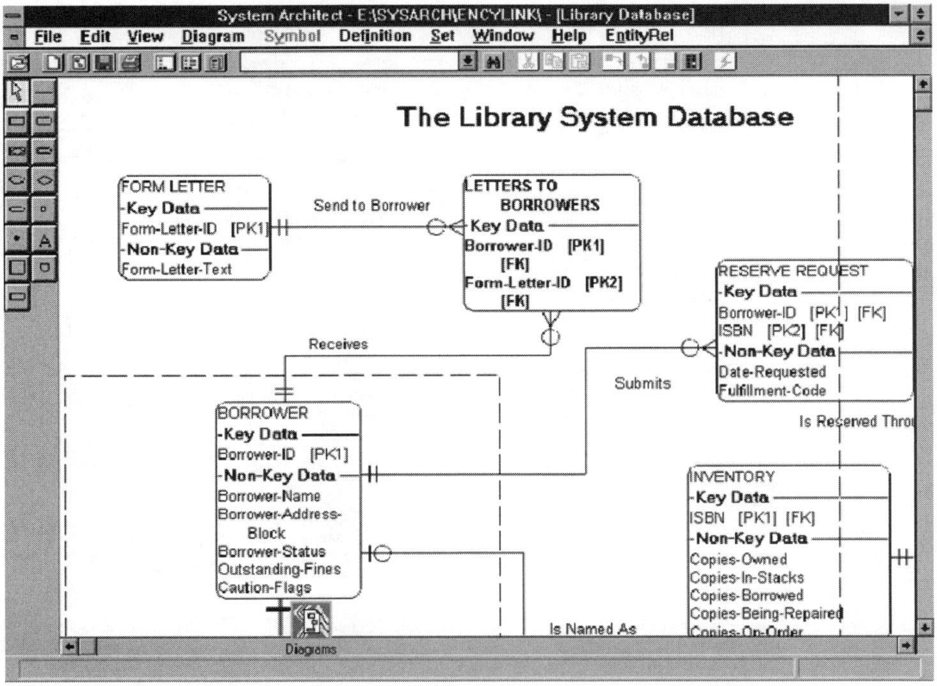

System Architect can also provide reverse-engineering features for database development. This allows database modelers to turn existing physical database schemas into database models. You can import structures from existing databases including tables, indexes, primary keys, foreign keys, stored procedures, triggers, defaults, rules, and views. The reverse-engineering facility supports all of the databases mentioned above. If you're using CASE, I recommend strongly that you consider using reverse-engineering facilities such as this. They save time, trouble, and don't typically make mistakes.

ERwin. ERwin from Logic Works, Inc. also provides bidirectional links with data models and most popular relational databases. ERwin is strictly a database modeling tool, and does not support process design features like System Architect (see Figure 4-12).

The general concept of ERwin is to create a logical database model, then map that model to a physical database schema. From there, you can generate the DDL (database definition language) you'll need to create the database schema on the target database such as Sybase, Oracle, or Informix. ERwin supports reverse-engineering features as well, building logical and physical models directly from existing databases.

Figure 4-12 *ERwin.*

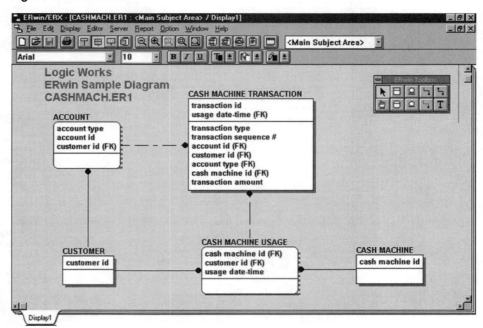

Importance of Getting the Database Right

Obviously, a proper database design and selecting the correct database technology is critical to the success of your client/server system. In many instances, the database is a neglected client/server component since users have no idea what front-end application their database connects to. Out of sight, out of mind.

In my experience, most performance problems are traceable to a database problem. This can involve overnormalization of the database, the wrong database model for the job, or an undersized processor. These problems are easily avoided if you just take the time to do your homework, and implement some of the concepts in this chapter.

Selecting a
Database Server

Now that we know about various types of databases and how to design a logical and physical database, it's time to turn our attention to the selection of the physical database server software. Once again I will cover this topic from the perspective of the client/server developer, looking at only the essential information.

You should remember that you need to get the details about databases from the database vendors. Things change quickly, and technology cycles through the client/server database world about once every two years. What's so today, ain't so tomorrow.

Database servers (client/server databases running on a server) are the heart of all client/server systems. They provide the central engine which ties the clients together. Considering that fact, the lack of thought that goes into evaluating and selecting many database servers always amazes me. If a team spends more time arguing about front-end development tools, they often end up with a database server that can't handle the basic requirements of the application. Or worse, they select a database server that can't scale to the user and processing load.

Server Activities

Database servers don't just provide data to clients that request it. Database servers do a lot behind the scenes to assure that the information is processed correctly and can handle any problems that servers will encounter. For example, database servers use sophisticated concurrency control features to provide locking mechanisms that protect data from multi-user access. This assures that two users who go after the same piece of data won't destroy the data in the process (the so-called "deadly embrace"). Database servers also secure the data, optimize database queries, cache data, and track metadata on behalf of the front-end application. Databases also provide APIs which let developers access the services of a database, including information processing.

Database servers provide referential integrity and two-phase commit. These features assure that things go right during the normal course of database processing. Referential integrity ensures that every foreign key finds a match in a primary key before it allows an update. For instance, a database server may reject an update to the sales table unless the customer number already exists in the customer table. This check is independent of the front-end application. A two-phase commit assures that your data will still be there when the hardware decides to crash since it commits the data to physical I/O not once, but twice.

Other tricks that make database servers valuable include the use of stored procedures, triggers, and rules. These mechanisms provide another location for application processing, which gives the client/server developer a means of placing some of the processing load on the database server. This feature is behind the fat server, fat client argument, or how the developer partitions the application between the client and the server.

So there you have it. Not only are database servers reliable repositories for information, they can also automatically fix problems, protect data from damage, keep out the unwelcome, and even provide a location for application processing. Pretty amazing little beasts, and they get better all the time.

Database Server Basics

Let's back up for a moment to the basic architecture of the client/server model. The idea of client/server is to do all the database processing on the database server, using all the native resources of the database server including disk, memory, processor, and operating system. The client and the server operate independently of each other. This, of course, is the essence of client/server. The effect is to reduce the load on the network, and the clients don't have to deal with any aspect of database processing. The client application simply makes a request (through an API) and only the requested information magically appears in local memory.

When you look at client/server, you may think that database servers are commodity products: one is just as good as another. I've found that selecting the right database server software can be risky. Selecting the wrong server is the fast route to system failure (as a case study shows).

A Case of Database Exhaustion

A good friend of mine built a large client/server system to support over two hundred clients running an order entry system. This was his first client/server system, and when he worked up the budget to build and deploy the application, he only allocated about 3 percent of the total cost of the system to the selection of database server hardware and software, as well as the hardware and software itself. The result was a quick read through a few magazines to select a database (I call that management by magazine), and the purchase of a low-end server to support it. "It's just the database, right?" he said.

Things went along well for a while. After eight months of development, the application performed well in the test lab with ten clients connected to his database server of choice. After one long year of application development, my friend deployed two hundred clients to the same server and found very different results. The number of client connections required much more memory than the server could support. The operating system began to thrash, and crashed shortly after the 105th user logged on. This happened before any actual application processing began. The database server literally died of exhaustion.

My friend talked his way out of the situation and maintained his job. However, it took two more months before he got a server in place that could support his user load, and the company spent many more dollars than originally anticipated. With a little planning, additional testing, and some common sense, all of this could have been avoided. Never neglect your database server.

I have to say that there is no foolproof method to select just the right database for your client/server development project. There are many things to take into account. You must consider the power of the platform that houses your database server software, SQL standards, and how the database supports application features such as stored procedures and triggers, as well as the added value of database administration and monitoring tools that come bundled with your database.

Of course, you can always select a database server that is much too large for your application, which assures that it will never run out of steam as the user and processing loads increase. But selecting a database server that's too big means investing a lot of money in hardware and software, and never realizing the return. I've seen project after project select high-end multi-processing RISC servers that cost as much as $200,000, where a $10,000 server would work just as well.

On the other hand, I've seen architects and developers select a server that has no chance of supporting the user and processing load of the application. This results in "server saturation," and the application simply does not work (see the case study). You don't have to make such mistakes. There are steps you can follow that assure the database you select is in the ballpark. I'll list those steps at the end of the chapter, but first you need to arm yourself with as much relevant information as possible about database servers. That's why I wrote this chapter.

IT'S A RELATIONAL WORLD

As I mentioned in Chapter 4, there are a number of database models, but one rules the world: the relational model. Unless special circumstances exist (e.g., a requirement of tracking very complex data structure, or the need to support a data warehouse) I recommend that you limit your database shopping to the relational world.

This does not mean that the relational model provides advantages that make other models obsolete, only that the relational model maps to most problem domains. What's more, it's easy to learn and use. For example, when teaching my database class at a local college, I found that my students took much longer to get the hang of the hierarchical and object-oriented data models than the relational model. At their core, relational databases are tables, and nothing more than tables.

Things continue to change. As interest in object-oriented development tools and data warehousing increases, so has interest in object-oriented databases and multi-dimensional databases. However, relational database vendors such as Oracle, Sybase, and Informix plan to solve those problems through relational database technology, and through the concept of a universal database server (as discussed in Chapter 4).

Despite the dominance of relational databases, I see some good fits for other models. For example, object-oriented databases (such as GemStone from GemStone Systems) store databases as persistent objects; thus they make good fits for client/server development tools that support the object-oriented development model exclusively, such as all Smalltalk tools (see Chapter 12). Since the application does not have to translate data to and from the object to the relational model, the tools perform better. You may find that object-oriented databases make a better home for complex data structures and binary data (digitized images, video, and sound), such as the ones required by repositories.

Of course, multi-dimensional databases (such as Easbase Analysis Server from Arbor Software Corp.) provide a good fit for OLAP front-ends. Since this model is just the "racking and stacking" of data, end-users find it easy to drill through to find the information they need. Keep in mind that universal databases can appear as object-oriented and multi-dimensional to clients who need to see the data that way.

Bottom line? If you have don't special needs, as I mentioned above, you don't need to stray from the relational database model. Relational databases are less risky to use. Most client/server development tools (and developers) support them, and will continue to do so.

DOES THE PLATFORM COUNT?

It's just after lunch (last year) and my phone rings. On the other line is a coworker. "Hi, Dave. I'm building a client/server system, and I'm finding that Visual Basic is totally unacceptable. The performance is terrible." "First time I've heard of that," I said. "Are you sure it's the front-end application that's causing your performance problem? What database server are you running?" "Watcom," he said, in a very strong voice. "What platform?" I asked. "Does it matter?" answered my coworker. I put down my coffee cup. This would be a long phone call.

Guess what? With over fifty users connected, my coworker was running a Win32 version of the Watcom database server under Windows 95 on a 486/66. Of course, the platform could not put forth enough disk I/O, processor cycles, and memory to make the database a good fit for more than just a few users. Fortunately, my coworker saw the error in his ways, and now runs his database server on something much bigger.

The platform determines the overall performance of the database server. Period. For example, Oracle on a 486 will not run as fast as the RISC version. The database server depends on the services of the host operating system. The platform's ability to provide efficient disk services, caching services, and network services is the foundation of a high-performance database server. Selecting the right platform for your database is as important as selecting the database itself. Okay, I'm off my soapbox.

For those of you who don't know much about hardware, don't worry. Here's the skinny. With only few exceptions, x86-, RISC-, and Sparc-based servers are the best processor platforms for database servers, in both single and multi-processing incarnations (depending on the user and processing loads). While x86 works well for one to fifty users, when the user load rises past that, I find that RISC and Sparc-based servers are a better fit (such as the RS/6000 and the Sun SparcServer respectively). Of course, it depends upon your database engine's ability to use the processor efficiently. Only pilot testing can answer that question. My advice is to test, test, test.

On the operating system side of things, Unix and Windows NT seem to provide the best bang for the buck, since Windows NT has moved into the high-end server domain once dominated by Unix. Both support multi-processing hardware, which provides granular scalability through the addition of processors.

Unix is a confusing beast. There are many flavors that run everything from PCS to monster servers. Unix is sold under many names including SCO Unix, UnixWare, Solaris, HP/ux, and AIX. When bundled with hardware, these operating systems come at a high cost. High-end Unix servers can cost as much as $50,000, depending on the number of processors and the configuration.

To exploit the best features of Unix, or any other operating system, database vendors such as Oracle, Informix, and Sybase have to master the native operating system's (e.g., Unix's) ability to support many simultaneous client connections. These connections are supported as threads, or as stand-alone processes (more on this later in the chapter). A database should capitalize on the operating system's I/O performance, memory management, and task management capabilities. Some do. Some don't.

Things could change in the world of high-end operating systems for database servers. Windows NT continues to rise in popularity. Windows NT offers an operating system that provides all the goodies of Unix, including pre-emptive multitasking and support for multi-processing, and is much easier to use. Microsoft's SQL Server is one of many databases that take advantage of native Windows NT capabilities. Other database vendors are moving in this direction as well.

The More Processors the Better.   Today's advanced servers come with more than one processor in the machine. Such computers allow DBAs and architects to add as many processors in the computer as required in one computer without having to network several computers together. This multi-processing computing is called tightly coupled multi-processing, and is the preferred architecture for most multi-processing database servers (see Figure 5-1).

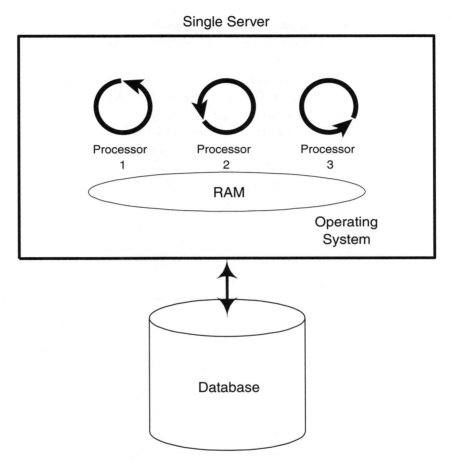

Figure 5-1 *Multi-processing Database Server.*

Tightly coupled CPUs allow for easy administration with high performance and scalability. Scalability is the ability to make the machine any size desired for any number of connected users. Of course, there are limitations to technology. The size of the machine is related to the number of processors installed; therefore, we can install processors as we need them.

For the DBMS to find the additional connected processors, multi-processor computers (tightly coupled) and computers clustered together (loosely coupled), it needs to run an operating system that can address the additional CPUs. The Unix operating system provides the computer hardware manufactures with a flexible base platform to build the multi-processing operating systems. However, Windows NT is coming on strong as the operating system of choice for multi-processing database servers.

Parallel Query Processing. Databases should know how to take advantage of multi-processing architectures directly, without depending upon the host operating system to distribute the processing. With the advent of large databases (known as very large databases (VLDBs), 1 terabyte or larger) and the interest in data warehousing, there is a need for database servers that take a "divide and conquer" approach to database processing.

Databases that support parallel processing by letting the operating system allocate the database processing among processors (known as "shared everything"), or by allowing the database server to allocate the database processing despite the OS ("shared nothing"). The shared nothing approach requires that you purchase a special database that supports this architecture (see Figure 5-2).

The basic idea is that these special servers break up a database query into subqueries. Although the architecture can vary, each processor usually has a

Figure 5-2 *Parallel Database processing.*

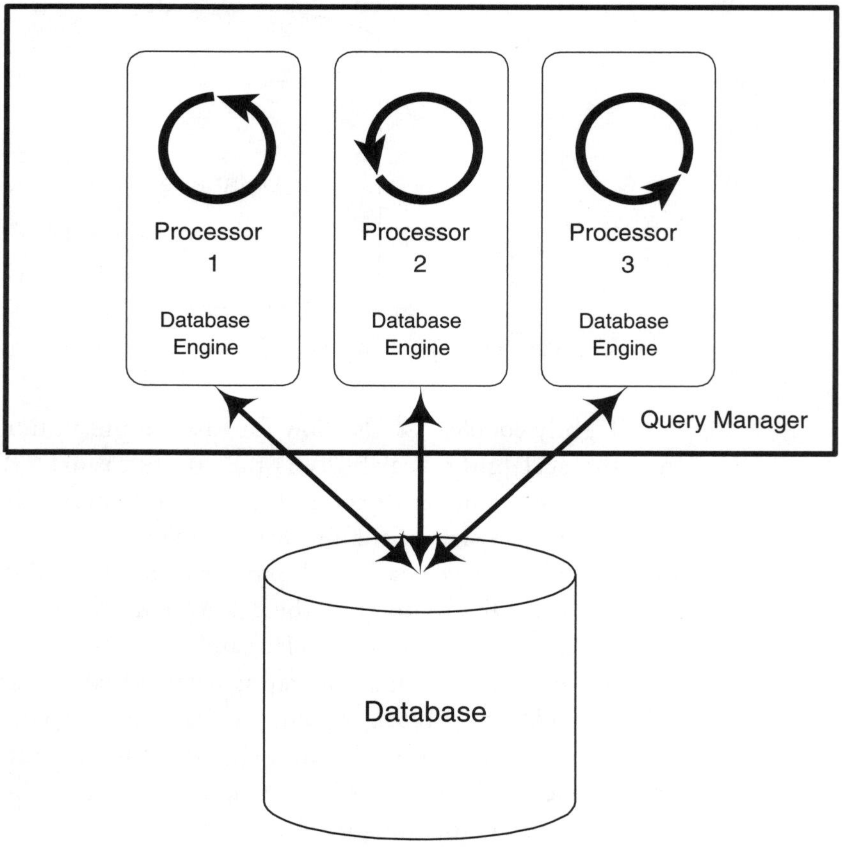

single database engine running on it. I call these mini-engines. When the query manager receives the request, it allocates the processing among the mini-engines. When processing is complete, the query manager combines the result set and returns it to the client (see Figure 5-3). This is a simplification of the process, and this mechanism varies from database to database, but the concepts are the same.

Although we've done parallel database processing for some time now, parallel processing is just moving out of the experimental stage to mission-critical production databases. Prices continue to come down as well, with a million dollars being my predicted cost for the hardware and the software within just a few years. Today you can purchase a server, OS, and a database that supports parallel query processing for as little as $50,000.

There are several parallel databases available, including Oracle's Parallel Query Option, Sybase's Sybase MPP, and Informix Dynamic Server. These databases are becoming commonplace in Fortune 500 companies as they provide organizations with the ability to manage large data stores and improve response time. Before long, all databases will provide parallel query capabilities.

Bypassing the Operating System. Although the operating system has a lot to do with the performance and efficiency of a database server, there is a trend among database vendors to bypass the operating system and get at the system resources directly. This has the effect of improving performance since there is always overhead when the server gets at the system resources through the operating system. In a sense, databases are becoming substitute operating systems that communicate directly with the various hardware systems on the server.

Examples of this are all over the database world. Most popular database servers, including Informix, Sybase, and Oracle, bypass the native file system and go directly to a special physical disk partition (known as the raw disk partition). Thus, the database does not have to make an operating system call to perform a simple disk read, which results in improved I/O performance and a faster database server.

Although each database provides a different approach, most databases allow the DBA to set up a raw disk partition as an option. Unless there is a good reason not to use a raw disk partition, you're usually best off using one. You should know that you'll need special utilities provided by your database vendor to back up the database.

Beware—if you plan to set up your database where the database server performs operating system-level activities (e.g., raw disk reads and writes), then that server should only support database processing. If there are other

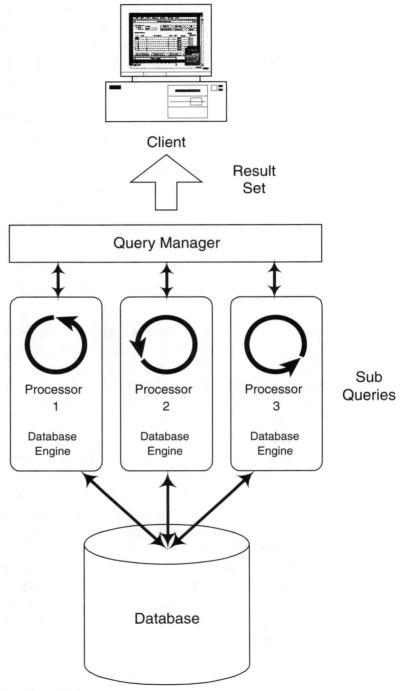

Figure 5-3 *The query manager.*

applications or processes on the server, they'll be shoved aside by the database server process, which takes what it needs without regard to the operating system. It's never a good idea to configure servers to pull double duty, such as acting as a file server and a database server at the same time. Worlds collide, and neither uses work well.

Today, databases perform other tricks that make them more like operating systems than database processors. Many attempt to provide an extra bit of performance by running the database server process as a kernel level process. This means that database processing occurs in spaces in the operating system which are reserved for the operating system, such as Ring 0 on x86 processors. The best example of this sort of architecture is Oracle for Netware. Netware, an operating system for a file server, can run applications native to the Netware environment as Netware loadable modules (NLMs). Since Netware does not provide Ring 0 protection, Oracle (as well as other databases that can run as NLMs) can run there and does. This has the effect of increasing database server performance, since the database runs at the highest level—but a bug in the process running at Ring 0 can lock the server. Because of this architecture, Netware-based servers provide a great platform for Intel-based database servers. That is, if you already have a need for a Netware file server in your organization.

Replication. Most of today's databases provide replication features as part of their product offering. Simply put, this means the DBA can set up two or more database servers in master-slave relationships which allow them to automatically share data. As the master database is updated, so is the slave database that exists somewhere else on the network. You can also set up the replication mechanisms so that databases update each other as the data changes over time. The time increment in which they update another replication server is known as latency. Usually this is anywhere from one minute to one day, depending on the requirements of the database and the application.

The problems that replication servers solve are performance and reliability. For example, I maintained a client/server system with users in the United States and London. The database server was physically located in the United States near the United States users. The wide area network (WAN) that connected the London users to the database server left a lot to be desired. On many occasions that network went down, and the London users were left without access to critical data they needed to do their job. Enter the replication solution.

When installing a replication server in both the United States and London, the London users would connect to and use the replication server located in London. As the U.S. clients updated their replication server in the United

States, the servers synched up with one another so all users were essentially using the same logical database. The latency was five minutes; thus the information was never more than five minutes old.

The beauty of using a replication server in these circumstances is that the users were not dependent on the reliability of the WAN. When the WAN went down, the users simply continued to use their local database. When the WAN connection was restored, the database servers synched up automatically. Performance for the London users improved as well, since they could make a speedy local connection to their server, avoiding the link to a database server over the slower WAN.

SQL FUNDAMENTALS

I have to tell you that I've been frustrated with the direction of structured query language (SQL). The promise, at first, was for the unification of SQL so that all database and front-end development tools could communicate using the same language. That was over six years ago. The SQL server vendors largely live in their own proprietary world. They all speak different languages and dialects.

As I write this book, there is no sure-fire way to communicate with various databases via a common set of SQL. There are many standards that everyone seems to pay lip service to, but it seems no one wants to build these standards into their product. If you think about it, if everyone used the same SQL language, middleware such as ODBC and IDAPI would be passé, and the world would be a better place.

International Standards Organization (ISO). There are several standard versions of SQL that databases adhere to. These standards are set through a joint agreement with the American National Standard Institute (ANSI) and the International Standards Organization (ISO). Although a bit boring to deal with in the moving and shaking world of client/server, it's important that you learn these standards before you select your database. Skipping through the hype, I think there are three SQL standards that you should address: SQL-89, SQL-92, and SQL3. I'll make it quick.

SQL-89. SQL-89 is the first significant standard, and it's beginning to show its age. What's more, SQL-89 is pretty much the most useless of all the ANSI SQL standards. To create SQL-89, ANSI looked at all the existing relational databases of the day to support SQL features common to all the products. They created the standard around the available products, and everyone was SQL-89-compliant.

As you may have guessed, the SQL-89 standard did not move the world any closer to a unified SQL standard. Also, vendors did not let conformance to the standard stop them from making their products even more proprietary to set them apart from their competitors. Databases continued to move in different directions, and anytime I see SQL-89 compliance in documentation or marketing material, I laugh.

SQL-92. Things began to change for the better. The ISO SQL-92 standard, created just a few years ago, filled in missing details left out of SQL-89. Finally, a standard that steered the database vendors in the same direction, but most of them resisted. As a result, many relational databases don't comply with SQL-92. One of the early adapters is Borland's Interbase. Other database server vendors are beginning to release products using SQL-92 this year. Hopefully, this trend will continue.

I think it's important that the database you select conforms to SQL-92, for many reasons. First, SQL-92 provides support for SQL agents, which are programs that generate SQL on behalf of the client. Second, SQL-92 supports SQL client/server connections, which converse with SQL agents to connect to an SQL server. Third, SQL-92 outlines support for embedding SQL into modern languages such as C++. Finally, SQL-92 supports dynamic SQL for advanced data types such as BLOBS (binary large objects), and standard error codes and diagnostics. Of course, you can get many of these same features in databases that are not SQL-92-compliant. They just don't support all of these features consistently.

SQL3. As that late night infomercial says "But wait, there's more!" There is a new standard on the horizon. SQL3 will have even more features to improve SQL-92, including Object SQL capabilities that support the object-oriented features of encapsulation, methods, user-defined data types, and inheritance. This is the standard to watch as client/server databases evolve.

LOOKING AT CLIENT CONNECTIONS

The number of client connections that the database server can support determines the scalability of the client/server system. For instance, database servers that require a high resource-per-client can't support that many clients since resources (memory and processor) run out. As clients log in to the server, they hit a wall where the database server runs out of resources and performance takes a turn for the worse, or the operating system begins to trash and crash. The trick is to determine the percent of resources that each connection requires, and use that number to determine the capacity of your database server. Databases servers that utilize resources efficiently can support many more users.

There are three basic ways that databases handle client connections: process-per-client, threading, or a mixed approach. When using the process-per-client approach (see Figure 5-4), each client connection requires its own process on the database server. For example, fifty clients would require fifty processes. This is a good approach since all the connections function in their own address space in the database server operating system. Thus the connections work in their own domain, protected from other ill-behaved processes that may do them harm. What's more, the process-per-client approach is a

Figure 5-4 *Process-per-client approach.*

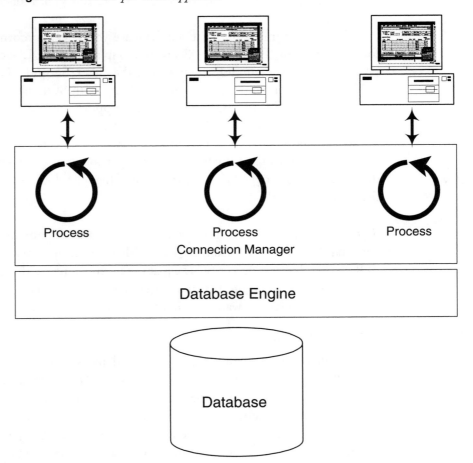

natural fit for multi-processing operating systems that allocate the connection processing across processors.

There are disadvantages to the process-per-client approach. Using a process for each connection consumes a lot of CPU and memory. In many instances, this approach requires that two or three processes run to support a single connection. I've seen database servers that require 5 MB of memory per connection. This approach is also plagued by context switching and interprocess communications which are required to support this architecture. Each of these functions comes with the process-per-client approach that requires additional overhead. Databases that use this approach include DB2/2, Oracle 6, and Informix.

With the threading approach, the database server runs all connections and the database in the same address space (see Figure 5-5). The connections, therefore, run as threads. Threads are simply lightweight processes that can run without the same resource requirements as true processes, and they do not require context switching. With threading, the connections can use their own internal schedule and they do not depend on the operating system's native process protection mechanism. You'll also find that this approach is easier to port from platform to platform (e.g., Windows NT to Unix) since threads do not depend on the native features of the host operating system.

The downside to database servers that use the threading approach is that the threads are vulnerable to server crashes due to other rogue processes or threads. Unlike processes, threads aren't protected. You'll find that threading does not equally distribute the operating resources among running threads, and a single thread can tie up a single processor, denying the other threads and processes its use (if the operating system allows it). Databases that provide connections in threads include Sybase System 11 and Microsoft SQL Server.

I've found that connection management through threading is the best approach for database servers due to the low overhead they place on the operating system. For instance, Sybase System 11 only needs 60 KB of RAM for each client connection. Sybase uses an SQL server process, called the dataserver, to launch threads each time a client logs on to the database server. There is also a thread for the database engine, database devices, and even a thread to support logging. As mentioned previously, the process-per-client approach can require as much as 5 MB of RAM per client. Thus the threading approach means your database server can support many more connections, thus more clients. Clearly this is the wave of the future, and should be first on your list when you shop for database servers.

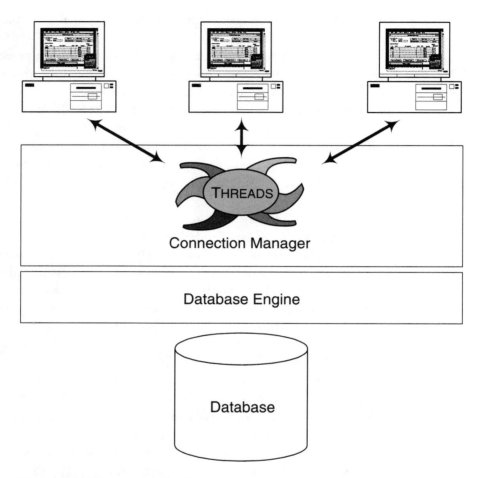

Figure 5-5 *Threading approach.*

A few database servers use a mixed approach to connection management. This means the database uses a combination of threading and process-per-client. Oracle 7, for instance, uses the hybrid approach by using a network listener that runs as a multi-threaded application. The network listener makes initial connections by assigning a thread called a dispatcher to each client who attempts to log on to the server, which places the message from the client into a queue. There is a shared-server process that takes messages off the queue using FIFO (first in, first out). Each message carries a request for the database server. Once the database engine executes the request, the same process returns the response set back to the client using the same process. If this seems a difficult process to follow, you're right. However, it does offer a few distinct advantages. This architecture provides a protected process environment, but does not have to assign a process for each client connection. On the downside, the use of a queue can cause performance problems.

STORED PROCEDURES, TRIGGERS, AND RULES

Stored procedures, triggers, and rules allow client/server developers to place portions of the application processing load on the database server. These features provide the developer with the ability to program the database server itself to perform any number of application-related tasks, or just to protect the data. By providing a mechanism to process on the database server, there is a reduced strain on the network.

Stored procedures allow the client/server developer to partition the processing load between the client and the database server: a proprietary mechanism. Stored procedures and triggers are not typically portable among database servers.

Stored procedures are just a collection of SQL statements and procedural logic that developers store and execute inside the database. Client/server applications invoke them through a messaging mechanism supported by the database server. For example, a developer can send a message to a Sybase database to tell the database to invoke a stored procedure that sorts the data and prints a report. Since the stored procedure actually executes on the remote database server, the client is free to continue processing.

Oracle's Developer/2000, for example, uses the native Oracle stored procedure mechanism to partition applications between Developer/2000 clients and Oracle database servers. Since both ends run the same dialect of SQL (PL/SQL), it's just a matter of moving code from the client to the server.

Triggers are stored procedures that are automatically activated by data-related events such as an update or a delete request. Triggers are most useful for enforcing database integrity rules such as deleting all sales records from the sales table for a particular customer when a customer gets removed from the customer table.

A rule is a type of trigger that checks the data before an update to assure that the data meets certain business rules. For instance, DBAs and developers generally don't let clients enter negative numbers into tax tables, or allow zip codes in the database that don't really exist. Good DBAs will set up a database that protects itself from such data anomalies, regardless of the types of clients who access the information.

CONSIDERING SECURITY

In most client/server systems I've worked on, security is an afterthought. It's not that people don't want a secure system, it's just that they don't want to put in the work or the cost required to make a database secure.

If you want to lock up your client/server system, your database server is the right place to start. Most databases provide their own internal security system that requires users to log in to the server before they can make requests or get data. Databases also provide several layers of security, including the ability to protect databases by table, column, and row. This means a DBA can lock certain users out of portions of the databases, for any reason. This is a good idea when sensitive data exists on the server, or when developers need to partition a single database server to support several applications and user groups.

For example, I worked on a client/server system where human resource data (including the much sought after payroll file) existed with the sales database and the inventory database. The DBA could lock unauthorized users out of the database, tables, and columns they were not allowed to update or view. If you attempted to access the data with any sort of front-end tool, the database server would return an error message.

Security varies from database to database, and may depend on the native features of the operating system. You need to check with your vendors before you consider locking up your data. If you're really concerned about security, you may want to check into databases that comply with government security standards such as C2 and B1. These security standards mean they will keep a close watch on user activity, detecting intruders as well as aging passwords. Informix, Sybase, and Oracle provide secure versions of their databases. You should know that these databases cost more, and may not provide the same level of performance due to the overhead of the extra security (e.g., auditing).

ADMINISTRATION

Finally, you need to consider database administration and monitoring tools that come with the database. Database administration tools allow the DBA to perform such activities as backing up the database, adding users, and tuning the database to optimize performance. If the tools are not a part of the database, you'll have to purchase them from third-party tool vendors, or do without.

Performance-monitoring tools allow DBAs to keep an eye on the database server. These tools watch I/O, cache, memory, processor saturation, and other aspects of the database server. The larger database server vendors such as

Oracle, Informix, and Sybase bundle basic performance-monitoring tools with their products. I've found that third-party tools provide the most features, but you'll have to fork over anywhere from $1000 to $10,000 for each tool.

A Quick Look at Sybase

Don't think we can leave this chapter without a closer look at one database. Let's take a look at the database I know the most about—Sybase.

Taking a bird's eye view, you'll notice that Sybase supports all major data types, including scalar data types such as numeric data, string data, date/time data, money data, and other types such as "TIMESTAMP" and "SYSNAME." Along with data types, Sybase provides support for constants such as integer, decimal, and float. What's more, Sybase can store binary information such as BLOBS, and through its new universal server product, can store objects and multi-dimensional data.

Sybase was one of the first databases to exploit the server concept, and the architecture supports client/server from the ground up. The server database must maintain a special system database called the master database to maintain database tables created by client applications. This master database stores data that pertains to the SQL server connections with the clients, other servers on the network, security parameters, and all other databases currently controlled by the Sybase SQL server.

Sybase creates two other databases during the Sybase SQL server installation. The first is the temporary database, for temporary storage of data during normal operations. The other is the model database, which provides a template when the client/server developer creates a new database.

Another interesting feature of Sybase is its use of database objects. These objects provide the user or the programmer with the ability to reference tables and attributes by shorter "object names." This object referencing lets the SQL server locate the objects specified without "qualified names" in tables from objects the current user created and currently owns. Database indexes are managed in much the same way as in other SQL database systems, and are always associated with a base table. The owner of the table can call and drop indexes at any time. As with other DBMSs, the use of indexes speeds up database operations, especially when many related tables are in use.

Also included in the Sybase SQL server is a catalog. The Sybase catalog is a collection of information that pertains to several objects of interest to the system. As explained earlier, objects can represent base tables, views, indexes, databases, application plans, or security parameters. These objects are maintained by an identification number that provides access information about the stored objects.

Security built in to Sybase provides protection of the data from unauthorized users. This security can protect the database at the table level, as well as columns and rows within the table. Users can have established access privileges on any given object in the catalog, meaning the rights can be granted or revoked based on the user's ability to update, delete, or alter data on the server in a particular object.

Other advanced features in Sybase include an advanced method of data distribution that allows data to be maintained over a network on several SQL servers. The fault tolerant facility of Sybase allows for system crashes without any downtime.

The open server facility lets other 3GL applications communicate with the Sybase SQL server through a common API. This is the native middleware connection to the database, and developers can also access the SQL server through an ODBC API. Finally, the Sybase product allows other DBMSs to access information on the Sybase server through the use of a "gateway." This means other DBMSs, such as Oracle or Ingres, can share information on the Sybase server as if the server were one of its own.

Distributed Databases

Although client/server is a relatively recent concept, data distribution among many database servers is an established practice. Client/server and reliable networks have reduced the need for distributed databases, and while you still find a few of them, replication and multi-tiered client/server can pretty much solve the same problems. While the products are passé, the architecture of a distributed database system is not. It's certainly worth a quick look.

Distributed databases present a single database view to all users, when the data is actually stored all over the building or all over the country. Connecting the data requires the DBA to specify where the data is on the network and the methods of communication.

It is the goal of each distributed DBMS to allow the user to access all stored information as if it were stored locally. So, as a user brings up client information on the screen, the address information may come from the computers located in Los Angeles, the sales information may come from the computer in Dallas, and the history information may come from the local database server. Of course, the user (and the developer) should not notice the distribution of the data.

In addition to the user not noticing where the data comes from, machine failures should also be transparent. If the computer in Los Angeles goes down, the user should not have to reconnect. When the computer comes back on line, the user should again have access to the data without a disruption of the application software.

The heart of the distributed database system is the network data dictionary. Not only does the dictionary need to provide the metadata, or information about the data such as format, length, and description, it must also provide the location of each portion of the data. The network data dictionary provides information to support navigation through the network, much as a data dictionary supports navigation through a database.

To provide full transparency, distributed data cannot be stored as a single copy. Single copies of data allow failures of one machine to impact the user since some of the required information becomes unavailable. Maintaining consistency among these copies becomes a complex task, but one that is left up to distributed database vendors such as Oracle and Computer Associates, who both sell distributed version of their Oracle and Ingres databases.

All queries in a distributed database keep data location and routing details from the users. All queries have to be decomposed into component parts where each component refers to the appropriate remote portion of the data. The queue gathers the data and presents it to the users. That data may come from one or several locations, including the local computer.

As you can imagine, the concurrency control for distributed systems is strange. For example, locking is not considered a good approach to concurrency control in a distributed DBMS. The locking functions require a great deal of processor overhead in a distributed system, since each occurrence of an item to be locked must be locked at each occurrence. Therefore the network may become bogged down while it keeps track of the locks.

Deadlock may also be difficult to detect in a distributed system since the system needs to be concerned with locks at the local node as well as locks across the nodes. Time-stamping can be a good approach to resolve concurrency control problems in a distributed DBMS. With time-stamping, the message traffic is reduced to the time-stamp information. Time-stamping is a good way to avoid deadlock situations in a distributed system, as long as you keep all your remote servers on the same clock. The recovery control in a distributed database system can be easily implemented if the data is replicated at another node. When a database is partitioned, the recovery controls become more complex.

The Procedure

This is lots of information for a single chapter, so I'll sum things up here through a procedure you can follow when you select a database:

First, you need to completely understand your requirements. Define what your client/server application will do, the number of clients, and who will use it. From this you can determine the processing load you will place on the server.

Second, you need to consider your clients. What applications run on the clients that require database access?

Third, you need to consider the middleware layer you use to connect to the database. A TP monitor provides a connectivity scheme very different from standard database middleware (e.g., ODBC). You have to take this into consideration.

Fourth, what database server features are important to you and your application? This list should include things like stored procedures, triggers, and administration tools.

Fifth, select at least three databases for consideration. Using these databases as candidates, select platforms for the servers and install them to create your test bed. Test each product using simulated application. Record performance, ease of use, programming, and efficiency results.

Sixth, make sure you consider cost. The fastest server may not be the best buy if you have to pay twice as much per client. Calculate cost on a per-user basis.

Finally, don't take this stuff too seriously. Remember, it's only software.

6

Using the Object-Oriented
Development Model

You can't avoid object-oriented development when you build client/server applications. The object-oriented development model and client/server are joined at the hip. Client/server tools dig deeper into the object-oriented development model, and developers are finally getting the hang of how to leverage the power of objects in their own client/server applications.

The object-oriented development model is nothing new, but it was not until the interest in C++ arose that the power of object-oriented development become a part of mainstream application development. Today all client/server tools support object-oriented development in their own proprietary way. During the last few years, development organizations dove in head first to object-oriented development, spending millions on people and tools. The object-oriented development model is not just another paradigm shift; it's a success story driven by client/server and intranet development.

This chapter is a springboard into our detailed discussion of object-oriented client/server development tools that we cover in the rest of this book. Take time to understand these concepts, and learn how to relate them to available client/server tools and technology. I'll examine the state of the art in object-oriented client/server development tools, including some object-oriented fundamentals, object standards, and how to leverage objects for client/server development.

Using this information as a foundation, the maze of complex and abundant object-oriented client/server development tools will be a bit easier to understand. I'll let you know just what you need to know to see through the hype that surrounds object-oriented development. I'll let you know what works and what doesn't.

An Object-Oriented World

The object-oriented tool industry will earn over $2 billion in 1997. That's up from just $379 million in 1993. What drives hordes of developers to objects is the fundamental belief that tools which use the object-oriented development model allow developers to build applications with standard reusable components, and thus build applications faster with superior quality. Unlike the structured development model, developers can program from the generic to the specific, reusing as much code as possible throughout the application.

I've found a paradox in this industry. Despite the fact that most client/server development is object-oriented, developers are still learning how to do object-oriented development. The fact is, when using objects, you have to think objects, and it's going to take some time before we are completely over the structured development model that was part of our lives for two decades. As new developers enter the work force, they are not as corrupted and are easier to make object-oriented. If you are not object-oriented, now is the time.

Object-Oriented Concepts

There are three basic concepts that I use when explaining objects: objects, messages, and classes. These concepts don't come to you without some degree of abstract thinking. For now, try to look at the programming model as the forest. We'll get to the trees later.

Classes and Objects

First I'll take a quick runthrough, then we'll hit the details. Classes are templates or blueprints for objects. They define the data encapsulated inside the objects and how the objects will behave and communicate with other objects (see Figure 6-1). Therefore, an object is an instance (a run-time version if you

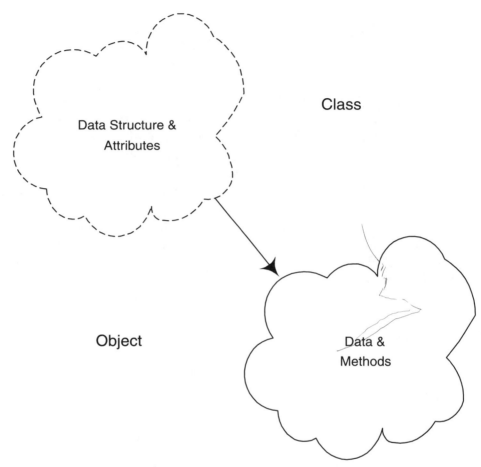

Figure 6-1 *Classes define objects.*

will) of a class (see Figure 6-2). Messages are sent from objects (sometimes devices like a mouse) to objects to invoke methods that exist inside an object (see Figure 6-3), and methods are functionally equivalent to small programs that carry out some activity.

Watch Out for Object Terminology Reuse

One of the frustrating things that I run into in the world of client/server development is the use of many terms that mean the same thing, and the use of interchangeable terms. The most abused are class and object. Vendors and even fellow authors have a nasty habit of calling classes objects and objects classes. There is a difference. For example, most specialized client/server development tools call classes objects, since they want to emphasize that their tool is object-oriented, despite the fact that they might actually be describing classes. As a rule, I'll use their definitions for their tool to avoid confusion in the forthcoming chapters. For now, however, I would like to set the record straight before moving forward with the book.

A *class* is a software implementation of an object type. It defines the methods that exist in each object that the class defines. A class also defines the operations that control how the data encapsulated inside the object is manipulated.

An *object* is an instance of a class, and objects can be real or abstract. Objects can store data, as well as methods to access the data, and an object may contain other objects.

Figure 6-2 *An object is an instance of a class.*

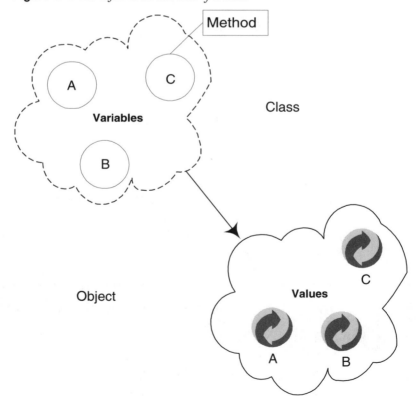

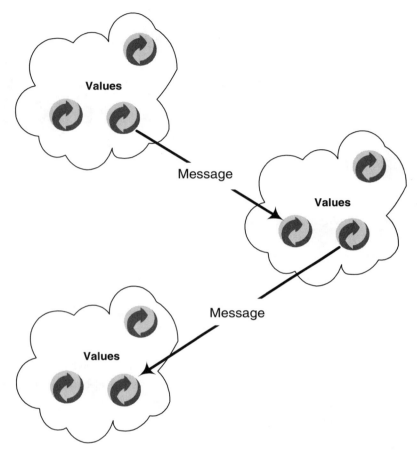

Figure 6-3 *Objects communicate via messaging.*

Let's look at an example to illustrate the differences between objects and classes. If Ford builds a Taurus, the design drawings for the Taurus are like a class. If Ford builds a Taurus, the design drawings for the Taurus are like a class. A Taurus that rolls off the Ford assembly line is an instance of that design or class: an object. Since cars do things such as allow the driver to steer, move forward, and move in reverse, those are methods that exist within our Taurus object (see Figure 6-4). Since a Taurus has a color, make, and model, consider those properties of the object (see Figure 6-5).

Of course, the concept of an object varies among client/server development tools. PowerBuilder, for instance, has both visual and nonvisual objects. Visual objects are GUI windows you can see such as data windows, data entry screens, and data grids. Nonvisual objects are objects that simply perform application processing and don't contain visual features. In the JYACC JAM 7

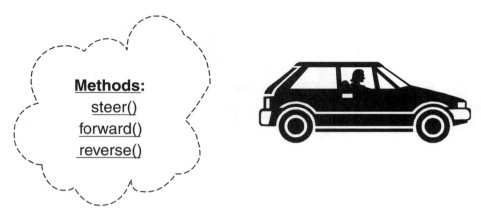

Figure 6-4 *Methods of a Taurus object.*

world, every object is a visual screen, and in the world of Smalltalk tools every-thing is an object—including databases, devices, and GUI controls.

A class is not a stand-alone concept. Classes exist with other classes in formations known as class hierarchies. Class hierarchies allow classes to inherit features and functions from other classes that exist above them in the hierarchy. This relationship is functionally equivalent to your relationship with your mother, father, and grandparents. They exist in a family tree, and you inherit their characteristics (hair color, eye color, height, etc.) through genetic inheri-tance. We'll cover this in greater detail below. Right now it's time to take a closer look at the trees.

ENCAPSULATION

Encapsulation is the process of packing data and methods together in an object. The object hides the data this way from other objects that exist in the memory

Figure 6-5 *Properties of a Taurus object.*

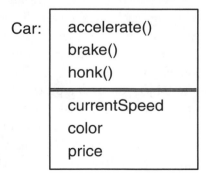

space of your application. Since encapsulation hides the information, encapsulation also protects the data with methods that surround the data which must be invoked to get at the data. This enforces the business rules of an application, and protects the data from corruption by other objects (see Figure 6-6).

Since encapsulation hides the details of the object characteristics from other objects, other objects can only get at the information by sending a message to an object. The object responds to the message without letting the other object know how the operation actually works. Kind of sneaky, no?

So what does this all mean? Using the concepts of encapsulation, developers can create objects that have their own little personality. Or, if you will, a single universe that functions independently of other objects, making them easy to modify. When changing an object, other objects that run in the same memory space are not affected.

MESSAGE PASSING

As just touched on, objects communicate through messages. If you come from the structured world, messages are like function calls, invoking preprogrammed

Figure 6-6 *Encapsulation.*

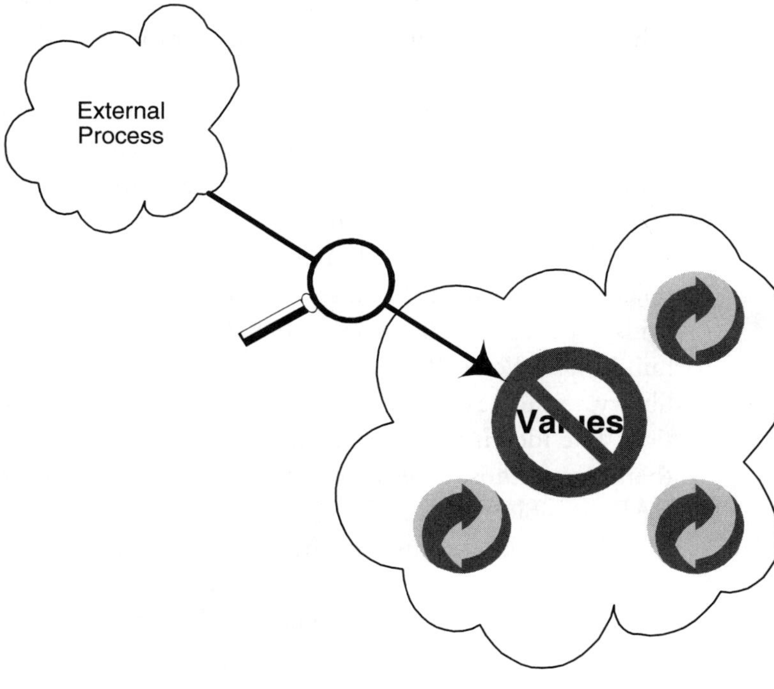

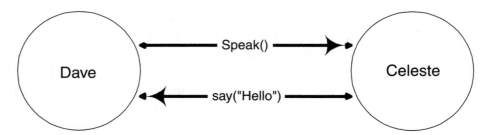

Figure 6-7 *Objects invoke other object services through messaging.*

procedures. In fact, when using C++, sending a message to an object is identical to invoking a function call.

Objects direct messages at methods that exist inside of other objects (see Figure 6-7), or messages may come from devices like a keyboard or a mouse. If there are results from invoking a method, such as a result set, the information passes back to the calling object as messages. This, of course, is controlled by the developer.

THE POWER OF INHERITANCE

Inheritance is the real power of object-oriented development. Using inheritance, developers can reuse any object in an already developed intra-application, or better yet, reuse objects that others have built. That means inheritance is the object-oriented mechanism that allows developers to "program through plagiarism."

Inheritance means that developers can create objects and link them together to take advantages of the services that each object offers. Developers use inheritance to link to existing object libraries using features of prebuilt objects that exist in the library.

For example, PowerBuilder comes with an extensive library of prebuilt objects. Included in the library are prebuilt objects to create data windows, grids, database log-ins, and graphs. PowerBuilder developers know this, and build their PowerBuilder applications around the existing PowerBuilder library, reusing as much of the existing objects as possible in the new application. The idea is to create an application by integrating existing objects, and then extend those objects to create the final application. This is what makes RAD possible.

Let's take a simple programming example. As we build a client/server application, we would look to the object library for standard issue data windows. Of course, the nice people who built the object library don't know the

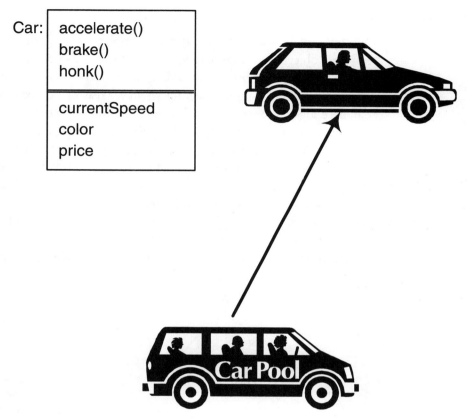

Figure 6-8 *Reusing objects to create new ones.*

specific requirements of your application, and thus created a generic data window with some properties you may want, and some properties you don't want. Since the tool uses the object-oriented development model, you can create your own instance of the object by linking to it and inheriting its features (see Figure 6-8). Once the features (methods and data) are in your own domain, you can alter them to fit your exact needs. You can throw away what you don't need, keep what you do, and add the missing features. After you create your new "hybrid" object, you can check it back into the object library for reuse in the application, or for use by other developers in other applications.

As I mentioned previously, each tool has its own way of dealing with inheritance. Some deal with it visually by passing visual objects down through a hierarchy, while others deal with objects on abstract levels. Let's look at some general features of inheritance, including the use of multiple inheritance.

MULTIPLE INHERITANCE

Multiple inheritance means that a single object can inherit characteristics from multiple objects (see Figure 6-9). For example, I can create a new object from two or more existing objects, providing me with the power to combine the methods and data into a single object for whatever reason. For example, I combined a database log into a window with a data window, providing a hybrid object that worked well for my application. Using the car analogy, we can combine a Taurus with a Corvette to create a very funny-looking but fast family car.

As you can see, this is a powerful concept. Many developers depend upon it. However, as with any powerful programming concept, it can be dangerous. Since you combine methods and data that exist in more than one object, you run the risk that the methods and data won't get along, and you could create bugs that are difficult to track down. Remember, when you inherit from an object, you inherit from all of the objects that the object inherits from as well.

Figure 6-9 *Multiple Inheritance.*

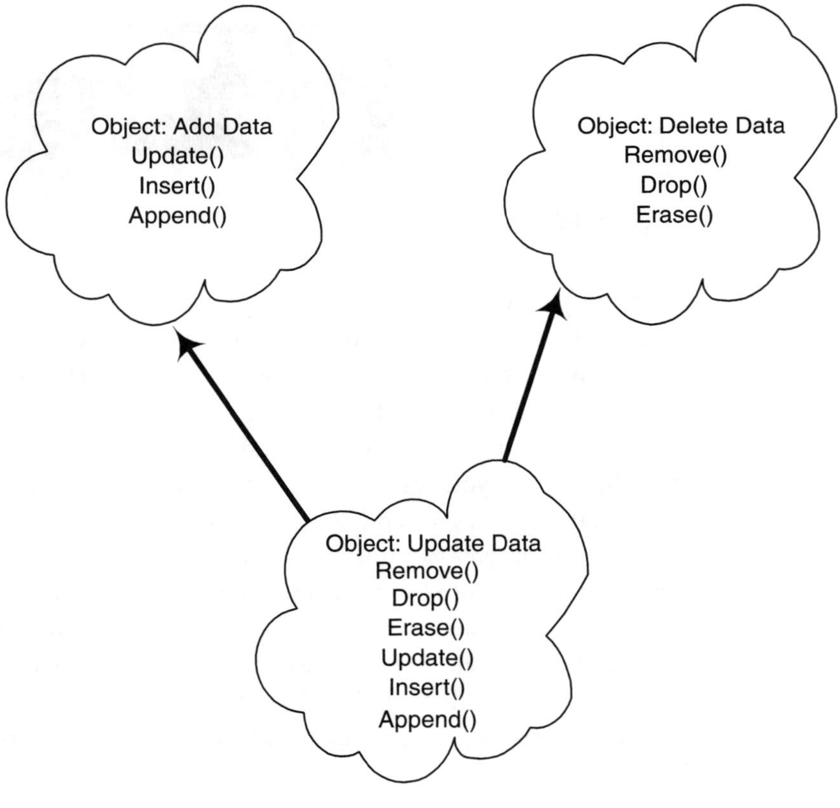

Therefore, you have to track back down two or more inheritance paths to locate and correct problems.

Because of the dangers associated with multiple inheritance, many tools don't offer it. PowerBuilder, for instance, only supports single inheritance. SQL Windows is one of the few specialized client/server tools that supports multiple inheritance. Traditional tools vary as well. What's more, while the all-object Smalltalk supports only single inheritance, C++ supports multiple inheritance.

To Be or Not to Be—Single or Multiple Inheritance?

The question of single or multiple inheritance use lingers on. I've heard both sides of the debate, and here's my take on it.

The proponents of multiple inheritance (the C++ crowd) argue that multiple inheritance is truly object-oriented, and provides the developer with the flexibility and power required to solve complex programming problems. When programming in C++, I've found that multiple inheritance comes in handy from time to time.

Those who think multiple inheritance is an evil abomination (the Smalltalk crowd) argue that multiple inheritance comes with the danger of mixing objects that should not be mixed. Bugs resulting from multiple inheritance are difficult to track down. I've found that to be true too.

If your tool or language supports multiple inheritance, it's okay to use it, but use it with some degree of caution. Know the objects that you combine, and know what objects they are linked too. If you use an object library, make sure you have good documentation, and ask the library vendors which objects mix and which don't.

I would not recommend the use of multiple inheritance to beginners, since it has a tendency to add complexity as well as problems. Professionals seem to be able to make multiple inheritance work to their advantage. Chances are, your tools won't support multiple inheritance anyway, so there is nothing to worry about. Think of multiple inheritance as a chain saw. In the hands of the untrained it can kill. But if you're careful, you can get things down quickly.

POLYMORPHISM

Another object-oriented term to drop in your next job interview is polymorphism. Polymorphism in another mechanism that lets you reuse code. It gives developers the ability to use several versions of the same method or operator that functions differently when used in one object than it does in another. The word "polymorphic" means "taking many forms."

Object-Oriented Lifestyle

Object-oriented is more than a way to develop applications. Developers can apply it across most life-cycle activities, including requirements, analysis, design, testing, and business process re-engineering. You'll find that building and deploying object-oriented client/server applications requires more thought about the application design than developing applications using "traditional" techniques. Thus I suggest you spend some time learning about the concepts in Chapter 7, where I discus object-oriented analysis and design in more detail.

Object-Oriented Approaches

Okay, now that you know the basics of object-oriented development, I have some bad news. Object-oriented development tool vendors don't consistently support the concepts you just learned about. Fact is, client/server tools and languages approach objects differently. It's helpful to break up the tool types into a few categories: pure, hybrid, and specialized.

PURE OBJECT-ORIENTED DEVELOPMENT

Pure object-oriented languages support objects, and nothing but objects. Client/server tools based on Smalltalk are the best examples of pure object-oriented development environments, including IBM's Visual Age, Digitalk's PARTS, Object Studio from Easel Corporation, and Visual Works from ParcPlace. I'll cover Smalltalk in detail in Chapter 12. Other pure object-oriented tools include the Eiffel. Eiffel also takes an all-object approach, but does not command the same market share.

When you build client/server applications with Smalltalk-based tools, you must resolve the fact that everything in the development environment is an object—and I do mean everything. If you want to access a relational database, you'll have to access it as an object. To get at a device, you'll have to treat it as an object as well. Messages are the primary means of getting things done.

The drawbacks of the pure object-oriented development model include the learning curve and available tools. If you don't already do things the object-oriented way, pure tools can be somewhat confusing. The toughest concept to get over is the fact that everything is an object, and so are classes. Thus, all objects are members of a class, and objects define the class. Before your head explodes from trying to grasp that concept, you should know that the pure object-oriented model leads to an "infinite regression." Smalltalk handles the infinite regression issue by declaring that "metaclasses" define all classes, and every single metaclass is a child of a single metaclass. The pure object-oriented model seems to be the exclusive domain of Smalltalk, and there are just a few Smalltalk tools available on the market.

Because of the complexity involved in forcing the developer into the object-oriented model, I doubt other tool vendors will go pure. Smalltalk has been losing market share in recent months. This is evident with the merger of Digitalk and ParcPlace into ParcPlace-Digitalk.

Once you learn Smalltalk, you'll probably like it. You can mix and match objects from the native object library to form your own client/server application. Once your objects are in place, you can extend them using the native Smalltalk language. Smalltalk compiles code incrementally, and new classes and objects work shortly after you create them.

Smalltalk-based client/server development tools, like other object-oriented tools, provide power to the developer through the object library included with the tool. When you select a Smalltalk development tool, you need to consider the fact that the library that comes with the tool defines its capabilities. Application development is just a matter of hooking up to the right objects, reusing objects, and avoiding coding as much as possible. The real challenge when using an object-oriented development tool such as Smalltalk is not just learning how the tool works, but learning the ins and outs of the library as well.

As with other object-oriented development environments such as C++ tools, PowerBuilder, and Visual Basic, there are a variety of third-party object libraries available to augment the standard objects that come with the native libraries. You'll find these libraries available in Smalltalk-related trade publications, or on the Web.

The up side to using the pure object-oriented model is that it forces the developer to use the object-oriented programming model, assuring that everything within the application exists as a well-designed (hopefully) independent object that easily reuses intra- or inter-application functions. Unlike C++, there is no way to drop back into the traditional structured model to solve problems in pure OO. Another downside is that it locks you into a few vendors that support a single language base. It will take time to learn pure objects. However, Smalltalk is not as proprietary as PowerBuilder, SQL Windows, and other specialized tools since it's based on an open language.

HYBRID OBJECT-ORIENTED DEVELOPMENT

The hybrid OO development model gives developers the best of both worlds. Hybrid programming languages and tools are built on top of existing traditional programming languages. Good examples of hybrid programming languages are Object COBOL, Object Pascal, and the most popular, C++.

C++, at least in my opinion, is the language that really propelled object-orientation into the limelight. It was derived from C, which quickly became the most popular programming language for the PC and Unix. C++ was a hit for two reasons. First, C was already in wide use in many organizations. Second, C++ is open and available from many vendors. Today, C++ is widely available on most platforms, and continues to dominate a segment of the client/server development marketplace. It is always the tool of choice for software vendors. The most popular C++ development environments include Borland C++, Watcom C++, and Microsoft Visual C++. I'll cover C++ in more detail when we discuss third-generation languages (3GLs) in Chapter 9.

Object purists argue that C++ provides developers with a confusing mixture of the object-oriented and structured development model. It's a bit too easy for developers to mix C and C++ code in an application, and never really take full advantage of the object-oriented development model. I have to admit that I've dropped back into C from C++ on occasion to solve problems that I could not figure out with C++. However, as I gained experience with C++, I stuck pretty close to the object-oriented aspects of the language.

Another feature of C++ that propelled it into the world of client/server is its use of a true compiler to deploy applications. Unlike Smalltalk, which uses an interpreter, C++ applications are fast and efficient. C++ is also one of the most flexible development environments. C++ lets developers build everything from device drivers to drawing tools to client/server applications, using the same language and tools.

C++ also provides the largest array of object libraries available, such canned objects for database connectivity, cross-platform development, and GUI construction (see Figure 6-10). Once again, you can purchase objects rather than build them yourself. This is almost always preferable.

One of the best examples of a useful C++ library for client/server development is Rouge Wave Software's DBTools.h++. DBTools.h++ is a C++ class library that lets C++ developers link to relational databases and make them appear as native C++ objects. When using DBTools.h++, developers don't have to drop back into the procedural portion of the language to gain access to remote data, as is the case when dealing with traditional ODBC or the native C libraries of the database vendors.

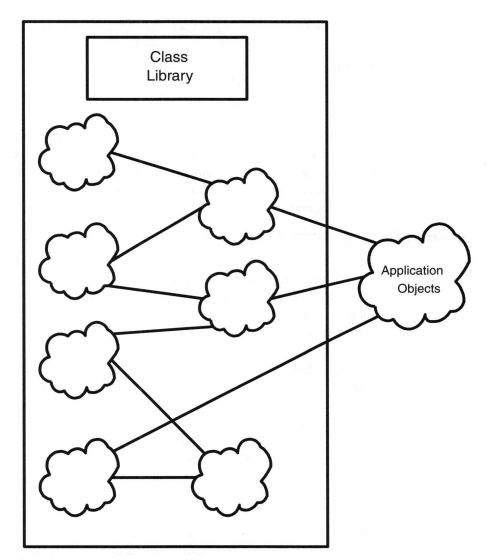

Figure 6-10 *Using an Object Library.*

What C++ object libraries you will have to deal with depends on the tool that you select. For instance, if you go with Borland C++, you'll use Borland Object Window Library (OWL). If you go to Microsoft Visual C++, you'll have Microsoft Foundation Classes (MFC) as your native library. These libraries provide most of the objects you'll need to create your C++ client/server application and include database connectivity, GUI controls, and even sample application objects that you can steal.

I have to admit that I like C++ (after all, I wrote a book about it), but there are big tradeoffs if you use C++ for your client/server application. C++ is a complex application, and difficult to learn. Count on about twice the learning time for C++ versus specialized client/server development tools such as PowerBuilder. You really need to first learn C, then learn about the object-oriented extensions of C++. C++ also operates very close to the metal. This means that developers need to think about allocating and managing memory directly. If you don't, bad things can happen such as memory corruption. What's more, C++ requires that developers learn complex and cryptic application programming interfaces (APIs). The end result is that it takes about twice as long to build a client/server application using C++ instead of specialized development tools.

SPECIALIZED OBJECT-ORIENTED DEVELOPMENT

Specialized OO development is really just a mixture of object-oriented implementations, with priority given to the concept of rapid development. This means that specialized development tools look at building the application as quickly as possible, using all sorts of object-oriented and "objectlike" approaches. Thus specialized development tools are the most complex of all the client/server development tools.

Specialized tools are built for a specific need, such as client/server development for Windows. These tools are the most numerous of the tools I'll discuss in this book after Chapter 8, and include biggies such as PowerBuilder, Visual Basic, Delphi, and SQL Windows. Specialized tools also include application-partitioning tools such as Forte and Dynasty, and cross-platform tools such as Unify, Uniface, and JAM 7. These tools only support portions of the object-oriented model, and the trick is to select the tool with the object-oriented features you really need.

Each tool's hodgepodge of approaches to objects makes applying the object-oriented development model difficult. However, everybody sells their tool as object-oriented. For instance, most specialized client/server development tools support single inheritance, and do so in their own proprietary way. JAM 7 supports inheritance through visual panels that the developer creates through inheritance. PowerBuilder supports both visual and nonvisual object inheritance. Visual Basic is almost not object-oriented at all, but has moved closer to the OO model with the latest releases. I still think it's a stretch to call Visual Basic object-oriented.

So how do you select a tool by its object-oriented nature? Developers first need to understand the object-oriented aspects of the tool. Let's take Power-Builder, for example. PowerBuilder developers can create a generic data window that contains all the columns they would like to use throughout an application.

This data window could also include color, size, fonts, and behavior. Once complete, developers can reuse that window throughout the application. When a developer makes changes to the window, such as adding the company logo, the changes automatically propagate down the hierarchy, changing all the objects that inherit from it. I use PowerBuilder as an example because I think it's a fairly typical specialized client/server development tool that supports specific portions of the object-oriented development model.

Of course, object purists don't like the specialized client/server development tools either. They argue that the lack of support for the formal object-oriented model and proprietary nature of these tools do not provide value in the long run to developers. The tool vendors argue that if they stuck too close to the object-oriented development model, the tools would be much more difficult to learn and use.

"Good Enough" Object Support

Having been in this business since the early '80s, and having heard from the pure, hybrid, and specialized client/server development zealots, I've come to my own standard for selecting a client/server development tool. I call it "good enough object support," or GEOS. GEOS means that the tool supports just enough of the object-oriented development model to make it useful for development, while it avoids locking the developer into a "paradigm." This means tools such as PowerBuilder, Delphi, and Object Pro are fine for most generalized client/server development needs, and support for the object-oriented model is good enough.

MIXING COMPONENT AND OBJECT-ORIENTED DEVELOPMENT

Objects aren't the only game in town. Component development is a recent addition to the world of client/server development. Component development involves the use of standard software components such as ActiveX (formerly OCX), Java, and OpenDoc components. This technology lets developers create applications by simply snapping components together to form an application, or more likely, to add functionality to an application. This is also the enabling technology of choice for intranet and Internet application development.

The difference between component and object-oriented development exists in the architecture. Components simply snap into the application, whereas objects inherit from other objects, which may inherit from still other objects.

For example, there is an ActiveX (formerly OCX) calculator that I use in many of the client/server applications I've deployed. Most client/server tools are ActiveX-enabled, therefore I just snap the component into my application, and place the code around it so the application knows when to invoke it, since ActiveX uses the standard interface. This is usually an all-or-nothing proposition, meaning it's difficult to alter the behavior of a component, unless the component developer has left hooks in the component to do so. The behavior of ActiveX components may be altered through aggregation, not inheritance. Aggregation, simply put, means embedding a component within a component to alter a component.

Using the component concept, developers can mix and match ActiveX components to form an application. Visual Basic, for example, is made up mostly of ActiveX components and uses the component architecture rather than the object-oriented model to create applications. Although objectlike, components are not object-oriented. Tool vendors have been confusing the issues as they hype their tools and technology.

A few specialized client/server development tools can mix the object-oriented model and the components nicely. Borland's Delphi, for example, can use ActiveX components (as well as Java with Borland's JBuilder) within an application as true objects that other objects may inherit from. This is the perfect marriage of objects and components. Other tools generally treat them as components with behavior and data accessible through the known OLE interface.

JUST SAY NO TO OBJECT-ORIENTED DEVELOPMENT?

I did a talk on object-oriented development a few year ago, and a gentleman came up to me afterward to tell me that he enjoyed the talk, but he wanted to build client/server applications without using objects. "Guess what?" I said. "That's going to be difficult." Despite the fact that today's tools still step all over the object-oriented development model, you really can't avoid using objects to build client/server applications. This is not to say that you can't force procedural C down the throats of your developers, but if you plan to bring the application in on time and within budget, you have to learn how to do things the object-oriented way. The gentleman I told this to put his head down and walked away. Sometimes you have to change to survive.

Mixing Objects and Tables

No matter how object-oriented the tools may be, we have to connect to a database some way, somehow. There are, of course, as many ways to do this as there are approaches to the object-oriented development model. I'll cover this in much greater detail in Chapter 12 when I talk about Smalltalk tools, but here let's look at this issue with a broader prospective.

When using the pure object model and pure object-oriented Smalltalk tools, we must treat data as persistent objects. Persistent objects are objects that reside in nonvolatile memory, and can exist after the application is closed. Pure object-oriented tools make relational databases appear as objects using wrappering mechanisms (sometimes called relational wrappers).

For example, VisualWorks provides an object-to-relational translation and mapping tool called ObjectLens and Visual Data Modeler. These subsystems of the tool let the developer map tables and columns to objects. Developers access the relational data as if they were accessing any other Smalltalk object. Other Smalltalk tools use similar mechanisms. Of course, if you use an object-oriented database, there is no need for a translation layer.

C++ and other hybrid object-oriented tools can access relational data as objects and nonobjects. For instance, I can drop back into traditional C to access data using native database APIs or ODBC. In doing so, I circumvent the object-oriented nature of the language and mix my application. Or, I can use C++ database access libraries such as DBTools.h++, or other native database access libraries that may come with the C++ tool.

By far the easiest way to access data is through the use of specialized object-oriented tools. Since these tools are built for client/server development, they have built-in mechanisms to access data. Most specialized tools don't access relational data as objects, but as relation data. For instance, PowerBuilder works directly with the database schema. Most developers will find it easier to deal with relational data as relational data (not as objects), with easy-to-use interfaces such as PowerBuilder database tools that graphically depict the relational database schema for the developer. I have to agree.

Object Standards

As you read this chapter (and as I write it), you might ask yourself, "Wouldn't object standards be nice?" I mean, you can mix and match objects in any tool, and potentially reuse every other object in the universe. This is certainly the Nirvana of object-oriented development. I have some good news here, and some bad news as well.

Although most object-oriented client/server tools promote the practice of object reuse, there is no de facto object standard. The Object Management Group's Common Object Request Broker Architecture (CORBA) is a specification that defines standard binary objects, sharable among tools that support the standard. (See Chapter 19 for more information on CORBA and distributed objects.) CORBA is tool-independent, meaning that you can build objects for Smalltalk using C++, and vice versa. Other examples of distributed objects include NeXT Computer's Portable Distributed Objects (PDO), and Sun's Distributed Objects Everywhere (DOE).

There are a few CORBA-compliant object vendors such as IBM's SOM/DSOM, Orbix from Iona, and Object Broker from Digital Equipment. CORBA defines the interfaces and communication mechanism between objects which reside locally, or across a network. Only a few tool vendors support CORBA. For instance, IBM's Smalltalk-based VisualAge can use SOM/DCOM objects.

The other standard object is not really object-oriented. Microsoft's Component Object Model (COM), and distributed COM (COM is the basis of OLE Automation [now called Active Server], ActiveX, and DCOM was once called Network OLE) are alternatives to CORBA. DCOM defines a standard interface that allows any COM object request broker (ORB) to communicate with any other COM object on the network. The strength of COM is tool support. Most client/server development tools, including PowerBuilder, Delphi, Visual Basic, and Visual C++, already provide the ability to create COM ORBs since they all support OLE automation. Microsoft created a standard from the tool support, where CORBA created the standard first, and now looks for the tools. The marketing power behind Microsoft could enforce the use of COM as our object standard.

On to More Objects

We did not cover everything about object-oriented development in this chapter, but you now have enough vital information to approach object-oriented client/server development, and most important, the know-how to get beyond the hype. This is just the beginning of the object-oriented discussion in this book. In the next chapter you'll find out what you need to know to design object-oriented applications. In later chapters we'll learn about the integration of objects in available client/server tools in more detail. By the end of this book, I hope to show you that objects are your friend.

Design Your Client/Server Application Right the First Time

Application design, to many, is an optional activity. With the advent of powerful specialized client/server development tools, developers put a sound application design down there with brushing after every meal. RAD (Rapid Application Development) is now the battle cry for many client/server development shops, and how passé to think before you code.

In many respects, the movement to circumvent the design process comes from our own industry. Specialized client/server tools such as PowerBuilder, Visual Basic, and Delphi promote rapid development and design through the tool. Speed is sexy, and sex sells.

However, I find that a sound application design provides a foundation for a sound client/server application. Skip it, and you'll pay the price with higher deployment costs, software quality problems, and possibly even project failure or abbreviated software life cycles.

Things change slowly. As client/server and the intranet become the platforms of choice for "business-critical" applications, more architects and developers will take a second look at application design. The sale of CASE tools, in decline since the decline of the mainframe, recently made a comeback. Development tool vendors see this trend too, and they now bundle CASE tools with their development tools, or provide interfaces with CASE. The linking of PowerBuilder and S-Designer is a good example of such a relationship. This trend will continue as organizations move client/server and client/server-enabled intranets to the enterprise.

In this chapter I'll take a look at what application design means to a successful client/server development project. Although a detailed discussion of application design is beyond the scope of this book, you should at least know you need it on your radarscope, if you are to find client/server development nirvana.

What's Application Design?

An application design is really just a series of activities that analysts, DBAs, developers, and end-users can participate in to assure that they all understand the users' requirements, that the requirements map to a sound application design, and that the design must be easily deployable to any development environment and database. Not an easy task.

We already discussed database design and development (Chapter 4), and the use of the object-oriented model (Chapter 6). We'll cover CASE in Chapter 15, so I won't discuss these topics here in detail. You should know that a sound application design and a sound database design go hand in hand. Moreover, with the continued interest in object-oriented technology, data and processing are becoming one and the same.

For the purposes of this book, we can define application design activities as those activities which take place before writing code, or generating the physical database schema. Application design activities include (but are not limited to) the gathering of use-cases (discussed later in this chapter), creation of an object model, the development of a data dictionary, or the generation of a state transition diagram. There can be as many as a hundred separate application design activities for large, complex systems, or two or three for smaller, less complicated systems.

For example, a large distributed application that I built just a few years ago required seventy-eight separate design tasks (gather use-cases, create object diagrams, etc.), and over fifty application design deliverables. Application design deliverables are outcomes of application design activities such as object diagrams, delivered to end-users, to developers, and sometimes to others on the application design team.

Sometimes systems are so simple that they require almost no formal application design. For instance, a simple client-tracking system I built for a friend of mine was designed and developed directly from a client/server RAD tool. I created the application right in front of his eyes, using the application development tool as my design environment.

Application "Desirements"

There are many ways to determine the application requirements (or the desirements) of your end-user audience. First you need to understand their business completely. Why? There is no way to build a system that automates their business if you don't know the ins and outs of their business. Sorry, but there is no way around this.

To understand a business, you must do your homework. Sometimes developers and application architects may only work in a particular industry to provide some consistent understanding of a business sector. For instance, consulting firms organize around business sectors such as health care, entertainment, manufacturing, and transportation. Developers and application architects use their basic understanding of a business sector to quickly understand an organization that operates in that business sector. I predict that this trend of specialization will only become more apparent as applications become more complex and specialized.

For now, we have a few tools at our disposal to assure that our understanding of how the application should look, feel, and behave is the same as that of the end-user. These tools require the use of a prototype, the use of Joint Application Design (JAD) session, and the use of user interviews.

JOINT APPLICATION DEVELOPMENT

Joint application development (JAD) provides one of the most successful methods of gathering desirements. JAD means that the end-users, developers, and application architects get together to talk about and jointly design the application. This is usually the outcome of a series of meetings where the end-users present their "vision" of the application, and developers work with the end-users to turn their vision into an application design.

A JAD facilitator leads JAD sessions to make sure everyone works together to meet the common goal. Everyone in the JAD session participates in the identification of data elements, processes, business rules, interfaces, user views, and other information relevant to the system design.

James Martin first described JAD, and he developed a set of steps and procedures that one can follow during a JAD session. The procedure even describes how the room should be set up, and where everyone should sit. A typical JAD session lasts two to five days, depending on the complexity and importance of the application. There may be three or four JAD sessions that take place throughout the design and development process. The JAD sessions are evenly spaced throughout the design and development process. You should hold JAD sessions off-site, away from distractions, and limit participation to those with direct responsibility for the system.

RAPID APPLICATION DEVELOPMENT AND PROTOTYPING

There is a gray area when it comes to the concepts of rapid application development (RAD) and prototyping. Many developers and application architects use the terms interchangeably. The differences exist, and it's important to make the distinctions.

RAD is a prototype-driven design and development technique, usually used in conjunction with a JAD. The outcome of an RAD is a working final system, without the use of a formal design. Users, developers, and application architects attend many JAD sessions, reviewing and suggesting and making changes to a working prototype until it meets the requirements. The system is then quickly put into service (see Figure 7-1).

Although RAD is fine for simple applications, in many instances it does not provide the rigorous method required to design and develop more complex systems. Remember, RAD means getting it wrong many times before getting it right once.

Figure 7-1 *RAD.*

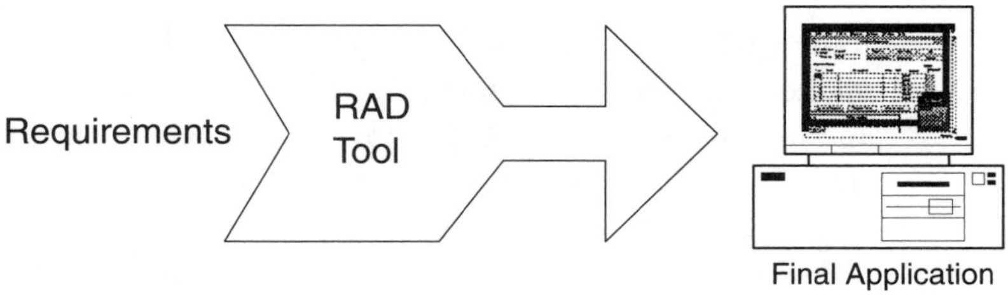

Requirements → RAD Tool → Final Application

Knowing When Rapid Application Development Is Bad

Rapid Application Development (RAD) promises to save everyone from the traditional "inefficient" object-oriented application development life cycles of yore. The idea is that rather than using the traditional waterfall model, we go directly to development (see Figure 7-2). This allows us to circumvent most of the object-oriented analysis and design activities that take so much time.

Figure 7-2 *Circumventing the waterfall.*

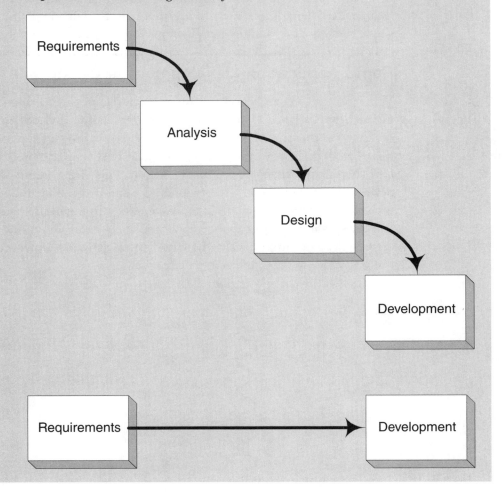

You have to admit this sounds good. RAD promises to build and deliver applications in days and weeks, not months and years. We don't have to deal with the time-consuming (and boring) design process, nor do we have to deal with the logical and physical structure of the application. Code first, ask questions later is the motto of RAD.

Is there a downside to RAD? You bet! As development organizations leap into the middle of the hype surrounding RAD, they find a collision of paradigms that bring about project failure after project failure.

I'm fighting this battle all the time. Most RAD advocates and vendors sell specialized object-oriented client/server development tools as "development without design." However, developers find that it's almost impossible to create an efficient, stable, and feature-rich object-oriented application when you exclude the preparation and planning. Another tradeoff in the making.

Rapid Application Development Is Cheap

When using RAD exclusively client/server development managers are seeking a cheap way out. They forgo the rigorous analysis and design activities described in this chapter for the cheap thrill of watching an application take form before their very eyes. This results in an RAD application that needs a lot of fixing and redeployment after release. This is the "rapid application development death spiral" (see Figure 7-3), and leads ultimately to trouble with the end-user, and failure of the system. Not to mention wasted money, and a very short lifespan for the application. It's one thing to use sophisticated object-oriented development tools that support RAD, it's another thing to move too fast to use them effectively.

Figure 7-3 *"RAD Death Spiral."*

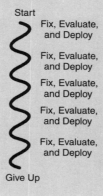

Start

Fix, Evaluate, and Deploy

Fix, Evaluate, and Deploy

Fix, Evaluate, and Deploy

Fix, Evaluate, and Deploy

Fix, Evaluate, and Deploy

Give Up

RAD tool vendors understand the allure of RAD, and they sell as much to the user community and management as they do to developers. In many cases that I've seen this results in a manager or CIO setting the development methodology for the organization using unrealistic expectations that surround RAD, and an awful lot of hype.

While object-oriented client/server development tools provide facilities for reuse, the RAD paradigm means that most developers won't have the time it takes to design their applications to make reuse a reality. Thus, reuse and RAD become mutually exclusive.

The fact is, reuse is not something that you stumble across. Both application architects and developers must put the time into the design to make reuse a reality. Using OOA/OOD methodologies, such as the ones described in this chapter, is a step in the right direction. Developers and application architects have to think through the object-oriented application before engrossing themselves in the RAD tool.

Can Rapid Application Development and Object-Oriented-Applications Get Along?

The things to remember about OO and RAD is that they move in different directions if you allow them to. There is a compromise that will not only allow developers to create well-designed object-oriented applications, but applications that perform well. Both developers and application architects need to follow a few basic steps.

First, make sure that the developers, application architects, and end-users have a clear understanding of the business problem. Don't become so immersed in the prototype that the business problem becomes obscured. This results in applications not living up to the requirements; failure will follow.

Second, set some portion of the life cycle aside for requirements, analysis, and design. Although it's tempting to dump some design activities for the sake of speed, client/server development managers need to ensure that everyone has a clear understanding of how the system design maps into an implementation of objects. This does not mean that all RAD projects need to have an all-out formal design effort, but there has to be some time allocated to map out class hierarchies, define objects, and figure out how all the components will fit together.

> The bottom line is that RAD is able to optimize the object-oriented client/server development effort by sacrificing design activities. In order to make RAD useful, developers need to take time to define how they will use RAD to complement the software development life cycle, not replace it. RAD alone is dangerous, but combined with other complimentary activities, RAD can be effective.

Developers and application architects will often use prototypes to help build their understanding of user requirements, both in the context of JAD and by simply working with end-users. Sometimes the prototypes become the final system, or a portion of the final system (as is the case with RAD). Sometimes they are tossed away for a more robust application. The difference between RAD and prototyping is that with RAD, the prototype becomes the final system, whereas the traditional prototyping approach facilitates discussion and provides a better understanding of the needs of the users since they have something in front of them to play with and critique.

Prototypes are early versions of the system that represent the look-and-feel of the system to the end-user. For example, in many JAD sessions, a developer will build a quick mock-up of the system to facilitate discussion during the JAD.

In most cases, prototypes only represent the proposed user interface and need not have all the functionality of the final system. For instance, there is rarely any need to connect the prototype to a remote database server. Local servers work just fine. It's also okay to have menus that lead nowhere, and data windows that don't yet exist. A prototype is always a work-in-process.

Prototyping tools can be any RAD or specialized client/server tool that can get a proposed system up and running, and allow many changes to the system. The best tools let a designer work quickly and easily. Examples of good prototyping tools include PowerBuilder, Visual Basic, and Delphi. Since these are fully functional client/server tools, developers can use portions of the system they build during the prototyping stage in the final system.

USER INTERVIEWS

While I found that JAD and the use of a prototype are the best ways to gather user requirements, sometimes JAD is not appropriate. For example, smaller systems that don't involve a large number of users often provide a good environment for user interviews.

To perform user interviews, simply meet with potential users to determine their requirements. There can be as many interviews as you want, but usually three days' worth is enough.

During these interviews, application architects will discuss the requirements with the users and gather information as they go. Subsequent interviews provide a review of the information gathered at earlier interviews, and a refinement of everyone's understanding of how the application will look and behave.

A prototype gives the user something to touch, feel, and critique. Prototypes prove time and again that a picture is worth a thousand words.

After the interviews, the application architect should understand all the business problems (the problem domain) that the application needs to solve. In addition, the architect should have an understanding of the logical data and application model, and the interface through the use of a prototype.

AVOIDING REQUIREMENTS DRIFT

"Requirements drift" is the inevitable shift in the underlying requirements of a client/server application as it moves through the life cycle. For instance, a bank system that I worked on a few years ago went a million dollars over budget when the requirements drift resulted in two system redesigns after the application moved out of the initial design phase. After its deployment, the system went through a third redesign for another million dollars. While every project encounters a little requirements drift, major changes in the base functionality of the system and database become counterproductive, not to mention expensive.

In many cases, requirements drift can be traced back to unreasonable users who look at client/server developers as people to serve their ever-changing mind. However, in other cases, I find that developers and application architects fail to manage their users properly, and/or understand the requirements correctly the first time. I'm finding more of the latter than the former.

For example, application architects and developers who don't manage user expectations will end up with users who expect their application development life cycle to be an interactive experience. This means that users will have great ideas late in the life cycle, and developers will have to perform a lot of "meatball" programming just to keep up. Developers are forced into a RAD life cycle, whether they like it or not.

To avoid this problem, let the user know that understanding and finalizing the application requirements up-front is essential to your ability to deliver a quality system on-time, and with the allocated amount of money. You'd be surprised how well users understand this and are willing to help.

Other problems with requirements drift deal with the application architects and developers who will not spend the necessary time to understand the application requirements. They guess at many of the requirements, and users—rightly so—make changes during development to get a system that meets their requirements. You must understand the requirements completely before you attempt an application design or develop the application. Seems logical. I can't count the number of times I see this simple rule violated.

How to Avoid "Analysis Paralysis"

Although I find that most development organizations lack the appropriate amount of analysis and design activities, there are a few who do so much analysis and design that the project seems to go on forever. I call this phenomenon "analysis paralysis."

Analysis paralysis means the overuse of analysis and design activities, and neglecting other life-cycle activities (e.g., development and testing). So how do you know when you're paralyzed? Watch for the first symptom when analysis and design activities seem to be consuming more than 75 percent of the development team's time from the project's inception to delivery of the final system.

There are no hard-and-fast rules about the amount of time one should spend doing analysis and design, since it depends on the complexity of the system. I don't feel that you should dedicate more than 50 percent of the time, money, and effort to analysis and design, especially when you consider the number of tools available today (e.g., CASE tools) to automate this process. However, this is a point of debate.

To avoid analysis paralysis, make sure you monitor the analysis and design activities. Watch for efforts that take much more time than they are worth, and adjust activities accordingly. The trick is to strike a nice balance between analysis design with other important life-cycle activities.

Object-Oriented Analysis and Design

Most client/server development tools are object-oriented. Therefore, developers and application architects not only need to understand the object-oriented development model (discussed in Chapter 6), they also need to understand that the object-oriented model requires a different approach to application design. Object-oriented analysis and design (OOA/OOD), simply put, provides developers and application architects with a way to map desirements directly to the object-oriented model, so you can map them into an object-oriented client/server development tool. In the last six years, OOA/OOD has gone from a topic of academic debate to realistic software development tactics. Today, OOA/OOD is the backbone of client/server development.

THINKING OBJECTS

The reason for selecting the object-oriented approach to a software development project lies in the power of the approach. Just as the structured programming revolution of the early '70s led to the structured analysis and design methodologies in use today, object-oriented programming is leading the way to OOA and OOD methodologies.

Methodology (or, a method) is a term that describes the procedures application architects go through to understand the desirements, and map them to a model that developers can implement using some sort of programming language and database. Methodologies usually entail two major components: a step-by-step procedure to approach and solve the problem, and a set of notation to define the problem and the solutions (see Figure 7-4). Notation is simply the collection of standard symbols and meanings the methodology uses. CASE tools automate the use of notation (see Figure 7-5).

Today, object-oriented client/server development leads the way to OOA and OOD methods. Although OO is a little wet behind the ears, it has several obvious advantages over the older structured techniques. The two have crossed paths many times (i.e., structured analysis and design for object-oriented software development), but today's application architects and developers go all objects.

What object-orientation brings to the table is the enhanced reusability of data and processes in the construction of software. In an object-oriented system, the data and the process are grouped into a logical entity: an object. Following the concepts of object-orientation, objects have the ability to inherit characteristics (methods and data) of one or more classes/objects.

This reusability through inheritance is the most compelling reason to move toward object-oriented technology. In short, we can do more with existing software, using fewer lines of new code. This makes the OO life cycle cheaper and more efficient.

What does this all mean? Object-oriented client/server development leads to the need for object-oriented analysis and design techniques to meet the specialized requirements of object-oriented development technology. I found that several advantages of OOA and OOD are apparent at first glance.

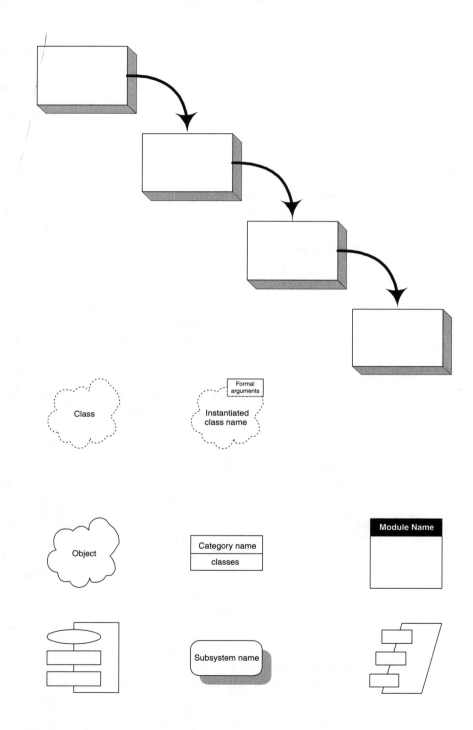

Figure 7-4 *OO Design notation.*

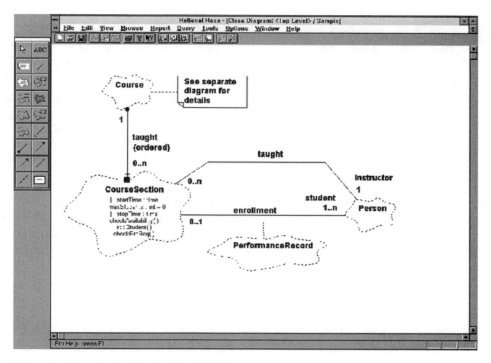

Figure 7-5 *Using CASE for OO Modeling.*

The most practical advantage is the ability to reuse analytical efforts. Object-oriented analysis and object-oriented design allow the analyst to organize information based on problem domain constructors. This provides a natural organization of processes and their associated data. Therefore the analyst or designer can reuse analytical efforts more efficiently than in structured methods where the data and processes are separated. These problem domain constructors eventually become real objects within the confines of an object-oriented program (e.g., PowerBuilder or C++).

Client/Server Becomes More Object-Oriented

Although object-oriented development has always been a part of client/server development, the tools always took a different view of the object-oriented model. However, a good object-oriented model created by OOA/OOD activities may not be easy to implement in a particular object-oriented client/server development environment. In other words, object-oriented became the buzzword, not necessarily the practice.

Things change quickly. Today's new specialized client/server development tools adhere closer to the object-oriented development model in its pure form. PowerBuilder version 5, for instance, is much more object-oriented than version 4, and can therefore provide a good home to a well-designed object model—the output of OOA/OOD.

Another advantage is the "back to reality" concept of OOA/OOD. OOA lets the analyst organize results in a more easily understood and natural fashion. As application designers, we tend to "overabstract" simple business events. The functional decomposition of structured analysis and design confounded this overcomplication. Quite simply, OOA represents the real world as we see it. People, places, and things found in an enterprise are objects. These objects have certain characteristics (data and behaviors).

Consistency is another advantage of OOA/OOD. OOA reduces the potential for differences between analysis activities. OOA accomplishes this by treating attributes and services as whole concepts, not the smallest unit of detail (as with functional decomposition of the structured world). OOA/OOD can also find and use common activities (objects) that benefit from one another through inheritance. This time saver is one of the most beneficial attributes of OOD and OOA. Overall, inheritance allows the use of common activities in a more logical way than structured analysis and design methodologies.

One last advantage of OOA/OOD is the ability to alter a system component without affecting the entire system: "change without pain." OOA/OOD allows us to place volatility into a domain and isolate certain areas of a system that often change (see Figure 7-6). This allows the system to react better to changes in the requirements. For instance, when using object-oriented development tools such as PowerBuilder, developers quickly learn to put portions of the application that constantly change in an object or group of objects. When an object's features change, the new features of the object automatically propagate to the objects that inherit from the parent (original) object.

OBJECT-ORIENTED METHODOLOGIES MADNESS

As previously mentioned, methodology refers to an assortment of notations and techniques used in system modeling and the entire life cycle's procedures. There are more than fifteen different OOA/OOD methodologies, all competing

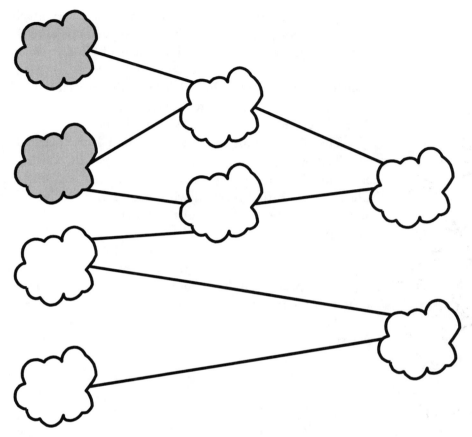

Figure 7-6 *Placing volatility into a domain.*

for the hearts and minds of application architects. In my experience, it does not make much difference which methodology you select, as long as it works well for you. You should consider the CASE tools that support your methodology of choice, and the availability of training and documentation for those tools.

There are two types of OOA/OOD methodologies: ternary and unary. Ternary methodologies are the natural evolution of structured methods using three distinct types of notation for data, dynamics, and process. In contrast, the unary type of methodology combines methods and data into objects. As you may guess from our discussions in Chapter 6, the unary type of methodology is more appropriate for object-oriented development, and thus makes better OOA/OOD methodologies.

Let's look at a few available methodologies. In the quick descriptions that follow, notice how many of the presented methods utilize similar techniques, concepts, procedures, and even notation. This is very much an overview. All these methodologies arose from books that you need to read to understand the methodologies in more detail. I'll list the books in the reference sections.

Booch. First, I have to admit that I'm rather partial to the Booch methodology. Don't let this sway you too much. Remember that methodologies are like shoes. One brand may not fit as well as another.

Here is something else to keep in mind. Booch, Jacobson, Rumbaugh (all described below) recently joined forces to create the unified method (see sidebar), a hybrid methodology that encompasses the best of all the methodologies. Clearly, the unified method will become the leading method due to the popularity of the methodologists who created it, and the methodologies it encompasses.

Grady Booch, the developer of the Booch methodology, described an object as a model of a real-world entity which consists of both data and the ability to expedite that data. Once the objects are located and defined, they are a basis for the modules of the system, or they are considered related objects.

The Booch diagram (see Figure 7-7) derives a set of objects directly from the specifications. The diagram demonstrates dependencies between the

Figure 7-7 *Booch Class Diagram.*

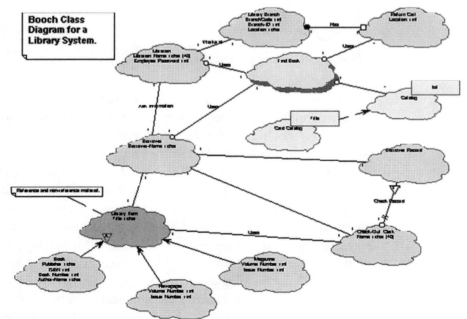

object-oriented language and the roles the objects play in the overall functionality of the system.

Booch relates structured design and object-oriented design as "orthogonal views" of how systems should be created. While object-oriented design structures the problem with objects that exist in the domain, structured design separates a system by modules (data and process) derived from data flow diagrams (DFDs). Booch argues that structured design works well with structured programming languages, but the structured approach forces developers to concentrate on execution of the program with little regard for the data. This results, as stated by Booch, in additional code and less data because structures are derived from processes, and the processes need to interact with data in the system.

In the Booch world, OOD is organized by objects via algorithmic abstractions. The Booch object model relates closely to object-oriented programming (OOP) in that each OOD module represents an object or a class of objects with reusability, modularity, and encapsulation stressed throughout the OOD processes. This close relationship with OOD and object-oriented programming lets the designers make business decisions before they create the code, which results in a better built, more efficient system. Those with OOP experience understand the benefits if they first consider how the classes and objects will be created and (more important) implemented.

Basically, Booch approaches the OOD program by creating four deliverables. First is the hardware diagram that presents the processors, devices, networks, and their connections. Second, the class structure presents the relationships between classes and objects. Third, object diagrams show the visibility of an object as related to other objects. Last, the architecture diagram depicts the physical design of a system.

Coad/Yourdon. Peter Coad and Ed Yourdon (one of the fathers of structured analysis and design) created a simplistic but effective approach to analysis and design using objects. Basically, Coad and Yourdon divide OOA as classes and objects. Objects are an abstraction of a problem's domain that reflect the abilities of a system to retain data, interact with data, and encapsulate values of attributes and services. A class is a collection of one or more objects with attributes and services, and includes an understanding of how to create new objects in the class.

A structure is the representation of a problem/domain complexity directly related to the system's responsibilities. Coad and Yourdon use this in terms of a Generalization-Specialization (Gen-Spec) structure.

A subject is a procedure to guide an analyst through a large, complex model. Subjects organize work based upon initial requirements. An attribute is some sort of data where each object has an independent value. Services are what the object can do (a method).

The diagram that Yourdon and Coad propose (see Figure 7-8) to represent the above concepts is basic. The significant characteristic of the object/class is defined within the object symbol. Now, if we are to relate one object to another, we employ Coad and Yourdon's connector and associations. Two or more objects may be associated by a connector. The connector, or association, can be of a Gen-Spec, whole-part, instance-to-instance, or a message connection.

Connecting the objects together using the Coad and Yourdon associations allows the analyst to study how the class/objects relate to one another. This ability to connect objects using several associations makes the Coad and Yourdon methods flexible and gives them the ability to react to most business problem domains.

Shlaer and Mellor. Sally Shlaer and Stephen Mellor outline a method of OOA that can use traditional tools from the structured world. This is a great method for keeping non-OOA CASE around a few years longer while reaping the benefits of OOA. Shlaer and Mellor use traditional entity-relationship

Figure 7-8 *Coad/Yourdon Diagram.*

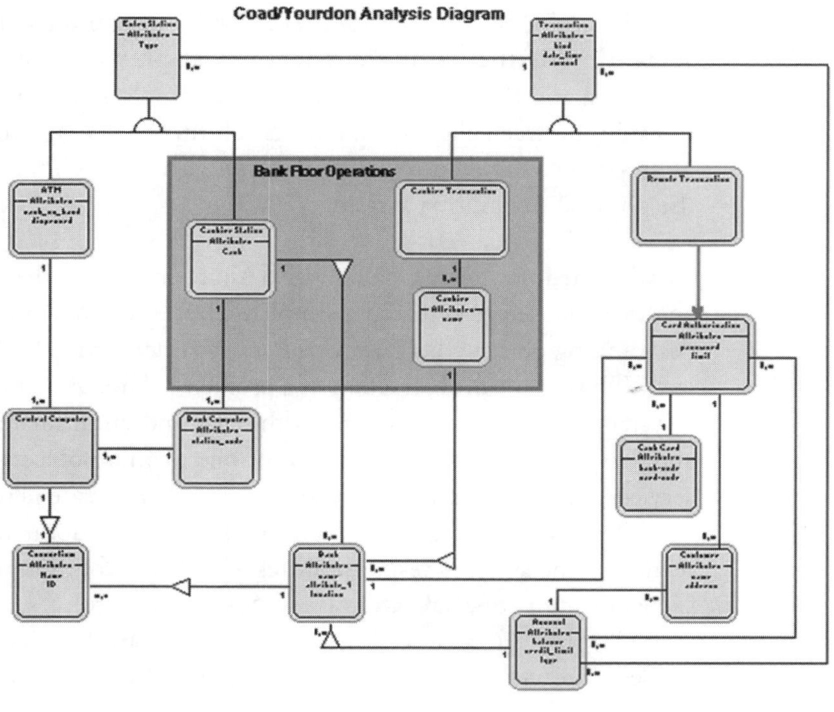

diagrams, data flow diagrams, and state-transition diagrams, mostly derived from Ward and Mellor's real-time system design methods (see Figure 7-9).

Shlaer and Mellor promote the following steps for OOA:

1. Construct an information model (entity-relationship diagram) that depicts objects, relationships, and attributes
2. Create a state model (state-transition diagram) for each object in the model. This diagram should contain all potential states to which that object might change
3. Create an object communication diagram that depicts all object state modes
4. Create a DFD for each state transition in the state-transition diagram, and a process specification to describe change in the state of the object
5. Create a data store on the DFD for each object in the ISD
6. Describe the boundaries of the system based on external events that may cross the boundaries
7. Create an external event list
8. Create a functional requirements list
9. Select OOD or structured design
10. Develop the program using an OOP (for example, C++)

Figure 7-9 *Shlaer & Mellor State Model.*

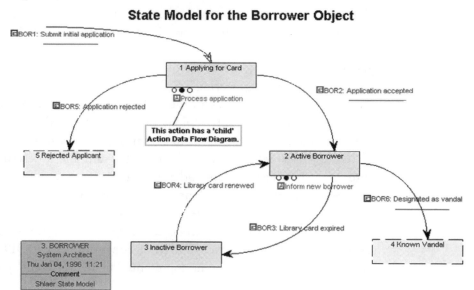

State Model for the Borrower Object

The Shlaer and Mellor OOA method differs from the structured approach by using a bottom-up, data composition approach to OOA. Remember, structured analysis uses top-down, and as argued by Booch, tends to create more code than is needed by OOD; this can cause problems if requirements change significantly over time.

The Shlaer and Mellor approach to OOA is a variation of data modeling that concentrates on the data or objects and how they are grouped. In this model, the objects are grouped by functions instead of processes. Messages passed from object to object determine the order of operations.

Shlaer and Mellor use three models to implement their method. The first model is the standard entity-relationship diagram (ERD, described in Chapter 4) where the entity represents objects, and relationships and attributes are depicted as they are in the standard ERDs. With this model, each object is presented as an entity in the ERD and in the data dictionary. Each object becomes a row in a table, and the ERD presents objects, attributes, and relationships.

The second model is a standard data flow diagram (DFD) which depicts processes that act on the objects defined by the ERD. This process model presents the processes for every state on the model. The DFD is standard and requires no new OOA symbols. The third and final Shlaer and Mellor model is the state-transition diagram (STD), which controls event-driven behavior of objects. This state model depicts the operation of each object or relationship on the ERD using a STD.

Many "true to the art" object-oriented analysts have criticized Shlaer and Mellor for not providing a method to depict messages or encapsulations, which are considered by many to be the critical advantage of OOA.

Jacobson. Jacobson, one of the oldest methods, uses a method called "object-oriented software engineering" (OOSE). It includes a focus on use-cases. Use-cases are models that represent the intended usage of the system. Although you can use use-cases as a methodology unto itself, I found that Jacobson provides the most value when you use it to gather requirements.

Use-cases definitions consist of a diagram and a description of a single interaction between an actor and a system. The actor is a user, or another object that resides in the system. Generally, you employ use-cases to gather requirements, since it's natural at determining how users interact with the system.

Also included in the method are categorizations of objects located in the enterprise, labeled interface, entity, or control. OOA/OOD models created with OOSE show partitioning represented by the different symbols (interface, entity, and control).

The interface objects model all functionality that represent the system interface. The entity object represents all functionality that relates to the actual information contained in the system, and the control object represents functionality that cannot be contained in the other objects. Later, the client/ server application designer places notations for attributes on the object notation. We can then further refine the model by grouping constructs into a subsystem. Basically, the model aims at logical and maintainable structure in the system.

Rumbaugh. This method was created at the General Electric Corporation, and is known as the object-modeling technique (OMT). Rumbaugh's is a well-tested, mature method, based on an information-modeling base. This method uses object model notation that supports information-modeling concepts (such as attribute and relationship), and object concepts (such as composition—called aggregation in OMT—and inheritance). You can also use Rumbaugh's method to characterize classes and instances (called objects). Figure 7-10 contains a typical OMT diagram.

Figure 7-10 *OMT Object Model.*

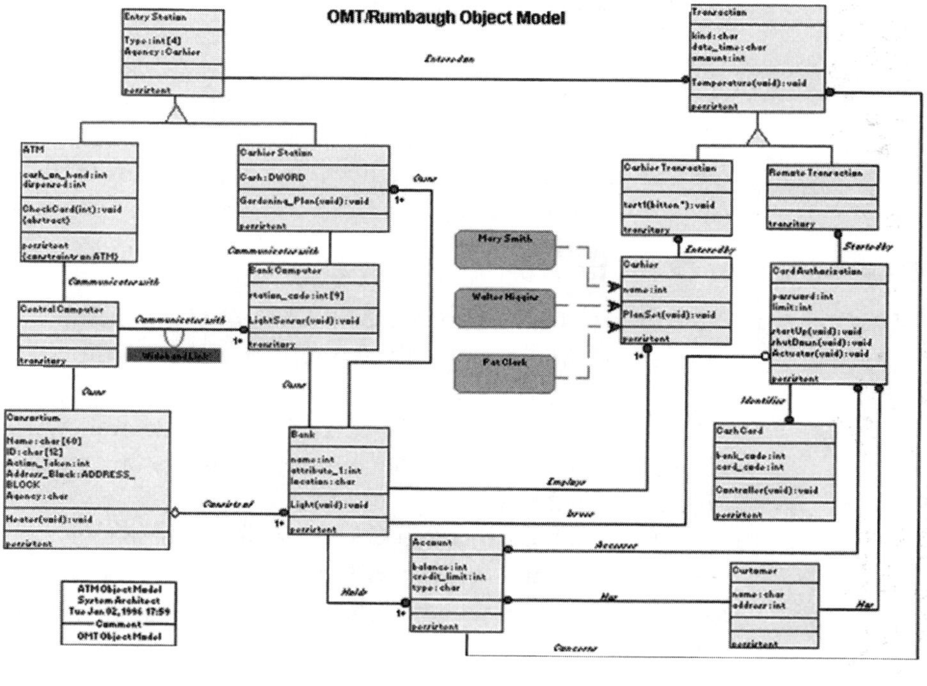

The strength of this method is the helpful notation, and the relatively conservative approach to object-oriented technology. Out of all the methods surveyed here, I've found that Rumbaugh has the best CASE support.

Bringing the Methods Together

If you think there are too many OOA/OOD methods, and they make the world more confusing than easy, you're right. However, there is a movement afoot to bring together the most popular methods—Rumbaugh, Booch, and Jacobson—into a single OOA/OOD design method called the unified method. If successful, this could provide client/server developers with one-stop shopping for methodology and CASE.

The driving force behind the unified method is Rational Software, the company that now employs all three methodologists. Grady Booch is the chief technical officer at Rational. Rational also hired Jim Rumbaugh, and merged with Jacobson's company, Objectory. Rumbaugh and Jacobson are collaborating at Rational with Grady Booch to merge their techniques and base the methods on common notation.

Although the unified method is still a work-in-process, it holds the promise of a methodology that everyone can agree upon. If you want to see this specification's progress, check it out on the web at http://www.rational.com.

Proprietary Methods. Some of the tools surveyed do not support any of the above "popular" methods, but support their own "home-grown" OOA/OOD method. Even though the methods are not popular or in use anywhere else, they should be considered at their face value. In other words; is the method useful?

OBJECT-ORIENTED COMPUTER-AIDED SOFTWARE ENGINEERING

Now that we have a basic understanding of OOA methods, and have surveyed some of the more popular OOA/OOD methods on the streets, let's take a look at the CASE (computer-aided software engineering) products that support OOA methodologies. We'll cover CASE in more detail in a later chapter (Chapter 15), so for now, let's limit the discussion to the unique features of object-oriented CASE.

As with the structured CASE products, these tools differ greatly in facilities, function, and technique. One must be very careful to select the tool to support the selected method. Remember, some methods (such as Booch) are supported by many CASE products, while others (such as Jacobson) are supported by only one. Therefore, when you select your method, consider the quality and availability of the CASE tools that support it. Let's look at a few of my favorite CASE tools.

System Architect. This is one of the strongest OOA/OOD tools available, and it's cheap. System Architect, from Popkin Software, provides a wide variety of support for most popular OOA/OOD methods supporting Coad/Yourdon, Booch, Rumbaugh, and Shlaer/Mellor. System Architect also supports most popular structured methods and data-modeling diagrams.

This is an effective tool that also supports a wide array of structured methods. System Architect is one of the many CASE tools presented here that operates in a Windows 95 environment, as well as OS/2.

Other features include requirements tracking through the entire OO life cycle, and the ability to integrate structured and OO design information in a single data dictionary. System Architect also provides rule checking, multiple views and representation of the object model and specifications, and advanced reporting capabilities.

Paradigm Plus. Paradigm Plus supports the most widely used object-oriented methods including Rumbaugh, Booch, HP Fusion, and their own ProtoSoft OOAD. The tool utilizes a "Paradigm Plus CASE Development Kit" (CDK) that lets ProtoSoft's users automate any software engineering activity, including the definition of objects, relationships, rules, notations, dialog boxes, menus, etc. As with the Envision tool, Paradigm can create a new custom CASE tool in a short time.

Other features of the product include multi-user capability using an object repository, a diagram editor, code generation for C, C++, Ada, and Smalltalk, and schema generation for relational and object DBMSs. In addition, this tool supports customization of report/code generation via a script language.

Rational Rose. Rational Rose is a graphical, object-oriented software-engineering tool. This object-oriented-only tool enforces the Booch object-oriented analysis and design method, and will eventually include support for the unified method (see sidebar). Rose supports the capture, communications, and consistency-checking of object-oriented technology. This tool supports visualization, which enables the analyst to create graphical representations of key abstractions and relationships.

Rose is now sold around deployment languages. For example you can purchase Rose for Java, Rose for PowerBuilder, and Rose for C++.

Putting It All in Perspective

The point I want to make in this chapter is that design activities are just as important as development activities. Maybe more so. Skip the design stage, fail to understand the business problems or the user's needs, and there is no need to build the system in the first place. It's doomed.

Although OOA/OOD methods and tools help work through the problem, they are not magic wands. Developers and application architects must ensure a good balance between OOA/OOD and development efforts to assure a healthy system. This is not as easy as it sounds, especially when you consider that we do this in an environment that constantly changes.

Finding the Right Tools

Selecting Client
Development Tools

This is the chapter where the rubber meets the road in client/server development. I've found that the selection of the wrong client/server development tool almost always results in failed client/server development projects. So why do we pick the wrong tools? The answer lies somewhere between the mega-hype that drives the client/server development industry (and now intranet development), the bitter reality of tools that don't deliver, and technology that does not work when it should.

You don't have to run the risk of project failure due to "tool tragedy." This is a classic case where a little bit of homework up front, with some testing tossed in, can assure that your tool of choice won't kill your project. The tragedy is that most development managers and developers won't study tools, and instead resort to "religious" decisions, or worse, "management by magazine."

So how do you select the right tools? The answer is to understand the enabling technology, the industry, and available products. Client/server developers and application architects need to take the time to understand a complex world in a constant state of flux. We need to understand how to select the best tool for the job, learn how to move from the requirements to the tool, and never work in the other direction. We need to know how to categorize tools and peal back the marketing hype to reveal the true capabilities of the tool.

In this chapter I'll make sense of today's state-of-the-art client/server application development tools. We'll look at the capabilities of the tools, create categories to better understand client/server tools, and look at the cost of the tools. I'll also provide a few examples of client/server tools you can purchase today for client/server and intranet development.

Avoiding the Holy Wars

The funny thing about client/server tools is that everyone has a favorite tool set to use. Tools are so near and dear to our hearts that it's almost a religious experience. The end result is the rise of zealots; developers and even application architects who refuse to consider other tools and technology when they build a client/server system. They have found their religion, and won't consider other leaps of faith.

As developers center around tool religions, I see a holy war of sorts taking place. Organizations wrap their development activities around tools, and developers refuse to consider other solutions. Fueling this religion fervor is the hype-driven marketing machine of the tool vendors, pitted one against the other. Trade magazines contribute to the problem as well. The result is a fragmented client/server development community that rallies around favorite tools.

The problem with holy wars is that developers limit their options when they approach client/server development projects. PowerBuilder is not always the answer, nor is Visual Basic, or high-end application partitioning tools. The application requirements dictate the tool selection process, and developers and application architects should always go from the requirements to the tools, and never from the tools to the requirements—which is, unfortunately, what usually happens. Don't grow attached to your client/ server tools!

Management by Magazine

Religious zealots sometimes present an obstacle to making the correct client/server tool decision, and then there are those who manage by magazine. This means the developers and application architects neglect to research tools by themselves, but use the latest magazine reviews to select tools.

Don't get me wrong, trade journals (and their Web sites) are an excellent way to learn about available technology, and even how tools compare with other tools in their class. But these reviews only cover the tools, and how they relate to *general* requirements. They cannot compare the tools to *your* requirements!

I'm often surprised when I get E-mail from developers who selected their tool based on an article I wrote (even though I always stress how important it is for the readers to apply their own requirements against the tool features). I always ask them if they considered their requirements. The answer is often no, and as a result, the tool may or may not live up to their requirements.

Client/Server Tools Defined

Client/server application development tools are any development environment, compiler, reporting tool, or even a framework that developers employ to build and deploy client/server applications. As I mentioned in Chapter 1, client/server has a few generally accepted ways of computing, and the tools usually run on the client and interface with the user using the native GUI, such as Windows 95, OS/2, Motif, or Mac OS.

Most client/server tools provide an integrated development environment (IDE) where the developer works to build a client/server application (see Figure 8-1). IDEs usually provide screen painters, object browsers, and code editors. IDEs also provide links to various database servers via a native (proprietary) connection layer, or through call-level interfaces such as ODBC or JDBC (Java Database Connectivity). These tools may connect to remote database servers, or connect to database servers that run locally in the same operating system where the tool runs (see Figure 8-2).

Client/server tools provide some sort of programming language, and almost all are object-oriented in some way, fashion, or form (even if it's just marketing hype). For example, PowerSoft offers its PowerScript 4GL, where Visual Basic provides VBA (Visual Basic for Applications). What's more, client/server development tools provide some sort of application distribution

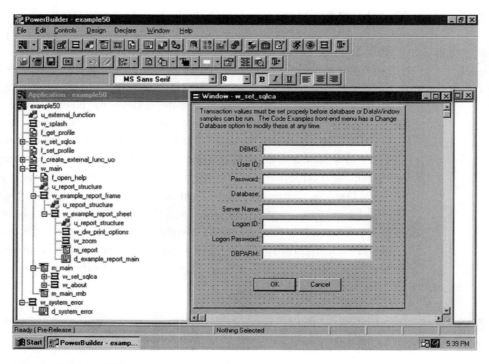

Figure 8-1 *An IDE.*

capability which lets developers create native executables or pcode, and interpreters for distribution to clients.

Applications created with client/server tools provide a few general services.
First of all, client/server applications interact with the users, perform general application processing, and interact with the database. The client/server application
translates input from the user into a database request, then returns data back to the
user through the interface. Sometimes the tools may communicate with a middle
tier, such as an application server that runs a TP monitor or distributed objects.

Client/server tools are of value to developers because all these complex
activities happen behind the scenes—the developer does not have to worry
about doing database requests through an API, or worry about the details of
interface processing and memory management (see Figure 8-3). The ability to
remove the developer from the underlying complexities of application development, middleware APIs, network communications, and database processing
is the real value of these tools. Thus, we can develop client/server applications
with a minimum amount of work and trouble.

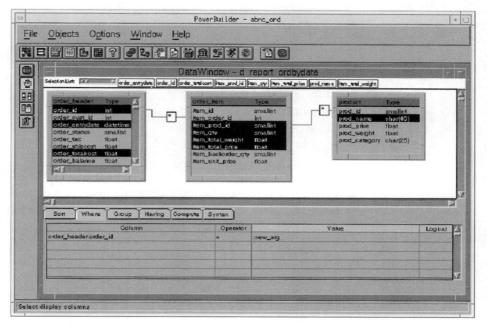

Figure 8-2 *Powerbuilder for Unix.*

Although most client/server development tools solve the same problems, they solve them in different ways. For example, all these tools provide their own proprietary development languages and object libraries. They all differ in how they provide the developer with user interface development tools, and how they link to a database, and even how much they cost.

Client/Server Tool Types

When I first began reviewing client/server tools, I found they were so different that it was difficult to place them in categories. For example, is C++ a real client/server development tool, or is it a language that can be part of a tool? As time marched on and tools matured, I found that certain tool types arose that made it easier to categorize these tools, which, in turn, made the selection process easier for client/server development projects.

So what did I come up with? As I see it, client/server development tools fit into one (okay, sometimes two) of the following categories:

- Third-generation language tools
- Specialized tools
- Multi-platform tools
- Smalltalk tools
- File-oriented database tools
- Reporting and DSS tools
- Code generators
- CASE tools
- Application partitioning tools

I have to admit that I encounter some tools that don't fit in any one category, but you'll generally find a fit for most tools. It's always helpful to use these

Figure 8-3 *A Client/Server Development Tool.*

Client/Server
Development Tool

categories as the jumping-off point for the tool selection process. What's more, it's to develop subcategories that better define the class of tools on your wish list. By no means is this a static set of categories.

THIRD-GENERATION LANGUAGE TOOLS

3GL (third-generation language) client/server development tools are simply traditional 3GL tools that use C++ or Pascal, and also provide database connections. Borland's C++, Microsoft's Visual C++, and Watcom's C++ are examples of 3GL tools that can do client/server. (I also discuss 3GL tools in Chapter 9.)

3GL tools are primitive when compared to full-blown specialized client/server development tools. However, they deliver blazing-fast native executables if client/server developers want to sacrifice ease of use for power. Today's 3GL compilers are very different from the command line compilers of the past. Tools such as Visual C++ provide powerful IDEs to create applications and look through class libraries, and compile and link applications. These tools also provide database links, but you'll have to access the database through the native features of the 3GL.

Third-Generation Languages Do the Intranet with Java

Just when we thought 3GLs (third-generation languages) would be a relic of our client/server past, interest in the intranet re-revolutionized 3GLs and the battle cry is Java. Java is a 3GL development language that looks a lot like C++ (see listing below). Java was built from the ground up for browser-based application development.

Using Java, developers can build applets. Applets are small programs that are downloaded along with HTML to the a Java-enabled browser where they execute inside the browser. The significance of Java is that it brings dynamic application behavior to the Web, which largely uses static text and graphics. Therefore, developers can create applications that can download into browsers, and they function like normal client/server client-side applications, disconnected from the Web server. A barrage of Java-based development tools have recently arrived on the market, including Symantec's Visual Café (see Figure 8-4), Borland C++, and Rogue Wave Software's JFactory.

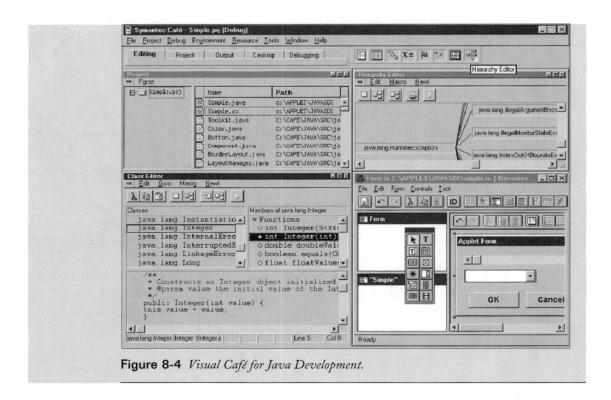

Figure 8-4 *Visual Café for Java Development.*

SPECIALIZED TOOLS

As I mentioned in Chapter 6, specialized development tools are highly proprietary client/server application development tools that provide everything the developer needs to build and deploy client/server applications. I call them specialized tools because they were built for a special purpose—to build client/server applications. This is unlike 3GL tools, which are built for general purpose programming. Specialized tools include tools that support RAD. Examples include Borland's Delphi, Microsoft's Visual Basic, and PowerSoft's PowerBuilder. Chapter 10 is dedicated to a discussion of specialized client/server development tools.

In addition to RAD capabilities, most specialized client/server development tools provide 4GL development languages, database connections built into the tool, an IDE, and some sort of approach to object-oriented development, as well as object libraries and the ability to use components such as ActiveX. Most employ the two-tier client/server development model, but a few (such as Visual Basic and PowerBuilder) also support application partitioning features.

I'm spending a lot of words on specialized development tools because they control the lion's share of the client/server development market. Most client/server projects use specialized client/server and the "fat client" two-tier architecture.

Client/Server Tools Move to the Intranet

As interest in the intranet moves to a hype-driven fury, specialized client/server development tool vendors look to move their tools quickly to the intranet. These tools include Delphi, PowerBuilder, Unify, Uniface, and Visual Works.

Delphi plans to Java-enable itself and release a Java version called JBuilder. JBuilder provides many of the features and functions of Delphi, but it can also generate Java code for use on intranets. PowerBuilder Web-enabled itself as well, which provides PowerBuilder developers with the ability to deploy PowerBuilder applications to the intranet using ActiveX. Both Unify and Uniface can deploy existing native applications to the intranet, and support the intranet like any other platform. Finally, Visual Works has a Web-enabled version known as VisualWave, which allows developers to deploy Smalltalk applications to the intranet (See Chapter 12 for more details on VisualWave).

Clearly, client/server and intranet development are joined at the hip. As more applications migrate to the Web, and as new client/server applications target the intranet, most client/server tool vendors will provide some sort of tool or feature to deploy applications to the intranet. If you're in the market for a client/server application, make sure it's intranet-enabled.

The interest in RAD that took the development world by storm in the early 1990s resulted in a by-product: specialized client/server development tools. Using these tools, developers quickly build applications by designing the user interface with an easy-to-use screen painter, then add behavior to an application by placing program code and data behind the interface. These tools let developers create applications right in front of the end-user. The developer doesn't have to deal with the complexities of a 3GL, middleware API, compiler, and network. Impressive demonstrations of specialized client/server tools drove salesman and development managers to predict the demise of the developer, since the tools were "so easy to use that users could create their own applications." This is a prophecy yet to be realized.

All specialized development tools provide some sort of IDE, which gives developers the ability to create databases, build windows and screens, add code, and compile and deploy an application from a single interface. The purpose of the IDE is to provide the client/server developer with a consistent look-and-feel. Some of the better IDEs I've worked with are PowerBuilder, Visual Basic, and Enterprise Developer from Symantec.

Another thing that specialized client/server development tools do well is provide easy-to-use database connectivity. This means that the developer need not think about how to hook up the application to the database since the application is generally built around the database (using repository development).

Most specialized client/server development tools provide their own proprietary 4GL that lets developers define the application behavior using an easy-to-understand development language. These programming languages provide familiar programming statements such as IF, THEN, ELSE, FOR, and WHILE. However, the idea behind specialized development tools is to define as much of the application as possible without programming, then use the programming language to fill in the details.

Specialized tools deploy applications to clients through run-time environments that include pcode interpreters and .DLLs for database connections. Unfortunately, most specialized client/server tools don't use compilers, and thus don't offer the same performance as compiled applications. This will change with the new release of PowerBuilder, with all releases of Delphi, and with a few specialized client/server development tools that can also compile speedy native applications. This trend is bound to continue.

So what do you have to pay? Compared to other high-end tools, most specialized development tools are priced to sell—usually from $1000 to $2000, depending on the options you select. You can get Visual Basic from $99 for the entry-level product ($499 for the professional version), where PowerBuilder may run you $2000 or more. You have to remember that the real cost is the productivity of the tool. A bad tool that's also cheap could require more development time to get an application up-and-running (if you get it running at all). Good tools, despite their cost, lead to good developer productivity as well as successful and maintainable applications. Those tools are a bargain at inflated prices, but watch out. Many tools are expensive and bad. Price is never a sure indicator of quality.

So are there downsides to using specialized development tools? You bet. The proprietary nature of these tools means it will be difficult to move an application you create with a specialized client/server tool to other tools and languages. What's more, if the vendor goes under, you're stuck holding the bag—a proprietary application without a supported development environment. The lack of object and component standards binds applications to tools. This could change as more tools migrate toward common object standards, such as those defined by CORBA and DCOM. For now, don't hold your breath.

MULTI-PLATFORM TOOLS

Multi-platform tools look like specialized client/server development tools, but with one difference. They let application developers create an application once, then port it to other platforms without modification (see Figure 8-5). For

Figure 8-5 *Multi-platform Tools.*

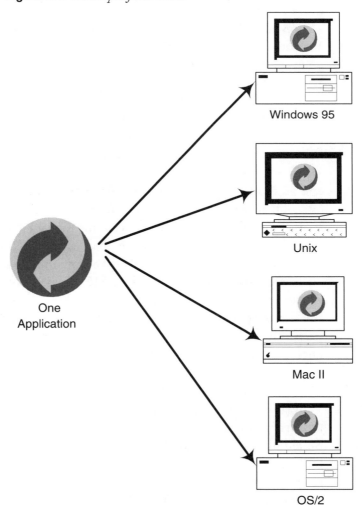

One Application

Windows 95

Unix

Mac II

OS/2

example, I could use a multi-platform tool like Uniface or Unify to build an application in Windows, then move it to the Mac and Unix without any changes to the base application. (I'll cover multi-platform development in more detail in Chapter 11.) Other examples of multi-platform tools include C/S Elements from Neuron Data, Galaxy from Visix, JAM 7 from JYACC, and Magic from Magic Software.

The value of using multi-platform tools (also called cross-platform tools and portable development tools) is that developers can support an organization that has a hodgepodge of client platforms. These tools protect the investment in an application by deploying the application to any number of platforms. Therefore, if organizations migrate from OS/2 to Windows 95, the tools can also migrate the applications.

Multi-platform tools work by placing a layer between the application and the native environments. When changing platforms, developers simply swap in a new native layer, and thus port the application to another platform. For example, you run Windows 95 run-time for Unify to run your Unify application on Windows 95. You use the Unix run-time version for Unix, and so on.

All multi-platform tools support cross-platform development in different ways. While some only support a subset of features native to the platform, others emulate the same look and feel across platforms. C/S Elements and Uniface are examples of tools that use emulation to bypass the native APIs, and go to the graphics layer of the operating system and GUI directly.

There are many downsides to multi-platform client/server development tools. First of all, many don't provide the native look and feel that application users demand. To become portable, they can't be all things to all platforms, and therefore can't excel on any of them. Second, multi-platform tools are notoriously expensive, costing as much as $15,000 per tool. Remember, most multi-platform tools charge by the platform, and you have to pay for each platform you deploy to. Finally, multi-platform tools are slower than their native counterparts. This is because they generally use interpreters, not compilers, when they deploy applications.

SMALLTALK TOOLS

Why am I putting Smalltalk tools in a category by themselves? They really are strange birds, and I just couldn't fit them into the other categories. Since Smalltalk was not created specifically for client/server, it's not a specialized tool. Nor is it a 3GL (third-generation language) (I would call it a 3.5 GL), although many Smalltalk tools such as Visual Works from ParcPlace-Digitalk support multi-platform development.

Smalltalk represents a different method of development. As mentioned in Chapter 6 and covered in detail in Chapter 12, Smalltalk uses an "objects, and nothing but objects" method of development, all wrapped in a sophisticated IDE. Smalltalk even treats relational databases as objects. The current list of Smalltalk tools includes Object Studio from Vmark Software, Inc., Visual-Age Team from Smalltalk from IBM, and Visual Smalltalk Enterprise and Visual Works from ParcPlace-Digitalk, Inc.

The upside to Smalltalk-type client/server tools lies in their power to leverage the best of the object-oriented programming model. There are also many downsides. For instance, Smalltalk uses interpreters exclusively, thus application performance can range from abysmal to just plain bad, depending on the tool. The tools cost a pretty penny too—almost twice the price of specialized client/server tools.

FILE-ORIENTED DATABASE TOOLS

Those of us who came into the world of client/server in the mid- to late '80's from the PC-based world of file-oriented DBMSs know how we evolved to bring computing power to the desktop through client/server. I spent a good portion of my early consulting time developing dBase III Plus systems for both single and multi-users, while working on large systems (COBOL, DB2, etc.) during the day. Little did I realize that the two worlds would collide into the revolution that is client/server.

Today, file-oriented database tools such as Visual FoxPro and Access from Microsoft, and Visual dBase and Paradox from Borland, continue their evolution to meet the needs of client/server databases. The most file-oriented database products are client/server-enabled, and support advanced development features you would find in specialized client/server tools. These include features such as object-oriented development, repository support, and, of course, support for the latest platforms such as Windows 95. They also link to popular database servers, and it's safe to say that file-oriented tools and specialized tools share many features, except price. Most file-oriented development tools cost just a few hundred dollars. What's more, many developers who still use file-oriented database tools want a migration path to client/server. That's the purpose of Chapter 13.

File-oriented database tools are designed to use databases that exist in files on the local hard drive, or they may exist on a shared drive on a LAN. Since files are passive and don't contain a database engine, the file-oriented database tools must provide the database engine within the tool (see Figure 8-6). Therefore, the database processing happens within the confines of the tool, along with any application processing needed. Even if the database physically resides on a

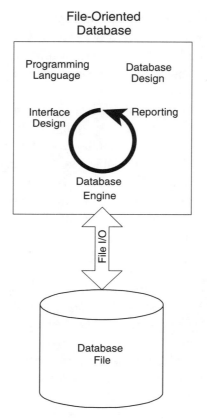

Figure 8-6 *File-Oriented Database Tool.*

shared network drive, the data is transmitted to the client over the network for processing. Therein you find the problem with file-oriented database development, especially when considering the multi-user application model.

The file-oriented architecture does not provide the same level of support for the client/server development model. The vendors retrofitted database connections and SQL capabilities to move into a new market, and performance does not quite meet that of "traditional" specialized tools such as PowerBuilder and Delphi. However, they offer a good fit for developers who want to create small-scale database applications with a migration path to client/server. Visual FoxPro, for example, provides an "Upgrade Wizard" that automatically replicates data from FoxPro files to popular database servers. Most file-oriented database tools plan the move to client/server as well.

Just when you think the file-oriented database tool market is dead, new products appear. Just a few years ago, Microsoft Access appeared and became the personal database of choice for millions of desktops. Since Access is a Microsoft product, it is ODBC-aware and can connect to any number of ODBC-ready databases (e.g., Oracle, Sybase, DB/2). More recently, Lotus Approach hit the streets. Lotus Approach provides nontechnical types with the ability to create and access simple databases that exist locally or on a shared drive. Approach can also access any number of popular databases through ODBC. However, both Lotus and Access offer limited application development capabilities. I would have to place them in their own easy-to-use personal database subcategory, which is not for developers.

REPORTING AND ON-LINE ANALYTICAL PROCESSING TOOLS

Reporting and OLAP (on-line analytical processing) tools allow both developers and end-users to access data that exists on any number of databases. (I'll cover this kind of tool in Chapter 14.) Reporting tools are more traditional, and provide developers and end-users with the ability to create simple reports (such as a monthly sales report, or a list of accounts receivable) and send them to a printer or the screen. Also known as SQL report writers, we distinguish these tools by their ease-of-use. Developers use them to visually design reports that work with client/server applications, and end-users use these tools to create ad hoc reports for any business reason. Reporting tools usually help the user assemble an SQL statement, and submit the statement to the database. Then the reporting tool processes the results that come back from the database (the answer set). These tools can also graph data as pie charts, bar charts, and line graphs.

OLAP tools are a new breed of reporting tool. They give end-users (sometime developers) the ability to make sense of data that exists in large databases or data warehouses. A data warehouse can be either multi-dimensional or relational, or a relational database made to emulate multi-dimensional. With OLAP tools, the end-user can slice and dice data to accumulate and summarize the information wanted, such as sales by region, sales by month, or sales by salesperson. OLAP tools offer more sophistication than reporting tools, and can perform advanced statistical functions to support executive information systems or general decision support systems (DSS).

CODE GENERATORS

Code generators are similar to specialized client/server development tools. However, they generate 3GL code for traditional compilers rather than provide their own proprietary application deployment mechanisms (e.g., pcode and interpreters). Using these tools, client/server developers can create the user interface, and define the behavior of an application with either a proprietary 4GL or native

3GL (e.g., C++). Code generators also provide database support, including links to popular databases and database design facilities. Once the developer defines the application, he or she hits a button and generates the code. The developer must then use a native compiler to build the executable for distribution to the client.

COMPUTER-AIDED SOFTWARE ENGINEERING TOOLS

CASE (computer-aided software engineering) tools (covered in detail in Chapter 15) let client/server developers design the client/server database as well as the application. Using a sophisticated diagramming subsystem with links to a repository, developers and application architects can design a client/server application all the way from a logical concept to a physical design. Some of these tools also generate code to create physical database schemas on popular databases, as well as generate code or components for popular client/server development tools such as PowerBuilder and Visual Basic.

APPLICATION PARTITIONING TOOLS

Application partitioning tools (covered in Chapter 20) are relatively new to the client/server tool market. Vendor claims that these tools provide the ultimate in scalability make them the latest rage as developers and application architects seek ways to quickly migrate to multi-tiered client/server development (See Chapter 17). The premier application partitioning tools are Forte from Forte Software and Dynasty from Dynasty Software. A few specialized and multi-platform tools, such as PowerBuilder and Unify, have retrofitted their tools for application partitioning. This trend continues.

With application partitioning tools, the developer can create a logical version of an application on a single workstation. To accomplish this, application partitioning tools use the traditional techniques of specialized tools, such as the creation of proprietary objects that exist in a single repository. Once the developer creates the logical objects, the developer then partitions the application so the objects can physically run on any number of application servers accessible by a network (see Figure 8-7). The objects communicate using a messaging mechanism, and the objects that run on all the servers create the partitioned client/server application. These tools also provide native links to popular database servers, and links to TP monitors.

The power of application partitioning is its ability to move objects from one server to the next as the application load increases or decreases. Moving the objects does not affect the application, and developers can move them as often as required. Another benefit is scalability. Remember from our discussion earlier in the book, traditional two-tier client/server applications don't scale well, which makes it

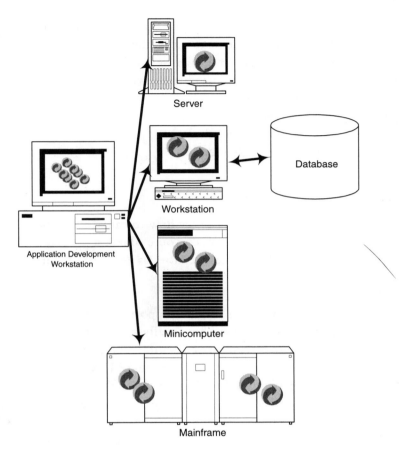

Figure 8-7 *Application Partitioning Tool.*

difficult to support over a hundred users. Application partitioning tools are naturally multi-tiered (or *n*-tiered), and can split the processing load among any number of application servers. Need to increase the capacity of your client/server application? Simply purchase more application servers to run your objects.

You have to pay a price for power. Typically, application partitioning tools run as high as $100,000 per development shop. These tools, like all specialized tools, remain proprietary. Object request brokers, such as those based on OMG's CORBA or Active Platform (COM, DCOM, ActiveX), may offer an alternative to proprietary application partitioning tools.

INTRANET DEVELOPMENT

One of the latest tool categories contains tools that create applications for the Web, either on the Internet or the intranet. Intranet development tools are really just traditional client/server tools that can deploy applications to the Web, allowing clients to access these applications using standard Web browsers such as Netscape and Microsoft Internet Explorer.

Using traditional client/server development techniques (such as interface painting, repositories, and links to popular databases), these tools deploy client/server applications by using a variety of Web-enabled technology such as HTML, CGI, NSAPI, ISAPI, Java, and ActiveX. (I'll cover intranet development tools in Chapter 23.)

Client/Server Tool Features

Okay, now that you know how to categorize tools, let's explore some of their common features. When you evaluate a particular client/server development tool or tools, use these features as your criteria for evaluation.

DESIGN FEATURES

Client/server tools need to support some design activities, but they do not have to be CASE tools. This usually means the tool offers a sophisticated object browser or navigator that guides the developer through the deployment of objects inside the IDE. For instance, Developer/2000's Object Navigator gives developers a graphical depiction of the application's layout. Developers can easily see how to add to the existing object, move objects around, or create new objects.

Along the same lines as application design, developers need access to database design features. Many tools, such as Symantec's Enterprise Developer (see Figure 8-8) and PowerBuilder, provide CASE-like features that let the developer graphically design a relational database to include tables, columns, indexes, keys, etc. With the database design complete, the developer or application architect can deploy the database schema to a target database. This should all happen automatically. If your client/server tool does not support database design and deployment features, you'll have to purchase a separate tool to do the job. For example, Magic requires that you use a CASE product to design and create the database. That's an added expense, and you'll have to teach your developer more than one development environment.

DATABASE FEATURES

You need to seek out tools with advanced database features. The tool should not only connect your application to the most popular databases, but manage

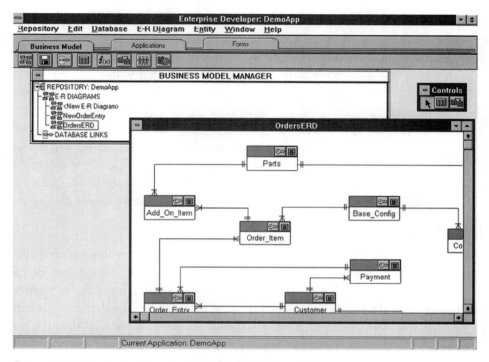

Figure 8-8 *Enterprise Developer's Database Design subsystem.*

those connections and provide you with good performance. Some tools, for instance, only provide ODBC connectivity to database servers. This can limit your ability to perform advanced database-related processing such as access to stored procedures and triggers (although ODBC now provides some of these features). The client/server tool should also provide a mechanism to tune your database connection to the target database. For instance, some applications are transaction-oriented, which results in a lot of single hits on the database, while other applications pull large amounts of information out of the database during normal processing.

REPOSITORY-DRIVEN DEVELOPMENT

Repository-driven development has to do with the way the client/server tool lets you add another layer of application logic and metadata (data about data) to the physical database schema. For example, when using PowerBuilder linked to an existing database, developers can add additional information about the data using PowerBuilder's Extended Attribute Set (PowerBuilder's repository).

This means that developers can let the repository know how to handle certain data elements (columns). The developer could define the "profit" column to always display negative values as red in the application. Also, the developer could define fonts and formats associated with data elements, and application logic such as business rules linked to that particular data element.

The power of repository-driven development is the ability to define how the application will handle certain data elements before it builds the application. Developers build the application on top of the repository, inheriting the attributes of the data from the repository. If developers need to change a business rule, they simply change it in the repository. The new rule automatically takes effect in all the application subsystems that use the business rule.

DEBUGGERS

Debuggers let developers find and correct problems with client/server applications quickly and easily. This means the developer can do things such as set breakpoints in the code where the application will stop processing while the developer examines variables, and other items that may indicate what's caused the problem. Debuggers also let developers step through an application to watch what happens as the application slowly goes through the motions. Good debuggers also provide the developer with the ability to spot problems by analyzing the application and making suggestions to the developer. Low-level 3GL tools, such as Borland C++ and Visual C++, provide additional debugging tools to monitor memory and the program stack on behalf of the developer.

INTEGRATED DEVELOPMENT ENVIRONMENTS

Integrated development environments (IDEs) offer a single interface to object browsers, code editors, database and application design subsystems, and application deployment mechanisms. While all specialized client/server development tools provide IDEs, they take different approaches. For example, while Delphi provides a complex set of independent Windows, PowerBuilder's IDE is much more simplistic. The right IDE really depends on the preferences of the developer.

PROGRAMMING LANGUAGES

All client/server development tools must provide some sort of programming language. Programming languages can be called scripting languages, or object languages, but all solve the same problem: They let the developer customize the application's behavior to meet the exact requirements of the application.

TEAM DEVELOPMENT

Finally, a good client/server development tools needs to provide team development facilities, or links to facilities that support team development. This means the tools will work in a multi-developer environment where developers check in and check out objects and code, and allow them to work on portions of the system without getting in one another's way (see Figure 8-9).

Most client/server development tools outsource this capability to third-party source code control vendors such as PVCS from Intersolv. Others build it into their tool, and usually sell it as an option. Developers and application architects need to understand the team development strategy of the tool. A good tool that does not support team development will not provide much value in a multi-developer environment.

Figure 8-9 *Using a multi-developer environment.*

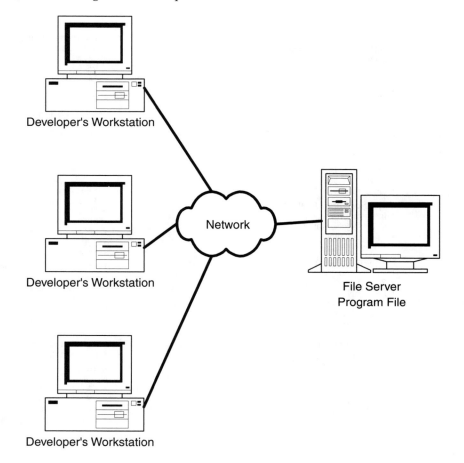

Selecting a Tool

After all that, the question remains: How do you select a tool? It's easy. First understand your application requirements. Second, understand the tool market and select a few candidate tools. Third, set up a matrix (see Figure 8-10) and list your requirements along the right side (team development, IDE, debugger, 4GL, etc.), and list the tools across the top. Finally, rank each tool 1 through 10

Figure 8-10 *Client/server tool selection matrix.*

Feature Weight 0 = not important 1= somewhat important 2=important 3=very important	Tool Features	Tool 1	Tool 2	Feature Weight 0 = not important 1= somewhat important 2=important 3=very important	Tool Features	Tool 1	Tool 2
	Repositories • Metadata • Extended data attributes • Object storage • Team development				**Performance** • Good • Fair • Poor		
	Database Design Facility • Logical database design • Physical database design • Schema generation				**Third party component integration** • OCX • VBX • OLE container • OLE automation server • Distributed objects		
	Database Connectivity • Sybase • Oracle • SQL Server • Informix • ODBC • Local/test database				**Platform Support** • Windows 3.11 • Windows 95 • Windows NT • OS/2 • Macintosh • Unix		
	Application Design Facility • Process model • Object browser				**Scalability** • 10 users • 50 users • 100 users • 200 users • 500 users • 1000 users		
	Object-oriented Features • Inheritance • Multiple inheritance • Encapsulation • Polymorphism				**Links to External Resources** • MAPI • Message-oriented middleware • CORBA • TP Monitors • Other		
	Programming Language • 4GL • 3GL • IF-THEN-ELSE • Looping logic • Ease-of-use • Database manipulation features • Object-oriented features				**Cost** • Per seat (developer) • Per seat (user)		

	Application Deployment
	• Deployment
	  –Interpreter
	  –Compiler
	• Debugger
	  –Set break point
	  –Variable watch
					Other Issues
					• Training availability
					• CM tool support
					• CASE support
					• Available talent
					• Frequency of upgrades		

on ability to meet your requirements (make sure you actually test the things). Also consider costs, the stability of the company, and other "soft" issues such as your labor pool and the availability of third-party training. Never rely solely on marketing literature, and try to avoid the input of zealots. The tool decision needs to be objective.

So now do you understand the tool market? That's my job as the author of this book, to explain it to you. In the next set of chapters we'll look at each type of client/server tool in detail. You can examine them as to their ability to meet your needs. May the best tool win.

9

C++ and Third-Generation-
Language Client/Server
Development Tools

Some people think that 3GLs (third-generation languages) such as C++, Pascal, and even COBOL belong with the pocket protector crowd, that they don't have a place in the world of client/server. They're wrong. Since their beginning, developers sought out the power of C++ and other 3GLs to deploy rock solid high-performance applications, and client/server was no exception. There is more C++ in the client/server world than you might think, which is the reason for this chapter.

Before we get moving, you should know that, although this chapter covers all 3GL client/server development tools, I'll concentrate on C++. Why? Almost all 3GL development in the client/server world takes place using C++. This is why I'll spend most of my time there. For you Pascal zealots, I'll have some stuff for you as well, at the end of the chapter.

C++ and Client/Server

During the last three years, C++ and "traditional" client/server seemed to move farther apart. Specialized 4GL client/server tools that support the sizzle of RAD-driven development are all the rage these days.

Despite the interest in RAD, C++ development tools still hold their own, and become more RAD-like every day. In the hands of skilled C++ developers, specialized client/server tools can develop applications almost as fast as RAD tools. The object-oriented capabilities of C++ allow developers to reuse most of the code, as well as support application frameworks (e.g., for database connectivity) that developers may leverage in client/server applications.

Consider Your Developers

When selecting a tool like C++, you need to consider many things. Often, planners do not properly consider the skills of developers and how C++ is applied in the application development process. C++ is not an easy language to master but you must completely master it when using it for client/server development. Count on as much as twice the training and ramp-up time to get your developers up-and-running.

So when is C++ not a good idea? Take the case of a good friend of mine who is a self-proclaimed C++ evangelist. Well, Mister Evangelist took over a client/server development shop and spent the first year of his job pushing the specialized client/server development tools out, and the C++ tools in, shouting words like "portability," "application performance" and "adherence to the object-oriented development model."

The problem was that the developers, who were used to easy-going specialized development tools, could not get the hang of C++ in the time required to keep up with the application backlog. Not having the time to get the hang of the language, or design the application properly, applications went out with C++ code that resembled COBOL. What's more, developers used their C++ compilers as a RAD tool. Not a pretty sight. Applications were delivered late and in poor shape. For example, a single application executable was more than 10 MB in size and GPFs appeared more on the screen than data.

I wish I could say that this situation ended happily, but it did not. An outside consultant was called in to solve the problem and my friend lost his job. He did find another one and this time he approached the integration of his love of C++ with a bit more caution. C++ is a good language but you need to know how and where to apply it.

I still rely on C++ to handle problems that specialized tools can't, such as talking directly to hardware, and linking to obscure APIs. In fact, with the popularity of the C++-like Java language, C++ made its way back into the hearts of developers. Java is a part of a few C++ development environments such as Borland C++ (see Figure 9-1). Microsoft even got into the act with its popular Visual J++ Java development environment (see Figure 9-2).

Today, C++ tools are full-blown client/server development tools, complete with IDEs, built-in database connectivity, and true object-oriented development, with links to COM and CORBA-based ORBs. Advanced development environments you'll find today include Borland's Borland C++, Microsoft's Visual C++, Symantec's C++, and Watcom C++, to name just a few. These tools are feature-rich and object-oriented, with an array of third-party tools and object libraries that developers can use to make C++ the best way to do client/server, depending on your application requirements of course.

C++

Like many good ideas in the world of computing, the origins of C++ are evolutionary, not revolutionary. Brian Kernighan and Dennis Ritchie developed the C language, the parent language of C++, at AT&T Bell Labs in the late '60s.

Figure 9-1 *Borland C++.*

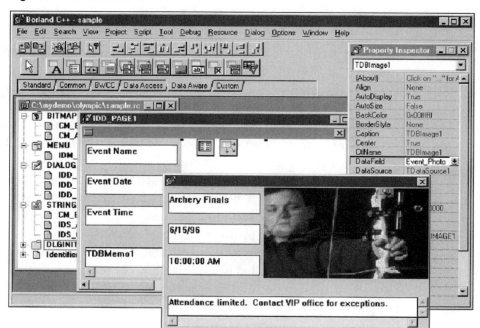

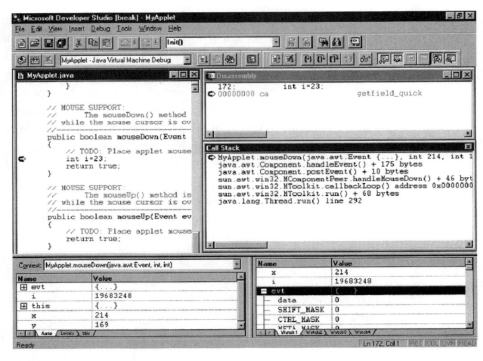

Figure 9-2 *Microsoft Visual J++.*

Their rogue project later became the basis of modern Unix and the native language of Unix C.

Long story, short. C is the native language of the Unix operating system where it thrived as the application development language for Unix. In the early '80s C found itself on the PC with new development tools such as Borland's Turbo C and Microsoft C. C provided a new way to develop PC-based applications, as well as device drivers and Terminate Stay Resident (TSR) programs. In the late '80s a movement began to create an object-oriented language. Rather than create a new language, C incorporated many object-oriented extensions that gave birth to C++.

C++ is a multi-platform language, and you can find C++ compilers for virtually every operating system available. Thus one of C++'s strengths (and the strength of most 3GLs) is its portability. However, today's C++ systems address particular platforms and their native APIs, which makes it difficult to write a portable C++ application. (See Chapter 11 for more details on multi-platform application development using C++.)

C++, THE DIRECTOR'S CUT

I find that the power of C++ lies in the flexibility of the language. C++ can merge native, application-specific, and third-party libraries into a single development environment. Therefore, I have the ability to customize the development tools to meet my exact needs—something that's difficult to achieve in other specialized client/server development environments. I can roll my own tool to handle GUI controls, database access, external messaging APIs, the Web, and application-related classes (see Figure 9-3). As with any other object-oriented tool, C++ tools are only as good as the libraries that come with the tool.

With C++, the libraries are everything. Rather than write the native operating system APIs directly into the application program, we use native API libraries such as Borland's Object Windows Library (OWL), or Microsoft's Foundation Classes (MFC) (see Figure 9-4). The developer simply inherits the features and functions of the library into the application, invoking objects that, in turn, call native GUI controls and native operating system calls (e.g., a disk write).

There are two good reasons to do things the C++ way. First, developers do not have to deal with the complexities of the native procedural API. Second,

Figure 9-3 *Using libraries to customize C++ development.*

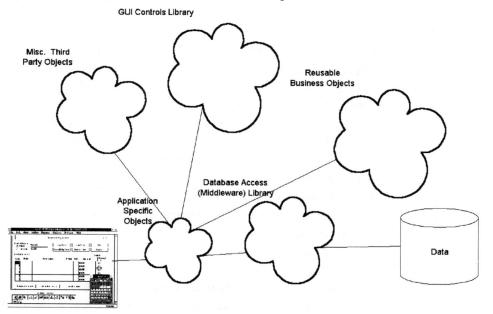

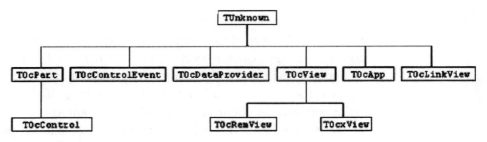

Figure 9-4 *Microsoft Foundation Classes (MFC).*

developers do not have to change the native API calls when the platform changes. For instance, when Windows 95 replaced Windows 3.1, the developer simply replaced the native Windows 3.1 libraries with the Windows 95 (Win32) libraries. The application absorbs the new features of the new API via the object-oriented inheritance mechanism of C++.

We can also extend this concept of native features support through libraries to multi-platform development. In Chapter 11, we'll talk more about how developers can purchase cross-platform C++ development libraries that support many different operating systems. The developer just swaps in the appropriate C++ libraries to support a particular platform. The same concept works for database connectivity libraries and business functions. These libraries come with the tool, or from third-party library vendors.

NEED FOR SPEED

If you need your client/server application to beat the clock in performance, you can't beat C++. Since C++ generates true native 32- or 16-bit applications using a true compiler, C++ can run rings around specialized client/server development tools that use interpreters.

On the downside, developers must wait for the client/server application to compile and link. In many cases, it can take as long as five to ten minutes to build a nice-sized client/server application. Therefore, C++ does not provide a good environment for developers who like to develop systems by trial and error. What's more, RAD can be difficult when you use C++, since you can't run the application as spontaneously as when you use true RAD tools like Visual Basic or PowerBuilder.

OBJECT-ORIENTED MODEL

As I made clear in Chapter 6, C++ is the benchmark for object-oriented tools. C++ adheres faithfully to the object-oriented development model by supporting inheritance, encapsulation, and polymorphism. The renewed interest in object-oriented development brought C++ and the object-oriented development model to specialized client/server development tools.

C++ TOOL TYPES

The C++ language is pretty standard. However, several types of C++ development tools exist for client/server and general purpose programming. I've grouped them into three categories: first generation, second generation, and third generation. Let me explain why.

First Generation. First-generation C++ development tools are standard command line compilers (e.g., cc hello.c). You can still find first-generation tool types with the Unix operating system, and command line compilers are a part of most modern C++ development environments. They support GUI application development, as well as traditional character-based development (e.g., ANSI terminal).

While first-generation tools give developers the ability to generate executables from C++ code, their standard features don't include IDEs, visual debuggers, and native connections to databases. Therefore, they are not well suited for client/server development.

C++ and the Intranet

So, how does C++ fit into intranet development? Most C++ development vendors have extensions for traditional Web-based development, with most building Java into their tools. Borland C++, for instance, is also able to do Java development and Microsoft Visual C++ is able to create ISAPI (Internet Server API) applications using a new version of MFC.

Over the next few years, we'll see C++ and Java merge as Web development grows. You can see the signs today. Most C++ development environments have some links to Java, either through extensions, through existing development environments or through new products that are really just a copy of their C++ development environment (e.g., Symantec's Visual Cafe).

Those that are C++ purists are purists no more. Most have moved to Java where they can leverage their C++ skills towards a more lucrative career. Java is everything C++ is, and much more. Java and C++ are bound to become one with nature.

Second Generation. Second-generation tools provide all the functionality of first-generation tools, but add advanced features such as IDEs, visual debuggers, and database connectivity. Developers drive these tools from the GUI, not the command line. They can edit, compile, and debug code from the same interface. The libraries that come with the tools determine database connectivity. Samples of second-generation C++ development tools include Visual C++, Borland C++, and Watcom C++.

Third Generation. Third-generation C++ development tools are the latest in the C++ arsenal. These tools are a cross between second-generation C++ tools and specialized client/server tools. Examples of third-generation tools include Optima++ from PowerSoft (covered below) and VisualAge C++ from IBM.

Third-generation C++ tools let the developers RAD their way through C++ development. As with other RAD tools, the developer creates the interface first, then adds the code behind the controls and windows to provide behavior. In this case, instead of PowerScript or Smalltalk, the developer uses traditional C++.

Database connectivity is easier as well. Unlike second-generation C++ tools that force the developer to leverage libraries, third-generation tools give developers the ability to create the physical database schema. They can also work directly with the database schema rather than through an API or object call.

While third-generation C++ development tools are just hitting the market, many traditional C++ developers will find a familiar home there. For instance, when I reviewed Optima++, I could begin simple application development tasks right away. The tool placed code visually into small granular objects, tied to GUI controls and data windows. This is the future of C++ development. I'll take a look at Optima++ later in this chapter.

AVAILABLE CLIENT/SERVER C++ TOOLS

There are dozens of C++ client/server development tools available for all sorts of environments. Let's look at a few of them for Windows-based client/server development: Visual C++ and Borland C++. I'll also take a quick look at Optima++.

Visual C++. I have to admit that I'm more of a Borland person than a Microsoft person, but Visual C++ is a pretty nice C++ development environment. Most C++ shops that I come in contact with use Visual C++, and I find that I use it more as time goes on.

Visual C++, like Borland C++, provides an easy-to-use IDE-driven development environment to build Windows 3.1 and Windows 95 applications

(Win16 and Win32). Visual C++ tries to be as automated as possible, and provides several application Wizards (called App Wizards, similar to the Borland AppExpert discussed next) that generate generic systems the developer can build into the final application. Remember, you should never have to start from scratch.

Visual C++ is a paradox. On one hand, it's a true object-oriented development environment. On the other hand, it's a component-based development environment in compliance with Microsoft's push for ActiveX. Visual C++ comes with a database of reusable application components known as the component gallery. Their components can be C++ classes, ActiveX controls, or OLE automation servers. The component gallery offers the developer a repository of components to browse during application development. Developers may even contribute custom components to the gallery for reuse by other developers in other applications.

MFC provides C++ developers with most of the objects they'll need for the application, including Win16 and Win32 controls. Developers can also layer custom objects into MFC using MFC Extension. MFC Extension is a DLL that gives developers the ability to add capabilities that are not present in the basic MFC classes. Like OWL, MFC supports native Windows features such as OLE, WinSock, MAPI, and access to Data Access Objects (DAO). DAOs are ways to manipulate data from within the development environment. Visual Basic also support DAOs.

Visual C++ is also ANSI/ISO-compliant, meaning that it complies with the American National Standards Institute's view of how C should work. This assures portability, if you stick to using ANSI-compliant C code.

Borland C++. Borland's C++ Developer Suite is typical of Borland products, and provides the most value for today's client/server developers (see Figure 9-5). With Borland C++, developers can create both 16-bit and 32-bit Windows applications, and the product now provides support for Java as well. Borland C++ also supports components such as ActiveX, OLE automation (and DCOM), and can even interface with the MFC.

Clearly, Borland shows its experience in the C++ development marketplace with subsystems such as AppExpert. AppExpert lets developers build applications quickly by simply answering a few questions. This is similar to Microsoft's Wizards. Borland C++ also supports multi-threading, and can link to most major databases through Borland's BDE (Borland Database Engine).

Developers build Windows applications with Borland C++ through Borland's GUI control library (OWL). OWL furnishes all typical Windows controls such as buttons, dialog boxes, and combo boxes. Developers simply link

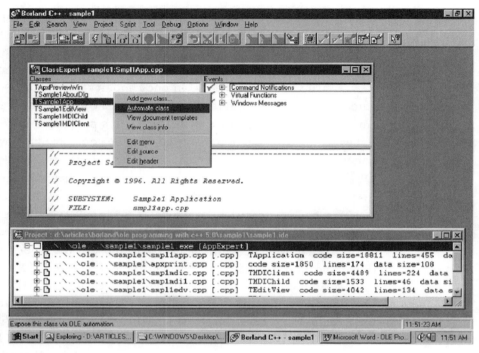

Figure 9-5 *Borland C++.*

their application hierarchy to OWL using the appropriate GUI control classes. Developers can inherit the control from OWL, then modify the object to meet the needs of the application. For example, I inherited a standard file dialog box from OWL, then added a company logo to it and changed the default colors. The same concept applies to data windows, menus, list boxes, or other GUI controls. You can do other things with OWL as well, such as make calls to WinSock, MAPI, WinG, and MCI.

Borland C++ Developer's Suite provides a full blown IDE (see Figure 9-1) which includes a 32-bit integrated debugger to help developers run down problems in the application code. Developers can even view low-level assembly code, and debug advanced applications by thread exploitation. Borland C++ comes with Win32 resource editors for interface designs, and can manage bit maps, icons, menus, cursors, and dialog editor. The product also supports ActiveX, as well as all C++ standards such as ANSI/ISO.

Although OWL is a powerful GUI class library, many C++ developers prefer MFC. Understanding this, Borland supports MFC compilation. I find that MFC is pretty much the same as OWL, but always stays ahead of the learning curve in terms of new features such as support for ActiveX and DCOM.

One unique feature about Borland's C++ development environment for Windows—version 5 was the first product to support Java development from the same development environment. This means that Sun's Java Development Kit (JDK) is part of the Borland development environment, which allows developers to create Java applets and applications. Borland lets you debug Java applications and applets as well.

C++ GOES RAPID APPLICATION DEVELOPMENT

There is clearly a trend toward C++ and RAD convergence. Traditional C++ development environments still do the majority of C++ development out there, but C++ tools that support RAD continue to make their way into many new client/server development projects. These third-generation C++ tools tightly integrate visual development and C++. Examples of these tools include Optima++, ProtoGen+ client/server suite from Protoview Development Corporation, C/S Development from Neuron Data, and VisualAge C++ from IBM.

Optima++ (covered next) gives developers the ability to use a component-centric architecture using ActiveX and OLE automation (see Figure 9-6).

Figure 9-6 *Optima++.*

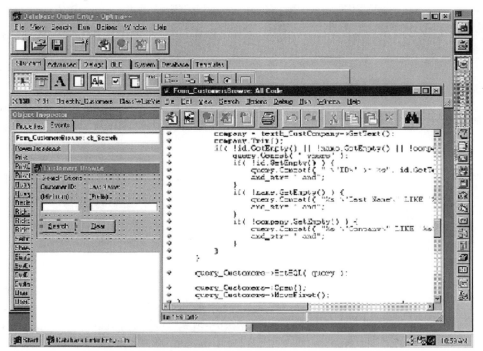

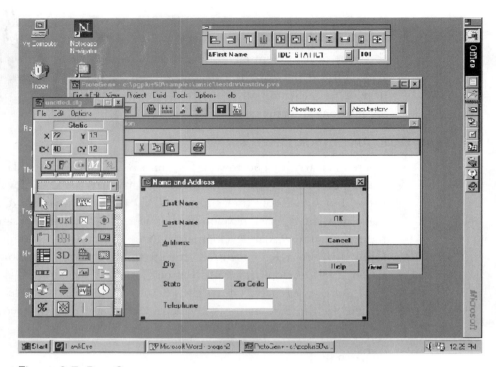

Figure 9-7 *ProtoGen+.*

Optima++ provides the RAD development capability of PowerBuilder, with the flexibility and object-oriented nature of C++.

ProtoGen+ Client/Server Suite approaches C++ by furnishing an advanced ANSI C code generator (see Figure 9-7). This way, developers create windows and database connections visually as they build their application. With the press of a button, ProtoGen+ generates submission-ready code for a C++ compiler. Developers can use the code as generated, or alter the code further to meet the requirements of the application.

VisualAge C++ (the C++ version of VisualAge Smalltalk), and C/S Elements can also mix RAD and C++. They both provide developers with the means to visually assemble the interface, then add behavior by coding in C++. The trend is to take C++ to RAD, and I'm along for the ride.

OPTIMA++

While Borland C++ and Visual C++ are good examples of second-generation C++ development environments, Optima++ offers a rare example of a third-generation environment. Optima++ is a full-featured visual client/server development language that gives developers the ability to use OLE automation and

ActiveX components within Optima++ applications. With C++ as its base language, Optima++ is also Java- and ActiveX-enabled for intranet and Internet development. You can even employ Optima++ for server-side application development using server APIs such as Microsoft's Internet Server API (ISAPI).

I would describe Optima++ as a cross between PowerBuilder and Watcom C++ (both owned by the company that puts out Optima++). Therefore, developers who know PowerBuilder will find many similar features in Optima++. For example, Optima++ supports DataWindows, reports, and OLE components with PowerBuilder. This means you can reuse PowerBuilder DataWindows within Optima++ applications.

Optima++ provides database support through data-aware controls. Optima++ drives database access the way PowerBuilder does.

When you build an application with Optima++, at first you'll think it's a typical RAD environment. That is, until you drill down to the C++ coding that must take place to build a true application.

Optima++ is very RAD-like in that you design and build the user interface first. This is the standard process where you select controls from a palette of controls that come with the tool. You can extend the controls on the palette using ActiveX controls.

After you build the user interface, you must then set the properties of the controls using a properties dialog. For example, you can set color and fonts, as well as simple actions (e.g., a button press calls a report).

Finally, Optima++ developers need to write the C++ code to handle all events that may occur while the program runs. This is where the majority of work comes in, and where C++ begins. How, you say? It's just a matter of clicking the right mouse button, then opening the code editor window. From here the developer enters the code into the code editor. Unlike traditional C++ tools, you don't have to enter the code into a source file (e.g., myapp.cpp).

The tool's ability to compile applications into native Win32 and Win16 EXEs differentiates Optima++ from other RAD or specialized client/server development tools. Optima++ applications run as fast as applications created with traditional second-generation tools, and much faster than traditional RAD tools such as Visual Basic. This means there is no RAD-performance tradeoff.

Optima++ is one of the best client/server development tools I've come across, perfect for those C++ developers who want a way to quickly deploy client/server applications and still leverage their knowledge of C++. What's more, you don't have to give up performance. Optima++ is on my A list, if you didn't already guess.

DATABASE CONNECTIVITY

So how do you connect C++ client/server applications to databases? It's easier than you may think. There are two basic ways to access databases from C++ applications and development tools: Use the native feature of the libraries that come with the tools, or purchase a database connectivity library from a third-party vendor.

Consider the native approach first. Borland provides a native database access subsystem called Visual Database Tools (VDBT). VDBT exists on top of the BDE (Borland Database Engine) (see Figure 9-8). The BDE exists in most Borland products such as Delphi, Paradox for Windows, and dBase for Windows. The BDE can connect to local or remote databases via native drivers or ODBC. Developers can create applications by dragging visual database components from a palette to a form.

Figure 9-8 *VDBT and the BDE.*

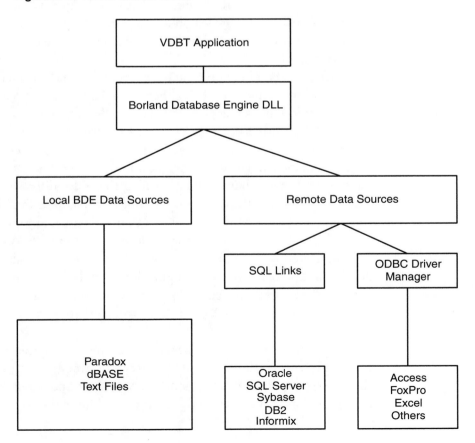

VDBT lets developers view live data while they build an application, and does not force the user to rely upon cryptic database API calls. For instance, in one of the first client/server applications I did with Borland C++, I had to use the native C++ API from Sybase. This meant I had to learn the API in great detail, and enter (and debug) the API call in time-consuming detail. I don't recommend it.

VDBT accesses data using the Microsoft COM. The COM architecture lets the developer access data using several techniques. For example, the tool can encapsulate the BDE API, which lets developers access the database through a database API call. Or the developer can exploit the COM wrapper using a native OLE automation interface to access the data. I recommend native OLE automation interface access over the BDE API.

Borland C++ developers access the VDBT using the dialog editor in the Borland C++ IDE. From there it's just a matter of establishing a persistent connection to the database using the "Database" function. The "Table" function retrieves data from the target database, and the "Query" function sends requests for data to the database. There are even ways to retrieve and display BLOB images from C++ applications.

Microsoft database access strategy is a four-letter word: O-D-B-C. When you use Visual C++ for client/server application development, there are two ways to access data. First, Visual C++ lets you go directly to the ODBC API. Or, you can use Microsoft's DAO (version 4). With DAO, you can manipulate data, as well as display and update data. DAO uses an OLE-enabled COM interface, which links to the Microsoft jet engine. You can also get to ODBC-compatible databases through DAO.

Sometimes it makes sense not to employ the data access features that come with the C++ tool. In this scenario, you can use any number of third-party C++-enabled database access tools. My favorite is DBTools.h++ from Rogue Wave Software.

DBTools.h++ handles all the low-level database interfaces for the developer, with no need to return to traditional APIs. DBTools.h++ is a C++ library that lets developers access databases as true C++ objects. Many developers find these a more natural way to process data from C++. DBTools.h++ ships with a core library that provides core database access functionality, and also includes another layer for native access libraries (e.g., Oracle, Sybase, Informix). In my experiences with DBTools.h++ in the Borland environment, the tight integration with the C++ language proved an advantage. It also supports portability since you can buy DBTools.h++ for several C++ development environments, even Unix.

Another third-party trick up my sleeve for the Visual C++ world is SQL*C++ from MITI. SQL*C++ gives developers a way to join queries directly from memory, and thus dramatically increase database performance. SQL*C++ also allows data to reside in arrays, rather than on the physical disk, which vastly improves performance.

Tradeoffs

As we can see, C++ provides an advanced client/server development environment, but there are clear tradeoffs when you use C++ for client/server development. First, C++ is a hybrid language. As mentioned in Chapter 6, this means that C++ supports structured and object-oriented development environments. Developers can mix and match object-oriented and structured code in the same system. Once again, worlds collide and developers circumvent the power of the object-oriented programming model. For example, mixed applications don't reuse as much code.

What's more, the C++ development language is complex. Budget much more time to learn C++ versus traditional client/server development tools such as PowerBuilder. C++ can be dangerous if you don't use it correctly. With second- and third-generation C++ tools, responsibility for memory management and other low-level programming activities lies with the developer. One false move, one bad pointer, and the application does bad things to your operating system.

On the upside, C++ development tools use a true compiler, C++ applications make the most of system resources, and they run like the wind. Modern C++ client/server development environments are as feature-rich as most RAD tools on the market. New C++-based client/server tools (such as Optima++ and VisualAge C++) make C++ easy to use and provide built-in database connectivity. Delphi already proved successful with its 3GL (Pascal). C++ could become the language of choice for a few other RAD tools as well.

Object COBOL

We can't spend the entire chapter on C++. There are a few other 3GLs out there as well, and you can certainly do client/server development from them. Object COBOL is an object-oriented version of COBOL that has shown limited success. However, Object COBOL provides a place for once mainframe-bound COBOL applications to run. What's more, it's object-oriented, which means you can employ encapsulation, inheritance, and other object-oriented features.

When I first heard of Object COBOL, I had to laugh. But today, many developers consider it a means to extend the life of older COBOL applications, and a way to port applications from the big iron. That saves money, and that's the name of the game.

Object Pascal

Object Pascal ranks second in my heart only to C++. Object Pascal, as sold from Borland, is a neat language to use. When I went to college, everyone had to take Pascal, so many already know the language. However, it took the release of Delphi to propel Object Pascal into the world of client/server.

Delphi uses Object Pascal as the native programming language (see Figure 9-9). Developers lay out the interface by dragging components from a palette, then use Object Pascal to define behavior. Delphi is an excellent two-tier client/server development tool, and its success ensures that Object Pascal will have a future, too.

Figure 9-9 *Borland's Delphi.*

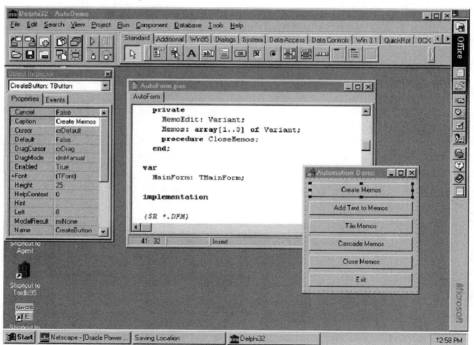

Making C++ and Client/Server Work Together

If I got any message across in this chapter, I hope you now understand that C++ should be in the running for your next client/server development project. Today's C++ tools provide updated, visual, and database-connected environments. C++ offers the ultimate in flexibility, since developers can build the tools around the application.

I see C++ as a good fit for client/server when an existing pool of C++ talent exists in an organization, or you have a special need to access devices or other low-level services, or you need to integrate many APIs into a single application.

C++ is not for everyone. If you want to throw together simple client/server applications, C++ can be more trouble than it's worth. For those tasks, specialized client/server development tools would be a better fit. C++ means you'll have to pay more attention to detail, consume more time, and budget extra time to learn about the design activities I talked about in Chapter 7.

C++ is also a good fit for those of you who want to dig into the wonderful-but-complex world of distributed objects, or if you plan to do three-tier client/server development with TP monitors. Portable application development also calls for the flexibility of C++. You'll see more portable client/server applications in the future, and C++ may be the only tool in town that can keep up.

Chapter

10

Specialized Client/Server
Development Tools

Now that you saw the rest, it's time to see the best. If any one category of tools has revolutionized the world of client/server, it would be the hundreds of specialized client/server tools that make up the lion's share of two-tier client/server development.

As I mentioned in Chapter 8, specialized client/server development tools are tools specifically built for client/server development. They are not general purpose tools like C++ compilers. They are tools that allow the developer to get to the final client/server application as quickly as possible. This means that they support RAD and prototyping.

Chances are, if you consider a typical two-tier client/server development project, specialized client/server tools are on the top of your list. They include bestsellers such as Visual Basic, Delphi, and PowerBuilder—tools that let the developer create applications as easily as I write this chapter. However, there are always tradeoffs.

In this chapter I'll focus on the concept of specialized client/server tools. We'll cover the different tools and development approaches out there, how the tools approach the development model, how each deploys applications and handles databases, and other aspects of client/server development. Just for giggles, I'll talk about a few of my favorite specialized client/server development tools in detail.

Different Tools, Different Approaches

If you get a chance, check out the *DBMS* Magazine's Buyer's Guide, found at http://www.dbmsmag.com. There you'll find hundreds of tools that qualify as specialized client/server development tools. Also, I'll list most of the tool vendors at the end of the book. The number has declined in recent months as some tool vendors went out of business and others merged. However, I still see the roll-out of new specialized client/server tools at the rate of about one every month, and that rate continues to pick up speed as everyone redeploys to the intranet. (See sidebar on page 216).

A consistent feature found in all specialized client/server development tools is lack of consistency. They all take different approaches to client/server application development, and all are pretty much proprietary. Despite the fact that the tools are very different, I broke them down into five common layers:

- The database access layer
- The repository layer
- The interface design layer
- The programming layer
- The deployment layer

THE DATABASE ACCESS LAYER

The database access layer of specialized client/server tools provides the developer with easy access to the target database. The layer acts as an intermediary between the target database and the tool, as well as application after deployment (see Figure 10-1).

The database access layer handles all the low-level native and ODBC API calls for the tool, and can perform such operations as reading a schema, data, and updating same as required during the normal course of using the tool.

This access layer must be database-independent, meaning it can communicate with a multitude of databases, both local and remote (database servers). This is done through an engine that exists within the tool that automatically loads and unloads the drivers required to access information on a particular

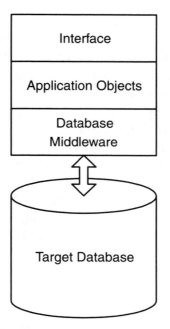

Figure 10-1 *Database Access Layer.*

target database. The drivers (just a concept at this point) contain all the information about a database, including native dialects, communication mechanisms, and other details.

For example, if I tell the tool to log in and begin communications with my Sybase server that runs remotely, I just provide the tool with information about where to find the database, along with my user ID and password. The tool can then log in to the server automatically. The same process occurs when I use Oracle as the target database, or Informix for that matter. The database layer makes all these diverse databases seem the same in the domain of the specialized development tool. You should be able to swap databases without changing the underlying application, if you run a typical fat client/thin server architecture.

If you decide to use ODBC rather than a native driver, the database access layer simply links to the database using ODBC. ODBC automatically translates the request through the ODBC driver manager, which loads and unloads the driver you need for a particular database. ODBC is helpful in that there may be no native support for a particular database from your tool. For instance, PowerBuilder supports most popular databases (the big three), but if you use one that is not supported, you can usually get to it through ODBC.

The database access layer lets developers get at the information in one of three ways. First, the developer can access the data as true application objects, which is the case with most Smalltalk tools and some specialized client/server development tools (e.g., Visual Basic's DAO). This model offers a more natural method of manipulating the data from the application, and does not make the developer switch from an object-oriented paradigm to relational, then back again. However, there is a performance penalty to pay since the tool has to go through another layer.

Second, the developer can access the data as relational schema (even if you use a nonrelational database, believe it or not). This means the developer uses the data as represented in the physical relational model, as tables, columns, and rows. I find this the most natural, since I think in terms of the relational database model anyway, and the tool still protects me from the low-level access issues, such as APIs.

Third, the developer can access the data via its native interface. This is simply the process of bypassing the database access layer entirely to go directly

Figure 10-2 *The Repository Layer.*

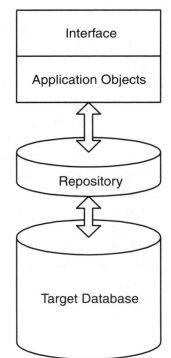

to the native or ODBC API. This is helpful if you want to invoke services of the database that you can't get at from the schema interface. For instance, some tools don't provide access to stored procedures and triggers, and this is a way to get at them. If you can avoid going to the native layer, do so. You'll give up portability across databases.

THE REPOSITORY LAYER

The repository layer builds upon the database schema, providing another layer for the collection of business rules and attributes about the data (see Figure 10-2). You can also call this the metadata layer (data about data).

The repository layer lets the developer store such information as the range of a value, the color and font that a column should use when it appears in an application, a business rule that must be met during data entry, even behavior such as triggering an event when a certain condition is met (see Figure 10-3). For instance, a column named Tax_Rate that stores the current tax rate for a retail sales system could have several other attributes set in the repository, such as a rule that it may never be a negative value and that its range must be 0

Figure 10-3 *Database design layer links to the repository.*

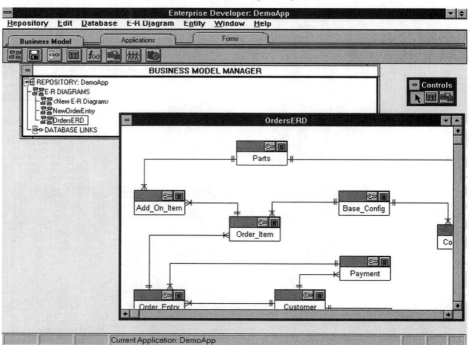

through 1.0. You can also set the default fonts and colors for the column, as well as a condition that when the Tax_Rate surpasses 15 percent, the stored manager is notified via E-mail. You really can do some powerful stuff with these repositories, previously possible only through programming.

The trick is to define as much of your application logic as possible in the repositories and avoid programming. Development should be just a matter of placing data elements on the windows. Since they know how to handle themselves, there is not much need to generate complex programs. What's more, once in the repository, you set the behavior and it automatically replicates itself anywhere it's used.

If you think that stored procedures and triggers do the same things, you're half right. While stored procedures and triggers can set up controls around data and enforce business rules, they don't know anything about the tool. Therefore stored procedures and triggers can't set other attributes and behavior native to an application development tool.

Some tools such as Oracle's Developer/2000 (see Figure 10-4) can leverage stored procedures and triggers as part of the way the repositories enforce

Figure 10-4 *Oracle Developer/2000.*

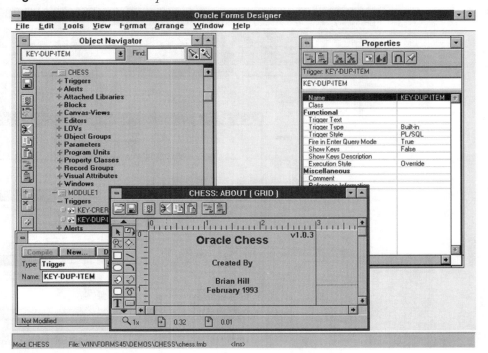

business rules, but tool vendors that want to decouple themselves from a particular database do things their own way.

These tool repositories exist in a number of locations—sometimes with the client, sometimes in shared files on servers—but in most cases they are simply layered into the target database. Take PowerBuilder's extended attribute set, for example. This is PowerBuilder's repository which actually resides on the target database with the data. This means the rules, although enforced at the client, exist with the data. This also means that other developers can also access the extended attributes from their tools. Uniface from Compuware, JAM 7 from JYACC, and Magic from Magic Software (see Figure 10-5) are examples of specialized client/server tools that support repositories.

More sophisticated repositories also allow the developer to store objects (such as data window objects) as well as column attributes. Thus there is a mechanism to reuse objects throughout an application, and developers use this feature to deploy a primitive inheritance mechanism. JAM 7, for instance, lets developers store screens in its repository, as well as inherit from screens in the repository to create new screens, which will also exist in the repository.

Figure 10-5 *Magic.*

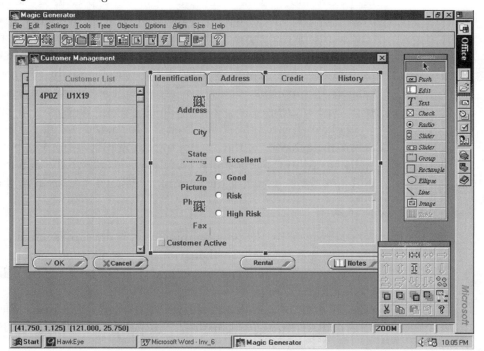

Finally, repositories provide the object-oriented aspects of many tools. Since the data element attributes are shared throughout the application, simply changing the attribute in the repository automatically changes the attribute in the entire application. For example, if you want a column to display on-screen as red not blue, simply change it in the repository one time, and the new way to display the column changes any object in the application that uses the column. The same rule applies for business rules and behavior.

THE INTERFACE DESIGN LAYER

The interface design layer is the subsystem that actually creates the screens, windows, and menus the users see. All specialized client/server development tools use some sort of interface design mechanism. Typically, the interface designers will provide a form window (the working area), along with a palette of GUI controls and data controls that the developer can drop onto the form. From there, the developer can modify the controls about the exact requirements of the application either by setting properties or through code.

Although I think most of them look the same, Visual Basic is a good example of an interface designer. The palette of GUI controls exists in one window, and the form exists in another (see Figure 10-6). Developers select controls from the palette and drop them onto the form. Some specialized client/server development tools, such as Visual Basic and Delphi, allow developers to extend the content of the palette through the use of ActiveX components that developers can check into the component repository. Since these tools provide developers with the ability to create components, developers can reuse the best components in the palettes. Components are also available from third-party vendors. Delphi uses the same type of architecture, as does Oracle's power objects.

Having placed the controls on the form, the interface layer lets developers define the behavior of the control by setting properties. The properties are generally stored in the repository. Developers also have the option of adding code to define the behavior of the control, which will also exist in the repository.

THE PROGRAMMING LAYER

As you may guess, the programming layer is the subsystem of the tools that lets the developer augment the behavior of an application through a programming language. Although some specialized development tools (such as Optima++) use traditional programming languages (such as C++), most use their own proprietary 4GL or scripting language. With names like Visual Basic for Applications (VBA), which is the native language of Visual Basic, and PowerScript, the

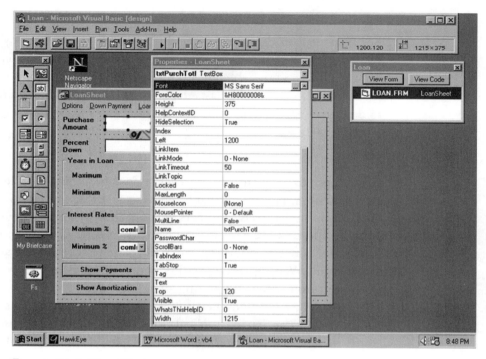

Figure 10-6 *Visual Basic.*

native language of PowerBuilder, these high-level languages attempt to provide an easy-to-use programming layer. This layer also provides a code editor, which offers the developer a programmer-friendly development environment with facilities such as context-sensitive help.

Programming languages, 4GL or 3GL, give developers the means to control program flow (if-then-else logic, for example) and the means to handle events for event-driven development. They also provide interfaces to databases (e.g., DBO), and a means to access low-level functions such as direct API calls. Although specialized development tools do provide you with a programming language, they don't place source code in files. They place source code in repositories.

A part of the programming layer is the debugger subsystem which helps the developer find and correct problems. This means that developers can set breakpoints in the source code, as well as watch variables, and even watch data as it moves into and out of the application. Good tools usually recommend corrections, and some even fix problems for you.

THE DEPLOYMENT LAYER

So what do you do after you build the application? Deploy it, of course. Deployment mechanisms give you the ability to generate applications that you can then load and run on clients. This subsystem offers a couple of ways to run the application: as a test, or as a deployed application. Then there are two ways to deploy an application: using an interpreter, or through a compiler. Let's find out how these work.

TEST MODE

Most specialized client/server development tools provide the ability to test the application. This means that by pressing a button, developers can see how the application looks, feels, and acts without having to go through a complete compile-and-link cycle (as is the case with 3GLs). This is the trait of a good RAD tool, since the developer can develop-test-develop-test to create the application. Waiting through a long compile-and-link operation can deter developers from frequently testing an application.

Since the application needs to run instantly, test modes usually use interpreters. Most specialized tools also use interpreters to deploy applications. Some tools test using interpreters and deploy using a compiler. Those tools support the best of both worlds, and it's the model I recommend.

INTERPRETERS

When an application development tool deploys an application using an interpreter, the application passes through the interpreter software, which in turn passes the application's calls to the processor (see Figure 10-7). The interpreter reads an application line by line from beginning to the end, telling the processor and native operating system what to do. Interpreters are nothing new, and have been a part of the 4GL world for years.

In many cases, the application code converts to pcode via a pcode compiler (not to be confused with a true compiler, see sidebar below). This just

Figure 10-7 *Using an Interpreter.*

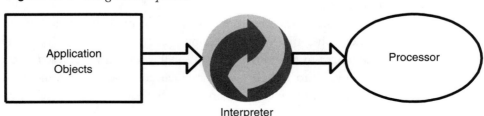

means that the code changes to a more efficient state for the interpreter. Pcode can't run without an interpreter. Examples of specialized development tools that use pcode interpreters are PowerBuilder version 4, Visual Basic, and Developer/2000.

The advantage of using an interpreter (pcode or source code directly) is that developers can run the application instantly with just a press of the button. This is a more natural way to develop applications for some developers. The downside is performance. Since the application must pass trough an interpreter before it gets to the processor, the application is less efficient (this means slow), and requires more system resources such as memory. Some specialized client/server tools mix interpreters and compilers.

For instance, one of the commonest complaints from PowerBuilder application users is performance. I've even seen performance of interpreted applications as a key reason to reject an application. PowerBuilder's use of an interpreter to support RAD is a tradeoff. Things got better with PowerBuilder 5. I'll tell you about that later.

Avoiding Compiler Confusion

One of the most confusing issues I deal with when I evaluate and recommend specialized client/server development tools is the deployment mechanism. The fact is, everyone claims "native compiler" capabilities, but when you peel back the onion, it's just pcode and an interpreter.

This is not really a deception since they do use "pcode compilers," but they still employ an interpreter to translate the pcode for the processor. Thus they don't perform as well as native compilers. However, pcode interpreters do perform better than source code interpreters.

So how do you tell? The easiest way is to look at the files that are loaded on the client. Generally, there should be a single EXE file that's application-specific. Watch out for DLL files that "have to" exist with the EXE for it to run (sometimes the DLLs have middleware responsibilities). The best way to find out is to peer into the EXE using a binary editor to see just what the tool created, but you need to know what you're doing.

This is a pet peeve of mine. I've had vendors out-and-out lie to me about the way they deploy. I've also had vendors tell me "that's proprietary information." If any of these things happen to you, I would seek another tool.

COMPILERS

Specialized client/server development tools that use compilers can create native executables that pass the application code directly to the processor. The direct approach is always best, and application speed/efficiency increases two- to three-fold compared to similar applications that run using interpreters (see Figure 10-8).

In the last year or so, many new specialized client/server tools (such as Delphi) hit the streets with native compilers as the native deployment mechanism. The ability to generate native code (16- and 32-bit) differentiated them from other specialized client/server development tools. I was blown away when I reviewed Delphi version 1, since it was one of the first tools that could do RAD and native compilers at the same time. The compile operation took only a few seconds, not minutes. Thus, testing an application during construction was not a problem.

After the success of Delphi, other specialized tools headed down the compiler alley. PowerBuilder version 5 (see Figure 10-9) learned how to leverage its Watcom (they bought Watcom, you know) compiler technology with PowerBuilder. Although not all native, PowerBuilder now provides a compiler that has dramatically improved application performance. Others are heading in the same direction.

Figure 10-8 *Using a Compiler.*

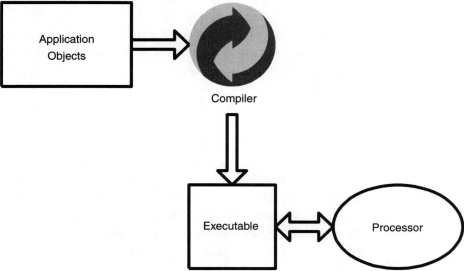

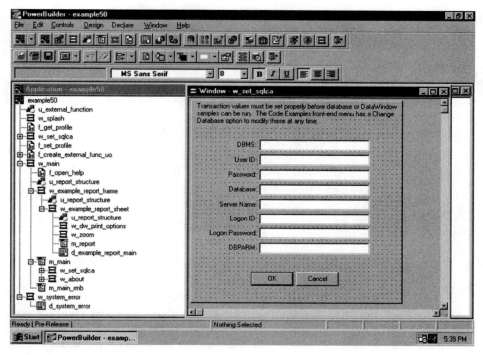

Figure 10-9 *PowerBuilder.*

Object-Oriented Abuse

As covered in Chapters 6 and 8, the object-oriented development model is an abused concept when you consider specialized development tools. It's not that the tools don't try to adhere to the object-oriented model, they just do so in so many different ways. PowerBuilder, for example, supports single inheritance, while SQL Windows supports multiple inheritance. Some tools, such as Visual Basic and Developer/2000, don't leverage the power of objects as much as they should, but are still sold as object-oriented development tools. I call this object-oriented abuse.

Looking at the problem from the tool vendors' point of view, the object-oriented development model is complex and must be watered down to make the tool simple to use. For example, PowerBuilder only recently allowed developers to create nonvisual objects, or objects that don't have to be tied to visual characteristics. This means developers can create more advanced-but-complex systems with PowerBuilder. Other tools continue to move closer to the object-oriented development model, including Visual Basic. We did our homework and learned from our mistakes. It's time to use tools that leverage the power of the object-oriented development model.

Proprietary Technology

Another concern about specialized client/server development tools is their proprietary nature. If you build an application with one specialized development tool, you can't move that application to other tools. Thus, when you select a tool, you walk down the aisle with it, especially when you consider the large amount of development time that goes into client/server application development. With proprietary technology, single-source tools are a risk.

I'm certainly not saying that you should be afraid of proprietary development tools—only that you consider the potential impact on a project tied inextricably to a tool and a vendor. I always tell people to create an exit strategy when they select a tool, or know what to do if the tool no longer becomes available or supported. If you do that, you'll work through the problem before it happens. The risk may be smaller than you think (see sidebar).

How Risky Are Proprietary Tools?

As mentioned a few times in this chapter, a clear disadvantage of specialized development tools is their proprietary nature. If the vendor goes away, so does support for your system, and thus your system. The question is: How much of a risk is this? While you should consider the risk, you should not let it deter you from selecting a product that meets your needs.

To date, I know very few cases of systems that were abandoned because the vendor went away. Generally speaking, most tool vendors don't go out of business and throw away a tool. They sell it to another company. I've seen this time and time again in the older file-oriented database development tool world. Look at dBase that Borland purchased from Ashton-Tate, and Clipper that Computer Associates bought (CA buys a lot of them). These products still exist today, and developers can still find support upgrades.

The same rule applies in the client/server world. ObjectView sold to Sterling Software, and Uniface is now in the hands of Compuware. Other tools are up for sale that you'll know about by the time this book hits the book stores. This industry will spend the next few years shaking out, and the sale of tools between vendors won't be that unusual.

The moral of this story is that while there is a huge risk that your tool of choice may be sold to another vendor, there is little chance the tool will go away entirely. Just keep in mind that this risk should be another factor when selecting a tool.

If you want to avoid this risk, look at tools with the largest developer populations. They are least likely to disappear overnight. Also, take a look at the financial situation of the tool vendors. A couple quarters of losses, and strange things can happen to the tool they sell.

Popular Products

There are more specialized client/server development products than any other tool type, and the list of tools grows monthly. What I would like to do here is quickly provide you with an overview of the most popular tools: PowerBuilder, Delphi, and Visual Basic.

POWERBUILDER

PowerBuilder is one of the premier specialized development tools, and it commands a large chunk of the market and developers' hearts. One of every two systems that I come in contact with is a PowerBuilder system. PowerBuilder has proved itself an effective development environment, and continues to lead the market.

PowerBuilder is multi-platform, but does not do multi-platforms well. For example, PowerBuilder has versions for the Mac, OS/2, and Windows (of course), but only supports a few flavors of Unix.

The strength of PowerBuilder is the advanced development libraries that come with the tool. Using these libraries, developers can mix and match objects to form the final application. The interface builder can use most native controls. PowerBuilder supports most major database servers natively, and can link to others through ODBC.

When you look at PowerBuilder, it becomes apparent that PowerBuilder's repository (the extended attribute set) drives application development. Developers define attributes for data in the repository, then build DataWindows for use in an application. Developers can assign events to DataWindows, as well as use PowerBuilder's proprietary PowerScript to add behavior to an application. Developers tie the applications together using a menu construction system, and deploy the application as a near-native EXE (with version 5). PowerBuilder 5 also supports primitive application partitioning features.

One advantage to using PowerBuilder is the number of developers who already use the product. The interest in PowerBuilder means you'll have lots of resources for information, including periodicals, user groups, and on-line discussion groups. PowerBuilder has also sparked a number of third-party libraries and add-on tools for use with the tool.

DELPHI

A Windows-only product, Delphi is a cross between Visual Basic and Object Pascal (see Figure 10-10). It's the newest of the tools I'll look at in this chapter, yet Delphi was one of the first to provide a native compiler for application deployment.

Delphi is more of a component development environment than an object-oriented development environment, but the product supports each paradigm equally well. Developers assemble interfaces on a form using any number of native Windows controls and ActiveX controls you can build or buy. Developers then set the properties of the controls, similar to Visual Basic. Here you can define colors, fonts, and behavior. Developers tie the Delphi application together

Figure 10-10 *Delphi.*

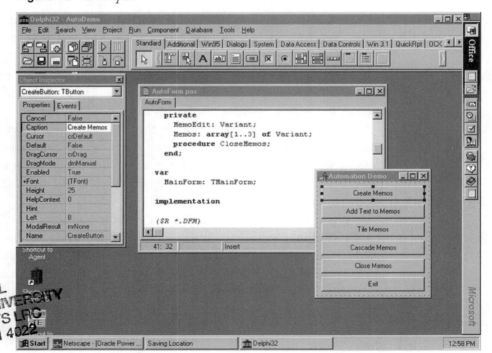

using Object Pascal, the native language of Delphi. Object Pascal is a 3GL, which makes it a bit difficult to use, but the code is encapsulated inside granular domains, which makes it a bit easier to manage. Delphi also supports the creation and use of OLE automation servers, making it Microsoft COM-compliant. Delphi supports most major databases natively, such as Oracle, Sybase, and Informix, as well as others through ODBC.

The real trick of Delphi is its ability to generate native EXEs. This is a by-product of Borland's vast experience with compilers, and this feature sets Delphi apart as a tool that generates the fastest application that uses the least amount of resources. I like Delphi, and think it should be in the running with the PowerBuilders and Visual Basics of the world when you select your tool.

VISUAL BASIC

Visual Basic is the 800-pound gorilla of the client/server world as one of the first RAD tools to dominate the Windows 3.0 market in the late '80s.

Visual Basic provides an interface developer subsystem that is the benchmark for other client/server development tools (see Figure 10-11). Using a

Figure 10-11 *Visual Basic.*

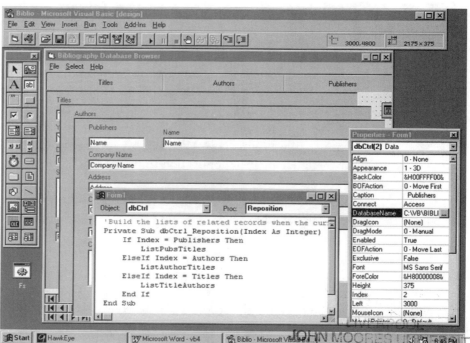

palette of standard GUI controls, developers simply select controls from the palette and place them on the form. Visual Basic provides several independent applications that run concurrently to make up the development environment. Visual Basic supports all database connectivity through 32-bit ODBC, and can generate applications in 16- and 32-bit Windows flavors.

Visual Basic offers the ability to extend the capabilities of the development environment. The professional edition of Visual Basic provides several additional ActiveX controls (like Delphi). Visual Basic's VBA (Visual Basic for Applications), the language that drives Visual Basic, is an event-driven programming language that looks like a cross between Basic and Pascal. VBA gives developers the ability to extend the functionality of a form, treating it as an object.

The real power of Visual Basic is its integration with the Windows NT and Windows 95 development environments, as well as its ease of use. I have to tell you, its use of an interpreter and ActiveX components makes it a bit slower than PowerBuilder or Delphi. Still, it's up there with other client/server development tools, and you can bet that Microsoft won't let other tools continue to lead this market.

Specialized Tools Move to the Intranet

Every specialized development tool has an intranet/Internet strategy. They all have products, subsystems, or add-ons that were just released, or are currently at the press release or beta release stage. Each migrates to the intranet in its own way, using various enabling technologies such as ActiveX, Java, CGI, NSAPI, or ISAPI. I'll cover all of this in Chapter 23.

The time to find out what your current or new tool vendor can do to get you on the Web is now. Work with your tool vendor to determine just how it will deploy your application to the intranet. Questions to ask are:

1. Do I have to change my application for the Web?
2. What additional tools and software will I need?
3. How much will it cost me?

If you want to move to the Web quickly, I would consider becoming a beta site for your tool vendor. The risk here is that your tool vendor won't move you to the Web soon enough, or won't have an effective Web strategy. You need to find this out ASAP, then make your decision.

Advantages

The are many advantages to specialized client/server tools. First, they are easier to use than general purpose programming languages (such as C++ compilers). They provide developers with an environment more conducive to development by using the layers that I described above.

Second, they support RAD. Developers can build and deploy client/server applications in fewer man-hours than general purpose programming languages. This cost saving translates into a cheaper overall cost of development (the real reason we use specialized client/server tools). However, many developers who use general purpose programming languages argue that hidden costs arise in deployment and user productivity that prove difficult to capture on the bottom line. I find that a good specialized development tool can deploy an application that looks, walks, and talks like a traditional application, with a lower cost of maintenance since RAD makes it easier to change and fix the application.

Finally, since these tools support RAD, it's easy to include them into the design process (see Chapter 7 for a detailed discussion of RAD). Developers can build systems right in front of the end-users. These are usually interface prototypes that become the basis for the final system. However, you should never try to RAD your way through a complex client/server system development project (see Chapter 7).

Tradeoffs

The downside of using a specialized development tool includes performance, scalability, and the proprietary nature of the tools. We beat the issues of proprietary nature and performance to death above, so let's talk about scalability.

Scalability refers to the tool's ability to support any number of users. This is generally an architectural limitation that has little to do with the tool. However, since most specialized client/server development tools only support two-tier, they lock you into an architecture.

Although you can integrate three-tier and multi-tier technology (such as TP monitors and distributed objects) with specialized client/server tools, they require much more time to make them work together. You can also turn to application partitioning tools that are simply specialized client/server tools that can deploy objects to additional servers as proprietary ORBs (See Chapter 20).

Most specialized development tools plan to address the scalability of application partitioning issue. PowerBuilder, for example, now allows developers to run nonvisual objects on remote servers. This trend will continue, but for now, specialized client/server tools are traditionally two-tier.

Tool Watch

So, how should you approach tool selection? Understand the different layers that specialized tools offer, and learn how to map actual tools to those layers. Review this chapter if any questions arise about layers during your selection process.

Having done that, consider the soft issues—how difficult is it to build applications with the tool, and how do these applications deploy? You also need to consider scalability, and interfaces that the tools support.

The difficulty lies in the number of tools out there, and the speed of technology changes. Don't try to consider every available product, or you'll drive yourself nuts. Select a few key players, and move through an old-fashioned selection process that takes all resources and requirements into consideration.

Multi-Platform Client/Server
Development Tools

The idea is so compelling that it's difficult to resist. Rather than write code and create a client/server application for a single client platform, developers can create an application that runs on several platforms. For instance, a developer might create a Windows-based client/server application that can also run on a Unix, OS/2, and Macintosh client. Seems too good to be true, or if it is true, why would we do anything else?

Multi-platform development tools promise an application development paradise where applications are all things to all platforms, and differences with various native operating systems are no longer a problem. However, there is a tradeoff.

Multi-platform development environments try to be all things to all platforms, with the emphasis on "try." Imagine if you met someone who claims to speak six languages, then you find out their fluency in five of those languages doesn't exceed general tourist lingo like "How much?" and "Where's the bathroom?" Yes, they would prove useful on a trip to, say, China, but how much of your native guide's explanations could they really translate? As with your general-purpose language expert, multi-platform development environments know the general lingo to get around many platforms, but since they try to know a little bit about many platforms, they can't, usually, excel on any of them. Any multi-platform client/server development tool available today warrants careful consideration of the issues associated with taking an application global.

In this chapter I'll take some of the mystery out of multi-platform client/ server development environments. I'll reveal the facts, let you know about the different types of tools, review available tools, and provide you with enough information so you'll know when to use them, and most important, when not to use them.

The Allure of Portable Application Development

Putting aside the technical limitations, there is a solid business need for cross-platform development. Client/server development is expensive, and it makes sense to develop applications that run on several platforms. Thus corporate development shops that support the typical hodgepodge of operating systems and processors simply can't pass up the value of multi-platform development. These tools leverage their investment in code, and adjust easily to constant changes in technology.

The idea behind portable code development is simple. Keep the code that interacts with the native operating systems (e.g., Windows NT, Windows 95, Unix, Macintosh) in its own layer. When you move applications from platform to platform, you simply swap in the native operating system and GUI layer of the platform where you intend to port the applications (see Figure 11-1).

In the early days, innovative C++ developers learned this trick as a way to move C++ applications from Unix flavor to Unix flavor, and sometimes to DOS and Windows. They would place most of the environment-specific code into their own set of objects. When they moved the application from platform to platform, they simply swapped in the native environment layers. Remember from Chapter 7, the power of object-oriented programming is its ability to place volatility in its own domain. This is a natural model for cross-platform development, where you place things that change (in this case, the platform) in their own domain.

Despite the power of traditional programming techniques, most developers find it almost impossible to make an application truly portable. A lot of recoding must always take place between platform moves. To solve this problem, vendors now offer a number of portable class libraries and 4GL tools that

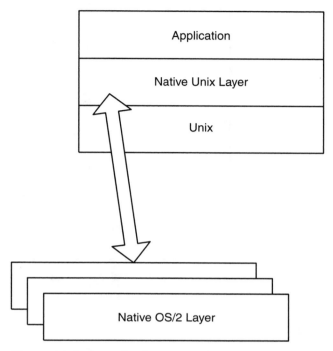

Figure 11-1 *Swapping Layers.*

make it much easier to develop portable applications, albeit much more proprietary applications.

These tools provide a layered API framework. The tools hide the code
that interacts with the operating system and GUI inside its own layer (see
Figure 11-2). Developers construct a client/server application on top of the
environment-specific layer. Thus they stay at a higher level of abstraction.
For instance, with a multi-platform development tool, you could program a call
to put up a message box as a proprietary API call, or as a high-level 4GL statement. The tools then translate the proprietary call into the native API as
required by the operating environment to put up the message box. The APIs to
do this vary from platform to platform.

By using proprietary API calls from 3GL and 4GL code, developers
don't deal directly with the native API layer. The tool handles the presentation
of the application within the native environments that the portable development tool supports. The idea is to write an application once, then port that
application without modification from platform to platform without having to
change the code.

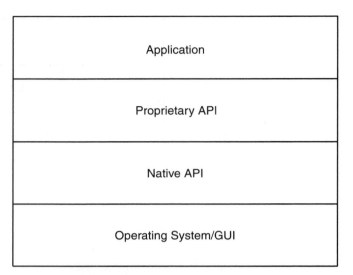

Figure 11-2 *Layered API framework.*

Approaches

Although the basic concepts of multi-platform development tools are the same, there are many techniques that tool vendors use to approach the problem of portability. I find that each tool vendor uses its own little proprietary method to provide a portable development environment, and it's difficult to place the methods in specific categories. What's more, as tools change, so do the approaches. However, four basic types of approaches arose when I tested these tools: the native, lowest common denominator (LCD), emulation, and hybrid approaches.

NATIVE

Before I tell you about the native approach, I should first tell you that I have yet to find a tool that provides a truly native cross-platform development environment. Therefore, when you consider the information in this section, consider the idea, not the practice.

In theory, the native approach to multi-platform development means a tool is all things to all platforms. No matter what platform the tool supports, it exploits all the features available through the native API, and still remains portable.

For instance, you can write an application that uses the native features of Windows 95 (e.g., threading) through the native Win32 API, and then implement the same feature on a Unix system. The problem is that the platforms are so different, and there are so many of them, that it's difficult if not impossible to support all the native features on them all.

A few tools have come close. For instance, most specialized multi-platform client/server tools (such as Unify, Uniface, and JAM 7) provide a consistent approach to delivery of applications on different platforms through their use of some features of the native API. However, they don't allow the developer to use all of them. The cross-platform C++ libraries don't do much better, but the developer can always go directly to the native API (Win32, X11, etc.) through the native C++ environment. When you do this, remember one key drawback. You can no longer port the application directly to other platforms. XVT from XVT Software is an example of a portable C++ development environment that comes close to native.

If you need to support all native features of all of the target platforms, you may find it better to build the application in portable C++ rather than employ a multi-platform tool. You'll have to do significant code changes when you move from platform to platform, but in the long run, it could be a better option. This is a well-established standard practice among many independent software vendors (such as WordPerfect and Lotus) who deploy applications to more than one platform. The large software vendors can afford to create teams of developers around platforms (e.g., a Windows 95 team, Unix team, OS/2 team). Many development organizations can't afford this luxury.

LEAST COMMON DENOMINATOR

The least-common-denominator (LCD) approach, the approach most cross-platform client/server development tools use, supports common features found within all environments. But, to maintain portability, developers must give up some native application features, and sometimes even native look-and-feel. In other words, LCD tools can't be all things to all platforms, but they can be some things to most platforms.

So what's the tradeoff? LCD does not support nonportable features such as Windows MDI (multiple document interface), OLE automation, or geometry management found in Motif. Nor does LCD provide a completely native look-and-feel, but the look-and-feel remains consistent across platforms.

Several problems arise with the LCD approach. A big problem is that applications may look out of place in their own native environment. A client/server system I built with a C++-based LCD tool looked like a Windows application, whether it ran on Windows, Unix, or a Macintosh. When we rolled the application out to the Mac portion of the organization, the users were so outraged to see an "evil" Windows lookalike application that many of them refused to use it. (Mac is almost a religion in some companies, you know.) There was a similar reaction from the Unix users, and thank goodness I didn't try to port it to OS/2. The LCD tool moved the client/server application without any code modification, just as promised. The issues arose over the lack of native look-and-feel that many users know and expect.

The ability to access to services of the native environment could be essential to the success of most client/server applications, especially since Windows 95 and Windows NT plan to build more application services into the infrastructure of the operating system (e.g., DCOM). We value an application's ability to exploit native features.

EMULATION

Obviously, the emulation approach to portability came from the hands of developers who hate to deal with native API. Rather than support only a subset of the API (as does LCD), emulation tools draw their own GUI controls for each environment and bypass the native API.

Open Interface Elements from Neuron Data is a good example of an emulation tool. To avoid the native API, Open Interface Elements writes directly to the graphics subsystem of each platform. What the user sees on the screen is not generated by an application program that invokes hundreds of native API calls (e.g., Win32). It's really just an image that exists in the graphics processing layer, such as Windows GDI (graphics device interface). The user is none the worse for wear, and unless someone pays close attention, it's hard to tell emulation from native.

Tradeoffs arise with the emulation approach as well. Since the application writes directly to the graphics layer (and not the native API), changes to the native API won't be reflected in the application. For instance, with an upgrade from Windows 3.11 to Windows 95, applications that use the emulation approach will still maintain the Windows 3.11 look-and-feel (if they run at all). Users will spot that, and you must buy the Windows 95 version of the portable development tool to fix the problem. This means another round of application testing, integration testing, and links to back-end database servers. In many cases, tool upgrades to keep up with operating system changes are four to six months behind the requirement.

Other issues with the emulation approach include poor performance. I noticed this problem with most of the tools that support emulation. This happens because the emulation tool's writes to the graphic layers of operating systems aren't as efficient as API calls. Emulation applications also tend to take up more memory, and conflict with other applications that must share the same environment.

HYBRID

The hybrid approach to cross-platform development remains unique, as well as rare. The hybrid approach combines the best features of the emulation and native approaches. Hybrid portable development tools attempt to use the native API as much as possible across all platforms. If a hybrid client/server development doesn't offer a feature (button, data windows, etc.) on a particular platform, the tool emulates it.

The resulting application should provide all the native features the users require, while the application remains completely portable. However, as with the native approach the tool vendor's job is much more complicated. C++ Views and ObjectStar are the closest I've seen to the hybrid approach.

SELECTING AN APPROACH

There is no best approach to portable development tools—as the tools exist today. For instance, there are no clear differences between the LCD and emulation approaches, and the only way to determine the efficiency of your tool is to test it in the environment where you plan to deploy your client/server application. As a rule of thumb, if you need to use cross-platform development tools, try to use tools that provide "close to native" support on the platforms most important to you.

If we all continue our migration to Microsoft environments as our preferred clients, the need for cross-platform client/server development will decline. This does not mean that many organization won't need to deploy single applications to multiple platforms, only that the number of platforms we deploy to will decrease. It's slowly becoming a Windows-only world. Also, as the intranet begins to become the platform of choice, developers will find that it is naturally multi-platform. Web-enabled applications can run on any platform that supports Web browsers. Not only does every platform sport a Web browser today, but so do devices such as cellular phones and personal digital assistants (PDAs).

The Intranet Is the Ultimate Multi-Platform Tool

While I spend a chapter of this book discussing the tradeoffs that arise in portable client/server development environments, interest continues to grow in the ultimate multi-platform application development platforms: the intranet. Today, the Web (this includes the intranet) is just another platform that tools can deploy to. As with single-platform specialized client/server development tools, most cross-platform tools support application development on the Web. These tools now support intranet standards such as CGI, HTML, ActiveX, and Java.

For example, Compuware's Uniface specialized cross-platform client/server development tool now provides Webenabler. Webenabler is a component of the Uniface products that lets developers build and deploy Uniface applications on the Web. This means that developers can create Uniface applications and port them to any platform that Uniface supports (including Windows, Unix, OS/2, and the Macintosh), and also port the application to the intranet for deployment to any platform (or device) that can run a browser.

But the tools don't make the intranet cross-platform. It's the intranet itself. Intranet developers can build Web-enabled applications with any client/server tool that supports the Web (and most do by now). These applications will execute on all platforms that support a browser. More platforms support browsers than any cross-platform tool can support. The costs are low, too. Intranet applications are inexpensive to build and deploy since developers pay the single-platform tool price, but still achieve multi-platform development.

If the intranet is cross-platform, then Java and ActiveX are the enabling technologies that bring dynamic development to intranet application development. Java is the most versatile. Developers can deploy Java applications as true cross-platform native applications that run with or without a browser. Since Java uses a bytecode interpreter vs. a native compiler, Java applications are out-of-the-gate platform-independent. Developers will also find new "easy-to-use" specialized client/server tools that support both Java and RAD. For example, Symantec's Café and Borland's JBuilder allow developers to visually create Java applications for direct deployment to intranets.

Today, the rise of the intranet as the next platform for client/server computing both hurts and helps the cross-platform tool market. It hurts the market in that specialized single-platform client/server tools can now deploy to multiple platforms via the Web. However, cross-platform tool vendors discovered that interest in the Web has created a new market for all Web-enabled client/server tools. What's more, since cross-platform tools already support more than one platform, their migration to the intranet is more of a natural process than a move from a single-platform development environment to the Web. The intranet is the future of cross-platform development.

Tool Types

I place portable client/server development tools in two categories: specialized cross-platform tools, and portable C++ libraries. If you go with portable C++ libraries, you'll look at products like zApp from Inmark Development Corporation, Zinc from Zinc Software Inc., and C++ Views from Liant Software Corporation. Specialized cross-platform tools bring 4GL functionality to cross-platform development. This category includes tools such as JAM 7 from JYACC, Uniface from Compuware, and Unify from Unify.

PORTABLE C++ LIBRARIES

Portable C++ libraries are C++ frameworks that work with existing C++ development environments such as Visual C++ or Borland C++. These libraries give developers the ability to access all operating system and GUI services using a proprietary API (see Figure 11-3). The API, in turn, implements the propri-

Figure 11-3 *Portable C++ Libraries.*

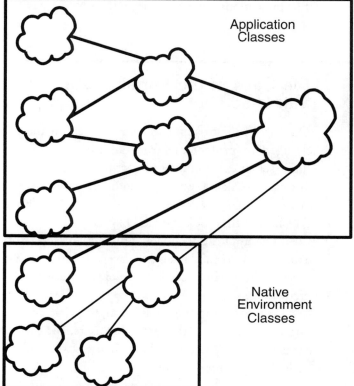

etary API call using native API calls (e.g., Win32 or Xlib). Since the API does not change from platform to platform, the C++ applications remain portable. The developer need only swap in the portable libraries that support a particular platform. If you need to access native features of the operating system, you can always go directly to the native API through the C++ development environment. However, you do so at the expense of portability.

The problems I found with these tools include adherence to the C++ programming model, ease of use, and performance. Since these tools force the developer to use a proprietary API, they often circumvent the C++ development model and lock the developer out of the language's productive features. If the developer does exploit these features, he or she must violate rules and the applications are no longer portable. These tools are also difficult to learn and use. You really have to learn C++ first, the development environment second, then learn the ins and outs of the portable C++ library, including each and every API call. Finally, performance can be a problem. Since these portable cross-platform development tools must translate an API directly into the native API using some type of cross-platform approach (such as LCD or emulation), the applications appear lethargic to users.

The Case of the Portable LCD Application with Lead Feet

The story you are about to hear is true, but the name of the tool has been changed to protect me from an Internet flaming. I once worked on a client/server development project that required Windows deployment. Since this was a project for the government, and at the time Unix was the government's standard, we needed a "glide path" to Unix as well. Enter a portable C++ library that took the LCD approach.

The application was a simple client/server application to manipulate data in an Informix database server, and took only three months to develop between three client/server developers and a DBA. The trouble began during testing.

While testing the application, the lackluster performance of the application annoyed both the tester and users. For example, when scanning down a multi-row database Window, the users watched while the application drew each character on the screen.

Needless to say, the application went back for a rewrite. With the tool vendor involved, the developers attempted to rewrite the application to provide better performance. After four months and lots of consulting hours from the vendor, it became clear that support for the cross-platform features of the tool came at the expense of performance. The developers changed tools and rewrote the application as a truly native application. The end result? Development and deployment cost four times the original estimate. All this because an LCD tool had lead feet.

SPECIALIZED CROSS-PLATFORM TOOLS

The problem with portable C++ object libraries is that you build an application in C++. Fortunately, RAD has arrived in the portable development market, and several high-level specialized tools on the market support cross-platform development. Rather than write applications around proprietary APIs, developers use easy-to-use 4GL development environments. These tools sit on top of the environment-specific features of the tool.

RAD is the battle cry of 4GL-driven cross-platform development tools. You can dummy up applications as fast as single-platform tools (such as Visual Basic and Delphi). The tradeoff is performance. Since 4GL tools drive applications through interpreters, speed often suffers.

SELECTING PORTABLE PRODUCTS

Soon we'll take a brief look at a few portable development tools I've run across. Before we do that, let's cover what you need to consider when you select a portable development tool.

First, consider the number of platforms the tool actually supports. Although tool vendors might say they support all major platforms, you will find platforms the tool does not support, or platforms with unequal support. For example, while all portable tools will support Windows and OS/2, only a few support obscure Unix systems such as Apollo. Try before you buy, and leave nothing to the imagination.

Second, since client/server requires access to data, make sure your tool of choice supports most database servers you need to link up to. Also understand what you need from your database vendor in terms of drivers. Make sure they support all major database servers on all platforms they support. In many cases, tool vendors charge extra for each database server you intend to access from the tool. Get those costs up front, and factor them into the cost of the final system.

Third, these tools should provide the developer with a means to design and deploy a database schema. There should be some way to create and maintain a database. Repository-driven development environments (such as Uniface and JAM 7) provide such features.

Fourth, understand the tool's approach to portability. Sometimes this is difficult to determine since many tools use some of each approach, and change from release to release. A good tool vendor will share those secrets with you, so you know what you're dealing with.

Fifth, check out the vendors. Once again, you're walking down the aisle with them. Vendor failure can mean a costly rewrite of an application using another tool. I hear all too often that a vendor goes out of business, and a business-critical application becomes an orphan looking for a new tool to call home.

Finally, test, test, and test some more. Never assume that a tool will support all features and functions on all platforms. Performance is often a problem, as is native look-and-feel.

VISION, Uniface, JAM 7, C/S Elements. The key players in the world of specialized cross-platform client/server development tools include VISION, Uniface, JAM 7, C/S Elements (a special client/server version of Open Interface Elements).

VISION, Uniface, and JAM 7 use similar development architectures (see Figures 11-4 through 11-7). All support some sort of repository-driven development environment. This means the developers build an application from the database up, but they must first define database elements, the rules associated with those database elements, and then the interfaces that display the data to the end-users. Uniface is more repository-driven than JAM 7 or VISION, and provides a robust repository. JAM 7 uses a visual repository, where application objects exist as visual windows (see Figure 11-7). VISION not only provides portable application development features, but application partitioning as well (see Figures 11-4 through 11-6 to see how VISION looks on the various platforms VISION supports).

All these tools provide GUI development environments linked to the repository. They also allow developers to create interfaces with the data, menus, and other visual application components. The idea is that you can create an application and a repository once, then deploy it to any platforms the tool vendors support. Platform support varies, so check with your tool vendor. Applications developed with repository-driven tools run through native interpreters.

Migration strategies to the intranet come with all these tools. Developers can deploy applications to the intranet as easily as they deploy applications to another supported platform. This usually involves the generation of HTML, CGI, ISAPI, NSAPI, Java, or ActiveX components that run on the Web server or within the browser of the Web client. The intranet looks like the future of cross-platform development.

XVT, zApp, Zinc, Object Star, C++ Views. XVT, zApp, Zinc, Object Star, and C++ Views all offer examples of cross-platform C++ development libraries. These tools vary greatly in features and functions, but most provide GUI development environments, database connection layers, and testing features.

The GUI development environments allow the developer to create the visual portion of the application. The developer then uses the traditional native C++ development environment to program the application. All these tools provide proprietary API mechanisms that place another layer between the developer and the native operating system. As previously mentioned, these applications are compiled into native executables.

Figure 11-4 *Vision for Open Look.*

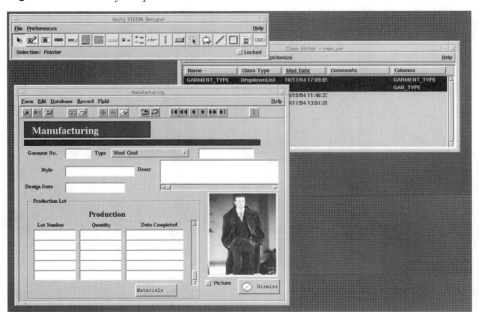

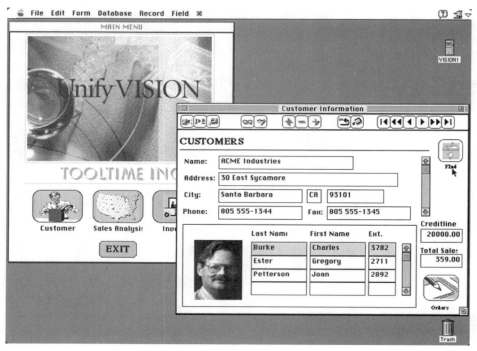

Figure 11-5 *Vision for Macintosh.*

Figure 11-6 *Vision for Motif.*

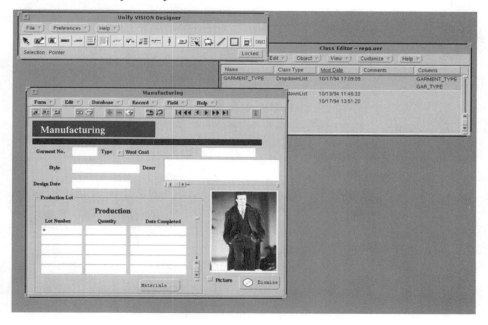

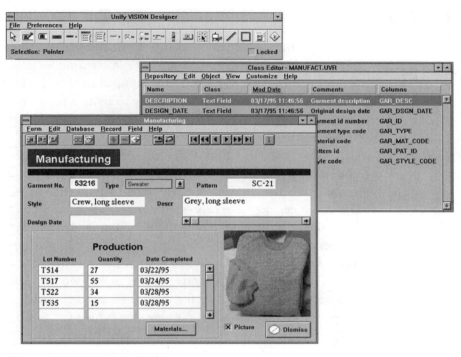

Figure 11-7 *Vision for Windows.*

Figure 11-8 *JAM 7.*

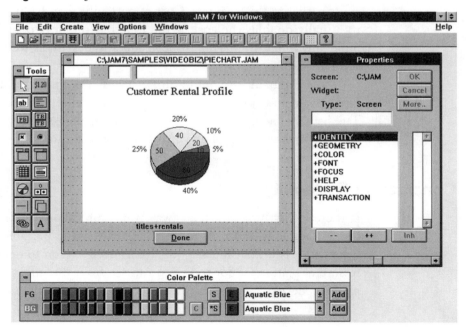

The Realities

Although there are many tradeoffs when you use portable client/server development tools, the allure of portability is too strong for developers and development organizations to resist. Many companies run a hodgepodge of processors and operating systems, and the ability to write a single application for all platforms seems like the right choice. Maybe so, but you need to understand the harsh realities.

The problem I find with cross-platforms development tools arises from the number of platforms we need to support. Portable tools can't be all things to all platforms (at least, not yet), thus they don't work well on most of them. For instance, most users can spot portable applications a mile away. They consider them "strange" and "out-of-place." Remember the popular portable development library that looked like a Windows application no matter where it resided? The Windows users did not notice, but the Mac users cried "foul."

Although it is a secondary issue, developers and users must understand the need to give up native features. For example, many portable development tools don't support native Windows features such as OLE and MDI, native help systems, or even features like cut-and-paste.

As already mentioned, you need to consider performance. Most portable applications don't run as fast as their native cousins. This is due to the overhead associated with application translation into native calls (see the case study earlier in this chapter). Cost of portability can be high as well. Portability usually doubles the cost of the tool and the developer hours required to build the application. Training considerations arise as well, due to the tools' complex natures.

This is not an attempt to turn you away from portable development tools. I only want to warn you of the tradeoffs that crop up when you go portable. The benefits of portable client/server development tools can largely outweigh the drawbacks. Let's explore when to use portable tools, and when not to.

Considering Portability

If there is anything you take away from this chapter, take the fact that you should look long and hard at your need to develop portable applications. The hype compels us, but unless you have a strong reason to deploy an application to several platforms, don't. As you can see from the information above, cross-platform development adds additional costs, complexity, and trouble.

If that does not steer you away from multi-platform development tools, you need to carefully consider the types of tools you employ. Portable C++ development libraries are great if you live in a C++ development shop, but they become complex development environments for standard client/server applications. What's more, you can't RAD your way through C++ development projects.

If you need portable application development tools and don't have C++ skills, I would recommend specialized multi-platform development tools. These are not wonder tools, but they do shield developers from the complexity of the underlying operating system, and provide a consistent development environment across platforms. At least, for the platforms they support.

If you need native features such as MDI, OLE, DDE, and Motif geometry, you need to find portable tools that support them, or return to native development tools. Things continue to get better, with more portable development tools that provide native features, but they must come a long way before they support all native features.

Determine your own application requirements first, then research the different portable development tools available (they change about every six months). Once you have all the information, invest in testing time to assure that your candidate tools function as promised. Then, and only then, select the right tool for the job. Don't be afraid to leave a tool behind if it's not a good fit, or you could end up throwing a ton of money down a rat hole.

Cross-platform development tools still have legs in a world where everyone runs different types of platform. While I don't recommend portable client/server tools unless you really need them, tool vendors continue their quest to be all things to all platforms. In a few years, we may finally get there.

As we retool for the intranet, we could find that Web browsers provide a consistent layer between the application and the underlying operating system. For example, since the Netscape Web browser runs on a number of platforms, so do Web-enabled applications. Developers can rest assured that the applications they run inside browsers can run on OS/2, Windows 95, Windows NT, Unix, and the Macintosh—without modification. I think most of the cross-platform development market will go the way of the intranet.

Smalltalk
Client/Server Tools

Smalltalk, the first true object-oriented language, is more than twenty years old and still going strong as a platform for client/server development. Although Smalltalk does not have the market share of specialized client/server development tools such as PowerBuilder, Delphi, and Visual Basic, Smalltalk does provide unique features that other client/server development environments have yet to replicate. That is why I put Smalltalk in its own tool category, and why I dedicated a chapter to the discussion of Smalltalk-enabled client/server development tools.

Object History

Smalltalk is the product of a Xerox research team that included Alan Kay and Adele Goldberg. Although Alan Kay recently retired, Adele still speaks at conferences and currently works for ParcPlace-Digitalk (a Smalltalk-based tool vendor).

Early versions of Smalltalk focused on research projects and academic articles. I spent a lot of my college time playing with Smalltalk, cutting my teeth on the only object-oriented language around at the time. Smalltalk was also the first environment to employ a GUI, and featured object-orientation before it was cool to be object-oriented.

Over the years, a few companies adapted and sold Smalltalk, including Digitalk, IBM, Vmark Software, and ParcPlace. They created commercial versions of Smalltalk that dominated the Smalltalk industry during the rise of client/server.

IBM sells VisualAge. VisualAge is a "visual development environment" based on IBM's version of Smalltalk. PARTS is Digitalk's Smalltalk product, and ParcPlace's product is VisualWorks. In 1996, Digitalk and ParcPlace merged to form ParcPlace-Digitalk. The combined companies now market new versions of their products that combine the technology of their previous products, a few of which are Web-enabled (see VisualWave sidebar later in this chapter). You can also find Smalltalk in the public domain, offered by the Free Software Foundation (GNU Smalltalk). Vmark Software sells the Smalltalk-enabled Object Studio.

Smalltalk Today

Today's Smalltalk offers truly portable, reusable code that supports all types of applications. Similar to a fourth-generation language (I call it a 3.5GL), Smalltalk is easier to learn and use than other object-oriented languages such as C++, but not as easy to learn as the 4GLs of specialized client/server tools. The client/server movement continues to drive Smalltalk's rebirth as development organizations finally realize the benefits of object-oriented development environments and the advantages of code reuse. Since Smalltalk forces the developers into the object-oriented development model, they can't help but reuse objects and code.

Complex applications need new methods to approach programming, and many developers find that Smalltalk can effectively break down complexity into smaller, reusable, independent objects. The goal is to hide the complexity of the underlying system and provide the developer with a truly portable application. However, despite the superior architecture and its faithful adherence to the object-oriented development model, Smalltalk has experienced only mild success in the world of client/server development.

Cross-Platform

Using portable Smalltalk environments, developers can write an application once, then move the code that exists inside Smalltalk images from one platform to another without modifying the application. Smalltalk applications developed within portable Smalltalk environments (such as Visual Smalltalk Enterprise— the new Smalltalk product from ParcPlace-Digitalk, and VisualWorks from ParcPlace-Digitalk) can run on Windows 3.11, Windows 95, Windows NT, OS/2, Unix, and the Apple Macintosh.

However, platform support varies. For instance, IBM's VisualAge supports OS/2, Windows, and AIX, but does not offer wide-spread Unix support as effectively as VisualWorks. PARTS does not support Unix at all. All provide connections to various databases directly from the Smalltalk development environment, but you need to find out exactly what database connections the product offers before you select a tool.

Pure Object-Oriented Development Model

Since Smalltalk is a true object-oriented language (unlike C++, which is a hybrid), everything in the environment is considered an object and all the work is carried out through objects that communicate via messages (see Figure 12-1).

Figure 12-1 *Everything is a Smalltalk Object.*

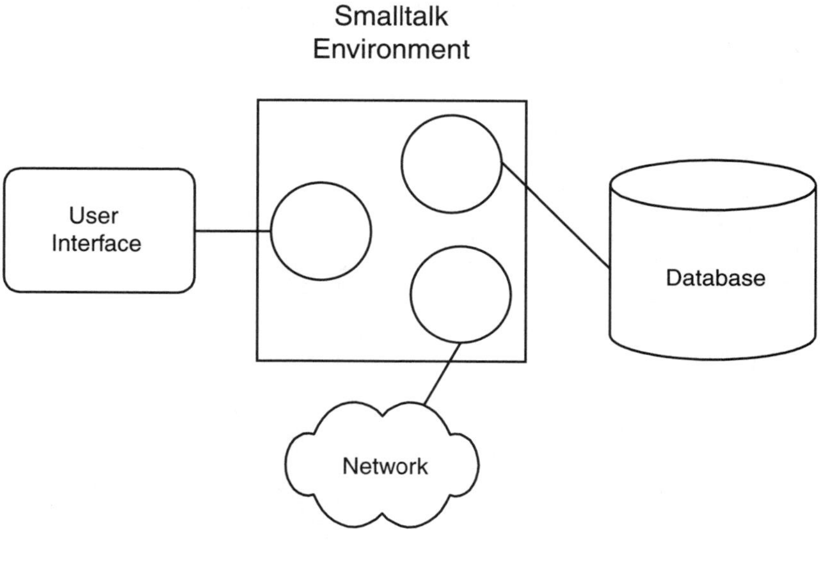

Smalltalk development uses a sophisticated multi-windowed interface with mouse controls, pop-up menus, and other graphical user interface (GUI)-type features. In fact, Smalltalk originated GUI environments, which are the basis of Windows and the Apple Macintosh.

Smalltalk's most important feature is the extensive library of classes that come with the language. These "canned objects" support a variety of functions such as serial communications, graphics, file I/O, database connections, and so on (see Figure 12-2). The developer uses the objects required to construct the application, and assembles most of the application from existing objects. IBM's VisualAge, for instance, relies on this concept to give VisualAge developers the ability to assemble an application almost entirely from pre-existing objects included with the tools. Customization of the objects with the Smalltalk language is usually required when you build an application.

Of course, not everything comes with Smalltalk. You can incorporate third-party objects into the Smalltalk environment to provide extra functionality. Most Smalltalk tool vendors have alliances with many smaller companies who develop third-party objects for their environments. This is one of the greatest benefits of a truly object-oriented development environment. Developers

Figure 12-2 *Smalltalk Class Libraries.*

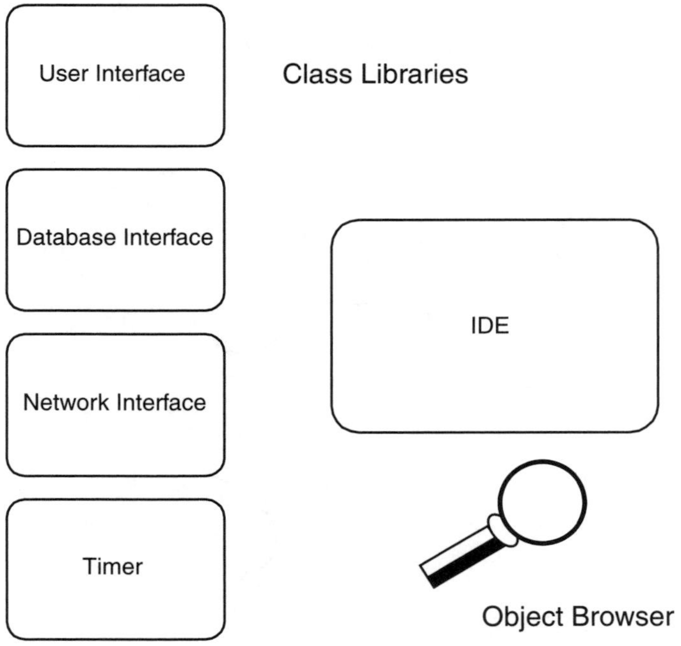

Class Libraries

User Interface

Database Interface

Network Interface

Timer

IDE

Object Browser

can trade objects like baseball cards, and extensive corporate object libraries can provide developers with the foundation objects they need to build new applications.

Everything's an Object

As you can see from other chapters, object-oriented tools don't support the object-oriented model in the same manner. Each tool has its own approach to object implementation, from the "almost object" tools such as Visual Basic, to the "pure object" tools. Smalltalk is a pure object-oriented language from the ground up. Everything inside the Smalltalk environment exists as an object, method, or class. Therefore, developers must use the object-oriented model exclusively to get things done.

If you don't have much experience using objects, Smalltalk can be a bit confusing. For instance, since everything is an object, so are classes. Yes, this also means that every object is a member of a class, and objects also define classes. If you follow this, you may be asking yourself if such an architecture could lead to infinite regression. The developers of Smalltalk thought of that problem. They declared that metaclasses define all classes. Metaclasses inherit from a single metaclass.

Got to tell you, programming in Smalltalk is an acquired taste. First and foremost, developers need to learn the ins and outs of using the objects-and-only-objects approach to develop their client/server application. Then, developers need to understand the Smalltalk object library that comes with the particular Smalltalk tool, and learn to mix and match objects to create the application. Smalltalk developers can then extend the capabilities of those objects, using the Smalltalk language to customize the objects for the application. Those objects, in turn, are reusable for other applications.

Smalltalk compiles code incrementally, and new classes and objects become effective inside the Smalltalk environment at the time the developer creates them. This feature makes Smalltalk work well as a RAD tool, and also makes Smalltalk fun to use since you can immediately see the fruits of your labor.

Smalltalk tools use interpreters to run Smalltalk applications, which results in good news and bad news. The good news is that you can create objects and run the application with the new objects instantaneously. The bad news is that interpreters mean applications that run much slower than compiled applications (such as C++ compilers, and even Delphi).

When you look at Smalltalk tools to build client/server applications, you need to look closely at the object library that comes with the tool. For instance, while VisualAge and VisualWorks are both Smalltalk tools, they come with a very different set of object libraries. Remember, if the Smalltalk tool vendor does not give you an object, you'll have to build it yourself, or buy it on the third-party object market.

After you master object-oriented development, you'll spend most of the up-front time for your first Smalltalk client/server project learning the object libraries that come with the Smalltalk tool. Once you understand how to use the object library, you'll find that most of the programming is already done. Building applications is just a matter of creating new custom versions of existing objects. Smalltalk objects are seldom developed from scratch.

RELATIONAL WRAPPERS

You may ask yourself: If everything in the Smalltalk development environment must be an object, how do Smalltalk development tools access relational databases, which are very nonobject? The answer is: relational wrappers.

Relational wrappers are special objects that exist in Smalltalk development environments to provide a translation layer between objects and relational database tables. This translation layer allows other objects to interact with relational databases as objects. This layer automatically generates the SQL to access information in relational tables, and converts data into objects (or, data that's accessed via objects) as the data returns from the database servers (the result set).

For example, VisualWorks, a ParcPlace-Digitalk product, provides data-to-object mapping mechanisms called ObjectLens and Visual Data Modeler. Both mechanisms give developers the ability to remap relational databases (like Sybase, Oracle, or Informix) to make them appear as persistent Smalltalk objects. The Visual Data Modeler lets developers manage relationships between the tables and objects. ObjectLens is really just a set of Smalltalk classes that provide the Smalltalk environment with the ability to access tables as native Smalltalk objects.

ParcPlace-Digitalk's Relational Database Interface supplies a relational database interface to most major database servers on the market. This interface provides Smalltalk database connectivity for most major database servers by allowing the Smalltalk environment to address each database, table, or record as a native Smalltalk object. The extensive list of supported databases includes Microsoft SQL Server, Sybase, and Oracle, and most IBM database servers and database gateways.

The ParcPlace-Digitalk database interface lets applications perform such complex activities as examination and modification of the data dictionary contents of an SQL server, including source code and database objects (stored procedures, triggers, rules, and defaults). This interface can also read rows in groups from the database, which allows developers to break large queries into smaller result sets, and offers many other database processing features.

The PARTS Relational Database Interface lets the developer create applications that work independently from the connected database. Thus developers can use a local PC database (such as dBASE IV) for testing, and then deploy the application later against a remote database server with live data. This tool also lets the developer leverage the power of SQL extensions (such as Sybase Transact SQL).

OBJECTS BOUGHT AND SOLD

The world of Smalltalk developers is a small one. I find that those who use Smalltalk love it. And those who love Smalltalk may often get together with other Smalltalk developers to trade objects.

The religious use of the object-oriented development model is what makes this practice so easy. Unlike the component model (e.g., VBXs), where you're basically stuck with the feature of a particular component, Smalltalk objects may be modified to meet the exact needs of an application. For example, an object that does sophisticated financial applications may be plugged into the class hierarchy, then the methods and data associated with financial application processing are propagated down to the objects that need them. The developers can take an object as is, or modify the object to meet the requirements of the application.

When Smalltalk Is not a Good Fit

I'm taking a risk in writing this sidebar. There are thousands of Smalltalk zealots out there that cruise books and magazines looking for those that denigrate the ultimate object-oriented language. Those that have crossed them have disappeared, never to be heard from again.

The fact is while Smalltalk is a good fit for many client/server applications, those applications that must perform well (at least at the interface layer) won't find a happy home with Smalltalk. Take the case of my last client/server project using Smalltalk.

It was an inventory application. Performance was a critical success factor due to the fact that those managing the warehouse had to beat on the application to pump product out of the door as fast as possible. While

Smalltalk did a good job of building the application, the use of an interpreter made the application appear sluggish. No "snap," as explained to me by my client. By the way, they were the ones who selected Smalltalk, not me.

While there were a few performance improvements that could be made with this application, the core problem was the deployment mechanism of Smalltalk. We could have thrown expensive hardware at the problem but with the number of machines we had to deploy, this solution was out of the question.

To solve the problem, we had to rewrite the application using C++. The warehouse workers were very happy with their speedy new friend. The moral of the story is: Before selecting Smalltalk, make sure you consider your performance requirements.

OBJECT BROWSERS

A tool common to all Smalltalk development environments is an object browser. With an object browser, developers can surf through the library of Smalltalk objects to select the right object for the job. Once the developer finds the object or set of objects, the developer can extend the functionality of any number of objects by using the browser as an entry point to enter Smalltalk code.

Browsers are typically graphical, and depict the class hierarchy as it exists in the Smalltalk environment. Simply place the cursor over an object, and you can edit the source code, view the data, or examine all the methods associated with a particular object. Browsers are at the heart of all Smalltalk development environments.

BUILDING YOUR INTERFACE

All client/server tools must have some facility to build a user interface. Smalltalk tools are no exception to this rule. Although each tool uses its own approach to build the user interface, most Smalltalk tools provide developers with a palette of GUI controls that the developer can use to assemble screens. Each GUI control is usually a Smalltalk object. Therefore, the developer can change the characteristics of that object (color, look, feel, behavior, etc.).

Smalltalk developers drag GUI control from the palette onto a canvas. They arrange the control on the canvas where they can modify the control to meet the particular needs of the application. A testing facility usually exists to test the interface during its construction. The test facility lets developers check out the look-and-feel of an application without having to compile it into native code. Remember, Smalltalk development tools use an interpreter; thus the developer can run the application at any time without a compile.

Smalltalk Tools

I've looked at most of the available Smalltalk development environments and found that all provided advanced client/server development capabilities. I also found there are more differences than similarities, despite the fact that they all use Smalltalk. Let's look at a few of the most popular Smalltalk tools that are client/server-ready.

VISUALAGE

VisualAge from IBM comes in two flavors: VisualAge that uses Smalltalk, and VisualAge that uses C++. The Smalltalk version is one of the first tools to sell itself as a "visual programming" environment, or a sophisticated tool so easy to use that end-users can create applications simply by moving and connecting icons which represent objects on a screen (see Figure 12-3).

For example, a VisualAge developer would design a data window using the VisualAge screen designer, then connect a data query object to the data window by drawing a line between the data windows and an icon that represents a database query. The line represents a connection that defines a message-passing mechanism between the data windows and the data query object. When running the application, the user interacts with the data window, which in turn interacts with the database query objects (which interacts with the database, of course). This chain of linked events provides behavior to the application. This is the concept behind visual programming.

This is, of course, a simple example. Typical VisualAge projects would define lots of links between lots of objects to meet the requirements of an application of normal complexity. What's more, while you can define up to 80 percent of the functionality of an application, you'll still have to define the remainder of the application using Smalltalk programs.

VisualAge should be a consideration if you develop for OS/2 clients, or if you really like the visual-programming model (see Figure 12-4). You should know that I did have some performance concerns with VisualAge.

VISUALWORKS

VisualWorks from ParcPlace-Digitalk is the classic Smalltalk development environment that supports more platforms than any other Smalltalk tool. Visual-Works allows developers to define an application by using its sophisticated

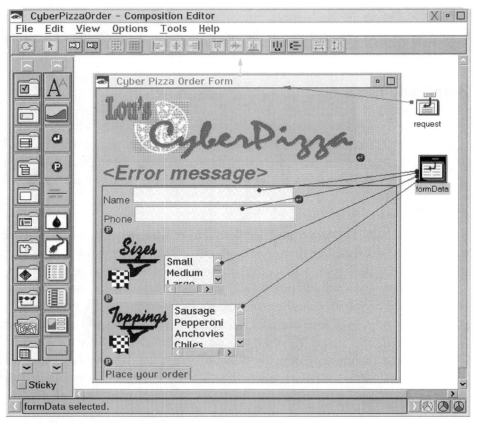

Figure 12-3 *VisualAge Web Development.*

object library that developers can access through built-in object browsers (see Figure 12-5). Most objects come with VisualWorks, including objects required to connect to relational databases.

The multi-platform capabilities are what really set VisualWorks apart from its competition. For example, I developed a VisualWorks application on a Windows 3.11 platform, then moved the application to Solaris, HP/ux (versions of Unix), and OS/2, without any changes to the application. VisualWorks uses the emulation approach to support the largest number of platforms.

As previously mentioned, the ObjectLens (see Figure 12-6) and relational interface components give developers the ability to link to any number of popular relational database servers, and map relational data into Smalltalk objects for use by the applications. VisualWorks Visual Data Modeler builds upon ObjectLens features by providing a means to build, define, and link the database objects to one another. This facility offers a more natural approach to

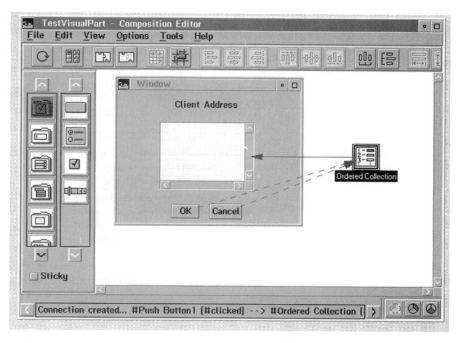

Figure 12-4 *Visual programming with VisualAge.*

Figure 12-5 *VisualWorks.*

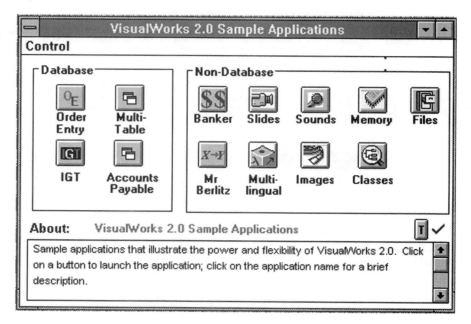

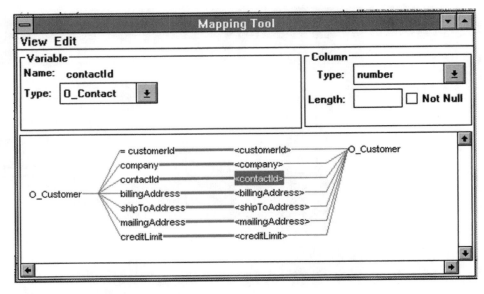

Figure 12-6 *ObjectLens.*

database development, since each Smalltalk object represents a business component (see Figure 12-7). Business components contain attributes and behaviors, not just the two-dimensional rows and columns of relational databases.

Figure 12-7 *VisualData Modeler.*

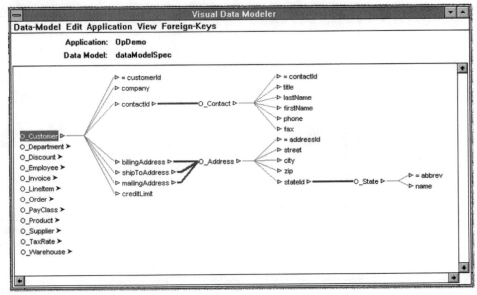

PARTS

PARTS works very much like VisualAge. With PARTS, developers can create applications visually using Smalltalk objects (see Figure 12-8). PARTS lets developers build applications by visually linking existing parts (Smalltalk objects) together.

Inside the PARTS development environment you'll find three types of parts: visual parts, nonvisual parts, and accessory parts. Visual parts create the user interface, nonvisual parts bring behavior to an application, and accessory parts access external resources (e.g., the file system). As with any other Smalltalk environment, the developers can modify the objects at any time for any reason to customize the objects for the applications.

PARTS uses relational wrappers to provide access to popular relational databases. You can use the wrappers to connect to Sybase, SQL Server, Gupta, and Oracle. Developers can also create multiple connections for each type of database. PARTS also supports Web development through a Java-enabled version of PARTS (see Figure 12-9).

Figure 12-8 *PARTS.*

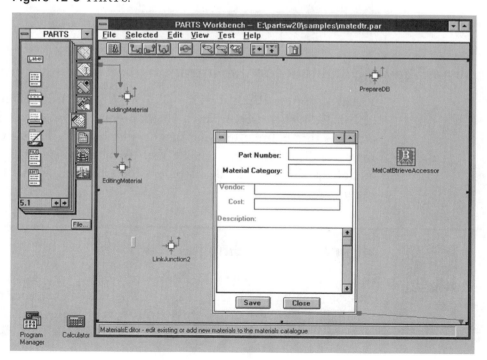

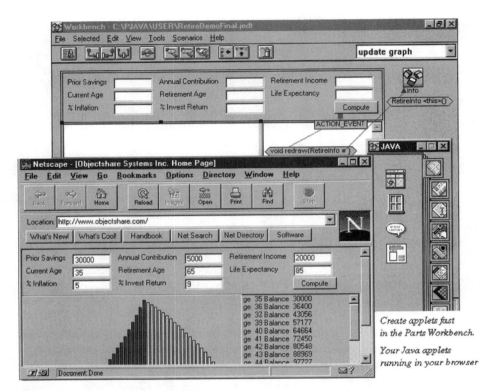

Figure 12-9 *PARTS for the Web.*

VisualWave: Smalltalk for the Intranet

VisualWave from ParcPlace-Digitalk is a Web-enabled version of their popular Smalltalk client/server development products. VisualWave is one of many products that promise to bring rapid application development (RAD) to the Internet. VisualWave is actually a Web-enabled version of VisualWorks, and one of the first intranet development tools to bring RAD to the Web (see Figure 12-10).

Intranet Driven Smalltalk

For those in the intranet and client/server development community who consider Smalltalk a "legacy" language, you need to consider the fact that Smalltalk drove one of the first Web development tools: VisualWave (described in detail in this chapter).

VisualWave was created when those at Parcplace-Digitalk attempted to use Smalltalk as the development environment for their own intranet. VisualWave grew out of that project and it was one of the first true RAD development environments for Web development that I saw on the market.

Today there are many other examples of Smalltalk for the Web as well, including PARTS and VisualAge (also described in this chapter). While Smalltalk is not getting much attention these days as a client/server development language, the use of Smalltalk for intranet development could re-grow interest in Smalltalk, and thus re-grow interest in client/server development. At least that is what the Smalltalk vendors are hoping for.

VisualWave, like other Web development environments, removes the developer from the complexities of Web development by offering features such as automatic creation of HTML files and CGI processes. This Smalltalk-based tool provides the Web application developer with an integrated environment to build, test, debug, and deploy the application from a unified work space. The

Figure 12-10 *VisualWave Development Environment.*

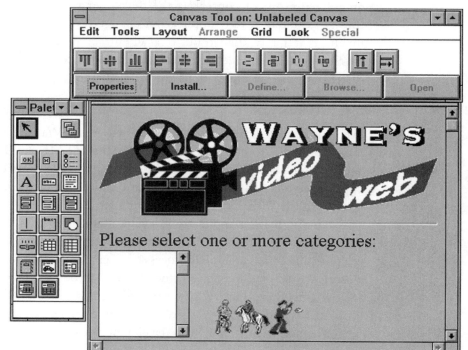

tool is proprietary in nature, but Smalltalk is an open language. VisualWave supports most database servers and platforms, and provides a session manager that allows the Web application to work with user-generated events rather than the Web's traditional static text and graphics.

VisualWave provides an easy-to-build layer between the complexities of Web development (HTML, CGI, Java, etc.) and the application. True Web application development requires that the developer learn the details of HTML, including support levels and verification processes. To add input and output services, the developer must also learn CGI, as well as an enabling language (such as C, C++, or Perl) to implement the CGI portions of the application. If the developer wants dynamic functionality within the application, then Java is one of the few places to turn. However, Java development is functionally equivalent to C++ (without the use of pointers), and developers must also learn an elaborate class library. The end result is that a typical Web application could require that the developer learn three development environments—HTML, CGI, and Java—to create a single application.

Ongoing maintenance activities add cost to Web development projects since Web applications are dynamic environments by nature. The reliance on low-level development environments greatly increases this cost, which can quickly spin out of control as the developer tries to patch his or her way through the day-to-day application changes. Web applications change at a much greater rate than traditional client/server applications. A high-level development environment would make ongoing maintenance less of a burden, since most low-level operations are handled automatically.

New Problems, New Tool

Web application development tools (such as VisualWave) handle the low-level programming automatically, and generate the HTML, CGI, NSAPI, ISAPI, and Java applets required to serve the needs of the Web application. The developer simply defines the application at a high level, often visually, within the domain of the Web application development tool.

The high-level application development layer puts the developer back into an amicable visual application development environment. Web application development becomes a familiar process of assembling application components on a form, and adding functions to those objects through a programming language such as Smalltalk. The Web development tools generate the application in a form understandable by standard Web browsers such as Netscape and Mosaic.

The addition of new Web development technology has a downside that many organizations fail to factor into their Web development tool decisions.

Most of these tools move the developer from Web standards such as HTML and Java to proprietary technology. Although this speeds up the complex Web application development process, the proprietary nature of these tools moves developers away from emerging Web standards. This creates a dependency on the tool and vendor, and could create a problem if this new industry moves in different directions, or if the vendor or product becomes unstable. Thus developers should approach these tools with the full knowledge of the tradeoffs they face by going from open to proprietary Web development technology.

PARCPLACE-DIGITALK'S VISUALWAVE

VisualWave provides Web development through an adaptation of its Visual-Works Smalltalk development environment. Like other Web development products, VisualWave removes the Web developer from HTML forms design and CGI programming, and forces the developer into Smalltalk's object-oriented paradigm. VisualWave also provides standard client/server development facilities such as links to database servers, and VisualWave uses its Database Connect for DB2, Oracle, and Sybase connections. Since VisualWave is a pure object-oriented environment, the developer must link to these databases as objects using an object-wrapping mechanism (see previous description).

VisualWave automatically generates the HTML and CGI interface for a Web application. The developer builds an application using VisualWave's graphical environment which automatically deploys on the Web. VisualWave provides a canvas editor to "paint" the Web application interface by dragging and dropping from a standard set of widgets. The layout editor automatically translates the canvas into HTML. As with other Smalltalk tools, VisualWave provides developers with an object browser, object inspectors, a symbolic debugger, a change list manager resource finder, and workspaces.

VisualWave furnishes a personal Web server to create and test Web applications. Using this miniserver, developers can invoke Web applications with any supported browser. When the behavior of the Web application meets expectations, developers can deploy the application using VisualWave Server.

The ParcPlace Smalltalk language used with VisualWave is a nonproprietary, ANSI-standard object-oriented programming language. VisualWave supplies over nine hundred classes and 24,000 methods prebuilt for Web applications. VisualWave is an all-object-oriented tool, meaning there is no mechanism for procedural or structured development. This is a significant paradigm shift for those who are unfamiliar with the object-oriented development model. Although the Smalltalk language itself is not proprietary, the extensive Web-enabled Smalltalk objects libraries that come with VisualWave are proprietary.

For all practical purposes, this binds the developer to the tool, despite the fact that this is an open language.

VisualWave applications are binary-portable across Windows, Macintosh, OS/2, and most popular Unix systems as images. This lets developers build an application on one platform and move it to other platforms without alterations to the application.

With VisualWave, developers can incorporate dynamic graphics into Web applications. VisualWave also includes an image-to-gif converter. Any image drawn by the application can be displayed on the Web browser at the client. This is useful in distributed business graphics (such as real-time market information), but the end-user must reload the page to update the graphics since it does not provide true dynamic application capabilities (such as Java or OCX applets).

VisualWave generates the HTML required to send the application to the end-user who runs any standard browser. Currently, VisualWave supports the advanced HTML extensions from Netscape, and maintains compatibility with browsers that don't support HTML extensions.

VisualWave offers a complementary server product: VisualWave Server. VisualWave Server supports a wide variety of Web servers (such as Netscape, NCSA, and WebSite) using the CGI interface. VisualWave Server also provides security features such as authentication and security for VisualWave applications using the capabilities of the native Web server.

VisualWave's Application Development Environment (ADE) releases developers from the need to use several tools to create sophisticated Web applications. The code is portable across several platforms. VisualWave came out several months ago, and thus has a jump on newer tools such as second- and third-generation Web development tools. However, VisualWave does not currently support Java or OCX applets which provide end-users with dynamic Web applications.

BUILDING VISUALWAVE APPLICATIONS

VisualWave calls its applications "live applications," or Web sites that have the power to interact dynamically with the Internet and intranet clients who use them (see Figure 12-11). For all practical purposes, VisualWave applications are true client/server applications deployed to another platform—the Web.

VisualWave provides an integrated approach to Web application development. The Web application developer stays inside a single environment versus the traditional approach of using an HTML editor, graphics editor, scripting language, etc. Some of the unique development features provided with the tool include a personal Web server, hot loading, browser accommodation, Smart HTML, session manager, and client/server integration.

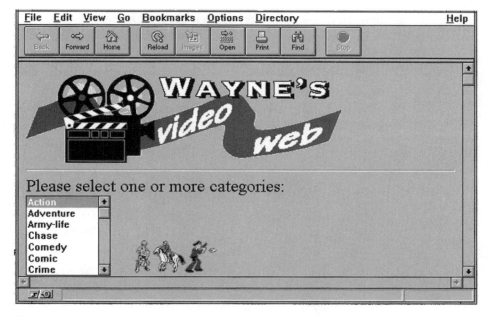

Figure 12-11 *VisualWave Application.*

The personal Web server provides a test environment for your Visual-Wave Web application. The Web server exists inside the development environment, available at any time for application testing. This allows the developer to see what the Web user sees, without having to use an external Web browser.

The hot-loading option lets developers load changes while the application runs on the Web server. This means that the Web application need not shut down to load changes, which results in a "hot load." This is a valuable benefit since continued service is an import feature of Web sites.

The browser accommodation feature lets the developer adjust to ever-changing Web standards. VisualWave applications automatically determine the type of browser that a client uses, and with its knowledge of browsers, it generates custom HTML for that particular browser. Those who run the latest Netscape version will use an HTML stream that makes the application look its best. The use of Smart HTML means VisualWave can provide dynamic presentation logic, which allows users to customize the information they want to see.

The session management feature of VisualWave gives VisualWave applications the ability to track states, something the traditional Web cannot do. In the Web, every page is independent of all others. Leaving a page and then returning resets the page, or returns the page to its original state. Web applications need to track the states of numerous clients connected to the Web server, and allow the user to return to a Web page and view it in the state the user left it. Although this is simple in the world of application development, it's much more difficult when using the stateless platform of the Web.

VisualWave uses the concept of a session to manage client connections. A session remains active during the user's entire interaction with the application, and keeps track of the state of the client's interaction. Thus the Web application resembles a traditional desktop application using no particular order of events. This is a key feature of Web-enabled development tools such as VisualWave.

Designed to layer into the current infrastructure, VisualWave includes support for twelve popular platforms (Windows NT, OS/2, Macintosh, and several Unix flavors), links to legacy and client/server databases, and offers built-in integration with object request broker (ORB) vendors. This allows the developer to link VisualWave applications to existing corporate databases for external Web and internal intranet applications. As a result, Web browsers can become the front end to all types of corporate and customer information. For instance, banks can use VisualWave to build customer applications that access account information directly from a Web browser. Basically, any application we can build in a traditional client/server environment can be Web-enabled using VisualWave.

VisualWave is best suited for developers who are familiar with Visual-Works or Smalltalk. The pure object-oriented paradigm is difficult to learn for non-OO developers, and can be restrictive for those who don't know how to use it properly. VisualWave plans to integrate Java development into the tools, but for now it's a traditional HTML/CGI Web application development environment. Moreover, the tool is proprietary, which binds the application to the tool.

VisualWave does many things well. The tool removes the developer from the complexities of the underlying Web technology (HTML and CGI), and the session manager allows the developer to deploy truly interactive applications on the Web or intranet. This is a complete environment which does not require integration of many Web development products (HTML editors, Web database connections, CGI development tools, etc.) that may not work and play well with others. The database support makes it easy to retrieve database information from your VisualWave application, and VisualWave is one of the most experienced Web-enabled application development tools on the market today. Best of all, it's Smalltalk-based.

ParcPlace-Digitalk is in the process of releasing a Web-enabled version of PARTS as well. This product will employ Java instead of CGI as the enabling technology.

Future of Smalltalk

Although Smalltalk is not the perfect development language, this object-oriented language is as close as they come. Using Smalltalk, developers can make the best of available software. Although they can't do everything, Smalltalk tools enhance the development environment so that no task is unattainable. Smalltalk environments and the tools that support them keep getting better all the time. In addition to being the oldest object-oriented development environment, Smalltalk is on its way to being the most successful.

There are some drawbacks to Smalltalk. First of all, most Smalltalk tools and applications that I dealt with in the past had a tendency to perform poorly. This is something that kept Smalltalk out of the mainstream world of client/server development tools. Things continue to change quickly in the world of Smalltalk. As I write this chapter, new products are in the works (e.g., the Web-enabled version of PARTS, and ParcPlace-Digitalk and IBM are looking for other new markets for their Smalltalk-enabled tools). If you do consider Smalltalk, do your research first.

File-Oriented
Database Tools

At one time I debated whether to keep this chapter in the book. I'm glad I did. While researching the audience for this book, I found that most of you will work your way down to client/server from traditional big iron shops. However, I found that more readers than I expected will move up to client/server from older file-oriented databases. I'll tell how to do that in this chapter, as well as discuss the details of file-oriented databases, their advantages and limitations.

You may remember from Chapter 8 that file-oriented database tools are tools that access databases as files, and they were not built for use with database servers (although most file-oriented database tools now work with database servers). This means that the database engine resides at the client with the application—a cheap model to deploy and maintain, but one that does not perform or scale as well as the typical two-tier client/server, not to mention three-tier and multi-tier client/server.

File-oriented database tools hold a special place in my heart. In the early days, I did a lot of moonlighting for small firms that needed simple database applications to solve special problems such as inventory management, billing, commission systems, and even a system to count the number of political commercials. Before the client/server revolution of the late '80s, these tools provided the most bang for the buck, and they were very capable.

The Case of the Blasted Database

Years ago, before this whole client/server stuff took off, I was a mainframe developer by day and a file-oriented PC database application developer by night (trying to earn enough to buy my first house). One of my best night-time consulting clients was a local advertising organization. It had an application that ran its business, keeping track of over 50,000 customers and over 100,000 transactions per year. Five data entry clerks moved data into the application 40 hours a week.

The application, as you may have guessed, was a traditional high-use, transaction-oriented application, probably better suited for a mini- or mainframe computer at the time. However, the organization was ahead of its time creating the application using dBase II for CPM, later moving it to dBase III for DOS and then to dBase III for LANs.

Everything worked fine with the application except for one thing: From time to time, okay almost every week, a database file was blasted (that means corrupted). Due to the handy automatic backup routine, there was never much work lost, but it was a frustrating problem nonetheless.

After some testing I determined that the problem was a combination of the database software's inability to protect the file properly in a high-use multi-user scenario and the number and volume of transactions that we were pumping through the system. An upgrade of the database software only reduced the number of times the file blew. I was, however, able to eliminate the problem by writing another routine to monitor the database and move data into the file at a much slower pace, simulating a single user. Of course, this was at the cost of performance.

So, how did I solve the problem in the long run? Well, as soon as I could, I convinced my client to move the data to a database server, and create a client/server application. At the time that was like telling someone to take an experimental drug. Since the database processing and concurrency control were more effective in this model there were no more instances of database corruption and my client lived happily ever after.

No, the moral of this story is not that file-oriented databases are evil, only that you need to match the application requirements to the architecture and the enabling technology. In this case file-oriented databases, at least the state-of-the-technology at the time, was a bad fit. Too bad it cost me and my client a lot of time and trouble before we discovered that. We are both much more savvy these days.

During this time we saw the rise of DBMSs such as dBASE II, III, III+, and finally IV, as well as dBASE clones such as FoxBase (which later became FoxPro) and Clipper, R:BASE 5000 and Paradox. While you can still find most of these tools today, they are very different now from the DOS tools they were then. Little did we know that these products were the prototypes for specialized client/server tools that appeared shortly after the birth of Windows 3.0, and still dominate the market today (see Chapter 10).

It is difficult to distinguish today's file-oriented database tools from specialized client/server tools. They provide traditional file-oriented database processing capabilities, and the ability to link to remote database servers for client/server. They also migrated from the structured development world of the '80s to the modern object-oriented world of the '90s. They remain a part of modern small systems development, and will be around for some time.

Hybrid Capabilities

What kept file-oriented databases going for such a long time was their ability to adapt to a changing marketplace. Once upon a time, you could only find tools to create single-user applications meant to run on a single PC. When LANs became all the rage, the PC-based databases of the time began to offer multi-user versions of their products that gave developers the ability to create applications that allowed multiple users to share a single file. Today, file-oriented databases can connect to all sorts of databases as remote database servers, and still retain their file-oriented capabilities.

DATABASE FILE ACCESS

There are a few differences between file-oriented and client/server development tools. Client/server development tools always count on another process that runs locally (usually on another computer connected to a network) to perform all the database processing on behalf of the client. This is the basic model of client/server. For specialized client/server tools to access data, you always need a remote database server, or a database server that runs locally (e.g., Watcom Database Server software, which runs locally on Windows for PowerBuilder).

File-oriented database tools are built to access database files that exist on the local hard drive, or a network file system. All the database processing occurs within the tool. This model simplifies things, since developers don't have to deal with setting up local or remote database servers for the tool, nor do they have to stop and start servers.

Since the database engine exists inside the tools, the database file is nothing more than a location on the file system for physical disk storage (see Figure 13-1). Database files can be as simple as ASCII text, or as complex as indexed binary files. Sometimes the data and indexes exist in separate files (e.g., the dBASE classic .DBF and .IDX files), and sometimes they exist in the same file. Some databases (such as dBASE) use fixed record formatting, meaning that the database uses a certain amount of disk space to store a record regardless of whether the information exists in the record. Variable record storage means the database only uses the physical disk space required to store the information in the database.

During the normal course of database processing, portions of the file must be loaded and unloaded into the database engine on the client to process the data. I call this the "obese client" model, since everything occurs at the client (see Figure 13-2). Sometimes the information exists on a local drive where it's easily accessible and secure. Sometimes the data exists on remote files systems where it's shared by any number of users who use any number of tools (see

Figure 13-1 *File-oriented database architecture.*

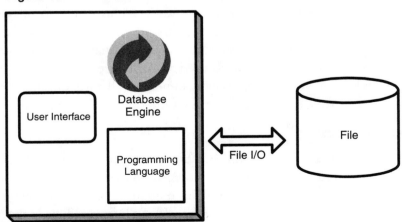

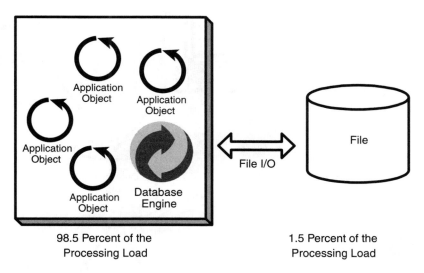

98.5 Percent of the
Processing Load

1.5 Percent of the
Processing Load

Figure 13-2 *Obese Client Model.*

Figure 13-3). The obese client model is the Achilles heel of file-oriented database tools, and the reason we continue to move away from this model.

MULTI-USER ACCESS

Although file-oriented databases work fine for those who build applications or manage data on a single PC, problems persist with their use in the multi-user environment. The problems include performance, concurrency control, security, and scalability.

Performance. When a file-oriented database (or application instance) runs on a client, and the client accesses a database file that exists on a file server, the database or application must load and unload portions of the file into and out of the engine. For instance, if you need to find a particular customer in a customer database, and you need to search on a nonindexed column, you must load the entire file into the engine across the network. Since these files are usually too big to fit in memory, the database engine must load and unload the files. This eats up network resources and kills performance.

Before I pan file-oriented database development all together, I must admit that a few file-oriented tools have sophisticated caching schemes that provide a dramatic increase in multi-user performance. You need to work with your DBMS vendor to understand how things work behind the scenes. I find

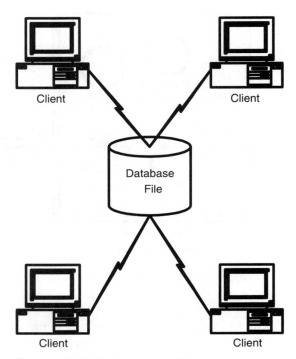

Figure 13-3 *Sharing remote files.*

that descriptions of performance in documentation rarely match the product's actual performance.

Just to put things in perspective, I did a benchmark after I converted a customer from a file-oriented multi-user database application to a small-scale client/server system. While it took 1.23 minutes to locate nonindexed customer information in their 20 MB customer database files, it took only 5.6 seconds to find the same information in a remote database server.

Remember the differences in the architectures when you consider the file-oriented database approach. The tool must read each data record. When you use the client/server approach, the application simply sends a request to the database server, which then processes the request remotely within the engine of the database server and returns only the requested data (the result set). If you move to client/server from the world of file-oriented databases, you need to understand these differences.

Concurrency Control. Concurrency control is another issue when you use file-oriented database tools. The key issue here is that the chance for disaster increases with the user load. Let me explain.

File-oriented database tools handle concurrency control through the native file and record locking mechanisms that are already built into the network file server operating systems. Examples of file server operating systems include Novell's NetWare and Microsoft's Windows NT.

You may open database files for read-only access (the safest route), or clients can lock an entire database file to perform such operations as adding data to the file, or just lock a single record to perform edits. Multi-user versions of file-oriented databases know how to lock and unlock records and files from the client. The mechanisms the file servers offer are primitive in contrast to what modern database servers can do for concurrency control.

I find that the trick to building multi-user file-oriented database applications such as these is to leave the database alone whenever possible. Whenever I build multi-user database applications, my motto is: "Only bother the database when you need to read and write data, and only when it's absolutely necessary." When I must read and write data, I must also build logic into the application to assure that the record is not locked before you edit or update it, and the file is not locked before you add data. Neglect this step and you risk damaging the database file since other users could change the file at the same time. This can lead to "deadly embrace," which means two or more users go after the same portion of the file, and in doing so, corrupt the file. Most client/server database vendors provide protections against deadly embrace. I once watched a day's worth of data go after a deadly embrace (luckily the network administrator backed up the files nightly).

Modern file-oriented database-oriented development tools can auto-lock the database files. This means that they decide when and how to lock the database file, based on the operation you try to perform. You can get into trouble with this as well. Some tools allow you to set up the database engine to avoid problems. For example, you can set up a database to perform optimistic or pessimistic file and record locks. Despite the advances in multi-user file access, I always have problems with it when I build systems that support more than a few dozen users. Either they get locked out of the database when they need it most, or they corrupt the data at the most inconvenient times. The long and the short of it is: File-oriented databases were not built for multi-user access, and they don't provide the advanced concurrency control that most systems require. You can show me many instances where highly skilled users programmed their way around the limitations, but the rule still holds true.

Security. Since security is typically built into the services of the database server, most client/server developers don't have to think about it (and rarely do). Users must have a valid password and user ID to access the data on the database server. Database servers can also lock certain users out of particular rows, columns, or tables, at the discretion of the DBA. This provides granular security that lets the developer customize security around the requirements of the application.

File-oriented databases can provide similar security features, but not with the same granularity of the traditional client/server world. For example, almost no file-oriented database can provide security down to the row and column level.

The security issues lie, once again, with the architecture. Since the database is really a file, the only security features that exist are the file and record level security built into the file server operating system. For example, while you can keep people out of a file, the file server operating system knows nothing about a database, and thus does not know how to restrict access by rows and columns. Many file-oriented databases use a one table, one file approach. Thus, you can keep users out of tables by keeping them out of files.

Many file-oriented databases, such as Visual dBASE and Visual FoxPro, let developers encrypt tables. This does not keep people out of the database, but they see only scrambled data. Security is not a strong point of file-oriented databases.

Scalability. Actually, file-oriented databases do fairly well when they scale up. The bottleneck occurs at the shared database file access, and there lies the risk as well. Despite the use of file and record locking, as you reach a larger user load, you can count on blasting the file a few times a month.

The numbers of clients you can scale to depends on the database engine of your file-oriented database and the efficiency of your file server operating system. I've seen as many as 130 users share a single database file in an occasional-use client tracking application for a sales organization. I also saw the file corrupted on a regular basis. The organization threatened to add more users, and now it runs on client/server architecture and the same tool. More on how that works follows.

Using the Batch Trick

When you hear the term "batch," do you conjure up a vision of large main-frame computers? Batch can get you around some of the multi-user limitations and risks. The trick that I use when I build a file-oriented database application is to keep transaction tables (such as line item details for sales transactions) in their own file.

You manage these files by placing them on the local disks of the clients. Since each client runs its own copy of the transaction database, there is no risk of file corruption due to concurrent use, and the users never get locked out of their own copy of the file. If you really want to keep the files on the file server, you can easily name the files after the user's log-in ID name, or after the workstation number, or some other unique name. That works as long as one transaction file exists for each client who enters transactions. At some set time, usually during a nightly batch run, the transaction files update a master transaction file, then the administrator deletes them (see Figure 13-4).

The advantage of using this batch trick is that users won't get in the way of one another. You can have them access reference data (such as the client database) as read-only. Also, they update transaction files on the local client; performance increases since they don't have to send and receive files down a network. I found that some users prefer this design, since they can correct the data before they send it to the master file.

This trick's disadvantage is that you won't have the current transaction information available during the day. Thus, it's difficult to see how the sales staff performs on an hour-to-hour basis. If you want access to more timely data, consider true client/server.

If this sounds a bit like a kludge, you're right. However, sometimes the kludge solves a problem without the use of additional resources. Sometimes kludges are the best solutions.

Figure 13-4 *Updating the master transaction file.*

Transaction File — Update → Master Database File

Migration to Client/Server

As I already mentioned, most traditional file-oriented database tools also support the client/server model. These hybrid tools include (but are not limited to) Visual FoxPro and Microsoft Access from Microsoft, Visual dBASE and Paradox for Windows from Borland, and Lotus Approach. I'll talk in more detail about a few of these later.

The reality is that most traditional file-oriented database tools do client/server about as well as most traditional client/server tools. Keep in mind that most of these vendors also produce specialized client/server tools (e.g., Borland's Delphi and Microsoft's Visual Basic) and they share client/server tricks across tools.

Visual FoxPro, for instance, leverages Microsoft's Jet database engine and 32-bit ODBC, features that are also an integral part of Visual Basic. dBASE and Paradox both use Borland's Borland Database Engine (BDE) to access a database. BDE is also a part of Delphi, and there are many other examples.

These tools link to remote database servers which act as the database engine. A request that would normally go to a local database engine that communicates with a file, now generates SQL which gets sent to the server.

To the developers (and the users, for that matter), the way they create applications and use the database remains the same. The only difference that some may notice is better performance for large database queues, but slower response time for some transactions.

A few tools offer everything you need to move to client/server. Visual FoxPro, for example, provides Upgrade Wizard. Upgrade Wizard is a tool that automatically migrates a file-oriented database to a true database server (see Figure 13-5, and the description below). The translation of file names to table names is automatic, as is the creation of indexes. I tested this with the latest release of FoxPro, and successfully sent one of my existing applications to client/server without doing anything more than answer a few questions for Upgrade Wizard. Other tools have similar features, or you can purchase third-party utilities that solve the same problems.

WHEN TO USE WHAT MODEL

So what will it be, database-oriented or client/server? You should consider the file-oriented DBMS architecture if your application's requirements do *not* include the following needs:

- Highly granular security (row level, column level, etc.)
- On-line transaction processing (OLTP) capabilities, and access to the data in real time
- Advanced concurrency control
- Logging, roll-back/roll-forward recovery

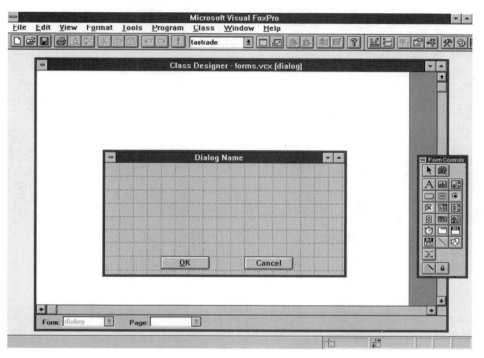

Figure 13-5 *Visual FoxPro.*

- High-speed application processing
- Support for more than fifty users—now or in the future
- Support for automated recovery operations
- An application processing load shift to a shared processor (e.g., application server or database server)

As developers, we must learn to provide solutions that offer the best value. File-oriented architecture is still a good fit for small work-group applications—applications that don't require full-blown database servers for database processing.

Features

Just like specialized client/server development tools, file-oriented database development tools provide certain features and subsystems. The common features of most file-oriented tools are object-oriented development, scripting and programming languages, and application generators.

OBJECT-ORIENTED DEVELOPMENT

Although most file-oriented database development tools existed well before the object-oriented revolution, most file-oriented development tools now support the object-oriented development model. Typically they are hybrid tools that support both legacy structured applications and newer object-oriented applications.

For example, Visual FoxPro supports traditional FoxPro applications, which means you can run applications created with the old MS-DOS versions of FoxPro or FoxBase. However, Visual FoxPro also supports the event-driven world of Windows development, meaning it can open and close windows, and offer developers GUI interface development tools.

PROGRAMMING LANGUAGE

All file-oriented database tools provide some sort of programming or scripting language. The type of language and its capabilities are a function of the tool you use. Visual dBASE, for example, provides a Pascal-like programming language that lets developers take complete control of an application. Visual FoxPro uses a variation on dBASE, and Microsoft Access uses Visual Basic's native VBA.

APPLICATION GENERATORS

"Why start from scratch?" is what I always say. Most modern file-oriented database tools provide an application generation facility. With these subsystems, the developer answers a few questions, visually creates the database, then generates a basic application. Visual FoxPro is a "Pro" at this, using the famous Microsoft Wizard system to create base applications. Developers can use the application as is, or modify the application to meet the exact requirements.

File-Oriented Database Tools

Okay, so what's out there? There are still many file-oriented database tools available today. I do have my favorites, and they are Visual FoxPro, Access, and Lotus Approach. Before we end this chapter and move on to client/server issues, let's look at a few file-oriented database tools.

VISUAL FOXPRO

Visual FoxPro is today's menu special at Microsoft for file-oriented database tools, and it's one of my favorites (see Figure 13-6). The reason I like FoxPro is

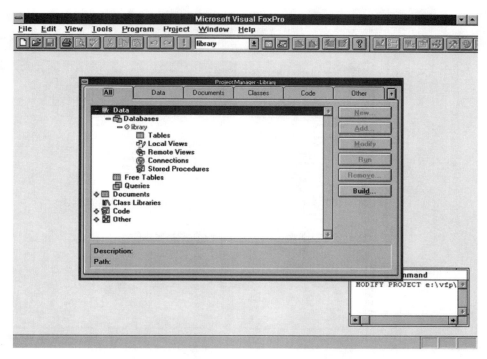

Figure 13-6 *Visual FoxPro supports the object-oriented development model.*

twofold: First is Microsoft's support for the object-oriented development model. Second is the tool's ability to switch from file-oriented to client/server, and then back again.

You build a FoxPro application the same as if you go client/server or file-oriented. You have to deal with four main components: the project manager, the database designer, the visual class designer, and the forms designer.

The project manager gives the developer complete control of an application. An application is really a collection of files, documents, objects, and database files. The project manager gives the developer access to all these application components within a visual hierarchy that the developer can expand to review detail, or collapse to look at the application from a higher level.

The database designer (see Figure 13-7) is actually a mini-CASE tool that exists inside FoxPro. Developers can display all tables, views, and relationships that make up the physical database design. They can also create a physical database schema using this same interface, and the tool offers advanced features such as the ability to link tables by dragging and dropping them in the tool.

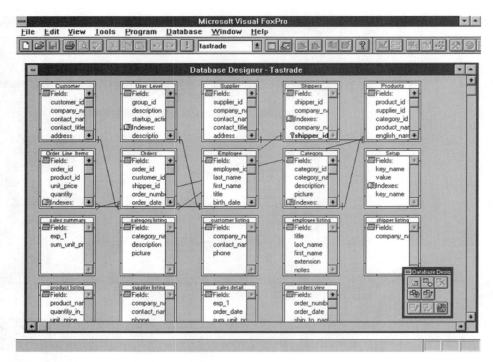

Figure 13-7 *FoxPro Database Designer.*

Unlike other file-oriented database tools—but consistent with modern, specialized client/server tools—Visual FoxPro provides a repository. The repository, known as the database container, contains all related tables, local views, remote views, and connections. Upon opening a database container, all connections for that database become active (local views, remote views, stored procedures, tables, and relationships).

Using the visual class designer, developers define custom classes by building their own properties and methods into the application. Developers use this tool to create classes that become available for reuse throughout the application. To use a prebuilt visual class on a form, developers select the Choose Class icon to get at the visual class. Classes are defined through the dBASE-like FoxPro programming language.

The visual forms designer is a true GUI interface development tool that provides all standard Windows 95 controls. Developers may align objects using a toolbar, and they can bind objects and data to controls using FoxPro's environment designer. As with the interface designers of specialized client/server tools, developers can build forms by dragging and dropping fields and controls onto the form.

Developers can access remote databases as local file databases using persistent application-level connections. Developers establish these connections by creating a remote view on the FoxPro database container. When creating a particular connection, the developers use a subsystem known as the connection designer. The connection, which really exists in a database, provides information to the application for connection to the remote database server. As an example, for each connection, developers can specify database, user ID, password, etc.

FoxPro provides an impressive array of Wizards as well, including a Fox Wizard to help developers create data-entry forms for a single table, or a one-to-many form. There is also a Report Wizard, Label Wizard, Graph Wizard, Mail Merge Wizard, and Setup Wizard.

As I mentioned earlier in the chapter, FoxPro takes you to client/server with just a click of a button. The Upsizing Wizard lets developers create database server versions of a Visual FoxPro database, thus saving the time it would take to do the migration by hand.

LOTUS APPROACH

With FoxPro, as well as Visual dBASE and Paradox, I'm talking about full-blown file-oriented databases that work just as well for application development as they do for personal database system. However, there is a class of tools that simply provide small database management systems, primarily for single-user office automation applications. They can also do application development if you really need them to. The best examples are Lotus Approach from Lotus, and Access from Microsoft. Let's take a quick look at these products.

Lotus Approach (see Figure 13-8) is not aimed at the application development market, but at the nontechnical business user. Approach provides an efficient tool to manage small single-user databases, and to generate basic applications. Lotus Approach also allows developers to share data via a shared database file, or even with remote databases services that are accessible through ODBC and native drivers.

Approach provides the proprietary LotusScript for application development, along with built-in security that restricts access to data by users and groups. There are also primitive OLAP capabilities (such as the use of cross-tab reports and top-value filters). You can get all this for about $100.

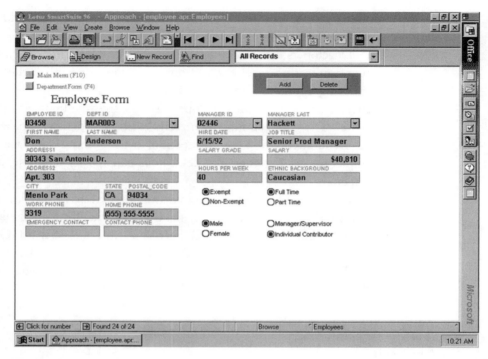

Figure 13-8 *Approach.*

MICROSOFT ACCESS

Access is a personal DBMS, and is part of the popular Microsoft Office Suite of products. Access offers advanced features for its small price tag (around $300, if purchased by itself). The product supports 32-bit multi-threading, and a database design facility that was the benchmark for many specialized client/server development tools available today.

Access provides handy features such as the Table Analyzer Wizard that walks the user or developer through the process of designing and deploying a database (see Figure 13-9). For example, this Wizard can automatically create a multi-table database and keys from a flat file.

You will find advanced reporting and query tools as well, such as a Filter by Selection button and a Filter by Form. Access also works with the native Windows 95 briefcase system to synchronize data as it moves from one computer to another. The database design facility of Access is as sophisticated as a tool costing six times as much (see Figure 13-10).

Access uses Visual Basic's VBA. In addition, you can use ActiveX components when you create an application and program Access to act as an

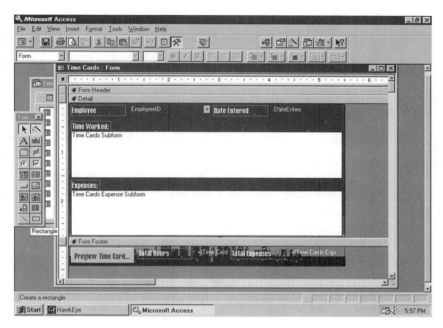

Figure 13-9 *Access.*

Figure 13-10 *Access Database Design Feature.*

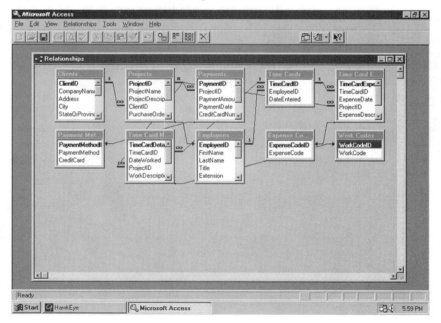

OLE Automation Server, or as a client. Database server access is through ODBC, or you can use the Access database file format in single- or multi-user configurations.

Future of Databases and Files

If you read between the lines in this chapter, you may ask yourself: Do file-oriented database tools have a future? Sure they do. I'll tell you why.

While client/server offers an application development solution for high-end database applications, it will cost you a pretty penny to build these applications. Consider the cost of the network, development time, tools, and the database server. File-oriented applications can be built for about half the cost, depending on what you want to do. The tools are inexpensive (around $500), and there is no need for a remote database server. The tradeoff is performance, scalability, security, and concurrency control. In other words, for small work-group class applications with a few users, file-oriented database tools work just fine.

I do advise that you select a tool that has some sort of migration path to client/server. This will give you a place to run as the user load increases, or as application requirements change. If you build your application in a file-oriented tool that does not do client/server, you could end up redeveloping the application with another tool.

You will continue to see file-oriented database tools for use with single-user database applications. For these applications, Access and Approach work fine, and they'll only set you back a few hundred bucks. As an added benefit, you can take these applications to client/server as well when the need arises. I like to keep my options open.

Reporting and Decision Support Tools

Reporting tools have been around since databases first showed up on mainframe computers. They give developers and end-users the power to turn data into information. Reporting tools may create accounts receivable reports, sales reports, end-of-year reports, or reports to base critical business decisions on.

Today's client/server-enabled reporting tools can reach from clients to servers to extract data. Their GUIs put a friendly face on modern reporting tools. Their features include the ability to generate desktop publishing-quality reports and graphs for the screen, a printer, or a Web server.

Although most client/server developers don't get very excited about reporting tools anymore, they are an essential part of most client/server applications. What's more, they are one of the few tools that are easy enough for nontechnical end-users to drive. In this chapter I'll take a quick look at the technology behind client/server reporting tools. We'll also look at the next generation of reporting tools that support traditional reporting requirements and on-line analytical processing (OLAP).

Reporting-Tool Basics

Reporting tools perform a few basic functions. First, they provide the end-users or developers with an easy-to-use user interface that lets them select data from a database server. They can choose ways to sort the data, and select data using criteria (e.g., WHERE SALES > 10000). Report developers may also act on the data further through simple and complex calculations.

Typical reporting tools know about the physical database schema, and will guide the user through the column selection criteria by providing a menu of available columns, as well as the data type of the column (numeric, character, BLOB, etc.), and how to act on a data type. The tools then prompt the user to enter the sort order, and guide them through selection of the criteria.

Second, reporting tools assemble the SQL statements behind the scenes. Since the tool generates the SQL, the developer or user doesn't need to know SQL. Once the SQL statement is complete, the tool sends it to the target database where the request is processed.

Finally, the reporting tool receives and processes the result set returned from the database server. The reporting tool formats the data, and displays an image on the client, or sends the report directly to the printer.

Of course, this description is very simplistic. Most of today's reporting tools go well beyond these basic capabilities, each offering features to set themselves apart from the competition, and they often operate in their own proprietary way. For example, some reporting tools (such as Crystal Reports from Seagate) allow developers to snap-in reports as ActiveX components. Others automatically exchange data with spreadsheets and word processing documents. Still other reporting tools provide sophisticated programming languages to create turnkey applications. I'll cover this in more detail later.

Moving to On-Line Analytical Processing

Although reporting tools have enjoyed a stable market presence for the last decade, the use of on-line analytical processing (OLAP) tools have given the reporting tool vendors another area of growth. As you may remember from Chapters 1 and 8, OLAP tools are designed to give end-users the ability to slice and dice their way through data, morphing the data into information to make correct business decisions (see Figure 14-1). OLAP is an example of a decision support system (DSS).

So what's the difference between traditional SQL reporting tools and OLAP? A few things, but they become more alike as the months pass. Tradi-

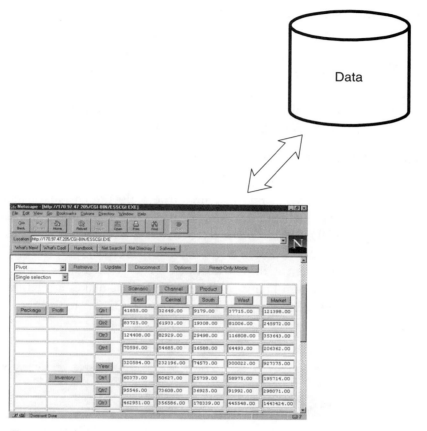

Figure 14-1 *OLAP.*

tional relational reporting tools provide general-purpose reporting services and are usually linked to a two-dimensional relational database. OLAP tools are built from the ground up for decision support activities, but they still provide many traditional reporting capabilities. Also, OLAP tools are built to use multi-dimensional databases (known as multi-dimensional OLAP, or MOLAP), or they can emulate a multi-dimensional database using a relational database (relational OLAP, or ROLAP). While general purpose SQL reporting tools send reports directly to the screen or to paper, OLAP tools are interactive. This lets end-users drill through the data to locate and make sense of information. OLAP tools have a tendency to provide more powerful calculation functions, with an ability to aggregate data, calculate penetration, contribution, period comparisons, ranking, and nonaggregatable metrics. As with anything client/server, the types of tools, and capabilities vary greatly.

MULTI-DIMENSIONAL ON-LINE ANALYTICAL PROCESSING

MOLAP is traditional OLAP, meaning that OLAP tools (such as IQ/Vision from IQ Software) are connected to a true multi-dimensional database (such as Red Brick or Essbase). They let the users move through the data easily, perform such operations as aggregation, statistical functions, and visual depiction of the data, which are all built into the tool (see Figure 14-2). All of this is interactive. Traditional reporting tools don't have these capabilities.

RELATIONAL ON-LINE ANALYTICAL PROCESSING

ROLAP takes a more practical approach to OLAP. Rather than make the end-users create and maintain a true multi-dimensional database, they can use any relational database (e.g., Sybase, Oracle, Informix). ROLAP can do this since ROLAP tools make relational databases appear multi-dimensional by changing the models in-flight to the client (see Figure 14-3). This is usually done on the client within a subsystem of the tool. For example, PowerPlay provides a subsystem known as Transformer that makes a relational database appear as multi-dimensional. Therefore, the OLAP tool links to relational data, but

Figure 14-2 *Essbase for the Web.*

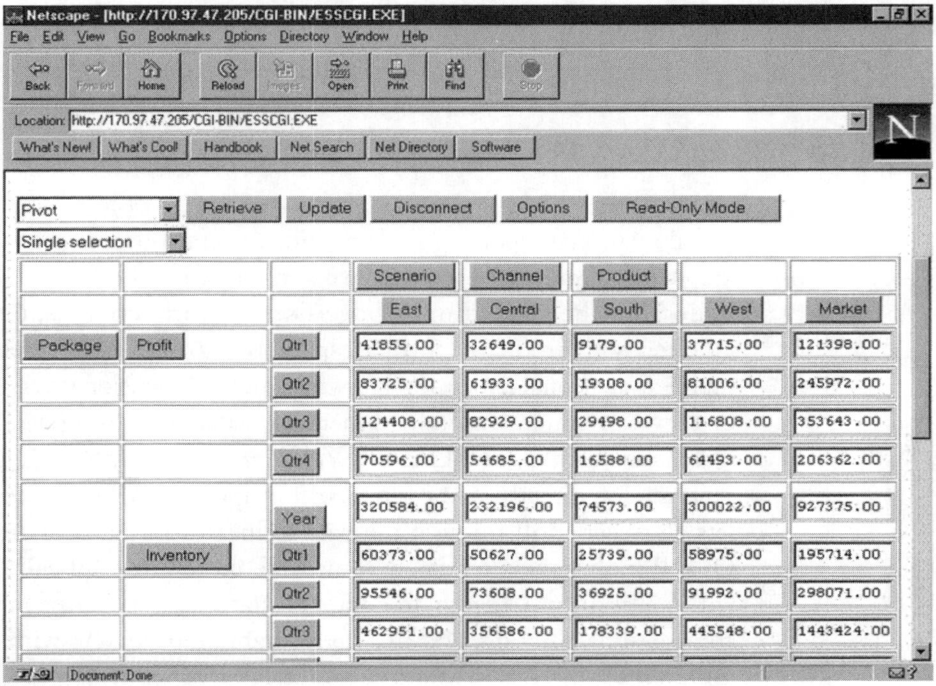

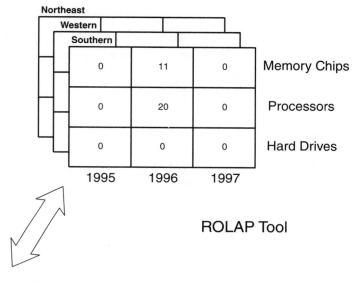

ROLAP Tool

Year	Region	Item	Sales (Thousands)
1996	Southern	Processors	20
1995	Northeast	Hard Drives	10
1997	Western	Hard Drives	22
1996	Western	Memory Chips	30
1995	Northeast	Processors	45
1995	Western	Hard Drives	5
1996	Southern	Memory Chips	11

Relational
Database

Figure 14-3 *ROLAP.*

remaps the data to multi-dimensional domains for the purpose of OLAP. If you think there is a performance penalty to pay, there is. However, I have not found it to be much of a problem.

Examples of ROLAP tools include PowerPlay from Cognos (described in detail later in this chapter), and Business Objects from Business Objects. These tools allow developers to map dimensions from a relational database. End-users use these dimensions to surf through the data. ROLAP tools convert the requests to SQL, which are then sent to the database server to return the data as dimensions. The best of both worlds.

RELATIONAL VERSUS MULTI-DIMENSIONAL ON-LINE ANALYTICAL PROCESSING

The tradeoff of ROLAP versus MOLAP is capabilities for money. Since MOLAP uses specialized technology (such as multi-dimensional database technology), the buy-in is heavy. Count on a million or more dollars as the admission price. Generally, MOLAP exists in an environment where multi-dimensional data warehouses (or data marts) already exist. What's more, multi-dimensional databases don't work with other non-OLAP front-ends. Therefore, you can't hook other front-end tools to multi-dimensional databases as easily as relational databases.

The pro-MOLAP crowd promotes the fact that relational databases don't provide the end-user with the performance or flexibility of true (real cube) multi-dimensional databases. I'm a fan of deploying data warehousing with relational databases since they keep my options open for simple data warehousing applications. I can do many things with relational databases, and only a few things with multi-dimensional. Consider MOLAP for high-end single-user data warehouses, ROLAP for everything else.

ROLAP tools grew naturally out of traditional reporting tools, and provide lower-cost alternatives to true MOLAP. They require less setup time, and can work with existing relational databases. MOLAP requires that someone purchase and integrate a multi-dimensional database (such as Red Brick from Red Brick, or Essbase from Arbor). These ROLAP tools provide the best of both worlds. Unless you really need to slice and dice data on a continuous basis, I would say that ROLAP is the way to go for general-purpose OLAP.

Features

Although these tools vary widely in features and functions, there are a few features which I find common to most of the tools. They include layers, automatic SQL, formatting and fonts, tool integration, and development capabilities.

LAYERS

Layers provide developers with the ability to create a custom universe that puts another logical layer between the physical database schema and the end-user. Layers solve a lot of usability issues, and protect the users from themselves.

We employ layers in reporting tools to give end-users the means to access the data as they see the business (see Figure 14-4). For example, rather than display five tables that relate to sales information, with layers, developers can create one logical access layer known as sales. End-users will find it easier to deal with a single sales database than with five cryptic tables. What's more, you can rename columns with more meaningful names, and apply business rules in a layer. Reporting-tool vendors call layers different things. For instance, Business Objects (the reporting tool, not the concept) calls layers 'universes.'

Layers also allow you to create different layers for different users. For example, I can create a very high-level layer with just a few groupings of data for a CIO of a company, and I can create layers with more granular detail for those in on-the-line positions. Remember, the database remains the same. The layer is placed on top of the database by the reporting tool.

Layers also protect users from themselves. For example, if reporting tools that talk directly to relational tables are too confusing, you'll find that users will constantly generate erroneous reports. Typically, they do not use the tables and relationships correctly. The results are reports that don't reflect reality, which become the basis for bad decisions. Using layers, developers can establish the way in which users access the data, and thus reduce the chance of pilot error. SQL is a tricky language, and it's easy to make mistakes if you're not careful.

Figure 14-4 *Using Layers.*

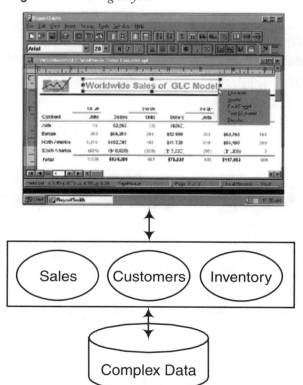

AUTOMATIC SQL

The automatic structured query language (SQL) feature of reporting tools simply means that the tool generates the SQL on behalf of the end-user. The reporting tool prompts the user for table and column selections, as well as criteria such as if TAX_RATE > .20, and sort order.

Using this information, the reporting tool generates the SQL automatically. Many tools (such as Esperant from Software AG) even allow you to view the SQL as it's generated and edit the SQL statement before sending it to the database server (see Figure 14-5).

Database server connectivity is the same as specialized client/server tools. The reporting tools link to the database server using native database drivers, or through ODBC.

PUBLISHING

Data turned into information can also be turned into attractive information. Most reporting tools provide publishing capabilities, including the ability to set fonts, color, borders, headers, and footers. This allows the end-user to prepare

Figure 14-5 *Esperant.*

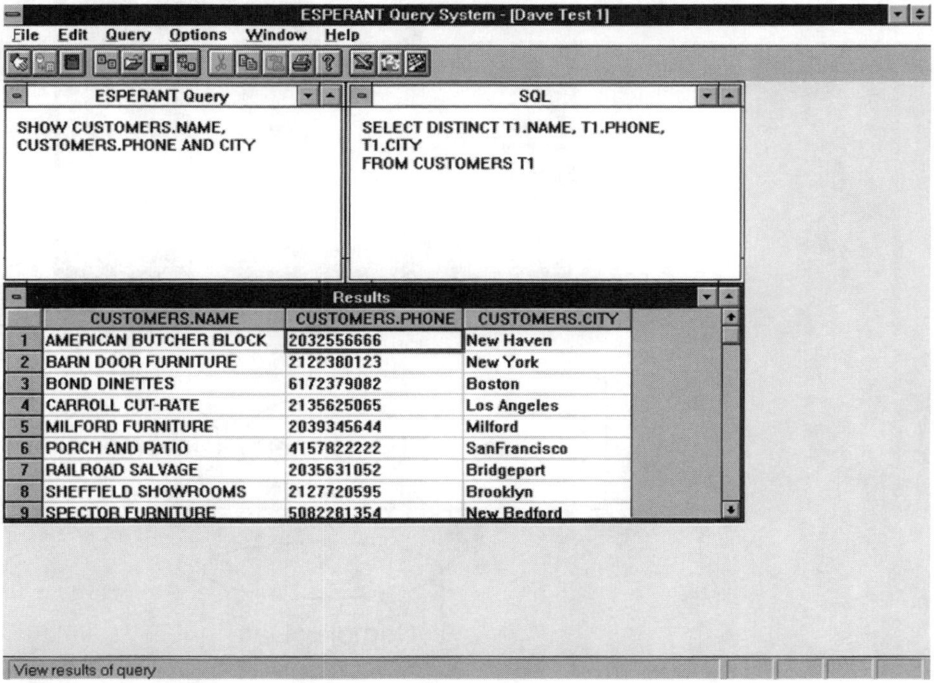

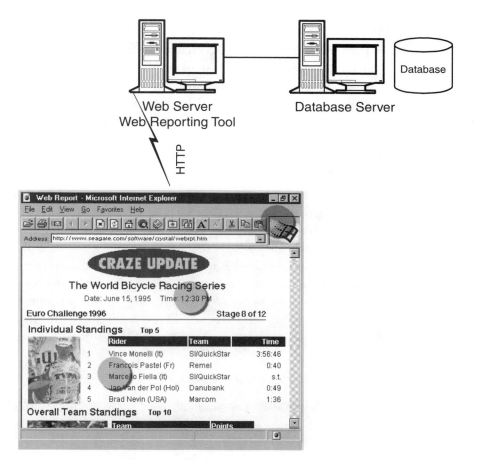

Figure 14-6 *Generating reports to the Web.*

formal live data reports without losing download time to a word processor or a desktop publishing package.

Today, publishing also means sending reports to the Web (see sidebar later in this chapter). Reporting tools not only generate reports to the screen and papers, but can generate custom HTML for use on a Web server. This provides report developers with the ability to distribute a report as a Web page (see Figure 14-6), accessible by anyone with a Web browser. For example, I'm working with a sales organization that generates weekly sales reports directly to its Web server. This allows the sales staff to view the report at any time, local or remote, without wasting paper (they always have the option to print). If you distribute a lot of paper now, I recommend that you look at doing this. Typically, this is an intranet application.

CHARTS AND GRAPHS

If you've heard the old saying that a picture is worth a thousand words, then you know why it makes sense to display data as charts and graphs. Report developers simply let the reporting tool know what data points need to be included in the graph or chart. Select a chart type, and generate the chart using live data to the printer or screen (see Figure 14-7).

TOOL INTEGRATION

Although many development tools such as PowerBuilder include reporting tools, most development environments bundle third-party tools (such as Delphi's ReportSmith, and Visual Basic Crystal Reports). The idea is that developers build reports to work with applications they develop using specialized development tools, then they simply snap those reports into the application.

While some reporting tools operate independently from the client/server application (albeit callable from an application through some sort of process-to-process link), a few reporting tools can generate components that integrate seamlessly into the application. These reports exist within applications as ActiveX components, or are accessible as OLE automation servers.

Figure 14-7 *Charts and Graphs.*

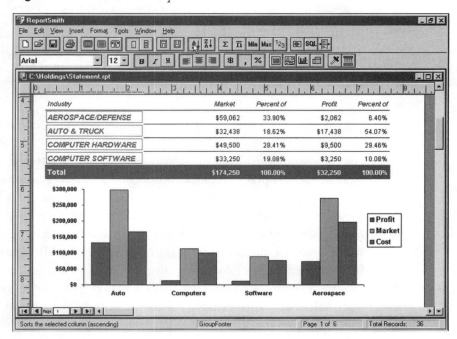

DEVELOPMENT CAPABILITIES

Finally, many reporting tools provide programming capabilities. This does not mean you can create complex client/server applications. That would be the reason specialized client/server application development tools exist. However, you can create reports that prompt the user for information (e.g., data to search for in the database) and act upon the data returned from the database server. Like specialized client/server tools, these are generally easy to use, but proprietary 4GL or macro languages.

Reporting Products

So, what client/server reporting tools are out there? Many reporting tools run on Unix, Macs, mainframes, and PCs, but I have a few favorites for client/server. ReportSmith (from Borland) and Crystal Reports (from Seagate) are my top two.

REPORTSMITH

ReportSmith is a simple, general-purpose query and reporting tool that lets both developers and end-users work directly with live data (see Figure 14-8). ReportSmith can display the reports visually (WYSIWYG) on the screen, or send the report to a printer. Not only does ReportSmith display live data in reports, it can also display live data as you create the report. ReportSmith supports cross-tabs reports, which means report developers and end-users can layer multiple rows and columns, as well as edit or pivot the data (if required).

ReportSmith allows you to do almost anything with your report. Report-Smith can even create reports that contain more than one report format. For instance, you can show columns in form reports, multiple cross-tabs, or any combination of the two. You can calculate derived fields and summary values in a report, and report developers can aggregate functions (e.g., sum, average, minimum, maximum, count, first, and last). What's more, you can sort the data in any order, by value or custom group specifications.

ReportSmith can create a report using multiple heterogeneous databases, which allows the report developer to create Master/Detail type reports. For instance, you can get the master information out of the customer database that resides on a Sybase server, and the detail sales information out of the sales database that resides on an Oracle server.

To enhance performance, ReportSmith provides a true draft mode to build and edit reports using only a subset of the database, which increases

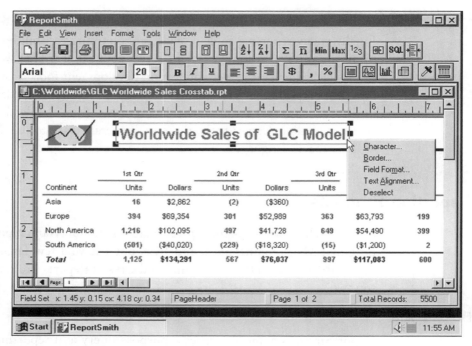

Figure 14-8 *ReportSmith.*

performance. ReportSmith offers local and server processing objects, allowing report developers to tune the report for better client/server performance. You'll also find that ReportSmith can create most types of charts and graphs, including bar charts, line charts, and pie charts.

ReportSmith offers limited development capabilities as well, and includes an embedded macro language that supports OLE and Dynamic Data Exchange. This provides seamless integration with other client/server development tools such as Visual Basic, PowerBuilder, and Delphi (ReportSmith comes with Delphi). ReportSmith report developers can create user-interface procedures, or access DLLs to extend the capabilities of the tools. ReportSmith supports most popular databases such as Oracle, Sybase, Informix, DB2, or file-oriented databases using dBASE and Paradox formats. If all else fails, you can access data through ODBC.

CRYSTAL REPORTS

Crystal Reports (see Figure 14-9) is not only a competent development environment, it has Microsoft behind the product. Like ReportSmith, Crystal Reports visually creates all kinds of reports for display to the screen or printer.

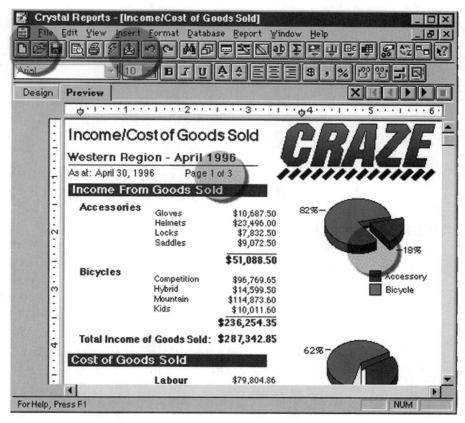

Figure 14-9 *Crystal Reports.*

Crystal Reports gives report developers the ability to create subreports, multiple detail-section reports, form-style reports, mail-merge reports, conditional report, multiple summary cross-tabs reports, and Web-ready reports (see sidebar). The subreport capability lets report developers create different views of data in one report for convenient viewing. Thus the report developer need not create multiple reports to solve the same problem.

Crystal Info Brings Three-Tier to Reporting Tools

If you think reporting tools are strictly two-tier, you haven't seen Crystal Info. Crystal Info is a three-tier reporting system that gives developers the ability to access powerful reports without taxing the clients or the network.

Unlike traditional two-tier client/server reporting, Crystal Info publishes information in folders. The folders exist in a middle tier, and are sharable among workgroups of users. The clients communicate with the middle tier, which, in turn, communicates with the database server for the information. The benefit with this architecture is the ability to support a large number of users, and the ability to share business logic on a central server.

One of Crystal Reports' best features is the ability to export reports to over twenty formats (including HTML). As an option, Crystal Reports can even send reports to end-users automatically via E-mail. Crystal Reports can link to most relational databases through ODBC.

Crystal Reports also provides development capabilities, allowing report developers to create advanced reports and then integrate them with Windows-based client/server tools as an ActiveX component. Crystal Reports supports VBX, MFC (Microsoft Foundation Classes), VCL and NewEra Controls and class libraries. They are included with Crystal Reports. Using these mechanisms, the application invokes the Crystal Report engine. Visual Basic and Visual C++ (as well as many other client/server development products) ship with Crystal Reports. There is no royalty to distribute reports.

Reporting Tools and On-Line Analytical Processing for the Web

All reporting tools have some sort of strategy, or actual products to deploy reports to intranets. The general idea is to generate HTML for storage on a Web server rather than send the report to the screen or printer. However, a few reporting tools are more sophisticated, such as OLAP tools which must be interactive. Some, such as Focus from Information Builders Inc. (IBI), use a Java front-end from their reporting tools.

WebLAP

The advantage of using the intranet to deploy OLAP is that there is no client software. Therefore it's just a matter of accessing the OLAP capabilities through a Web browser (such as Explorer or Netscape). This places the power of OLAP where it really belongs—with anyone who needs to access information to make business decisions. In other words, the intranet and OLAP bring the power to the people.

A good example of the marriage of OLAP and the Web is DSSWeb from Micro Strategy. DSSWeb lets Web users slice and dice their way through data using a standard Web interface (see Figure 14-10). DSSWeb performs traditional OLAP calculations such as penetration, contribution, this period/last period comparisons, ranking, and nonaggregatable metrics. DSSWeb also lets users view data in several formats, including maps, grids, charts, and graphs.

As with any other OLAP tool, DSSWeb lets you drill down on reports to find additional details. Or you can set up the OLAP reports to auto-prompt for filters to find new data as it's needed.

DSSWeb is a Web server-based application that uses the ROLAP model. This means it runs in the same machine as the Web server, and can pump HTML down to the DSSWeb clients through the CGI Web server

Figure 14-10 *DSSWeb.*

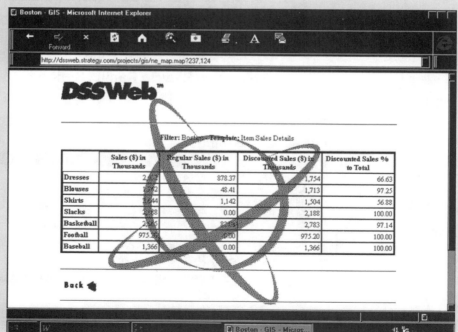

API (more on CGI in Chapter 23). DSSWeb gets at relational databases using 32-bit ODBC. What's more, DSSWeb provides remote administration capabilities that give administrators the power to manage report DSS Web sites anywhere in the intranet or Internet.

Crystal Web Reporting

A good example of an intranet-ready traditional reporting tool is Crystal Reports. With its latest release, Crystal Reports can generate reports as HTML documents for use on Web servers (see Figure 14-11). This is another convenient mechanism to deploy reports to many end-users, providing access through Web browsers.

Figure 14-11 *Cyrstal Reports Web.*

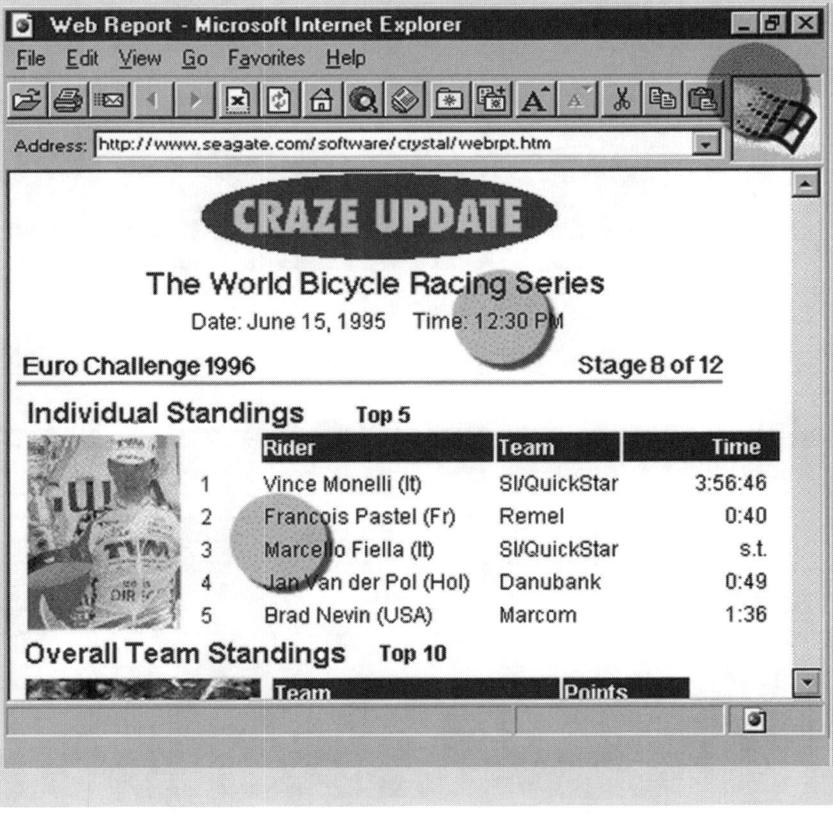

As an option, report developers can configure Crystal Reports to automatically generate predefined reports on the Web. So, at a predetermined date and time, the report can refresh itself with new data, generate itself on the Web server, and make the report available to anyone with a browser.

Crystal Reports also provides a Web activity reporting tool that lets the Web master view the Web server activity logs through a formatted report. This is helpful for Web server management, but I would not buy Crystal Reports specifically for that purpose.

With Crystal Reports, end-users can select reports from an HTML page, and then automatically generate that report for viewing and printing from their Web browsers. This means that any number of users will have access to useful corporate information, without having to install and configure Crystal Reports or any other reporting tool. That's the power of the intranet.

PowerPlay

Now that we have covered general-purpose reporting tools, let's look at an OLAP tool to balance things out. One of the better general-purpose OLAP tools available is PowerPlay from Cognos (see Figure 14-12).

I like PowerPlay for several reasons: First, it's relatively inexpensive compared to the other OLAP products. Second, it supports ROLAP.

PowerPlay is a suite of four programs that give report developers the ability to create OLAP and non-OLAP reports and graphs. The programs are PowerPlay Explorer, PowerPlay Reporter, PowerPlay Transformer, Cognos Portfolio, and Cognos Scheduler.

PowerPlay Explorer provides end-users with the ability to point and click their way through the data using an easy-to-follow interface. Transformer provides the virtual cube capability of the tool (ROLAP) by automatically transforming two-dimensional relational data into multi-dimensional data for use by Explorer or Reporter. Portfolio organizes PowerPlay reports using interactive briefing books, accessible by the report users.

Reporter is the core of PowerPlay, providing report developers with the ability to build interactive and automated reports in any number of formats

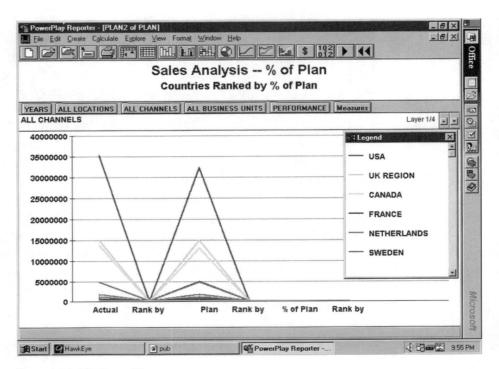

Figure 14-12 *PowerPlay.*

(including cross-tab, columns, and free form). As an option, you can tell Reporter to use "Visual data depiction." This means you can generate pie, line, and bar charts, as well as simple point and correlation graphs.

Reporter sifts through the database and result set, selecting only the data you need to work with. After submitting the database query, the developer can build ad hoc calculations, as well as build data filters and sort the data.

With Reporter, developers can create reports by dragging and dropping data elements from the multi-dimensional virtual cube. This view is called the category tree. All reports include a dimension line that depicts the available dimensions, and the level of detail each dimension can show.

PowerPlay reports are true OLAP in that they are interactive. This allows report users to drill down to more detail by simply double-clicking on a category button on the report. To create a chart or graph, click on a button at the top of the PowerPlay window. PowerPlay is classic OLAP.

Should You Use a Third-Party Reporting Tool?

Many of you already use the reporting tools built into specialized client/server development tools (such as PowerBuilder). The question is: Should you use a third-party reporting tool? That's an easy one.

Most specialized client/server development tools work with the most popular third-party development tools, but most bundle reporting tools. Unlike PowerBuilder (where the reporting tool is native to the development tool), most of these bundled reporting tools are decoupled from the main development environment. For example, Visual Basic bundles Crystal Reports, and Delphi comes with ReportSmith. Most 3GL tools don't come with reporting tools at all, nor do Smalltalk tools.

My advice is to ignore the bundling (there is usually a reason they throw it in), and evaluate as many reporting tools as possible on their own merits. For instance, ReportSmith could be a good fit for your Visual Basic application, and Crystal Reports may be a better fit than Report-Smith for your Delphi application. It really depends on the requirements of the application. Sometimes you may need to use more than one reporting tool.

For example, on a two-tier client/server application using Power-Builder, I found that the PowerBuilder reporting subsystem lacked many of the capabilities my clients required. Thus we created all the reports using Crystal Reports. However, I found that while Crystal Reports works well for application-driven reports, it lacks some features we needed in an ad hoc reporting tool. Therefore, we selected Business Objects as our ad hoc reporting tool for use by the end-user. I find that this mixing and matching of reporting tools is typical when using specialized client/server development.

As with specialized client/server development tools, you should create a table to help select your reporting tool. Place your application requirements down one column (bar charts, colors, real time, custom programming, etc.), and the tools across the top. Rank each tool for its ability to meet the requirements (I usually use 1-10). Add up the score and you have your tool. If it's close and one tool comes bundled with your development environment, you can use that as a tie breaker.

"Reporting from Washington, D.C."

Reporting tools are one of the few things in client/server that seem to work consistently. Since they use a simple model and they are relatively mature, I'm rarely disappointed by reporting tools, and they keep getting better.

Things we need to work on include tighter integration with development tools, and better support for OLAP in traditional reporting tools. It would also be nice to see reporting tools driven by the dynamic Java technology, as well as the traditional HTML, CGI, and HTTP for Web-enabled reporting applications (see Chapter 23). We are still honeymooning with the Web, and we'll see these capabilities in the near future.

The real challenge is to create reporting tools that are both sophisticated enough to handle the most complex reporting jobs, and simple enough for nontechnical end-users. We are not there yet, but we are moving quickly.

Computer-Aided Software Engineering Tools and Client/Server

In Chapter 7 I talked (briefly) about software design and development, and described a few of the most popular object-oriented analysis and design (OOA/OOD) methodologies. Although these methodologies describe what to do, and sometimes how to do it, you need CASE tools to really make OOA/OOD happen—CASE tools that work with your client/server development tool of choice.

CASE (computer-aided software engineering) technology promises to make software design and development "easy." While CASE is not the "silver bullet" the CASE vendors promoted in the late '80s, today CASE provides good value for application architects. CASE knows how to communicate with most popular databases and client/server application development tools. I would not consider taking on any but the most simplistic client/server development projects without arming myself with some sort of CASE tool.

In this chapter, let's take some of the mystery out of CASE, and look at what CASE tools are, what they say they do, and what you can really do with them. I'll take you through a few of my favorite CASE products and let you know how well they work with other client/server components such as the application development tools and databases.

Hype versus Reality

CASE technology is hype versus reality. In the early days of CASE, vendors promoted this new technology as a means to replace application developers. The idea was that application designers could quickly design the application with these tools, press a button, and the application would appear right before their eyes. You don't know how many times I was called into the offices of MIS executives to be asked why we were not a part of this "revolution" that could potentially save millions of dollars and reduce the application development backlog.

The hype, as it always does, eventually leads to reality, but development organizations ran to CASE in droves. CASE tools sold for as much as $100,000 per tool, and required workstations that cost $10,000 and up to run. They were not user-friendly, and you could count on a month of training before application architects (more popularly known as analysts at the time) could get up to speed with the tool.

As you may guess, the CASE technology of the time did not live up to the hype. Development organizations tossed out CASE tools like candy-bar wrappers. CASE took a lashing from the press, and everyone declared CASE dead. Vendors renamed products to distance themselves from CASE, and even magazines with CASE in their names dropped the term quickly. Was CASE dead?

Putting Too Much Faith in CASE

In the late 1980s, CASE was making a big splash. CASE was poised to remove application development backlogs and remove the developer from the payroll. Or at least that's what most of the Fortune 500 (including an organization that I was working for at that time) believed.

I was in meeting after meeting, viewing slide presentations about this "magic" technology, and I spent my days reading articles in the trades on the joys of CASE. Was this really a revolution?

Not even close. While CASE tools did provide a way to automate some of the analysis and design work we were doing, I found that the code generation was a joke and the database schema generation better left to the humans. The end result was the use of a $100,000 tool as nothing more than a glorified paint program. CASE was considered a failure and a few people even lost their jobs over it.

The real failure was not CASE but our inability to distinguish hype from real capabilities and potential from the quick fix. CASE was not a failure but simply a technology that needed a few years to mature. Still stinging from the letdown in years gone by, both CASE vendors (those that survived) and application architects are viewing CASE for what it is: Another tool that assists the application architect, developer and DBA in their system design and development activities.

I don't work for that company anymore but I'm sure whatever is the "hot & hyped" technology, they'll consider it to be the next magic bullet. I've yet to find the magic bullet of software development. If you find it, send me an e-mail.

Computer-Aided Software Engineering Comes Back

Despite the early failings of CASE technology, interest in CASE began to re-emerge at the beginning of the client/server revolution (see Preface). Client/server tools are based in the object-oriented development model. The OO model required a different design approach and new methodologies were created to support object-oriented development (see Chapter 7 for a short description of the most popular OOA/OOD methodologies). With the advent of client/server databases, developers and application architects sought new ways to design and deploy relational databases that would let them move directly from the model to the physical database.

Considering what I just said, there was a need for a tool set that could handle complex object-oriented application design using the state of the art in object-oriented analysis and design methodologies. There was also a need for tools that could do logical and physical relational database design (see Chapter 4). CASE technology filled that need, and the object and client/server revolutions put CASE back on the developer's radarscope.

Methodology Automation

Today, CASE tools provide good value for most client/server development products, with practical capabilities at a practical price. CASE tools, with many times the power of the old CASE tools, are affordable at $100 to $2000, depending on features and functions. CASE tools are easy to use, they run in standard Windows desktops, and can link to popular client/server development tools (such as PowerBuilder and Visual Basic) that allow CASE tools to turn design information into real application objects. They link to most popular database servers, to read and write schema information automatically.

Typically, developers employ CASE technology to automate a particular analysis and design methodology (e.g., Booch, OMT, or Yourdon/Coad). CASE supports both the notation (the symbols used to depict the system) and the process that the methodology employs. CASE tools also keep a repository of the design information (such as objects, properties, methods, as well as tables, columns, relationships, and databases). Using CASE to do the application design, you can move quickly through the design process since the tool works with you.

Many modern CASE tools walk the application architect through the design phase and provide on-line assistance, as well as the capability to reverse-engineer existing applications and databases. Clearly, the trend is to move CASE closer to the client/server components, and to put CASE in the hands of developers. CASE is becoming a standard add-on from most specialized client/server development tools.

Types of Computer-Aided Software Engineering Tools

CASE tools, like everything client/server, take different approaches to solve problems. A common problem with many technical "revolutions" is that the idea evolves to encompass terms or features beyond its true definition. CASE is no exception, and many vendors put CASE labels on their non-CASE tools. It's helpful to use a few basic categories to separate CASE products by capabilities. I like the traditional CASE types: upper CASE, lower CASE, integrated CASE (ICASE), and meta-CASE. However, today these types are running together.

"UPPER CASE" (UPPER COMPUTER-AIDED SOFTWARE ENGINEERING)

Upper CASE tools deal with high-level design activities such as object and database modeling, and they can also track limited repository information. Upper CASE tools deal with the methodology, and not with the deployment details of the application. Therefore, upper CASE does not handle application details such as the physical database, or implementation of object models.

"LOWER CASE" (LOWER COMPUTER-AIDED SOFTWARE ENGINEERING)

Lower CASE tools deal directly with application deployment, and not with the application design. Code generators, interface designers, and even reporting tools are traditional examples of lower CASE tools.

INTEGRATED COMPUTER-AIDED SOFTWARE ENGINEERING

ICASE (integrated computer-aided software engineering) combines the capabilities of upper and lower CASE tools, and includes both application and database design in the same tool. Not only does ICASE support most high-level design activities (such as object and database modeling), but the ICASE tools can perform lower CASE activities as well (such as code, interface, and database schema generation).

ICASE is the type of case tool for client/server developers, since we can design the application and database at a high level, as well as generate interfaces, objects, and DDL. Examples of ICASE for client/server include System Architect from Popkin (see Figure 15-1), and Rational Rose from Rational (see Figure 15-2). Since ICASE is where we are today with CASE technology, I'll limit the discussion to ICASE for the remainder of this chapter.

A good example of ICASE is System Architect. System Architect supports most structured and object-oriented design methodologies, as well as logical and physical database design. Through add-on features, it can also re-engineer existing applications and databases, and generate application objects and database schemas (see a description of System Architect later in this chapter).

Figure 15-1 *System Architect.*

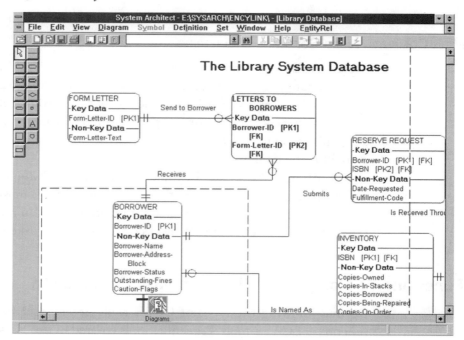

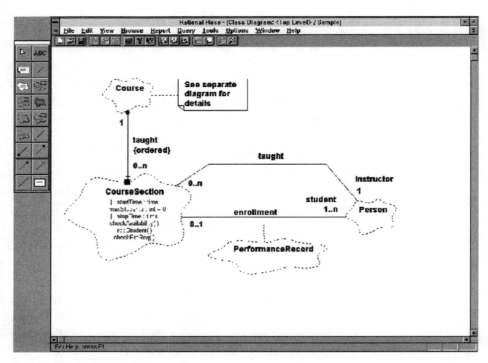

Figure 15-2 *Rational Rose.*

META-COMPUTER-AIDED SOFTWARE ENGINEERING

Meta-CASE tools don't promote a particular methodology. Instead they allow the application architects to build a custom methodology into a particular CASE tool. For example, if I don't find any of the off-the-shelf methodologies useful, I can make one up, or use portions of a few methodologies to create a hybrid methodology. However, meta-CASE tools usually come with a few prebuilt methodologies.

With meta-CASE tools, you can customize both the tool's notation, as well as the repository that drives the tool. Meta-CASE is most useful for organizations that need to automate a custom methodology. In my experience, this is a pretty expensive venture. It always costs more to be different.

Functions of Computer-Aided Software Engineering

Beyond knowing the types of CASE tools, it's helpful to understand the functions of CASE tools. Like other tools covered in this book, I found several features common to all the tools. Common CASE features are diagramming, repositories, interface design, schema generation, reverse engineering, team support, and object generation.

DIAGRAMMING

The diagramming features of CASE tools provide the application architects with the ability to create object and database models using common notation from popular methodologies. This means that application architects can draw the application, and depict the object hierarchy using notation that developers can understand (see Figure 15-3).

If you use drawing tools such as Microsoft Paint, PowerPoint, or Visio, you'll have no trouble using the diagramming tools of client/server CASE. By the way, Visio is a drawing tool that supports CASE features (see Figure 15-4).

Figure 15-3 *OOA/OOD Notation.*

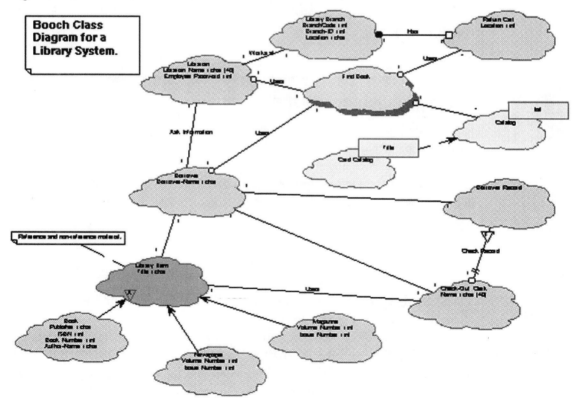

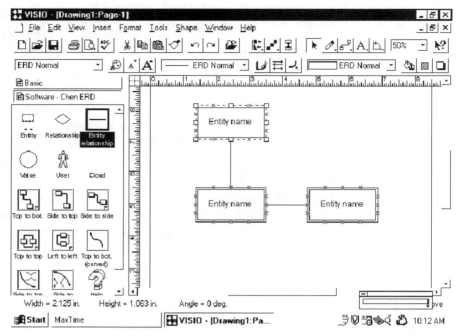

Figure 15-4 *Visio.*

CASE Publishing on the Intranet

Like reporting tools that have Web publishing capabilities, many CASE tool vendors provide their users with the ability to publish diagrams on Web servers. This allows anyone with a Web browser to view them. This is a great feature if you're looking to share object models and logical database diagrams with others on your intranet. I recommend that you consider it when evaluating your next CASE tool.

REPOSITORIES

Most CASE tools use a repository. Like the repositories found in specialized client/server tools, CASE repositories keep track of application information such as objects, object properties, interfaces, and metadata (data about data).

Application architects fill these repositories with information when they design the system. For example, when you create new objects on object diagrams with the diagramming subsystems, the tool automatically stores object information in the repository. The application architects can access the repository from other subsystems of the CASE tool (such as the database modeler, or the interface builder). The repository is also the resource for the code and schema generation system. It's the heart of the CASE tool.

The best examples of repository use are the Designer/2000 and Developer/2000 client/server development tools from Oracle. Designer/2000 (see Figure 15-5) is really Oracle CASE, redeployed to work with client/server. As application architects build database and application diagrams (Oracle CASE is not really object-oriented), the application information automatically resides in the shared repository (an Oracle database).

Developer/2000, the client-side development tool of Developer/2000 and Designer/2000, reads information from the share repository to create the client-side application. Other vendors (such as PowerSoft) have a similar strategy, but they team with third-party CASE vendors that can share information with the client/server tool. For example, Microsoft teamed with Rational Rose to provide their CASE features for Visual Basic. We'll see more of these teaming agreements in the future as we begin to build more complex client/server systems.

Figure 15-5 *Oracle's Designer/2000.*

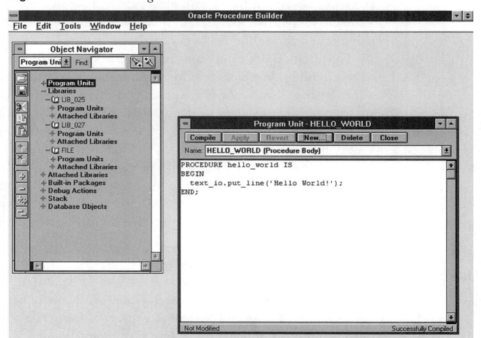

INTERFACE DESIGN

CASE tools also provide an interface design subsystem to create the user interface using standard native GUI controls. These subsystems are similar to the interface painters of the specialized client/server development tools, but they don't provide a true development environment. Once created, the interfaces may be exported to application development environments, or used as an interface prototype to facilitate a requirements discussion for the end-user. They also allow application architects to tie objects into interface components.

As a rule, I would not waste my time using interface designers that come with the CASE tools. You're much better off using the interface designer that comes with your client/server development tool (sometimes they are the same, as is the case with Developer/2000 and Designer/2000). This way you can be sure that the interface you build will work with your development environment. There may also be a difference in the types of controls each interface design subsystem offers.

SCHEMA GENERATION

Most client/server CASE tools that support database design (including ERwin from Logic Works and System Architect) come with some sort of schema generation subsystem. Along with the logical and physical database design that you define with CASE tools, the CASE tool can also generate DDL (Database Definition Language) for the target database.

For instance, you can create a database with three tables, columns, keys, and relationships. Just press a button and the tool creates the physical database on the database server in a few seconds (see Figure 15-6). This also makes it easy to implement changes to the database. In many instances, the database designer does not have to learn the native features of the target database, only its location and how to connect to it. The tool handles the rest automatically.

Since many of you try to avoid process-modeling CASE by RAD-ing your way to successful client/server development, database-oriented CASE seems to be the most popular use of CASE in the client/server world. Tools like ERwin (described later in this chapter) that do database design exclusively are my favorites to work with.

OBJECT GENERATION

Unlike schema generation, object generation is a little tricky. Some CASE tools (such as Rational Rose and System Architect) can generate objects for target development environments (including C++, PowerBuilder, Visual Basic, and

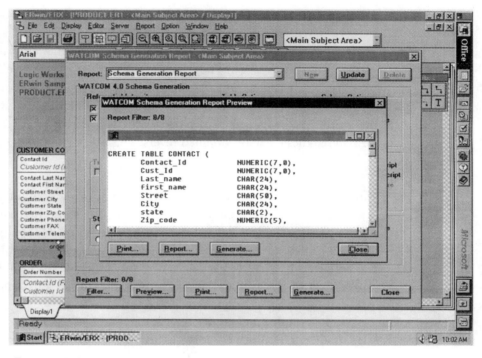

Figure 15-6 *ERwin generates DDL.*

Smalltalk). As a rule, they can only generate simple objects. You can count on a significant amount of work to get them to meet application development requirements. Also, don't count on the ability to regenerate objects over and over again. Generally speaking, it's really just a "one way, one time" process.

Things will improve as CASE tool vendors and client/server development tool vendors learn to work better together. Rose, for instance, promotes its latest CASE products as having the capability to send and receive design information from the development tools. It organizes its product lines around development environments to make this possible (see a description of Rational Rose later in this chapter).

REVERSE ENGINEERING

Reverse-engineering capabilities of CASE refer to the tool's ability to read application and database information from existing applications and databases. Typically, this means pointing the CASE tool at the application objects, and generating object-models automatically. Or pointing the CASE tool at a database—and the database model magically appears before your eyes.

Of course, your CASE tool must support the target development environment or the target database for this to work. While early attempts at reverse engineering proved limited, today we don't have to start from scratch to make changes to an existing application. The database-oriented reverse-engineering tools seem to work better than the process-oriented tools. It's easier to keep up with database technology than client/server application development tools. Rational Rose is one of the few tools that does process-oriented reverse engineering well, where ERwin handles database-oriented reverse engineering without a problem.

TEAM SUPPORT

Finally, CASE tools need to support a design team, or multiple-user access. This means that many application architects can share the same design information (such as object definitions and entities). This is usually accomplished through a shared repository. Team design support allows CASE to coordinate the activities of a team of designers, and bring together all the work into a single view of the system design. This is a handy feature since most client/server design teams contain three to ten people.

For example, you can assign the database design effort one or two database modelers, assign the interface design to a single architect, and assign the process design to the rest of the team. As they work through the system design problem, they'll identify objects, data elements, use cases, and other aspects of the system, and capture these data points in the repository. Once in the repository, they are automatically sharable among others on the team. Typically, team features involve an extra charge. They sometimes employ traditional code control systems (such as Intersolv's PVCS) to divvy up the design components.

Computer-Aided Software Engineering Products

Today there are only a handful of CASE tools that support client/server, but I saw an emergence of new tools in the last year. The market is slowly expanding as client/server moves from simple to complex application development problems. Prices fall and capabilities go up. Here are a few products I recommend.

RATIONAL ROSE

Rational Rose is a pure object-oriented process modeling CASE tool that supports the Booch OOA/OOD methodology, but continues to head toward support for the combined Unified methodology (see Chapter 7). In addition to providing all the upper CASE functionality, Rose can generate and reverse-engineer code from Java, Forte, Smalltalk, C++, Ada, PowerBuilder, and Visual Basic.

Rational Rose and Microsoft recently teamed up to bring CASE to Microsoft development tools. This could propel Rose to the top of the CASE world. Rational Rose is available on SunOS, Solaris, AIX, HP-UX, and Windows (of course).

Rose applies the Booch notation for OOA/OOD, and automates the process behind the Booch method. You can also use Rose to capture your analysis model, and transform your application model from analysis to design. From there, you can refine your design and perform such activities as determine different views on the same object model, and exchange the design information with the target tool. For example, Rose can generate PowerScript for Power-Builder, as well as generate visual objects, nonvisual user objects, and windows. Rose can also exchange design information with ERwin through an agreement with both vendors.

Rose is one of the first tools to support "round-trip engineering." This means that Rose can send design information to your development tool, where you can refine the design into an application. Rose can also read the application to update the design model. Although I would not recommend that you go from the design to the application and back again too many times, this is a step toward the nirvana of CASE technology—the ability to layer into your development environment of choice. I'm excited about Rose's direction.

SYSTEM ARCHITECT

System Architect is the Swiss army knife of the CASE world (see Figure 15-7). System Architect supports over eighteen types of methodology notation (including Gane/Sarson, Yourdon/DeMarco, and Ward/Mellor), and OOA/OOD methods (such as Booch, Coad/Yourdon, and OMT). System Architect also supports data-modeling features (such as Chin Bachman) and IDEFO/IDEF1X entity relationship diagrams. Application architects can even mix and match methodologies as required by the application. For instance, you can link a child diagram of one method or diagram type to a parent diagram that uses another methodology.

System Architect includes handy features such as the ability to use an "Auto Name" facility that prompts application architects for information as they enter notation on a model. The System Architect repository is called the encyclopedia, and this is the heart of any design you do with the tool. You begin a new diagram by selecting a methodology from the methodology menu.

System Architect uses the top-down decomposition method. This means you can create a child diagram from any notation in a model. For instance, you

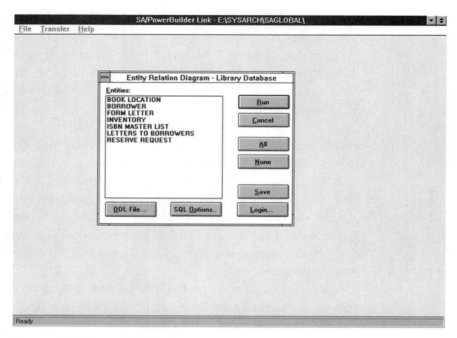

Figure 15-7 *System Architect.*

can click on a symbol that depicts an object to further define the inner workings of that object. This is also the facility that allows you to mix and match diagram types as you build your application design.

System Architect can reverse-engineer most popular databases, and generate schema for those databases. You can also do GUI design from System Architect, and share design information with PowerBuilder's Extended Attribute set.

ERwin

ERwin is one of few CASE tools that only does databases, but it does them very well (see Figure 15-8). ERwin is my tool of choice for database design since it can both reverse-engineer an existing database and generate DDL for a target database. I find the fully attributed database model easy to understand and use. ERwin also supports links to popular client/server tools (including Visual Basic and PowerBuilder).

To create a database, simply create the entities and relationships for the logical and physical design. You can then move into the physical design, where you define columns, keys, and data types. Having done that, it's just a matter of generating the DDL for the target database, then sending the DDL to the target database to commit your design to a physical database schema.

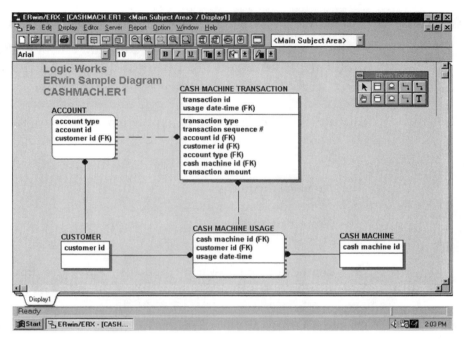

Figure 15-8 *ERwin.*

S-DESIGNER

S-Designer is really a set of four modules: ProcessAnalyst, DataArchitect, AppModeler, and MetaWorks. ProcessAnalyst provides application architects with a tool to create data flow diagrams to capture requirements information. DataArchitect is for database designers, and provides conceptual and physical data modeling to read and write schema information. AppModeler provides application architects with the ability to generate native objects using the Data-Architect models. AppModeler can create objects for PowerBuilder and Visual Basic. MetaWorks provides team features to S-Designer, allowing a team of application architects to access a central dictionary.

When using S-Designer, the idea is to provide a "point A to point B" automated development process. Application architects can create database models by reverse-engineering existing databases. S-Designer can also generate base documentation for the database design. Using the data model, S-Designer generates native application objects, and shares the information with native tool repositories. If you use PowerBuilder, you should take a look at S-Designer (as well as Rose and System Architect). If you don't use PowerBuilder, skip S-Designer.

A Case for "CASE" (Computer-Aided Software Engineering)

As you can tell from this chapter, I'm a big advocate of CASE. This is logical since I'm also an advocate of a rigorous design and architecture process for client/server. CASE makes the analysis and design process nearly painless. With CASE, you can send the design information directly to your tool and the database, and read from existing applications and databases.

The trick is to select the right CASE tool for the job. Things to consider include:

- Your methodology
- Your development tool
- Your database
- Costs

You need to pick your methodology *before* you pick your CASE tool. Your methodology should support the most efficient design and development process for you and your development organization. However, I would recommend that you select a methodology with good CASE support, the most popular being OMT and Booch. The Unified methodology is a newbee, but its success is a foregone conclusion, considering the forces behind it.

You also need to consider your database and tool. Your CASE tool should know how to talk to them. It does not make sense to select a CASE product that can't exchange design information with your client/server components. You'll have to work through the tradeoffs, and my advice here is to stick with the most popular tools, if you can.

Finally, you have to consider costs. CASE is only a good value if it's productive for you. CASE is cheap these days, but the cost of the tool is only part of the equation. You need to consider training costs, administration costs, and the cost of upgrades. You can't use a tool unless you know the methodology it supports. Kind of like using a word processor to write a paper in French when you don't speak the language. Also, many CASE products sell schema generators, object generators, and reverse-engineering subsystems as separate products with separate costs. Make sure you factor in costs for the components you need.

CASE has a bright future in the world of client/server, and I'm really looking forward to the next generation of CASE products. They will make my job even easier. Client/server developers and application architects need to learn how to use CASE efficiently, as well as how to use a rigorous process to assure the success of a client/server application.

IV

Creating the Right Client/Server Architecture

Chapter

16

Partitioning Your Client/Server Application

I have to admit that I'm excited about writing this chapter, for several reasons. First, the concepts of process and application partitioning, as well as of basic client/server architecture, are among the most confusing, and least understood ideas. Today, application architects and developers are making architectural mistakes costing millions of dollars—mistakes that could have been avoided with just a little bit of architectural knowledge, the willingness to open your mind to some new options and not blindly follow vendors.

Second, the concepts I'm revealing in this chapter, as well as the next four chapters, make client/server and the intranet ready for the enterprise. Traditional two-tier client/server can't scale, but three-tier and *n*-tier client/server can get us there. There is a tradeoff. You have to pay for scalability with higher complexity and higher development costs.

Finally, this is the most exciting area of client/server development. We are now solving complex problems with complex architectures, but the technology is adapting quickly. We're now able to scale with less complexity and less effort. Application-partitioning tools and distributed objects hold the future of partitioning. These technologies, however, are still evolving, and we must proceed with caution.

In the next four chapters I'll take a close look at the enabling technologies that will get us to enterprise level client/server. In this chapter we'll look at the architectural issues, and partitioning technology at a high level. Then we'll look at TP monitors, application-partitioning tools, and distributed objects. We'll not only learn what they are, but how to use them in the construction of client/server systems, and how to consider them as architectural tools.

Divide and Conquer

The basic concept of client/server is splitting the processing load between a client and a server. By sharing the processing load, and processing requests in parallel, client/server provides better performance, as well as decoupling the application processing from the data not only logically but physically.

Things, however, aren't always that simple. Today we are looking past the traditional client/server concepts, moving client/server away from the two-tier world to a complex world where applications are split across multiple processors and databases. What's more, they must maintain mission-critical characteristics such as fault tolerance and fail-over. We are not there yet, but we are moving in that direction both as a profession and as an industry.

ARCHITECTURE-DRIVEN

Application partitioning is really an architectural concept. A fundamental decision when building a client/server system is which base architecture to use, two-tier, three-tier, or *n*-tier (see Figure 16-1). After selecting a base architecture, the architect is charged with deciding where to place the application processes to best optimize available resources and meet the requirements of the application. There are many thing to consider, including user load, processing load, application type, cost of development, maintenance, and performance expectations.

User Load. When designing a client/server system, one of the first questions I ask is the number of users who will be using this system when it is deployed. I also ask how many users are expected to use the system after one, two, and five years (although no one ever knows who's going to use the system after five years).

Why am I so nosy? Well, the number of users the system is expected to support is a good indication of which base architecture works best. For

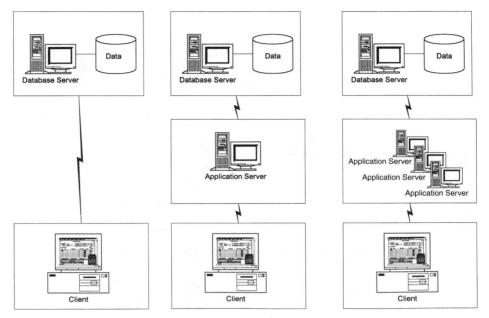

Figure 16-1 *Two-tier, three-tier, and* n-*tier Client/Server.*

instance, if the system is expected to support more than one hundred simultaneous users, I'll begin to lean toward three-tier and *n*-tier client/server architectures for reasons that will become apparent later in this chapter. If more than two hundred users are to reside on the system, this clearly indicates more than two-tiers (see Figure 16-2). However, you need to consider other issues too, including the ones that follow.

The number of users drives the architecture of the system because of the limitation of the number of users you can connect to a database server at the same time. Although each database has a different approach to supporting user connections (see Chapter 5), and thus provides different loading characteristics, you're generally going to watch a database server break at around two hundred to three hundred connections. This is due to the operating system running out of resources to support the connections, trashing, and finally crashing or performing poorly. Three-tier or *n*-tier client/server architectures are able to circumvent this limitation since they are able to funnel database connections through a middle tier.

Processing Load. The process load is the number of processor cycles, memory, and disk resources that an application requires from a particular computer to

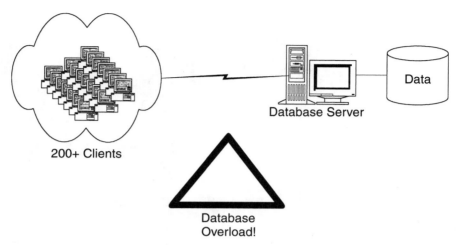

200+ Clients

Database Server

Data

Database
Overload!

Figure 16-2 *Overloading the server.*

get the job done. Although computational and disk-intensive applications require the most system resources, it's difficult to determine the amount of system resources by application type, because of the different deployment mechanisms that development tools use. For instance, compilers are more resource-efficient than interpreters.

The processing load that an application places on a server or a client directly affects the architecture. Process-intensive objects should be put in their own domain on their own application server. That's generally the rule of the middle tier in three-tier client/server. However, process-intensive objects may also be distributed between clients and database server.

Architects determine processing load through simulation and testing. Simulation tools are able to guess how much of a processing load an object will place on a computer. Testing means simulating the processing load and watching how the computer and operating system react. For example, some application objects may take an average of 20 percent of system resources during normal processing, where others will almost saturate a computer at 80 to 90 percent. The best approach is to mix simulation and testing, where the testing will prove out the simulation model and also validate assumptions for further simulation models.

Application Types. The type of application also impacts your architectural decision. As I suggested earlier in the book, there are several types of client/server application, including OLTP, OLAP, real-time, occasional use, and work-flow. OLTP (on-line transaction processing) applications are applications that exist around transactions. Examples of OLTP applications include sales-order entry systems, credit card transactions, even applications that count long-distance phone calls. OLTP applications are intensive, and require a large amount of system and database resources. What's more, they generally support a high user load, and provide the most value for the development dollar. The majority of client/server systems I've built are OLTP applications.

OLAP (on-line analytical processing) applications allow the end-user to slice and dice data to make business decisions. While there is a significant client processing load, OLAP applications are famous for being database-intensive. OLAP applications usually support only a few select users; however, as the prices of OLAP tools fall quickly, and OLAP moves to the Web, OLAP applications may become more commonplace. Since OLAP applications require direct access to the database, they are typically two-tier, but in most cases require high-end database servers supporting multi-processing.

Real-time applications are able to absorb and display information as it happens. Examples include process control systems that may control an entire petroleum plant, or market-watching applications that sit on the desks of stock-and-bond traders. In many cases they are intensive transaction-oriented applications as well, since the real-time information that's coming into the system is being stored to disk and acted upon in the application.

Occasional-use applications, as the name implies, are not used continuously. Examples include time-reporting and expense-reporting systems. Since these applications are not intensive, you can solve them using any number of architectures. The intranet is becoming a popular architecture for occasional-use applications, since they are there when you need them and don't require additional middleware or client application. More on that in Chapter 23.

Work-flow applications are able to automate activities we once did on paper. For example, if an invoice is received, it's entered into a database and automatically routed to a manager to approve payment. He or she does this electronically, then routes the invoice back to accounts payable where a check is cut. All of this happens using an elaborate system of networks, databases, and message-oriented applications. Since work-flow applications are not resource-intensive, most architectures work. I recommend traditional two-tier application development, tied to an electronic mail system. Lotus Notes supports such an architecture.

Cost of Development. It's been my experience that architects and developers don't often consider costs when selecting an architecture. However, the costs of developing some types of client/server architectures are significantly higher than others. Therefore, cost is a consideration.

As a rule, simple architectures cost the least. Traditional two-tier client/server, for example, generally provides the best bang for the buck. This is because the technology, specialized two-tier client/server tools and database servers, is relatively inexpensive and does not require a significant investment in hardware. What's more, two-tier client/server applications require only a portion of the development hours required by more complex architectures.

Complex client/server architectures, such as three-tier and n-tier, are the most expensive. Not only is the technology required to create the architecture (TP monitors, application partitioning tools, distributed objects, etc.) pricey, but you can count on about twice the development time as when using more traditional two-tier client/server tools. We'll find out why later in this chapter when I discuss three-tier and n-tier enabling technology.

Maintenance. Maintenance is a cost that few consider when building a client/server system. The amount of maintenance is directly related to the complexity of the system, as well as the quality of the system when deployed.

Simple systems are easier to maintain: There are not as many components to keep track of. Since client/server system components are dependent on one another, changing one component can require changes to other components.

Poorly designed and developed systems are difficult to maintain no matter what architecture you use. That's why it's important to devote a good deal of the life cycle to the requirements and design, and then follow through with a quality application development effort.

Performance Expectations Finally, architects need to consider the performance expectations of the end-users. While subsecond response time is always desirable, it's not always possible with low-end architectures and high user load. Once again, there are tradeoffs of performance, cost, and complexity. You need to understand the performance expectations up front, and modify the application if you need to.

Importance of the Architecture

I've found we are so focused on tools and trends that developers and application architects don't pay enough attention to the architecture. The problem is that architecture is where the power really is, and where you can spend more dollars than you need to—or not enough.

For instance, you can't get to two hundred or more users using two-tier, but three-tier and *n*-tier are too much for work-group class applications. The difference in price is not thousands, but millions, and I've seen millions wasted by bad architecture.

Architecture also means that developers and architects have a chance to think through basic features and functions that the application should support. This is where we think about response time and overall system throughput, and interfaces with other systems. We're also able to work through the growth of the system as application and user requirements increase. Systems that don't scale die an early death.

The moral of the story is: Don't neglect the architecture. It's the toughest problem to solve, but one you have to solve.

DYNAMIC VERSUS STATIC

Before we dig too deeply in the concept of client/server architectures, let's discuss the concept of dynamic versus static application partitioning. Static application partitioning requires the architect to select a location for the application processing at design time. Once committed, it's difficult (if not impossible) to relocate the processing (see Figure 16-3).

TP monitors are classic static application partitioning tools. Since TP monitor services (described in Chapter 18) are built using traditional 3GLs such as COBOL or C, once built, the services are bound to the TP monitor, meaning they are bound to the middle tier. If your processing requirements change, it's difficult to move the objects from the middle tier since you'll have to redevelop them using a client side development tool, or as stored procedures and triggers in the database server.

Dynamic application partitioning means that architects and developers have the option of relocating the objects among client, application server, and database server, at any time for any reason (see Figure 16-4). This provides the developer with the ultimate in flexibility since he or she doesn't have to commit to a particular partitioning scheme, and change moves the processing load around the architecture to meet the requirements of the application, and to improve performance.

Application-partitioning tools such as Forte and Dynasty are the best example of technologies that support dynamic partitioning. (See Chapter 20 for details.) Using these tools, developers can create a logical working version of an application, then move the application objects to other servers connected

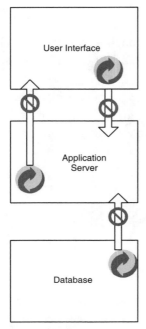

Figure 16-3 *Static Application Partitioning.*

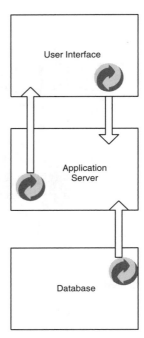

Figure 16-4 *Dynamic Application Partitioning.*

via a network. The application-partitioning tools can keep track of where the objects are executing and allow them to communicate, creating a virtual system. Application-partitioning tools provide developers with the ability to repartition the application so as to redistribute the processing load. This is usually a simple process of dragging and dropping objects, and does not require additional programming.

Other dynamic partitioning technologies include distributed objects. Distributed objects work very much like application-partitioning tools, but developers need to deploy the distributed objects on each system. Also, while sometimes the code is portable from server to server, sometimes it is not. I'll cover distributed objects in detail in Chapter 19.

Creating an Architecture

So if application partitioning and architecture go hand in hand, how does one create an architecture? It's really just a matter of a concept, followed by a logical and physical architecture. I'll walk you through it.

First, before you create an architecture, you need to do a lot of things, including understanding the requirements in detail, creating an application design, and considering all of the issues I've already mentioned. One of the most common mistakes in the business is architects that approach a problem with an predefined architecture, and try to make the problem fit the architecture. Bad idea. You have to stay flexible, and select an architecture that best fits the problem at hand.

LOGICAL ARCHITECTURE

Your first step in creating your architecture is to create a logical architecture. A logical architecture allows you to map certain application functions to conceptual architectural layers, without actually committing them to a particular tier or enabling technology. As with logical database design, this is helpful in understanding the goal and objectives of the architecture before drilling down to the details. I've followed this "rule-of-thumb" approach for years, and it always works.

When approaching a logical architecture problem, you need to perform the following steps:

1. Divide your application into logical objects
2. Define each object by its function in the application
3. Depending on what the logical objects do, group them around three layers: the presentation layer, the application layer, and the data access layer
4. Refine the model by moving some objects, that communicate often, to the same layer

The first step is dividing the application into many logical objects (see Figure 16-5). Most of the logical objects should come from object diagrams that are the product of the object-oriented analysis and design effort (described in Chapter 7). This is why I keep harping on the fact that OOA/OOD is critical to the success of your client/server project. Examples of logical objects are data entry forms, tax table calculations, and database sort operations. You can refine the objects down to such detail as GUI control objects, but that's a bit much at this level.

I'll typically put a list of all of the objects in a spreadsheet, or better yet manage them from your CASE repository. You can even place them on 3×5 cards, if you find that more useful. Whatever you decide to do, you need some way to manage all of these objects, since we are going to mix and match them.

Once you have a list of all of the logical objects that make up your application you need to define what each object does. Again, this information is gener-

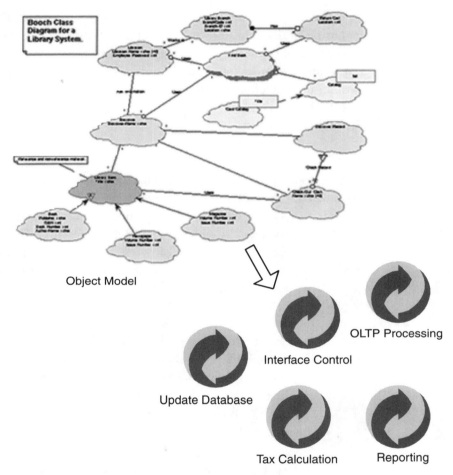

Object Model

OLTP Processing

Interface Control

Update Database

Tax Calculation   Reporting

Figure 16-5 *Dividing the application into logical objects.*

ally available from your OOA/OOD work, but feel free to refine the definition of an object at this point. For example, considering the tax table calculation object above, you need to define what that means, and if and what data the object requires. You also need to include the interfaces for the object, such as the user interface and data interface. Define what flows between those interfaces as well.

Next, you need to group the objects around three basic layers: the presentation layer, the application layer (sometime called the business logic layer), and the data access layer (see Figure 16-6).

The *presentation layer* defines how the application is presented to the end-user. These objects typically deal directly with the manipulation and control of the user interface.

The *application layer* objects provide the general application processing capabilities, and for most applications that is where the action is. What's more, you'll find that most of the objects reside at this layer.

The *data access layer* objects are easy to spot, since they are the ones that deal directly with the database. Objects that read information from a database, or objects that write information to a database, are the best examples of data access layer objects.

Once you have grouped the objects, it's healthy to refine the grouping by looking at how the objects communicate. Objects that are constantly communicating should be placed at the same layer, if they are not already. You'll find

Figure 16-6 *Presentation, application, and data access layers.*

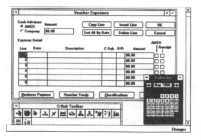

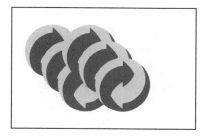

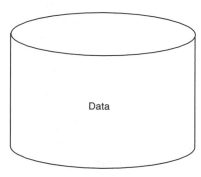

that from 2 to 5 percent of the objects need to be relocated. You need to update this information in your database, spreadsheet, or repository.

PHYSICAL ARCHITECTURE

Okay, now that we've come up with a logical architecture, it's time to turn our attention to mapping the logical onto the physical. Before we can do this, we need to select the enabling technology, such as TP monitors, application partitioning tools, specialized client/server tools, database servers, and distributed objects. This is because the enabling technology will define how the logical objects exist in the physical model. I'll explain more about the enabling technologies in this and the next few chapters.

Let's say our application is transaction-oriented (OLTP) and we decide to build our system using a TP monitor. The logical presentation layer objects will be built using whatever front-end development tool can communicate with a TP monitor (such as C++, PowerBuilder, or JAM 7). On deploying the application layer logical objects in a TP monitor architecture, they exist as TP monitor services inside the TP monitor environment residing on the application server (the middle tier). If you think that the data access logical objects will work best on the database server as stored procedures and triggers, you are half right. Depending on what the objects do, it generally makes better sense if objects dealing with data through simple read-and-write operations reside on the application server. Objects that are more database-extensive, such as large sorts, database reports, and automatic migrations, are best deployed as stored procedures and triggers. Remember, a TP monitor-enabled architecture is static, and you can't move the objects off the application server at will.

Mapping logical architecture to an physical architecture using an application partitioning tool is easy. It's just a matter of mapping the logical to physical objects, then partitioning the application between the presentation layer, the database, and any number of application servers. Remember, application partitioning tools support dynamic partitioning, so you can repartition at any time. Therefore, it's not as important to get it right the first time as it is when dealing with static partitioning technology (e.g., TP monitors), or semistatic partitioning technology such as distributed objects.

These are just general guidelines. When mapping most logical architectures to real technology, you'll have to consider the advantages and limitation of the particular products. For example, with the advent of the Microsoft ActiveX-based TP monitor, Transaction Server, we could find that TP monitors are no longer static. Transaction Server allows the developer to move

ActiveX components from the presentation to the application layer. I recommend that you pay close attention to the rest of the material in this chapter, as well as the rest of the book. These concepts are the future of client/server.

Two-Tier Partitioning

Let's dig a bit deeper into the partitioning paradigms. As you may recall, these are two-tier, three-tier, and *n*-tier. I will even add 2.5-tier, since I've been hearing about it a lot from vendors, and I would like to address it here. Since I've spent so much time discussing tools, technology, and architecture for two-tier client/server, I'm not going to go into it in this chapter in too much detail. You should know by now that two-tier client/server is simply the process of splitting the process up between the client and a database server.

Two-tier client/server systems are typically specialized client/server development tools building an application at the front-end, and a database server at the back-end. Traditionally, two-tier client/server applications have been "fat client" applications. However, the trend has been to place some of the application processing on the database server as stored procedures and triggers (see Figure 16-7). Specialized client/server tools such as Oracle's Developer/2000 make this easy, since objects can be moved between the clients and database servers (as long as it's an Oracle database). Other approaches aren't as easy. Typically,

Figure 16-7 *Using the database server for application processing.*

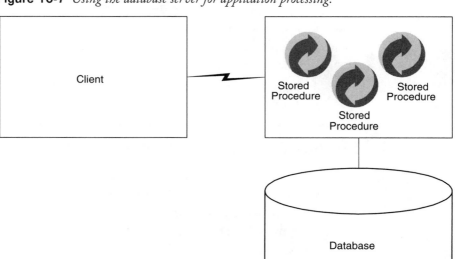

developers must code the stored procedures by hand in a different language from the one used on the client. The front-end application must know how to invoke the stored procedures and triggers from the client. Most front-end applications can, but a few can't. You need to check with your front-end tool vendor before electing to place some of your application processing on the database server.

A debate of sorts has been raging on during the last few years, arguing fat client versus fat server. I'll register my opinion in the sidebar.

Fat Server versus Fat Client? (I'll Settle This One, Once and for All!)

There is an ongoing debate about how developers should partition an application. At the core of the argument is the partitioning of the majority of the application logic on the server, or the client.

Traditional two-tier client/server means a fat client. Since the client/server development tools create client-side code, that's the path of least resistance. The database server simply exists for data access.

The problem that many have with two-tier client/server is that since the application is distributed to the clients, there is a lack of control. New client-side software has to be loaded on each client, when fixing bugs or changing application logic. What's more, placing most of the application logic on the client means slower clients.

Fat server advocates stress the advantage of placing most of the application logic on the database server using stored procedures and triggers. The client is a simple "thin" process that interfaces with the end-user, and in turn invokes procedures on the database server. This model means that you can make changes to the application centrally, and move the processing load off of the client, with the potential of increasing client performance.

My Answer: It's Just Another Tradeoff

The reality is that fat server versus fat client is a tradeoff. If you place all of the application logic on the database server as stored procedures and triggers, you aren't going to be able to support the same number of clients as you can when using the thin server model.

The bottleneck is the database server, and is best described through an example. When using the fat client model an application may only require an average of 2 percent of the database server's capacity. This is because most of the application processing is taking place on the client, and not the server. Therefore, you can support as many as fifty clients using the fat client architecture.

When using the fat server model, most of the application exists as stored procedures and triggers on the database server. The same application would require as much as 5 percent database server capacity per client. Therefore, you're only going to support twenty users using that fat server architecture. What's more, it's much harder to build stored procedure and triggers on the database server than it is to build client-side applications using today's sophisticated development tools.

Thus, while there may be some good reasons to place most of the application processing on the server, clearly the tradeoff is scalability. If you're moving toward a fat server architecture, I recommend that you look at three-tier and *n*-tier client/server architecture instead. I know that there are other views on this topic, but you guys will just have to write your own book.

2.5-Tier Partitioning

I'm placing a discussion of "2.5-tier" partitioning in the book because it keeps coming up when selecting architecture and client/server products. Simply put, 2.5-tier client/server means scrapping screens from existing mainframe applications. This means that a client application communicates with a local 3270 emulator which is in turn communicating with a mainframe. The application is able to scrape information from the screen, and display it to the end-user as if it was a native GUI application. These are easy to spot, since they look out of place with other native GUI applications. I've found that 3270 green screens don't map real well to GUIs.

The idea behind 2.5-tier client/server is ligament. Sometimes there are mainframe applications that cost too much to port to client/server. Screen scrapping allows organizations to maintain the investment in an existing application, as well as provide a native interface. However, there are many downsides. First, the application has a tendency to perform poorly due to the number of layers it must go through. Second, the application looks out of place. The biggest downside is the fact that you have to continue to play nursemaid to a mainframe. This is expensive.

Three-Tier and *n*-Tier Partitioning

The advent of three-tier and multi-tier (*n*-tier) client/server architectures has revolutionized what we can do with client/server. As I mentioned in the beginning of this chapter, traditional two-tier client/server can't scale to a large user and processing load. Three-tier and *n*-tier client/server solves this problem. Multi-tier and three-tier client/server architectures have other advantages too, such as the ability to place application logic in a single share layer. This architecture provides better maintenance, and "change without pain."

I'm going to spend the next four chapters talking about the technology that makes three-tier and *n*-tier client/server possible, such as the TP monitor, application partitioning tools, and distributed objects. This section will serve as an introduction.

TRANSACTION-PROCESSING MONITORS

TP (transaction-processing) monitors are software that can process transactions in behalf of one or many clients. TP monitors sit between the client and a resource. A resource can be a queue or an API, but most often is a database server (see Figure 16-8).

The basic idea is that a developer builds services within the TP monitor environment. Services are small programs that are able to interface with the TP monitor through an API. TP monitor services are usually built using a traditional 3GL such as C, C++, or COBOL, but lately a few high-end specialized development tools such as JAM from JYACC have delivered products that interface with TP monitor APIs. I'll cover TP monitor in detail in Chapter 18.

Examples of TP monitors include Encina from Transarc, Tuxedo from BEA, and CICS from IBM. Microsoft has just entered the TP monitor game with a COM-enabled TP monitor, Transaction Server.

TP monitors generally run on their own server, but they can run on the database server as an option. I recommend that you place the TP monitor on its own server, since you don't want the TP monitor processing to get in the way of the database server processing.

TP monitors are able to reduce application to a transaction level. Developers create most application functions as transactions, having a beginning, middle, and end. These are usually discrete functions such as updating a customer database with new customer information, or deleting rows from several heterogeneous databases at the same time. An application is the process of invoking one transaction after the other.

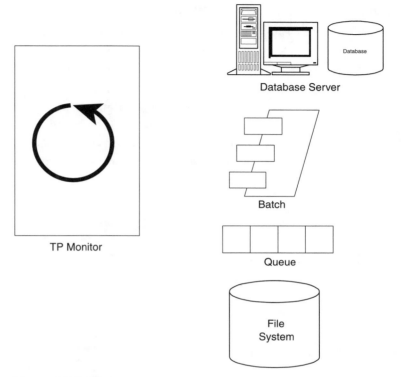

Figure 16-8 *Resources.*

Using this transaction model TP monitors are able to recover from problems that may occur while processing a transaction, bringing the system back to the state it was prior to invoking the transaction. This means that network and database problems won't leave your system or data in a undesirable state. Either the transaction works or it does not.

The beauty of transaction model that TP monitors is that the system is always reliable. That's the way ATM machines are usually tracked by TP monitors, which either process the transaction or don't. If a transaction failed in the middle of processing, the ATM machine might pass out money, without removing the amount from your account. TP monitors are products to use when you absolutely have to assure that something works.

Beside transaction processing, TP monitors can also perform load balancing. This means that the TP monitor is able to move processing around to maximize available resources. TP monitors can restart servers, and report trouble to a console. Of course each TP monitor does these things in its own proprietary way.

DISTRIBUTED OBJECT DEVELOPMENT

Taking a bird's-eye view, distributed objects are tool- and language-independent objects that can run on a variety of platforms. Distributed objects are able to communicate with one another using a common communications mechanism, where they can invoke one another's services (see Figure 16-9). I'll cover distributed objects in more detail in Chapter 19.

There are two flavors of distributed objects: those built using the Object Management Group's common object request broker architecture (CORBA) specification, and those built using Microsoft's distributed component object model (DCOM).

Figure 16-9 *Distributed Objects.*

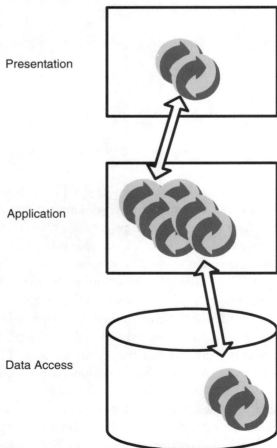

CORBA is the oldest and most widely deployed distributed object standard. Remember, CORBA is not a product, but a specification. There are several commercial ORBs based on CORBA, including IBM's SOM/DSOM, Iona's Orbix, and DEC's ObjectBroker.

The idea is that a client/server developer can build application services using one of these commercial ORBs, and distribute them to any server. Since they all use the same CORBA standard, they should be able to communicate with each other, finding and invoking object services. The developer is free to mix and match ORBs to create a flexible distributed system, not dependent on a tool, language, or vendor.

While CORBA-based ORBs may very well be the future of client/server, a few problems exist. First of all, performance is not what it should be, and ORBs sold by different vendors aren't able to talk yet. These problems are being addressed by both the OMG and the ORB vendors. For now, they are very much niche players. ORBs lack the tool support needed to succeed in the near future, but I believe they are going to be the future of client/server.

DCOM takes a different approach. Instead of creating, and having everyone agree upon a specification, Microsoft has built the ORB infrastructure into its operating systems. For example, if you purchase a copy of Windows NT version 4, you have DCOM available to you. It's soon going to be a part of Windows 95 too.

The idea behind DCOM is that any tool that can create OLE automation servers can share those servers with other OLE-enabled applications. This means that most of today's existing client/server development tools, including PowerBuilder, Visual C++, Visual Basic, and Delphi, can create ORBs for use over DCOM.

DCOM has just hit the streets, so it's anyone's guess how the ORB will do. Microsoft does a very good job at making high-end technology a commodity. DCOM could be another success story for Microsoft, if you ask me.

APPLICATION-PARTITIONING TOOLS

Application-partitioning tools offer the ultimate in scalability and flexibility, as long as you don't mind a proprietary solution. I'll cover application-partitioning tools in Chapter 20.

The idea behind application-partitioning tools is to create your objects, then distribute them over all available systems. Application-partitioning tools are dynamic applications, and allow the developer to redistribute objects when necessary. The objects are really proprietary ORBs.

Developing for the Masses

Architecture is everything in client/server, and a major portion of architecture is determining where to place the processing, and which enabling technology to employ. Your ability to do this correctly, the first time, will reduce the risk of another client/server failure.

While two-tier is okay for work-group-size client/server applications, bringing client/server to the enterprise means a much more innovative approach. The trick is selecting the right technology for the application requirements. While TP monitors are proven, they increase development costs. Distributed objects are not yet ready for high-end client/server, and application-partitioning tools are proprietary. Good architects must weigh the tradeoffs and determine the best approach. What's more, the technology is ever-changing, and you have to keep up.

We are at a crossroads in the world of client/server, finally moving into the domain of the mainframe. In building applications for the masses, we need to work on our bag of tricks, and understand which tricks to perform when.

Intranet Architectures

Think about three things when you build an intranet application: the enabling technology you want to use (Java, ActiveX, CGI, etc.), the architecture that works with your enabling technology, and the intranet tools you need to build the application around your architecture. This chapter outlines the architectural solutions for the intranet; we'll also begin to discuss intranet-enabling technology. Chapter 23 continues the intranet enabling technologies discussion, and reviews available intranet development tools.

This chapter lies between 16 and 18 to extend our architectural discussion to the intranet. Why? Whether you like it or not, the intranet is here to stay. If you do client/server today, it's time to prepare yourself for the intranet. If the overwhelming indicators hold true, the intranet will drive the direction of client/server for the next five to ten years.

Intranet Rising

Backing up a bit, the idea behind intranets is the use of commodity Web technology for internal applications. In other words, the creation of a "mini-Web," hidden behind the corporate firewall. The "mini-Web," or intranet, becomes a platform for the next generation in client/server applications development. Developing client/server applications for the intranet is the latest rage in client/server development, and takes up a good portion of this book (as well as the title).

For you old client/server developers, don't fear change. Embrace it. I don't think the intranet will replace client/server. The intranet simply extends its capabilities to a new platform. HTML replaces GUI APIs, Java replaces C++, and Web servers become interface deployment mechanisms. However, any new paradigm comes with new architectures (later in this chapter).

All (and I do mean all) traditional client/server development tool vendors now offer intranet development versions of existing tools, or brand-new tools. They offer intranet-enabled report writers, and OLAP tools as well. Most tools can even deploy existing client/server applications to intranets.

Figure 17-1 *Future demand for intranet application development will outpace the Internet.*

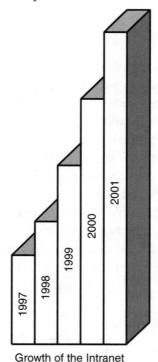

Growth of the Intranet

Uniface from Compuware, for example, provides a Web deployment mechanism to deploy an existing Uniface application as a true Web-enabled intranet application. Same goes for Unify, JAM 7, and dozens of other tool vendors. This intranet thing is not a trend, but an all-out paradigm shift in the business. Right now, vendors that lack a product or intranet strategy will find a sure-fire death in this business. The tools follow the hype, and the hype follows the tools.

Zona Research, Inc., predicts that intranet development will account for a larger market share than traditional Internet development by the year 2000. IDC Research states that future demand for intranet application development will outpace the Internet by five times in the year 2001 (see Figure 17-1).

John Deere Works

John Deere Works's Waterloo Division is one of the first adopters of an intranet. John Deere uses its intranet to integrate corporate data with agricultural information, as well as track test results of the latest equipment and access one-line documents.

The driving force that sent John Deere to the intranet was the multi-platform capability of the Web. Like many other companies, John Deere supports a hodgepodge of operating systems and processors, including Windows, Mac, and Sun workstations. Since Netscape Communicator runs on all these platforms, John Deere can integrate all its intranet applications within native browsers, on all platforms.

For instance, John Deere places its parts database on its intranet, accessible by any employee who needs to locate parts. The database can even produce an image of the part, displaying the image and text information on the same Web page. What's more, John Deere can send digitized sounds of equipment problems over its intranet, playable through the multi-media capabilities of the Web browser. This helps equipment technicians locate similar problems by simply matching the sounds.

For John Deere, the intranet provides its employees with an inexpensive alternative to traditional client/server. There is no need for concern with the complex problems of application integration, obscure middleware layers, or the pitfalls of multi-platform client/server development. The intranet saves them money, and that's the bottom-line benefit of the intranet.

INTRANET COMPONENTS

To understand the architectures of the intranet, I recommend that you first become familiar with the key players of the intranet: The Web client, the Web server, the database server, and the application server. I won't talk about the basics of these components in this book (since there are boatloads of books that do), but let's take a quick look at intranet components and the role they play in intranet architectures.

Web Client. The Web client is a personal computer (PC), or even a device that runs a Web browser, that can display HTML and graphics. The Web browser makes requests to the Web server, and processes the files the Web server returns. While many call this classic client/server, it's really closer to file-oriented. The Web client does not exchange messages, but entire files. The whole process is relatively inefficient, and resource-intensive.

Figure 17-2 *Web servers use an external process that runs on the Web server using Web server APIs or CGI.*

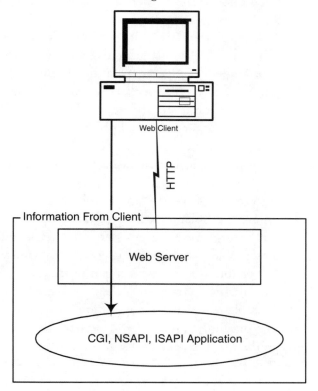

Web Server. Web servers, at their core, are file servers. Like traditional file servers, they respond to requests from Web clients, then send the requested file. We typically see HTML, graphics, and multi-media files (audio, video, and animation) stored on Web servers. Today we also store Java applets and ActiveX components on the Web server. We call all this stuff "content."

Today's Web servers pull double duty. Not only do they serve up file content to the hordes of Web clients, but they perform rudimentary application processing. With enabling technologies such as advanced HTML (e.g., HTML version 3), CGI, NSAPI, and ISAPI (described in Chapter 23), Web servers can query the Web client for information, then pass that information to an external process that runs on the Web server using Web server APIs. In many cases, this means users can access information on a database server, or link to real-time information such as the current temperature and humidity from a weather station (see Figure 17-2).

Database Server. Database servers work in the intranet the same way they work on more traditional client/server architectures. They respond to requests, and return information. Sometimes the requests come from Web servers that communicate with the database server through a CGI process. Sometimes they come directly from Web client communication with the database server via a CLI (call level interface) such as JDBC for Java, or ODBC for ActiveX (see Figure 17-3).

Application Server. Application servers work with intranet applications by providing a middle layer between a resource server and the Web server (see Figure 17-4). Application servers run traditional middle tier-enabling software (such as TP monitors or distributed objects). TP monitors communicate with both the Web server and the resource server using transaction-oriented appli-

Figure 17-3 *Applets are able to communicate with database servers.*

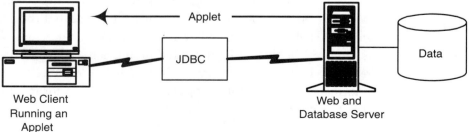

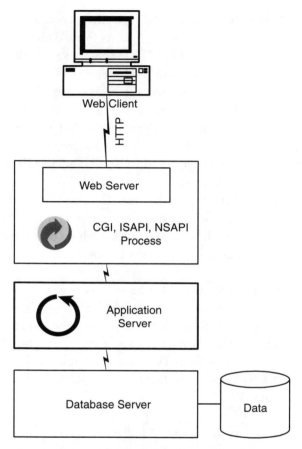

Figure 17-4 *Application servers working with the intranet.*

cation development (lots more on TP monitors in Chapter 18). As with three-tier client/server, TP monitors bring load balancing, recovery services, and failover capabilities to the intranet. The flexible APIs that TP monitors offer make communications with both the Web server and resource server possible.

Distributed objects perform similar functions, but they can exist on Web servers, database servers, and even browsers (e.g., Visigenic's VisiBroker). This is the latest in Web technology, and promises to "upgrade" traditional Web by replacing rock-solid Web standards such as HTML. See Chapter 19 for more information on distributed objects, and Chapter 23 for more information distributed objects on the Web.

The Fourth Paradigm

I see the intranet as the fourth paradigm of client/server. So what the heck are the other paradigms? If you read the book in order, you already know.

At the first paradigm we see traditional file-oriented applications. While not really client/server, they did let us share data. The second paradigm covers traditional two-tier client/server. Also, the second paradigm provides better scalability than the first paradigm. The third paradigm, three-tier and *n*-tier client/server, can solve the limitations of the second paradigm by placing a middle tier between the client and the server. This book covers all these paradigms in detail.

The fourth paradigm, the intranet, is really bits and pieces of the previous three paradigms wrapped up for Web-born applications (see Figure 17-5). For instance, when a client requests a Web page, the client is really requesting a file. When employing CGI (or NSAPI, or ISAPI, for that matter), they use the Web sever as the middle tier (see Chapter 23). Thus, it's logical to call this three-tier intranet (see Figure 17-6). When we employ Java or ActiveX, the system down-

Figure 17-5 *Changing paradigms.*

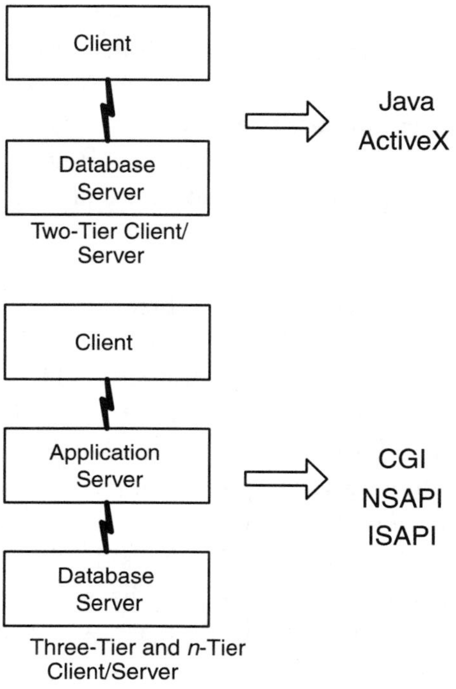

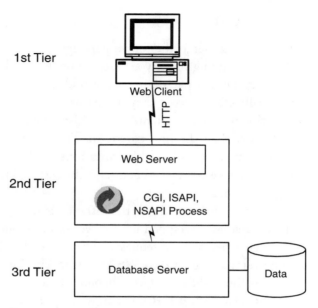

1st Tier

Web Client

2nd Tier

3rd Tier

Figure 17-6 *Three-tier intranet.*

loads the applets or components into the browser, which then links back to a resource server (e.g., a database server). Thus it's logical to call this architecture two-tier intranet. Finally, with the advent of distributed objects and TP monitors for the Web (e.g., Microsoft's Transaction Server), we are learning to create four-tier intranet. The client is connected to the Web server, which in turn connects to a distributed object or TP monitor, and then to a resources server. If you've kept count, that's at least four tiers (see Figure 17-7).

THREE-TIER INTRANET

As mentioned previously, three-tier intranet means we use a CGI application (or NSAPI or ISAPI) that can drive a Web server, interface with a Web client, and interact with a database server. The external CGI process pumps HTML dynamically back to the client using HTTP, customized for that particular client and particular user action (see Figure 17-8).

Since a CGI application can also communicate through multiple APIs (they are traditionally 3GL applications such as C, C++, or COBOL) and the native database API, the sky is the limit for the type of information you can send down your Web server. That's why you will use this type of intranet architecture not only for database access, but to access real-time stock market infor-

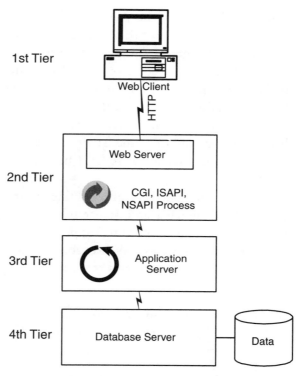

Figure 17-7 *Four-tier intranet (or more).*

mation, conduct electronic commerce, and communicate with applications such as SAP/R3 that use the application's API.

Search engines (such as Excite or Yahoo) provide the best examples of three-tier intranet. A Web client enters a word or phrase in an HTML displayed in the Web browser (see Figure 17-9). The user presses a button (or hits Enter) to pass the information to an external CGI application that runs in the native operating system of the Web server. The CGI searches for the Web pages using the search criteria. When the information returns from the query, the CGI application returns the results to the Web client by dynamically building the Web page for the client. Of course, you can use the same concept and architecture to build database applications for the intranet. A multitude of tools exist to make development of such applications quick and easy (see Chapter 23).

It's the CGI architecture that really made the intranet a contender for king of the client/server world. Using CGI, we can dynamically control what the Web client sees, as well as react to input from the user. This means we can deploy applications to the Web and thus the intranet. In this scenario, intranet applications can do most things we expect from traditional client/server.

However, there are many drawbacks to CGI. First, CGI emerged from the old days of the Web. Like HTTP, it's stateless. HTTP was only set up to transmit information to and from the Web server, and then it disconnects. The CGI application cannot track the state the user was left in since the server forgets everything once it hands the HTML back to the Web client. There are hacks to get around this issue. Tools such as VisualWave and NEXT Software's WebObjects implement these CGI hacks automatically so you don't get your hands dirty.

Behind the state issue of CGI, there are performance and efficiency issues as well. CGI launches an instance of an application to process a single client request using a "share nothing" approach to resource allocation. This means that if 1000 users access a Web-enabled database, they may launch as many as 1000 different CGI processes to perform an operation on behalf of the Web

Figure 17-8 *The external CGI process pumps HTML dynamically back to the client using HTTP.*

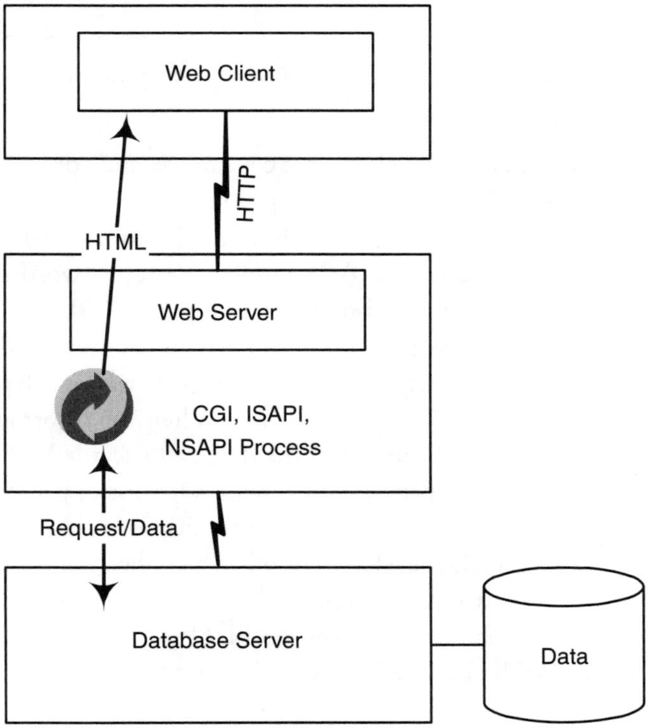

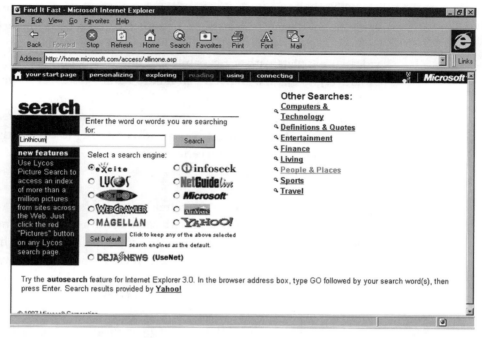

Figure 17-9 *Search engines.*

client. As you may recall from our discussion of the limits of two-tier client/
server from Chapter 16, the operating system can't handle all this processing, and
it dies a horrible death. CGI can't naturally perform load balancing, or create
links to shared resources.

The problems with CGI are obvious to those who develop applications
with it (yours truly included), and those problems limit the capabilities of
three-tier intranet. NSAPI and ISAPI are more efficient and speedy than
CGI, but they are proprietary. CGI can work across most Web servers, while
NSAPI is proprietary to Netscape Web servers, and ISAPI is bound to
Microsoft.

TWO-TIER INTRANET

Java and ActiveX provide the enabling technology for two-tier intranet. The
idea is that you download the applet into your server. The applet can function
while disconnected from the Web server as a typical dynamic client application,
and can run in a virtual operating system of its own. As an option, the applet
can link back to a database to access data for an application, just like traditional
two-tier client/server.

There are many features that make this architecture desirable. First, we can run our intranet applications disconnected from the Web server. The applet only connects to a database server to send and receive information. JDBC provides Java applets with the capability to link to any number of database servers as native Java classes. ActiveX can link to database servers as well.

The second major advantage is the ability to provide the end-user with a dynamic Web application. This means applets and ActiveX components that can respond instantly to user actions without having to constantly talk to a Web server, as is the case with three-tier intranet.

FOUR-TIER AND *N*-TIER INTRANET

The four-tier and *n*-tier intranet architectures are not widely used today, but their popularity is increasing as we seek a means to deploy mission-critical applications to our intranets. They provide developers with the flexibility to create Web applications that can scale and support all the advantages of distributed processing. Although this area is not yet cast in stone, I see three basic architectures emerging: TP monitors, CGI/distributed objects, and pure distributed objects.

Earlier we discussed the rules of an application server, and as we will cover in detail in Chapter 18, TP monitors add another layer for business application processing between the Web server and the database, and provide some advanced application processing capabilities to boot.

This architecture works by allowing the Web client to access the TP monitor services from a CGI application. The TP monitor then processes the transaction service, and communicates with the database server on behalf of the CGI process (if required). The information is then returned to the CGI process which pumps the results back to the Web client as HTML (see Figure 17-10).

Take the concept a bit further, and the CGI process can communicate with other middle-tier layers such as distributed object. As with our TP monitor example, the CGI application can access methods contained in a distributed object, or a group of distributed objects (see Chapter 19). Once we invoke a method, or a series of methods, the distributed objects perform application processing on behalf of the CGI process linked to a Web client. The distributed object can even access a database.

Once again, after processing, the information returns to the CGI process which pumps the results back to the Web client. Since the CGI process can communicate with any number of distributed objects that exist on any number of application servers, this intranet architecture supports *n*-tier and provides excellent scalability.

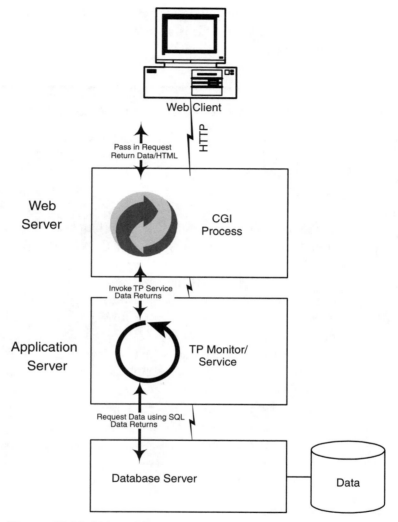

Figure 17-10 *Using a TP monitor.*

Take things ever further, and the advent of Web-enabled distributed objects means developers can place distributed objects at the client and the Web server. Rather than communicate with the Web server using traditional HTTP, the Web client runs a distributed object and communicates with the Web server using a native object protocol such as CORBA's IIOP or Microsoft's DCOM. Unlike HTTP, these protocols are dynamic and can use states, and thus make dynamic application development easier for developers. Developers can also mix and match distributed objects at the client, the Web server, the database server, and all points between to meet the requirements of the application. Once again, this is an *n*-tier intranet architecture, and provides good scalability.

Traditional Web Architecture Is a Dog

When we deploy client/server using traditional Web technology, we always encounter the same problem. Traditional Web technology was never designed to support application development. HTTP and HTLM, the basics of the Web, were built to download and view, not to process applications interactively.

Take HTTP, for example, the middleware for the Web. HTTP is a simple protocol that rides on top of TCP/IP. HTTP can only do one thing at a time, which gives intranet developers an easy architecture to work with. However, HTTP is inefficient and must establish a new TCP connection for each request. This eats a lot of resources and network bandwidth. What's more, developers cannot create multiple requests at the same time, over the same connection.

For instance, it takes four connections to request and download an HTML file with three images embedded in the HTML document: one for the HTML file, and three for the image files. Think about all the images and HTML files that support a typical application. You'll need plenty of bandwidth, and client processors that can hide the sluggish application. Although the Web is the way to go, we are actually taking a step back in time.

Intranet Drawbacks

You should know that the intranet, no matter which architecture you employ, is not a good fit for every application. The file-oriented features and stateless nature of most intranet enabling technology (see Chapter 23) limits what the intranet can do for you. For example, high-volume transaction-oriented applications, where the clients require subsecond response time, won't find a happy home on an intranet. If thousands of users invoke the same CGI process, you will see a system on its knees (see Figure 17-11).

Java and ActiveX are a step in the right direction, but not a large step. The "download once, run many times" (DORMAT) concept comes closer to traditional two-tier client/server, but brings the limitation of two-tier client/server

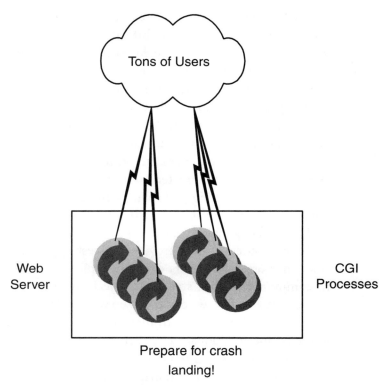

Figure 17-11 *CGI overload.*

with it. True mission-critical applications that use Java or ActiveX are not appearing on the desktops as quickly as expected. However, Java has the most support from the tool community, and new tools (such as Borland's JBuilder or Symantec's Visual Café) could make Java application development as easy as development with traditional two-tier client/server wonder tools, database connections and all. For now, approach intranet development with caution, ask a lot of questions, and test, test, test.

Working with Client/Server

The thing to remember from this chapter is that the intranet is just an extension of client/server. With the intranet, we add a similar but new architecture. The addition of an intranet Web server means architects must consider the capabilities of each architecture, as well as the enabling technology. What complicates things is that we are still playing with the technology, and it constantly changes.

Client/server developers can best leverage the intranet to complement the existing client/server architecture. As I mentioned, I would treat the intranet as just another platform—a platform with its own set of APIs, interface, advantages, and limitations. It's a platform that makes a good fit for some client/server applications, but not for others. For example, while the intranet offers a great media to distribute text and graphics, intranet technology cannot provide the performance an OLTP system requires to support a critical sales-order application. Not yet, anyway. I've seen organizations try it, and fail.

As technology presses on, we'll move to more dynamic intranet-ready application development technology (such as ActiveX and Java), with distributed objects waiting in the wings. Intranet applications remain unproven for high-volume transaction-oriented client/server. As tool vendors become better at these technologies, we could soon see widespread use.

Distributed objects provide the best approach to intranet architecture, since they offer developers dynamic application development, and the ability to communicate with standards objects such as CORBA and DCOM (see Chapter 19). In fact, we could end up with an Internet and intranet based solely on distributed objects, with distributed-object line protocols such as IIOP replacing the traditional HTTP. But it's too soon to define the formal role of distributed objects in intranet development.

From now on, the intranet will always be a part of client/server development. We can already see a sharp turn toward the intranet. For example, of the many systems I built in the past two years, all have Web capabilities, and thus exist in the fourth paradigm. I suspect you'll run into the same thing.

All client/server tools offer Web-enabled versions of themselves. All will produce HTML/CGI, Java, or ActiveX versions of their applications. What's more, new intranet-enabled client/server tools provide mechanisms to connect your intranet application to database servers, without having to deal with cryptic APIs.

I recommend that you embrace the intranet, and use the architecture I described in this chapter. Embrace the fourth paradigm of client/server, because it's embracing all of us. Your next step toward intranet development is to understand the available tools. I'll cover those in Chapter 23.

The Magic of
Transaction-Processing
Monitors

I like TP monitors. In fact, TP monitors are one of the best tricks in my bag of tricks to develop and deploy large-scale, large user-loaded client/server applications. That's why I dedicated a chapter to TP monitors.

TP (transaction-processing) monitors bring many things to distributed computing that you can't accomplish with traditional client/server development tools. I'm talking about scalability, fault tolerance, and an architecture that centralizes application processing. TP monitors provide virtual systems and single log-on capabilities, and can often reduce the overall cost of a system.

I constantly promote the virtues of TP monitors in an industry driven by hype, not solutions. TP monitors get little play at conferences, or from the press. Half the developers and architects I meet think that TP monitors are an outdated technology, and don't belong in modern client/server development. The other half think TP monitors are some next-generation supersoftware, yet to become a reality. Both assumptions are incorrect.

TP monitors are ready for prime time, and have been for a long time. Architects should consider the use of TP monitors with most distributed client/server systems. It's easier than you think to build applications around TP monitors. With products like Microsoft's Transaction Server (see sidebar), TP monitors could become a commodity product that's easier to use and deploy than more traditional high-end TP monitors.

In this chapter, let's look at TP monitors from a functional and a developer's perspective. We'll see where TP monitors make a good fit, how to build applications around TP monitors, available TP monitor products, and review tools built specifically for use with TP monitors.

Transactions in Action

TP monitors are nothing new. They originated in the mainframe days, and yours truly spent a good deal of his early days developing applications around TP monitors. Most mainframe databases came with TP monitors, which managed processes and coordinated access to the database. Whenever you use TP monitors, you need to divide complex applications into bite-size units called transactions. TP monitors control transactions from their beginning to their end, from the client to the resource server, and back again.

As I mentioned in Chapter 16, transactions are all or nothing. They either work, or they do not. They never leave a transaction incomplete. Thus, you can count on TP monitors to leave the system in a stable state. This provides the developer with a consistent and reliable programming model, and makes TP monitors a natural for distributed applications that must deal with many databases, queues, and batch interfaces running on heterogeneous platforms.

Transaction-Processing Monitors Make Complex Systems Simple

A common use for TP monitors is updating several databases during one transaction. For example, I built a system a few years ago that integrated several legacy databases into a single client/server system.

As part of the application, I needed to record a sale by updating the customer database that resided on a mainframe, the inventory databases that resided in an Oracle database, and credit-tracking databases that ran on SQL Server. Rather than update each database from the client, I integrated the application with TP monitors, and created a transaction server to update all the various databases on behalf of the client. How?

The transaction service was just a structured program that ran inside the TP monitor environment. I simply created a transaction service and named it "upall." The "upall" service was invoked by the client, which also passed the data in as parameters to the transaction service. The service connected to each database and updated it with the proper information, and returned the success or failure for each transaction. Therefore, I simply invoked the service from the client, and all the databases were updated automatically. Cool! I call this type of architecture a "virtual system," since a single interface allows access to a number of heterogeneous resources (see Figure 18-1).

Since this is an example of a true TP environment, the transaction does not commit all the database updates until all updates are complete. If there is a problem such as a database not working at the time, the TP monitor rolls

Figure 18-1 *A Virtual System.*

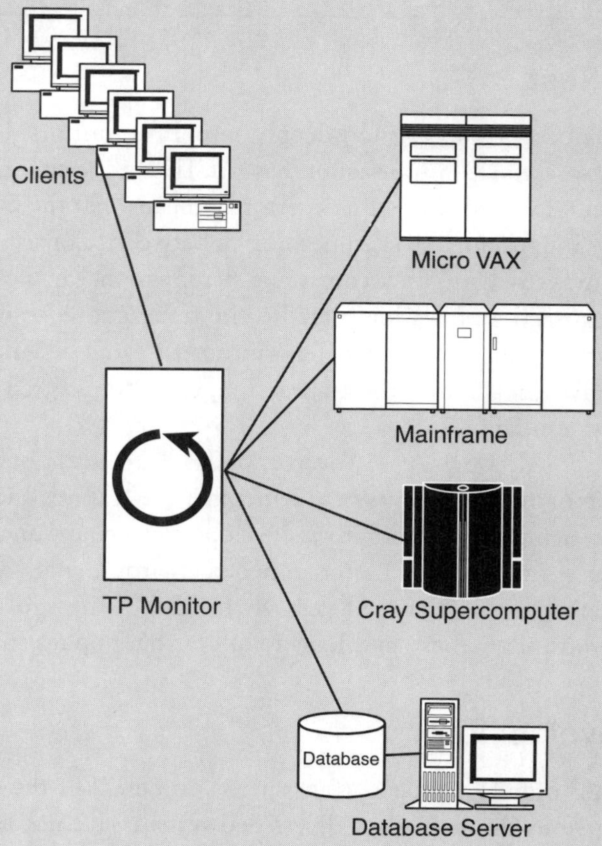

Clients

Micro VAX

Mainframe

Cray Supercomputer

TP Monitor

Database

Database Server

back the transaction as if it never happened. This assures that updates occur on all databases, or none. The TP monitor provides load-balancing services that allow the TP monitor to support a thousand or more clients (which this application does) and only use about seventy database connections per database. This means that the database servers themselves are not loaded down, and in at least one case, we saved on licensing costs.

This example application records as many as 5000 transactions a day, and is still going strong. What's more, it has never lost a transaction, or recorded a time when the databases were out of sync. A bad network connection between the monitor and a database server did stop the system one time. The TP monitor did not update the databases that were still working, which means the TP monitor did its job just as planned. As time goes on, databases will be combined to try to turn three databases into one. In the meantime, the TP monitor really saved the day.

The "ACID" Test

Before we can dig too deeply into TP monitors, let's discuss the concept of transactions. A transaction has "ACID" properties, meaning it's atomic, consistent, isolated, and durable. Atomic means that the transaction either completes, or it does not, never something in between. Consistency means that the system always remains in a consistent state, whether or not the system completes the transaction. Isolation refers to the transaction's ability to work independent of other transactions that may run in the same TP monitor environment. Durability means that the transaction, once committed and complete, can survive system failures.

Although ACID oversimplifies the concept of a transaction, in my humble opinion it's an easy way to remember the features and functions of TP monitors. When using TP monitors, developers can count on a high degree of application integrity—even in heterogeneous environments with different operating systems and databases. Even when other things go wrong often, TP monitors won't allow these problems to affect your application or data.

Scalable Development

TP monitors process transactions on behalf of the client, and can route transactions through many diversified systems. It's not unusual to see a TP monitor tie together a mainframe, a NT server, a multi-processing Unix server, and a file

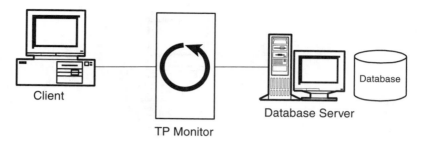

Figure 18-2 *TP Monitor accesses data on behalf of the client.*

server. TP monitors also provide load balancing, thread control, and the ability to automatically recover from typical system problems.

Although they are technically middleware, TP monitors are more than a simple middleware connection layer. TP monitors provide a place for the application code to run. Thus, TP monitors provide a location for business processing and application objects to run. For example, you can use TP monitors to enforce business rules and maintain data integrity, or you can create entire applications by building many transaction services and invoking them from the client.

There is a big difference between traditional two-tier architectures, and three-tier with TP monitors. First of all, the client no longer works directly with the database. The developer must build a transaction service. When the client invokes the transaction service, it accesses the database on behalf of the client (see Figure 18-2).

For example, a PowerBuilder application can access a TP monitor service through a DLL. The DLL sends a message to the TP monitor that tells it to invoke a particular transaction service (see Figure 18-3). The transaction service interfaces with the database. This means that the client is decoupled from the database, and can't work directly with the schema. Tools (such as Power-Builder) that use the schema for application construction don't have to deal with the database. You build a true thin client—almost a terminal—when you build client/server applications around a TP monitor.

DATABASE MULTIPLEXING

The real trick that TP monitors perform is to multiplex and manage transactions to reduce the number of connections and processing loads that larger systems place on a database server. With TP monitors in the architecture, you can increase the number of clients without increasing the size of your database server. Why? With a TP monitor at the middle tier, you remove the one-to-one, client-to-connection limitation of traditional two-tier development.

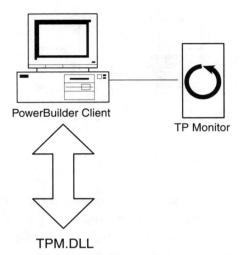

Figure 18-3 *Using a .DLL to access a TP Monitor.*

For example, a thousand or more clients can easily use a single processing mid-sized database server to access the database through a TP monitor. The TP monitor only requires about fifty connections to support that number of users. Since they can "funnel" the clients' requests, TP monitors remove the process-per-client requirement (see Figure 18-4). A client invokes the transaction services that reside on the TP monitor, and the services can share the same database server connections (threads and processes). Whenever a connection

Figure 18-4 *Removing the process-per-client requirement.*

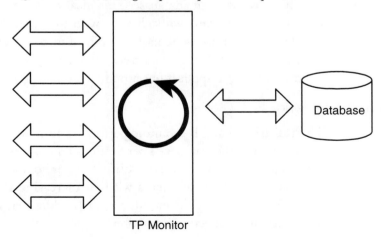

overloads, the TP monitor starts a new connection to the database server. This is the core of the three-tier architecture, and the reason three-tier can scale to high user loads.

LOAD BALANCING

As we just mentioned, TP monitors remove the process-per-client requirement, and funnel incoming client requests to shared server processes. When the number of incoming client requests surpasses the number of shared processes the system can handle, other processes start automatically. This is the concept behind load balancing (see Figure 18-5). Some TP monitors can distribute the process load over several servers at the same time, or distribute the processing over several processors in multiprocessing environments.

The load-balancing features of TP monitors also handle transaction priorities. The TP monitor can run some transactions at a higher priority. Developers use this feature to assure that VIP clients get top-notch service. TP monitors handle priorities through classes. High-priority classes kick up the process priorities. As a rule, developers use high-priority server classes to encapsulate short-running and high-priority functions. Low-priority processes (such as batch) run inside low-priority server classes.

Moreover, developers can assign priorities by application type, the resource managers a transaction uses, high and low response times, and fault-tolerant features that a transaction requires. Developers can also control the number of processes or threads available for each transaction, using any number of para-

Figure 18-5 *Load balancing.*

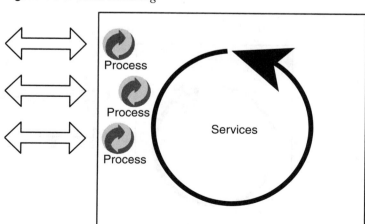

TP Monitor

meters. Of course, each TP monitor varies in features and functions, and you'll need to check with your vendor to see what its tool supports, where, and how.

FAULT TOLERANCE

As I mentioned, TP monitors were built from the ground up to provide a robust application deployment environment, and to recover from any number of system-related problems. TP monitors provide high availability by employing redundant systems. For instance, TP monitors use dynamic switching to reroute transactions around server and network problems (see Figure 18-6). The transactions work through a two-phase commit process to assure that the transaction completes, and that transactions never become lost electrons when hardware, operating systems, and networks fail. Two-phase commit also makes sure that you can perform transactions on two or more heterogeneous resources reliably.

For example, if there is a power failure, TP monitors notify all participants (server, queues, clients, etc.) of the particular transaction process of the problem. All the work that occurred thus far in the transaction is rolled back, and the system returns to the state it was in before the transaction began, cleaning up any mess it may have left. Sometimes, developers can build transactions that automatically resubmit themselves after a failure.

COMMUNICATIONS

TP monitors provide a good example of middleware that uses middleware. TP monitors communicate in a variety of ways, including remote procedure calls (RPCs), distributed dynamic program links (DPLs), interprocess communica-

Figure 18-6 *Dynamic switching.*

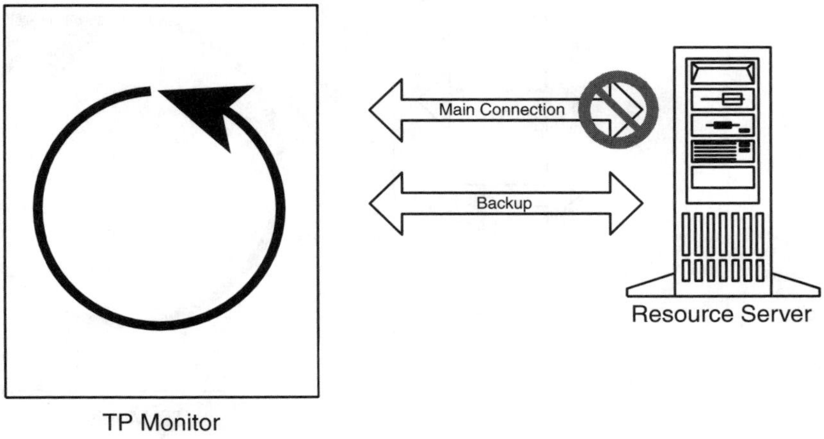

TP Monitor

Resource Server

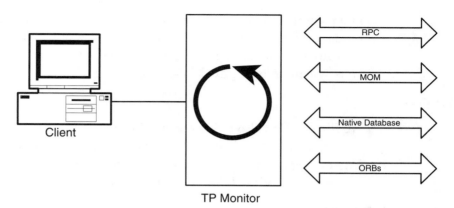

Figure 18-7 *Mixing middleware.*

tions, and message-oriented middleware (MOM). However, the RPCs that TP monitors use are specialized for use with TP monitors, and known as transactional RPCs (or TRPCs). Since TP monitors are simply APIs in an application, developers have the flexibility to mix and match all sorts of middleware layers and resource servers to meet the requirements of an application (see Figure 18-7).

Products

In the world of TP monitors there are four major players: NCR's Top End, Transarc's Encina, IBM's CICS/6000, and BEA's Tuxedo. Microsoft will also be a player in the TP monitor world when it releases Transaction Server, a COM/ActiveX-enabled TP monitor (see Sidebar). Let's take a quick tour through the big players, and look at a brief synopsis of each.

ENCINA

Transarc's Encina is a TP monitor closely coupled with the Open Software Foundation's Distributed Computing Environments (DCE). Encina accesses databases using XA, and works on most Unix platforms. The trouble with Encina is performance. The close ties to the RPC-bound DCE mean that Encina will take a few more cycles to process a transaction.

TUXEDO

Tuxedo, the market leader from BEA, provides the best platform support, including HTP, NCR, Pyramid, Sequent, Silicon Graphics, and Sun. The wide platform support makes Tuxedo the safest bet for a TP monitor, since you can always find platforms to run it. The last Tuxedo project I worked on ran the TP monitor on a PC running UnixWare (an Intel version of Unix). That low-end, inexpensive configuration itself was pretty speedy, but you can take the code to larger Unix systems as well. Tuxedo also supports a DCE connection (See Chapter 3).

TOP END

NCR's Top End also offers versions for most Unix platforms, including IBM, Sun, HP, and NCR. Top End is second only to Tuxedo in market share. Top End can exploit most multi-processing environments, and NCR tied it closely to the services of the Unix operating system.

CICS AND CICS/6000

IBM's CICS/6000 is a Unix version of IBM's mainframe-based CICS TP monitor. CICS/6000 works with IBM's RS/600 line of servers, and you can also find it on HP/9000s, and a few other Unix environments. CICS is an older TP monitor that can run existing CICS systems that may already exist in your organization.

The downside of CICS/6000 is its lack of support for a wide variety of operating systems, such as Windows NT. Another drawback is that CICS cannot run multiple copies of the TP monitor across servers. The upside is the number of years under CICS's belt, and the number of people who already know how to program in CICS. For example, I did a lot of CICS in the past, and picked up CICS/6000 in no time at all.

Microsoft Prepares Its Transaction Server (Formally Viper)

Microsoft will soon break into the TP monitor marketplace with the release of Transaction Server (TS). TS is the code name for its COM (Component Object Model)-enabled TP monitor, in beta as I write this book. The significance of TS is that it could make TP monitors a commodity product, and allow any COM-enabled tool to create transaction services.

Microsoft is serious about selling a TP monitor. They hired the top TP talent in the market from companies like Tandem, IBM, and DEC, and plans to release a TP monitor that can run ActiveX components as transactions (see Figure 18-8). Therefore, it's just a matter of creating an ActiveX component, managed by the TP monitor services. This could place the development of TP monitor applications in the hands of easy-to-use specialized client/server development tools such as Delphi, Visual Basic, and PowerBuilder. TS is also Internet-aware, and Microsoft built it from the ground up as a run-time environment for Web-enabled applications.

TS is actually a transaction-oriented repository for ActiveX components, and allows the ActiveX components to function as transactions. Clients invoke the ActiveX component as a transaction. The TS environment manages transactions the same way traditional TP monitors do.

TS is a true TP monitor that provides transparent distribution, reliable updates of databases, and a scalable development environment. Using the COM model, developers and ISVs will find it easy to deliver products that work with TS. TS also exploits DCOM and accesses Web server functions through Microsoft's native Internet Information Server API (ISAPI).

When available, you'll find versions of TS for Windows NT and Windows 95, and you can write TS transactions using any COM-enabled development tool. Microsoft SQL Server's Distributed Transaction Coordinator (DTC), a component of TS, is already a part of Microsoft SQL Server (version 6) that allows developers to distribute transactions over several SQL servers.

I think TS will be a success for several reasons. Microsoft will put its resources behind TS to make the product powerful and easy to use. Also, TS will let TP developers use off-the-shelf development environments to create TS transactions. Microsoft will sell at a price most can afford.

Microsoft is very good at making high-end products into commodities. This will be just another example.

Figure 18-8 *Transaction Server can run ActiveX components as transactions.*

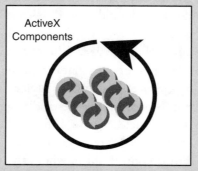

Transaction Server.

XA and X/Open

There are a few standards that define how TP monitors function: the International Standards Organization (ISO) and X/Open's distributed transaction process (DTP). X/Open is the one to pay attention to, since it defines the APIs TP monitors use.

In 1991, the X/Open XTP group created the transaction processing reference model, and in 1994 they published the distributed transaction reference model. This model defined the features of transaction-based systems, and how they communicate with outside resources.

An outcome of this process was the definition of the XA interface. The XA interface defines how a transaction manager and a resource manager (such as a database) can communicate. For instance, XA defines how Encina can communicate with Sybase.

The XA interface is a set of function calls, split between the transaction manager and the resource manager. Functions provided by the transaction manager allow the resource manager to tell the transaction manager that it's alive and well and ready to work with a transaction, or that it's resting and should not be bothered. XA provides other features too.

Those who develop three-tier client/server applications around transactions need to know the inner workings of XA. For TP monitors, XA is the gateway to the outside world.

Transaction Processing versus Stored Procedures

Some of you may wonder if stored procedures do many of the same things that TP monitors do. In some respects, they are the same. Developers create procedural programs that perform some predefined operation when called upon by a client application. Stored procedures and triggers can even support transaction characteristics.

However, they are very different beasts. TP monitors manage application execution through services that run in the TP monitor environment, away from the database. Since they are decoupled from the database, they are database-independent. Stored procedures and triggers remain proprietary to a particular database (e.g., Oracle, Sybase, Informix).

In addition, TP monitors provide advanced services such as load balancing and thread control. Also, where the presence of a TP monitor makes the system easier to scale, the presence of many stored procedures and triggers can reduce the number of users the system can support.

Developing Transaction-Processing Monitor Applications

Now that we know what TP monitors are, how in the heck do you build client/server applications with them? There are many ways, many products, and a few tradeoffs to consider.

The first thing to consider is the three-tier architecture. At the first tier is the client, who handles interaction with the end-user. At the second tier, the application server processes most of the application logic using the transaction facilities of the TP monitor. Some sort of resource manager resides at the third tier, such as queue, file system, or batch interface, but most often it's a database server such as Oracle, Sybase, or Informix (see Figure 18-9).

When we build applications around TP monitors, we build the client application within traditional development environments such as C++. Or

Figure 18-9 *Resource manager.*

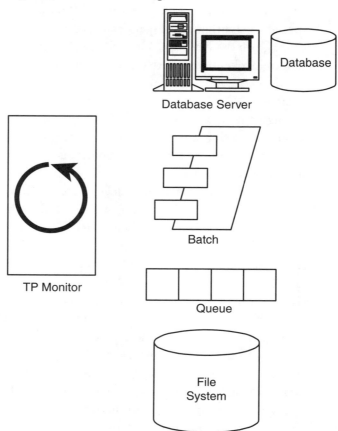

developers may use a specialized client/server tool that knows how to interface with a TP monitor, or any other development tool that can load and use a DLL. There are, however, tools built specifically for use with a TP monitor. Tools with this capability include Prolific's Prolific, PowerSoft's EncinaBuilder (it's really just PowerBuilder), and Encina for Windows.

When we build transaction services using a TP monitor and a traditional 3GL, we can access transaction services through the native TP monitor API. Usually, TP monitors support traditional 3GLs such as C and COBOL, but some support C++ as well.

To build transaction services, we define what functions the service will perform programmatically when access to TP monitor APIs is required to make it happen. Take Tuxedo, for example. The tpconnect() function call sets up the conversation with the participating service, tpsend() returns a response, and tpalloc() allocates buffer space.

Let's look at a typical Windows-based client/server development project. From a Windows client, access to a TP monitor and its services exists within special DLLs that developers can load from most client/server development tools. Once the developer loads the DLLs, they can work through the application to invoke functions that access transaction services running within the TP monitor. As previously mentioned, the service can then talk directly to the database on behalf of the client application, using interfaces such as XA, or through the native database API. Developers must build not only the client application using a particular development environment, but the TP monitor services. Remember, typical TP monitor services are 3GL applications that use the TP monitor API.

The problem that most developers run into is that they are decoupled from the database, and thus can't work with the schema. This is more of a problem for the specialized client/server development tool developers (Visual Basic, Delphi, PowerBuilder, etc.) since they usually work with the schema to construct an application. This is less of a problem with C++ developers, since they usually work with DLLs and APIs, and don't typically deal directly with the schema from the development environment.

The client application communicates directly with the TP monitor through a transactional remote procedure call (TRPC). In turn, the TP monitor talks to the resource manager using a native protocol or XA. Examples of resource managers are a native database API, ODBC, or a proprietary database-dependent network protocol such as Oracle's SQL*Net. As I mentioned, since you handle the creation of a transaction service through a 3GL interface, you have the power to integrate many API services into a single transaction.

Java Does Transaction-Processing Monitors for the Intranet

For those of you who think that Java and TP monitors are worlds apart, guess again. Since Java can access external resources (such as database servers) using native APIs, Java applets and applications can also access transaction services on TP monitors.

A intranet client downloads the applet from the Web server, where it runs inside the browser environment using a native Java byte-code interpreter. The applet can then invoke the services of a TP monitor on the intranet, or the Internet. The TP monitor, in turn, carries out the request and returns a status back to the applet.

The significance of this capability is the migration of Java to three-tier client/server. This will give Web-enabled application developers the ability to scale those sorts of applications to the enterprise. It's also a way to Java-enable existing three-tier client/server applications, since the transaction services are predefined.

FOURTH-GENERATION-LANGUAGE-DRIVEN TRANSACTION PROCESSING

If the above sounds like a lot of work to you, it is. Building a three-tier client/server application using TP monitors is a complex process, and it takes a lot of development time. Remember, developers are not only responsible for creating the client application, but also the application server middle tier. Until a few years ago, this meant 3GL development. Today, other options exist.

A few 4GL application development vendors have created products specifically for TP monitor, three-tier application development. A few of these monitor vendors that work with 4GL include NCR, Transarc, and BEA, and the products include Tempo from Four Seasons Software, EncinaBuilder from PowerSoft, and Prolifics from Prolifics. Let's take a quick look at them.

TEMPO

Tempo is a suite of products from NCR, the makers of Top End. It's the completest set of easy-to-program products that I've found for TP monitor development. That is, if you happen to use the Top End TP monitor.

Tempo provides an easygoing 4GL TP monitor development environment, and includes a modified version of SuperNOVA (a client/server development product from Four Seasons Software). Tempo consists of Top End's distributed application management services, Powersoft's PowerBuilder, as well as SuperNOVA. To build a Top End application, developers use PowerBuilder to build a list of Top End transaction service names, and to define their input and output parameters. This produces a data window object that developers can use from within the PowerBuilder tool. Developers invoke TP monitor services through PowerScript. That takes care of the client.

At the application server, developers use the SuperNOVA 4GL to build the transaction services. This replaces the traditional method of using a 3GL compiler and the TP monitor's API. Developers use a PowerBuilder application to access the TP monitor services they defined with the SuperNOVA 4GL. Since SuperNOVA is database-aware, it can communicate with most database servers through an easy-to-use interface. This gives developers the ability to see the database schema when they build SuperNOVA transaction services on the application server. Because SuperNOVA talks to Informix, Oracle, Sybase, and Ingres databases (along with any database accessible through EDA/SQL or ODBC), SuperNOVA can bring RAD to TP monitor service development.

EncinaBuilder

If you use the Encina TP monitor product, you'll find a version of Power-Builder to access transaction services on Encina. EncinaBuilder is really just an integration of PowerBuilder and Encina for Windows (a DLL) that gives PowerBuilder developers the ability to build an Encina client using the popular PowerBuilder.

Developers have access to a transaction service browser, which is native to EncinaBuilder. The browser lets the developers select the Encina services they want to add to their PowerBuilder application. EncinaBuilder can automatically create custom user objects such as data windows, DLLs, and transaction objects.

Prolifics

While Tempo and EncinaBuilder tie themselves to a particular brand of TP monitor, Prolifics (formally JAM/TPi; a sister company to JYAAC) from Pro-lifics supports several. Prolifics provides a TP monitor-ready version of JAM 7 for Tuxedo and Encina. Prolifics is another division of JYACC (see Chapter 11).

Rather than build transaction services with a 3GL, JYACC's idea is to build them with JAM 7's easy-to-use, specialized client/server development environment. Developers may use this tool to build the client and server sides of an application. Like Tempo, Prolifics can work directly with the TP monitor API, which removes the developer from the API's complexities. Moreover, since JAM 7 is a database-aware product, it can access databases directly without having to resort to a low-level database API. Developers can even specify database interaction graphically, and build the service with an easy-to-use scripting language that's part of the base tool. JAM 7 is multi-platform, and can run pretty much everywhere. Again, you can RAD your way through the development of common transaction services.

iTRAN

iTRAN, from Independence Technology, is another product to help facilitate TP monitor-enabled application development. The iTRAN tool kit works with Encina, Top End, CICS, and Tuxedo.

The key to iTRAN's power is its portability. The tool kit lets developers use traditional client/server development products (anything that can load a DLL) to create portable three-tier TP monitor applications. The TP monitor services appear as standard procedure calls to the developer and the development tool. The tool kit provides a translation layer between the application and the TP monitor, therefore the developer can swap TP monitors at anytime without having to change the client code (see Figure 18-10). You will find this helpful if you use more than one TP monitor, or if you want to protect your investment at the client.

THE GOOD NEWS

Good news? I already gave you the good news about TP monitors. They provide highly scalable and reliable development environments that can handle most user loads and recover from most problems. They are the best way I know to handle heavy-use client/server applications, especially in heterogeneous distributed processing environments.

THE BAD NEWS

The downside of using TP monitors includes the cost of building three-tier client/server applications. The extra development time, and the price of the TP monitors themselves drive costs skyward. The bottom line is that three-tier client/server development is complex, and requires a variety of skills to implement a system. A lot of frustrating integration work must occur, such as making your client talk to your TP monitor, and making your TP monitor talk to your database. They never seem to work "right out of the box" without a lot of technical support from the vendors.

As a general rule, budget twice the development dollars when you build TP monitor-based applications versus traditional two-tier client/server applica-

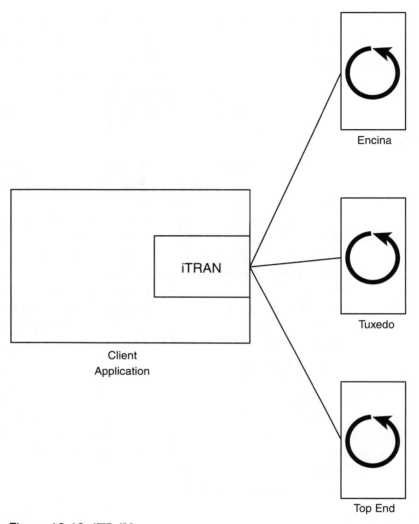

Figure 18-10 *iTRAN.*

tions. However, when you consider the cost per user and the number of users TP monitors can support, it could be a bargain.

The database funneling trick could mean a few less database licenses, but you'd better check with your database server vendor. Many of them have rewritten their licenses to include users connected through a TP monitor. The cost of TP monitors has put them beyond the reach of most small organizations. Many run around $50,000 per monitor, and plan right now to spend more dollars on training, support, and hardware.

To Monitor or Not to Monitor?

So, is your client/server application monitor worthy? Here are a few reasons to create your application around a TP monitor:

Mission-Critical. Your application is so important that it cannot fail. TP monitors can recover from almost any type of problem, if you set them up correctly. TP monitors also make an application highly available, with downtime reduced through redundant servers and the TP monitor's ability to reroute transactions around problems.

High Performance. Since TP monitors provide load-balancing features, they provide consistent performance. With user loads from one to a thousand, TP monitors can start and stop processes and threads as required, and even partition processing across servers or processors.

Scalability. TP monitors are one of the best ways to make your application support an ever-increasing number of users. Since TP monitors circumvent the limitations of two-tier client/server, they can take you where you want to go.

I would say that anyone with a client/server application that supports over a hundred users should consider using a TP monitor. That's about where we run into a performance and stability wall with most traditional two-tier client/server systems. I also think that TP monitors are one of the best tricks in the business. They saved my neck many times. They can save yours, too.

Working with Distributed
Objects and
Components

Distributed objects entered the systems scene in the early '90s, but their potential didn't reach the client/server development world until very recently. My long, turbulent relationship with distributed objects began over six years ago. In my opinion, today's distributed objects will soon move into mainstream client/server and intranet development. That's why it's important to include distributed objects in any discussion of client/server development.

Several recent events have renewed interest in distributed objects:

First, we now move in droves toward multi-tiered client/server. Developers find that the enabling technology of distributed objects can get them there. Distributed objects give client/server developers the ability to create portable objects that can run on a variety of servers, and communicate using a predefined and standard messaging interface.

Second, during the last few years, we only had one real standard, CORBA (described later in this chapter). Microsoft has just entered the distributed object marketplace with the distributed component object model (DCOM). DCOM promises to provide a distributed object infrastructure with Windows-based operating systems, and the ability to tie together applications created with traditional client/server tools. The object request broker (ORB) is also part of the operating system, and therefore it's a giveaway.

Third, we learned to take ORBs to the desktop through the use of components. Application components such as ActiveX and OpenDoc let developers create a client/server application by mixing and matching components. Kind of like building an application the same way we piece together a jigsaw puzzle. This is the nirvana of application development, the ability to assemble applications the way Ford assembles Mustangs from prebuilt component parts.

Finally, the rise of the Web renewed interest in distributed objects. Technologies and standards such as CORBA's Internet Inter-ORB Protocol (IIOP) promise to provide both an enabling technology for dynamic application development, and a better application-to-application, object-to-object transport layer. Now that powerhouse Web companies such as Netscape have put their weight behind ORBs, intranet developers will continue their rush to ORBs.

By the time this book hits the streets, I believe distributed objects and components will have a much stronger hold on the client/server development market. I see more development projects use these technologies, and I see a renewed interest at conferences and in the press. The interest in the Web will move things quickly as well.

This chapter provides the information you need to know about client/server development using distributed objects or components. We'll start from the conceptual level, and move through distributed-object and component standards du jour, and then into tools and trends. I'll fill you in on the good, the bad, and the distributed.

The General Idea

I became involved with ORBs in my early days of object-oriented development. As I learned to leverage objects for application development, the fact that objects are bound to tools limited my efforts. For example, a C++ tool (e.g., Microsoft Visual Basic) can only use a C++ tool. What's more, that C++ object is not only bound to C++, but typically bound to a particular C++ tool as well. I, along with most object developers at the time, wanted a way to mix and match objects to form an application.

So what's an ORB? Object request brokers provide developers with standard objects that communicate with other standard objects using a standard interface and line protocol (pretty standard, right?). Like traditional objects, (such as those found with C++ or Smalltalk), ORBS can access methods of other ORBS locally, or over a network (see Figure 19-1). That gives ORBs their distributed capabilities. ORBs can also exchange data and are platform-independent, able to run on many connected servers.

ORBs can pass requests from object to object. The clients invoke ORB services through the ORB Core and the IDL stub. Or you can employ a dynamic invocation interface (described later). The stub provides mapping between the language binding (e.g., C++ and Smalltalk) and the ORB services. That's how you make the ORBs do what you want them to do. The ORB Core then moves the request to the object implementation. The object implementa-

Figure 19-1 *ORBs are able to access methods of other local or remote ORBs.*

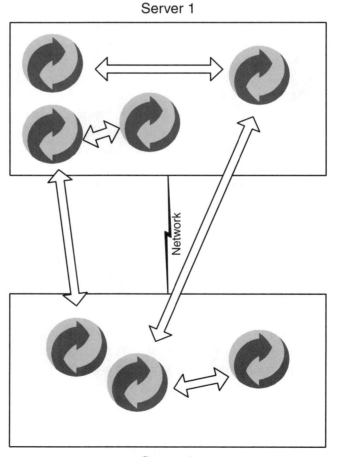

Server 1

Network

Server 2

tion receives the message through an upcall using the IDL skeleton or dynamic skeleton. More on this later.

Common Object Request Broker Architecture

It was 1989, I was developing some of the first object-oriented applications at Mobil. At that time, the Object Management Group (OMG), a consortium of technology vendors, began work on the first cross-compatible distributed object standard. The OMG includes the object powerhouse vendors—IBM, Apple, Sun, and many others. The OMG promised object reuse regardless of the platform, tool, or programming language—a common binary object to work anywhere for any application, an object that would let developers mix and match objects for distributed computing application development. This standard became the Common Object Request Broker Architecture (CORBA), first released around 1991 (version 1.1). However, a long road lay before us.

I read CORBA 1 with great anticipation. This specification would finally let me put down my C++ compiler and purchase objects to create my applications, now that the standard was in place. As with many things in the distributed application development world, there is always a catch.

The first CORBA specification came in two parts; the interface definition language (IDL) and the dynamic invocation interface (DII). Each of these components exists inside every CORBA ORB and provides a messaging service between ORBs either locally (intracomputer), or over a network (intercomputer).

The IDL, at its core, defines an object's structure and provides the developer with an API to access the object services during run-time. The IDL is what the CORBA ORB developers must deal with to build application-dependent features into an ORB.

The DDI is an API as well; it provides developers with dynamic construction of object invocations. In contrast to the IDL, DDI allows developers to do things while the objects run. The client can establish the objects and operations, including any parameters.

SHORTFALLS

CORBA 1 had many limitations. For example, it did not provide enough detail to allow ORB vendors to create CORBA-compliant ORBs that could work together. Therefore, while version 1 did define a common object standard, there was no real value without interoperability. CORBA 1 was a baby step.

The OMG released CORBA 2 in 1994 to solve the problem of interoperability. CORBA 2 provided specific syntax for a network protocol, and thus ORBs could communicate with one another. CORBA 2 also defined a TCP/IP-based Inter-ORB protocol backbone, as well as an Inter-ORB communication service to let components generate IDs for any interfaces they support.

The guts of CORBA ORBs remained the same, including support for an IDL and DDI. However, CORBA 2 includes mapping to C++ and Smalltalk. CORBA 1 only included mappings to C, a nonobject-oriented language. Go figure.

Today there are many CORBA-compliant ORBs available from commercial vendors. They include IBM's Distributed System Object Model (DSOM), Digital's ObjectBroker, Visigenic's Orbaline, and Iona's Orbix. Most have CORBA 2-compliant ORBs already available, while some are almost there.

COMMON OBJECT REQUEST BROKER ARCHITECTURE DETAILS

There are four main parts to a CORBA ORB: the object request broker (ORB), object services, common facilities, and application objects (see Figure 19-2). You will also find these features in other ORBs such as Microsoft's COM/DCOM, or even proprietary ORBs such as those sold by NeXT Software, Forte, and Dynasty.

Object Request Broker. The ORB is really an engine that shares information with other ORBs, and together creates a distributed application. ORBs exist as

Figure 19-2 *Parts of a CORBA ORB.*

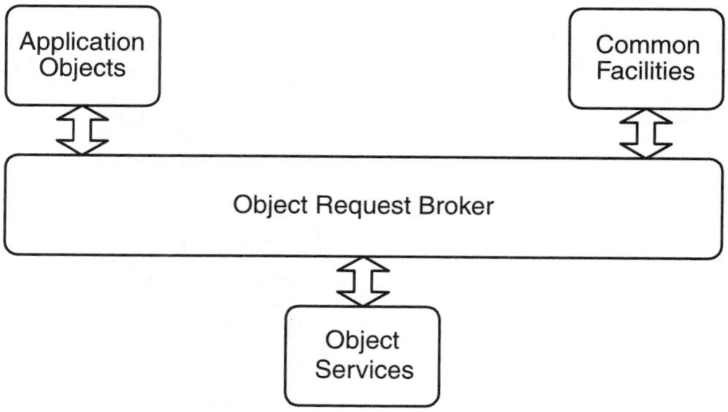

background objects, and function behind the application. We layer applications on top of ORBs that provide the distributed infrastructure. This is why ORBs make good middleware layers—many communication services already exist in ORB services (such as CORBA-compliant ORBs). Layering also provides heterogeneous application portability and interoperability.

Object Services. CORBA mandates object services, which are groups of services that leverage object interfaces for communications between services. These are the basic services developers expect in an ORB: security, transaction management, and data exchange services. Developers use object services as a base class of sorts, to build applications.

Common Facilities. Common facilities are a collection of services that link with the client, and remain optional for CORBA. This lets developers build component characteristics in CORBA-compliant ORBS. Developers think of common facilities whenever they need to implement CORBA-compliant, component-based objects such as OpenDoc.

Application Objects. Application objects support application development features of a CORBA ORB as defined by the ORB/application developer. Here is where the rubber meets the road in ORB development, where we can turn ORBs into something useful. We build these features of the ORB with the IDL. The IDL assures interoperability with other CORBA-compliant ORBs.

Object Request Brokers for the Intranet

Although the press has shown renewed interest in ORBs, that does not make ORBs another client/server success story. However, ORBs on the Web could change all that. As always, hype drives success.

What caused all the commotion was an announcement by Netscape that they would base their Internet infrastructure on the CORBA Internet Inter-ORB Protocol (IIOP). As you may gather from this chapter, IIOP is the way CORBA-compliant ORBs talk to one another. We now plan to have these ORBs communicate over the Internet and intranets.

Netscape promotes IIOP as the next version of HTTP, and promises to deliver new application development capabilities for the Internet and intranet incarnations of the Web. Netscape rules the roost in the world of Web browsers, with over 80 percent of market share and 20 million Web browsers in use. That's a tremendous amount of power in today's Web world, enough to make distributed objects an overnight success. IIOP-enabled ORBs will reside on the client and run inside an ORB-enabled browser. The browser will communicate with other CORBA-compliant objects that exist on the intranet or Internet.

IIOP isn't the only ORB player. Visigenic has already created a Java- and CORBA-based ORB for the Web called VisiBroker. Visigenic licenses VisiBroker to Netscape, and the next release of Netscape communicator will include VisiBroker as part of the browser. This is exciting news for the CORBA world. VisiBroker could finally make CORBA the standard for distributed object-based applications on the intranet.

Microsoft is in the game too, promoting DCOM as a means to deploy distributed objects to the Web. DCOM is described as ActiveX's answer to IIOP, and can use a DCOM-based binary network protocol using DCE-RPCs.

Component Object Model

What both complicates and drives the distributed object world right now is the emergence of Microsoft's component object model (COM). Microsoft invented COM just a few years ago, using its existing object linking and embedding (OLE) model as the design basis for COM.

Although the great ORB debate rages on, COM is as much an ORB as CORBA. ORB provides an object standard (that isn't really object-oriented) and a common mechanism for inter-ORB communications. COM is based on OLE automation (using the COM model), a standard on most Windows desktops and a feature of most Windows-based client/server development tools. For example, Visual Basic, Delphi, and PowerBuilder all support the creation of COM-enabled OLE automation servers—servers an application can share through DCOM.

There are several COM products, including OLE automation servers (which can function as ORBS) and ActiveX components. I'll take a quick tour of each.

OBJECT LINKING AND EMBEDDING AUTOMATION

OLE automation lets developers take advantage of the services of other OLE/COM-enabled applications. For example, you can access the services of a PowerBuilder application from Visual Basic, or run a Visual Basic object from

Word for Windows. OLE provides a standard interface to expose methods for access by other OLE automation servers or containers.

There are two kinds of OLE automation: the OLE automation controller and the OLE automation server. The OLE automation controller is really the COM client. The controller actually invokes the services of an OLE automation server through the common OLE interface (see Figure 19-3). OLE automation servers are ORBs that expose methods functions, available for use by other OLE automation servers.

There are two kinds of OLE automation servers: in-process and out-of-process. In-process servers are typically DLLs, and run in the same process and memory space as their clients (see Figure 19-4). ActiveX components offer the best examples of in-process OLE automation servers with some component features built in.

In contrast, out-of-process servers run in separate memory and process space from their clients (see Figure 19-5). Out-of-process servers are typically EXEs that communicate with other COM applications through some sort of lightweight RPC mechanism (intracomputer). As with any ORB, out-of-process OLE automation servers can invoke the services of other COM ORBs locally, or remotely through DCOM (described later).

ACTIVEX

ActiveX is a COM-enabled component that can be snapped into your application, or downloaded into your Web browser like a Java applet. ActiveX

Figure 19-3 *OLE Automation Controller and Server.*

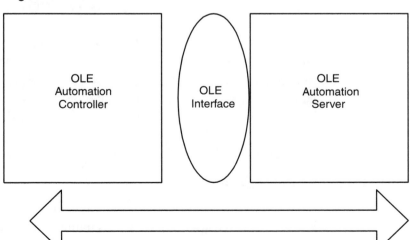

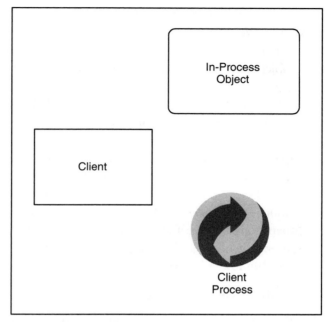

Figure 19-4 *In-process servers.*

(formally OCX) is Microsoft's answer to components and Java. ActiveX will be a major player in Microsoft's world. You will see ActiveX as an application component that works inside most Windows-based client/server development environments, and even on servers like SQL Server, Internet Information Server, and the new Transaction Server TP monitor (see Chapter 18).

Figure 19-5 *Out-of-process servers.*

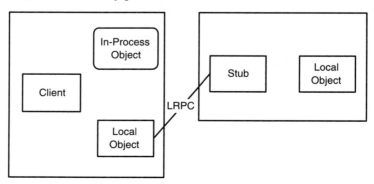

ActiveX components are really OCX components stripped down for use on the Web, although Microsoft no longer uses the term OCX. They use the OLE in-process server architecture, and can naturally link to other COM-enabled architectures such as DCOM (described next). Client/server developers can use ActiveX components inside applications when they use ActiveX-enabled development tools such as Visual Basic, PowerBuilder, and Delphi. The ActiveX support in these tools ensures ActiveX's success as a component standard, and could ensure its success on the Web as well. In my opinion, tool support makes or breaks a component standard (see OpenDoc sidebar later in this chapter for some preaching on that issue).

There is a downside to ActiveX. As with everything Microsoft, ActiveX is linked to Windows. Microsoft addressed this concern and made ActiveX an "open" standard, with the ActiveX standard controlled by an independent committee of vendors and developers. Microsoft also plans to port ActiveX to other non-Windows platforms such as the Macintosh and a few flavors of Unix.

MOVING TO DISTRIBUTED COMPONENT OBJECT MODEL

Of course, if you cannot distribute COM-enabled ORBs, you lose the power of COM. DCOM (now known as the Active Server) gives developers the ability to

Figure 19-6 *DCOM.*

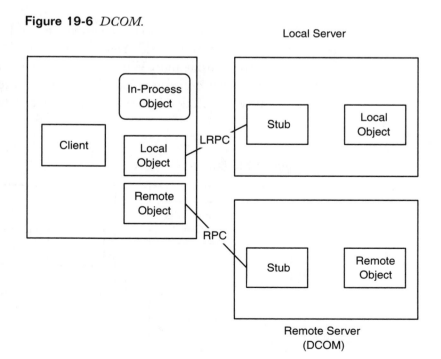

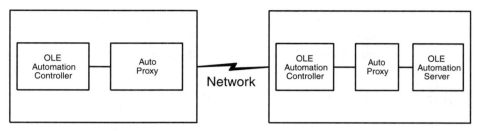

Figure 19-7 *Using DCOM to access remote COM ORBs.*

create OLE/COM automation servers, and make them available for other COM-enabled client/server applications on a network (see Figure 19-6). DCOM is not a commercial ORB, but part of the operating system. DCOM was first released with Windows NT version 4, and will be a part of the next release of Windows 95.

Unlike CORBA-enabled ORBs that require a lot of integration and coordination to make them work, DCOM makes life a little simpler. With DCOM, the COM-enabled application simply checks the registry of the Windows operating system to locate and use remote COM-enabled ORBs, finding and invoking the service it requires. For example, a client/server developer could create a COM ORB (an OLE automation server) that generates a sales report that any number of COM-enabled applications can use. Other COM-enabled applications that exist on the network can see and use the COM report ORB. They locate and invoke the ORB's methods through the Windows operating system's built-in DCOM mechanism (see Figure 19-7).

As I mentioned earlier, DCOM differs a bit from the CORBA architecture because it's built into the infrastructure of the operating system, and it is not a product of an ORB vendor. DCOM is backward-compatible with existing COM-enabled client/server development tools, and tools that were not created specifically for the development of distributed objects. These tools will find themselves in the distributed object business simply because DCOM can distribute the OLE automation servers they create.

CORBA has yet to attract the mainstream tool vendors. The lack of tools means a lack of interest in CORBA by the client/server development community. In contrast, COM is already a part of most Windows-based client/server development tools, including many tools covered in this book.

There are drawbacks to DCOM. I believe DCOM will always be a Windows-bound ORB. Therefore, if you operate in a heterogeneous computing environment, you're better off with CORBA. DCOM is still immature, and does not provide the performance of CORBA (not that CORBA is anything to write home about).

Microsoft has a habit of developing complex, high-end software (such as ORBs) into widely available commodities. The availability of tools and the popularity of Microsoft operating systems will assure a place for DCOM.

Component-Based Development

Component-based client/server development differs from the traditional object-oriented programming model since it mixes in some distributed objects. Developers reuse objects by embedding them inside an application with application development tools that know how to use a particular proprietary or standard component.

Mixing and matching components means that developers can purchase expertise they may not possess. For instance, vertical market component vendors from petroleum, financial, and retail industries offer developers specialized functionality that requires little or no custom coding. In some cases, developers can extend the components to meet the exact needs of an application, although the enabling-model (COM or CORBA) limits their ability to extend the capabilities of the component.

Object-oriented development, on the other hand, leverages existing objects by inheriting their characteristics into an application, and customizing the object to meet the exact requirements of the application. The problem with object-oriented development is that it's difficult to develop standard interchangeable parts, since object-oriented development occurs at a very low level in the language or the tool. For example, you must know how C++ works to use existing C++ libraries or frameworks.

Components usually contain fewer features and functions than applications, but they provide more services than a simple program function or an object. In many respects, components are "retro," and adhere more to the modular program model of the past than they do to object-oriented development. Developers use components and the tools that employ them to increase developer productivity, and to build quality in through reuse.

Components aren't perfect either. They don't provide the reuse granularity of true object-oriented development you get from tools such as Smalltalk, C++, and even PowerBuilder. Instead, components provide reusable features that eliminate the need to know component implementation details. In fact, components usually don't come with source code, where most object libraries and frameworks do. This means that developers can't subclass the objects and customize them to meet the "exact" requirements of the application.

The component market continues to grow. With $100 million in sales in 1995, the forecast sale of components will reach $1.65 billion by the year 2000, according to Dream IT, Inc., a research company in Boulder, Colorado (see Figure 19-8). In many respects, components will replace object-oriented development because the technology will live up to the promise of reuse.

COMPONENT TOOLS

Client/server developers may divide component-enabled development tools into several camps: those that use CORBA-based components such as Open-Doc, Web-enabled components such as Sun's Java and Microsoft's ActiveX (described earlier in this chapter), and proprietary components with loyalty to a single development environment. However, software components that exist on the user interface do not limit components. Interchangeable software components can also exist at the middleware layer, at the middle tiers, and as service layer objects on the back end. For example, as middleware layers, CORBA-based distributed objects can use the interoperability of the ORB to provide platform-independent connections.

Figure 19-8 *Component Market Places.*

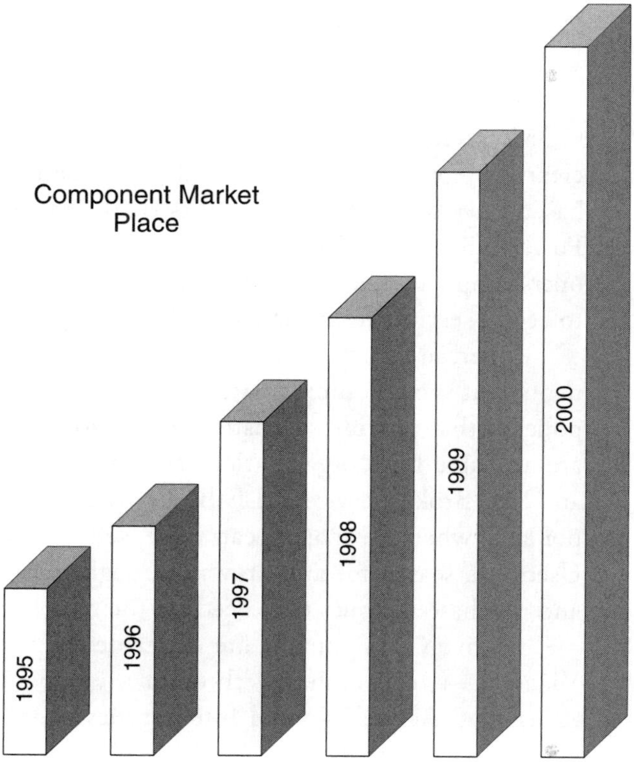

Most client/server development tools can "componitize" an application. For instance, Forte (from Forte Software) and Dynasty (from Dynasty Software) allow developers to create applications using a series of interworking proprietary object request brokers (ORBs). VISION from Unify lets developers assemble applications on a single workstation. Once the application works, developers can partition the application, or distribute objects to run on other accessible servers. We cover these application-partitioning tools in detail in Chapter 20.

The key to component-based application-partitioning tools is flexibility. Developers can not only mix and match components at the front end, they can also mix and match components that perform back-end processing, repartition an application, or swap in components as the needs arise. While they stand as a model of reusability, flexibility, and efficiency, the proprietary distributed component technology these tools employ won't work or play well with objects or components from other development environments.

Thus, standards are the key to practical component-based development, or the concept of a stand-alone language of independent objects that can plug directly into an application, document, or operating systems as easily as processor chips plug into a computer. That's the promise of both COM and Open-Doc, as they make their way into development tools.

ActiveX Tools

COM and its standard component incarnations, ActiveX and DCOM, are the clear leaders in the component development marketplace. Most Windows-based development environments (including Visual Basic and Visual C++, PowerBuilder, and Delphi) can use ActiveX objects inside applications. Developers simply instruct the development tool to embed the object, and tell it how to access services from the embedded object.

There are many ActiveX controls you can buy or download, from components that provide simple date and time functions for an application, to components that provide sophisticated spreadsheets and word processors. These are available from organizations such as ObjectSoft Corporation, that offers an OLE Broker service. OLE Broker is an online marketplace for OLE components, where developers can trade, sell, or give away ActiveX components. Users can search for and browse through components from various vendors, and purchase the ones they need for their application.

ActiveX components are either developed in-house with tools such as Visual C++, or purchased through a component vendor. Since Microsoft redesigned ActiveX for the Internet, developers may also download components for execution inside an application, or inside an ActiveX-enabled Web browser such as Microsoft's Internet Explorer.

The difference between ActiveX and Java is that ActiveX components are language-independent. However, many Java vendors are heading toward the language-independent route. ActiveX will leave the gate with a suite of popular client/server development tools that already exist. Java tools are still more specialized and not as mature.

At their core, ActiveX controls are traditional OLE controls extended for Internet development. Microsoft provides the ActiveX Template Library (ATL) for developers. In turn, ATL provides the library and includes example components. ATL is just a library of C++ templates that help developers create ActiveX controls from an existing base of code. While ATL hides the complexities of COM/OLE development from developers, they still need to understand COM to make the most of the ActiveX architecture.

ActiveX is not at all object-oriented. You modify ActiveX components via aggregation, not through traditional object-oriented features such as inheritance or polymorphism. This by itself does not seem to limit the capabilities of the component standard, but ActiveX components don't mix well in object-oriented development environments. However, Borland's Delphi can force ActiveX components into a class hierarchy. Delphi also provides some inheritance capabilities as a feature of the tool.

Product vendors show the most interest in ActiveX. Lotus, for instance, plans to repackage SmartSuite as a series of ActiveX controls by the end of 1997. Other product vendors include Visual Components, Inc. (in Lenexa, Kansas), which provides ActiveX versions of its spreadsheet and text editor for only $450. Microsoft also plans a set of vertical ActiveX controls known as Line of Business, or LOBjects. LOBjects cover specific industries such as retail, life insurance, health care, and manufacturing. We'll see LOBjects in late 1997.

ActiveX enjoys a vast amount of tool support. Most Windows-based client/server development environments employ, or will employ, ActiveX components in the construction of the application. Visual Basic (covered in Chapter 8), for instance, uses ActiveX exclusively. Developers can embed ActiveX components directly into a Visual Basic application, and Visual Basic provides a sample set of components with the tools. Visual Basic developers trade ActiveX components. The same is true of PowerBuilder, Delphi, Lotus Approach, and Microsoft's Access. All are ActiveX-enabled, and can share components using this standard component architecture.

Another ActiveX-enabled tool is NatStar from Nat Systems. NatStar is a distributed client/server development tool that can integrate with Visual Basic, PowerBuilder, and other tools that use ActiveX. Another OLE-enabled component development environment is Total Framework from Cincom System, Inc. Total Framework allows developers to build business applications by integrating components. For instance, WorkFlow Framework (part of Total Framework), provides developers with the ability to identify, model, and automate business processing. Assemble Framework lets developers construct business applications that represent real-world entities, and Persistence Framework allows developers to share business objects throughout an organization. OLE/COM integrates the three frameworks into an application.

Where's OpenDoc?

Although developers, especially those who work in heterogeneous environments, had high hopes for OpenDoc, it's a clear third in market presence when compared to the ActiveX and Java worlds. OpenDoc is an innovation of IBM, Apple, and Component Integration Labs, Inc., that recently released a working product after a long period of alpha testing. It's not clear if OpenDoc will gain the tool support it needs to succeed. However, a few innovative tools such as Oracle's Power Objects will support OpenDoc components (Power Objects supports ActiveX as well).

OpenDoc is CORBA-compliant, and a component version of IBM's distributed system object model (DSOM). OpenDoc, while available on Windows, is more prevalent on Unix, OS/2, and the Macintosh. OpenDoc components are made up of documents, parts, containers, applications, parts editors, parts services, and a parts viewer. Developers simply group Open-Doc components together to create an application.

Not considering the market share and tool support, OpenDoc has a lot of OLE-based components. For instance, OpenDoc faithfully supports the object-oriented development environment, including inheritance. In addition, the interface is more powerful and allows developers to do more with fewer API calls. OpenDoc extends beyond the bounds of Windows by allowing developers to build OpenDoc components on one platform, then run them on other platforms without modification. Other details developers need to consider include OpenDoc's support for irregularly shaped objects, overlapping parts, and the ability to have several parts active simultaneously.

The OpenDoc crowd, in an attempt to win developers, is now Java-enabled. OpenDoc components, following an agreement with IBM, Apple, and Sun, will allow developers to treat Java as an OpenDoc part so applets can work as parts for OpenDoc applications and allow Java access to OpenDoc objects. In addition to providing Java hooks, OpenDoc can also embed OLE-enabled components that provide OpenDoc developers with the best of both worlds.

IBM's SOM/DSOM does not have the component momentum, but it can integrate as a component in IBM's Visual Age (covered in Chapter 12). SOMObjects version 2 may now be downloaded over the Internet at no change. IBM is clearly on the OpenDoc bandwagon, and announced that the Justsystem Corporation of Japan will port its office automation software to OpenDoc. Unfortunately, it is one of few. The good news is that Club OpenDoc is open for business on the Web. Club OpenDoc lets developers share information, as well as development software and objects. You can reach Club OpenDoc at http://www.software.ibm.com/clubopendoc/. If that site is not active, assume the worst.

THE WEB FACTOR

The rise of the Web and the intranet as an application development platform is the real source of change in the way developers use components. Web-based application development attempts to move beyond the static text and graphics of HTML documents to full-fledged dynamic applications that receive, display, and process information like any other application.

Java is the key to dynamic Web application development, with ActiveX waiting in the wings. The secret to Java's success is its ability to execute applets (components written in the Java language) inside popular Web browsers such as Netscape Navigator (I'll discuss Java in more detail in Chapter 23). Web users download Java applets (components) along with the HTML document. The applet, written in platform-independent byte code, executes inside the browser via an interpreter. Java also secures itself from rogue applets preprogrammed to perform destructive actions.

Although Java is still new, the hype that surrounds Java flooded the market with tools to create Java components. For example, Sun's Java Development Kit (JDK) provides developers with the basics to create applets. However, innovative tool vendors such as Symantec, Borland, and Rogue Wave provide easy-to-use development kits that bring rapid application development (RAD) capabilities to the 3GL-like Java language. These tools provide developers with the ability to visually build, test, and debug applets for deployment inside Web browsers, or inside applications for general use. Although these are not development environments that use components, they are development environments that create components.

Other component-based development tools (such as OpenScape from Business@Web) provide OLE-enabled development capabilities. OpenScape's component approach lets developers wrap APIs for legacy systems (existing applications and databases) which establish the services via a common communication protocol (e.g., RPCs, ODBC, and OLE). OpenScape integrates with Netscape as a plug-in.

The influence of the Web as a component-based development platform is just beginning. Many in the client/server development environment suffer from integration problems, but integration of applications at the client with a Web browser makes most of these problems a thing of the past. As component-based development becomes easier on the Web, Web-based applications that use Java, ActiveX, or some other component-based Web technology will continue to gobble up more market share.

The Realities

There is good news and bad news when you consider distributed objects and their place in client/server development. While distributed objects do provide client/server developers with an advanced distributed architecture to develop and deploy distributed applications, there are issues that make them unsuitable for mission-critical client/server computing. For instance, most commercial ORBs don't perform well. I tested these things over and over, and would not use them for a high-performance transaction-based application. What's more, there are few recovery mechanisms built into ORBS (CORBA and COM), and most ORBs don't perform garbage collection functions, load-balancing, or concurrency control. This means they don't scale well, despite the fact that they support multi-tiered client/server architectures.

You have to consider middleware too. Most ORBs, COM and CORBA, use the synchronous communications model. They lack support for asynchronous messaging, and make a better fit for distributed computing and the Web. Finally, the ORB code is not portable from platform to platform. As with everything, the vendors and standards bodies plan to fix these problems with new releases of specifications and products. Until that happens, you'll have to wait. Again.

Components are a slightly different story. As developers move cautiously toward component-based development, tool vendors see the trends and create tools to meet the demand. ActiveX/COM did a good job of sneaking into popular client/server development tools while no one was looking. Thus, by default and market presence, ActiveX may become the standard component by numbers alone. Tools that employ ActiveX will hold the largest market share. If you do Windows application development, a tool's ability to use ActiveX should be at the top of your list.

Unfortunately, OpenDoc did not attract developers in the same number as COM. Clearly, Microsoft owns the desktop, and thus component architecture as well. OpenDoc will still be a factor in heterogeneous development environments that use OS/2, Unix, and the Macintosh. ActiveX won't dominate those platforms—for now.

The Web could very well be the component development environment of the future. Not only does it provide cross-platform development capabilities, it's also cheap and has momentum. Java, and development tools that create Java applets continue to dominate the market, with ActiveX gaining fast. I'll discuss the enabling technologies in more detail in Chapter 23.

Client/server developers, ORBs, and components are joined at the hip. We could easily have a single de facto standard for component and ORB-based development for Web and non-Web applications. For components and distributed objects to enjoy success, we all need to sing from the same sheet of music. And I can only dream.

Application-Partitioning Tools

Application-partitioning is, first and foremost, a client/server architectural concept. It's the process of distributing processing among computers available on the network. The task of selecting processes to run on the client, or the server, is an example of application-partitioning.

Second, and most common, application-partitioning is a concept that is linked to a set of tools known as application-partitioning tools. These tools are not unlike specialized client/server tools. However, they not only build objects for processing by the client, they also build objects that can process on any number of processors in addition to the client and the database server.

Application-partitioning tools are all the rage. In the world of client/server, developers always look for new ways to build multi-tiered client/server applications without having to resort to traditional application three-tier 3GL-bound processing layers such as TP monitors or distributed objects. Application-partitioning tools offer those benefits and more. Using these tools, developers can repartition, or reallocate, the process load by dragging and dropping icons on a computer screen.

Although I've found that application-partitioning tools do provide advanced features for multi-tiered client/server development, developers need to approach with caution. Many of these tools may be cost-prohibitive, and many developers may apply them where they should not be applied.

In this chapter, let's take a hypeless look at application-partitioning tools, with a close look at typical features and functions. Then we'll look at a few of the most popular application-partition tools so you can decide if application-partitioning is for you.

Breaking Up Is Hard to Do

When you design a client/server system, the most basic decision you'll have to make is how to divide up the processing between the client, the server, and sometimes an application server (see Figure 20-1). When using the traditional two-tier client/server model, developers split the processing load between the client (using any sort of front-end tool) and the server (using stored procedures and triggers). When using the three-tier client/server model, developers must employ a TP monitor or a distributed object to provide a platform for the application logic and processing.

Both the two-tier and three-tier model have several limitations. First of all, you have to divide the application between the client and the server at the

Figure 20-1 *Application Partitioning.*

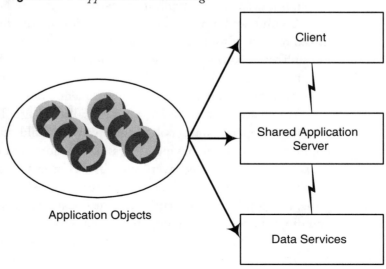

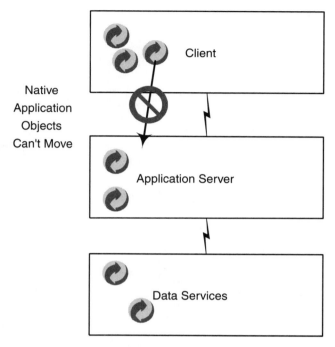

Figure 20-2 *Committing processing at the design stage.*

design stage (see Figure 20-2). Once committed, it's difficult to repartition the application logic and processing load since you must deploy them using the native features of the front-end development tool and the database server. Thus to move application logic from the client to the database server you must rewrite that portion of the application using stored procedures or triggers.

In many of the client/server systems I work on, developers begin with a good design and a good partitioning scheme. However, as with everything in system development, things change. Additional users require use of the system, the application itself changes, and/or the processing load increases on the client or the server. When using traditional two-tier and three-tier technology, it's difficult to adjust the application to fit to the changes.

Application-partitioning tools solve these problems by dividing an application into partitions, or chunks of application logic that execute on any available processor that is accessible over a network (see Figure 20-3). The real selling point of application-partition tools is not their ability to partition a client/server application, but their ability to repartition an application. This allows the developer to relocate application processing dynamically, as needed,

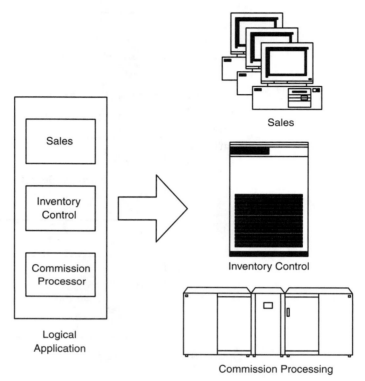

Figure 20-3 *Application partitioning using application-partitioning tools.*

without affecting the underlying functionality of the application. This also means no changes in the application code.

Scaling Through Distribution

Application-partitioning tools solve the same problem as three-tier client/server (e.g., TP Monitor and distributed objects) by providing developers with the ability to scale their applications to the enterprise (over a thousand or so users). For instance, when using an application-partitioning tool such as Forte or Dynasty, developers can specify that computationally intensive portions of an application run on the fastest processors available. A developer can specify that a portion of a financial application crunches the numbers on a high-end RISC server, while the less intensive processing occurs on a low-end PC-based server (see Figure 20-4). Moreover, developers can also specify that portions of

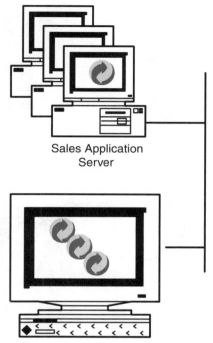

Sales Application
Server

Financial Application Server

Figure 20-4 *Placing objects on special servers.*

the application which support the largest number of users execute on an available multi-processing computer (see Figure 20-5).

The trick that application-partitioning tools perform is the ability to use all accessible computer resources that the tool supports for truly distributed application programs. What's more, the developer can tune the application through the dynamic application-partitioning capabilities of the tool.

Application-partitioning tools provide "fail-over" capabilities through process replication. Using these facilities, developers can program applications to reroute to replicated platforms when portions of the application fail (see Figure 20-6).

Types of Application-Partitioning Tools

I like to divide application-partitioning into a few distinct categories: proprietary ORB-based, ORB-based, and database-dependent. Let's look at how each tool type approaches partitioning.

Inventory Management (Super Computer)

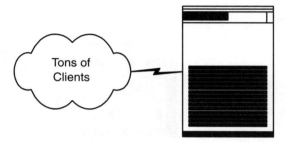

Client Processing (Multi-Processing Server)

Sales Order Processing (Single-Processing Server)

Figure 20-5 *Leveraging server power to support numerous clients.*

PROPRIETARY OBJECT-REQUEST-BROKER-BASED

Proprietary ORB-based application-partitioning tools, including Dynasty and Forte, are the original application-partitioning tools. These tools use their own ORB that they distribute to a number of servers which provide a location for application processing. The ORBs communicate with one another using a proprietary messaging mechanism (see Figure 20-7).

Developers build applications using this type of technology by building and assembling application objects within a typical application-development environment. Most application-partitioning tools provide their own "easy-to-use" 4GL and GUI developer. Once the developer creates the application

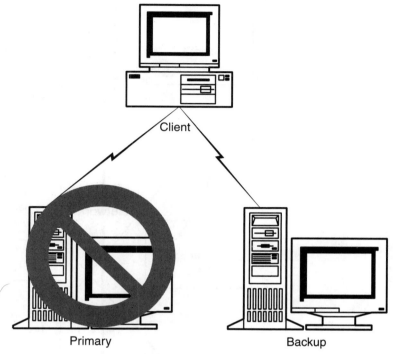

Figure 20-6 *Fail-over capabilities.*

objects, the application can be tested with all application objects running on the same client computer.

After the developer knows that the application works properly, he or she can partition the application objects to other available servers. This is usually accomplished by dragging and dropping the objects to icons that represent application servers available on the network.

In the background, away from the developer, an amazing event is underway. The application-partitioning tool moves the object to a remote server. When the object arrives there, an engine on the remote server generates native 3GL code (e.g., C) and compiles the code into a native executable (the ORB). Once running, the object can communicate with other objects that make up the application using a messaging mechanism. Or the object communicates with a middleware layer that moves interprocess information to and from partitions. The developer can do this as many times as needed, and can execute any object on any available supported server. I've seen configurations where twenty application objects each run on their own server.

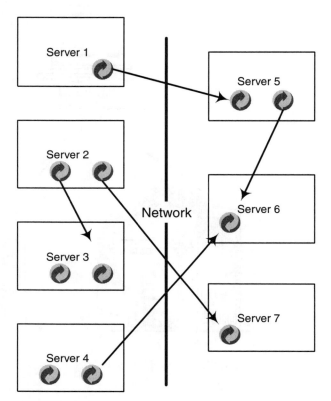

Figure 20-7 *Proprietary ORBs.*

The real fun is repartitioning the application. At any time, the developer can move objects from server to server, which automatically sets off the chain of events that moves the object, generates code, and compiles the ORBs on their new host (see Figure 20-8). While application-partitioning vendors describe this process as dynamic, you'll find that you need to shut down and restart the application for the new partitioning scheme to become effective.

Of course, a client/server application is useless without data. All proprietary ORB partitioning tools also connect to popular database servers (see Figure 20-9). All objects have direct access to database services. In addition, you can easily integrate TP monitors using these types of tools. Distributed objects are also supported.

There are advantages and disadvantages to this approach. The advantage is that you can create applications that support any size of processing load. As the user and processing load increases, developers can simply partition the

Step 1: Move logical object from the developer's
workstation.

Step 2: Generate native code for the target
platform.

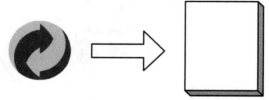

Step 3: Compile the code using a native compiler
to create the run-time object.

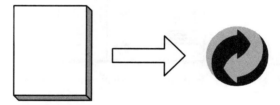

Figure 20-8 *Moving objects.*

application to more servers (see Figure 20-10). This architecture thus provides
the ultimate in flexible scalability.

The downside is that you walk down the aisle with the tool vendor. The
ORBs are proprietary and not based on available standards such as COM or
CORBA; thus they are not supported by other tools. When the tool vendor
goes out of business, so does your application.

OBJECT-REQUEST-BROKER-BASED

ORB-based application-partitioning tools, such as PowerBuilder and Visual
Basic, provide partitioning features that let developers create and use standard
ORBs. Developers can create the ORBs inside the tools, and run the ORBs on
any platform that supports them. For instance, Visual Basic creates OLE-
enabled ORBs based on the DCOM standard. These ORBs can reside on any
Windows NT and Windows 95 computer. The ORBs communicate using the

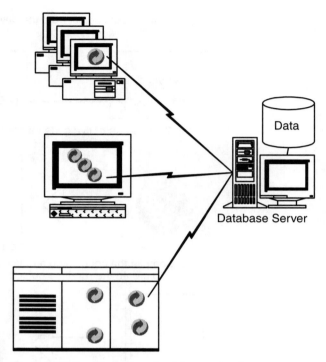

Figure 20-9 *AP tools work with most database servers.*

standard interfaces of the ORB (e.g., RPCs or LRPCs). CORBA-based ORBs work the same way, but don't have the same level of tool support as OLE and DCOM.

The benefit of using ORB-based development tools is that the ORBs they create are tool- and application-independent. This means any tool can create an ORB that is usable by any other tool or application which supports that particular ORB standard.

The tradeoff of using this open architecture is sizzle. The development tools are just hitting the streets, and they don't provide the drag-and-drop whiz-bang of the tools that use proprietary ORBs. DCOM makes any OLE-enabled development tool, by default, an application-partitioning tool, but the tools aren't really designed to support application partitioning. For example, you won't find a mechanism to drag-and-drop objects from server to server in PowerBuilder, Visual Basic, or Delphi. But you can create ORBs with Delphi, and use them from PowerBuilder or Visual Basic. As DCOM becomes a more widely accepted standard, specialized client/server tools will surely begin to support partitioning features.

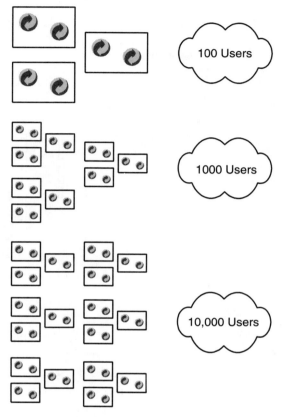

Figure 20-10 *Scaling with AP tools.*

DATABASE-DEPENDENT

Database-dependent application-partitioning tools can partition an application, but only as objects that run on remote database servers as stored procedures and triggers (see Figure 20-11). For example, the developer can create objects that form an application on the client, then distribute the objects between the client and the database server as required. As with proprietary ORB partitioning tools, the developer can easily repartition the application at any time.

The tradeoff here is deployment. Since these objects can only partition to available supported database servers, this provides nothing more than flexible partitioning capabilities to the two-tier client/server model. Indeed, this model does not provide the scalability of application-partitioning tools that can employ a server that is neither the client nor the server. Oracle's Developer/2000 is a good example of a database-dependent application-partitioning tool.

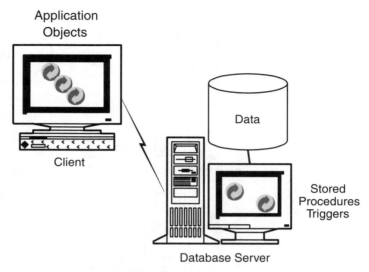

Figure 20-11 *Database-dependent AP tool.*

FORTE

Forte, introduced in 1994, is the newest and most powerful of the proprietary ORB tools. Built specifically for application-partitioning, Forte provides a C++ kernel (for ORB deployment)and a set of application-partitioning tools that let developers distribute application processes to any number of servers supported by Forte. Forte is multi-platform, supporting Windows 95, Windows 3.11, Macintosh, and the Motif/Unix. You can distribute Forte ORBs to a number of platforms, including OpenVMS, SG/UX, AIX, SunOS, HP-UX, and Windows NT. Forte can link up to Oracle, Sybase, and Rdb.

Forte is an object-oriented development tool, supporting classes, sub-classes, encapsulation, inheritance, and polymorphism. Developers use the event-programming model to build applications. Forte also supports threading, which allows objects to communicate with one another asynchronously.

Like many two-tier specialized client/server development tools, Forte uses a model-driven development architecture. This means the developer builds applications using high-level sharable service objects first (functionally equivalent to a repository), before extending those objects (called service objects) to meet the requirements of the applications.

The service objects are the objects that contain the business processing services. They exist in Forte's repository, sharable among other applications, or within the same application. The repository also stores metadata, defining the classes and objects from those classes. The repository is actually an OO DBMS.

All Forte developers share a single repository, and there is an object browser that lets developers locate, extend, and deploy objects.

You can't be a client/server tool without providing your own proprietary 4GL and GUI screen builder, and Forte is no exception. Forte provides a 4GL editor and GUI painter, as well as a debugger. You'll also find a version control mechanism to manage object sharing in multi-developer environments.

Building applications in Forte is no harder or easier than with nonpartitioning tools. This is due to the fact that the developer environment is separate from the deployment or partitioning environment. The idea is that the developer builds the application first, including the interface, data access layers, and application logic, then deploys the application as partitions, moving them to various available platforms.

The client components use the Forte interpreter (known as the Forte engine) to run the application at the client and server ends. The developer has an option of compiling the object into native code to enhance efficiency. Forte can generate a default application-partitioning scheme for you, but you have the option to override the default and repartition the application by dragging and dropping objects onto available servers, represented as icons. Forte provides a performance-monitoring tool to monitor the performance at each application server. This way, the developer can spot application servers that are over- or underutilized, and repartition the application to balance the load.

Forte links to a database by automatically mapping the database schema and data using an array that's native to Forte. Developers have to deal with the database on a native SQL level. Forte uses its own object to handle transactions.

DYNASTY

Now in its third major release, Dynasty is the "grandam" of application-partitioning tools (see Figure 20-12). Dynasty is also a fully object-oriented tool that supports classes, subclasses, encapsulation, inheritance, and polymorphism. Unlike Forte, which supports several types of clients, Dynasty has its feet firmly planted with Microsoft, and only supports Windows. Databases supported include Oracle, Sybase, SQL Server, DB2/2, SQLBase, and any database accessible through ODBC. Using Dynasty, you partition applications to DOS, Windows, Windows NT, Macintosh, HP-UX, SunOS, Solaris, AIX, and SCO Unix.

To build applications with Dynasty, you must first understand the ten object types which can make up a Dynasty application. They include: business objects, data objects, DataManager, DataStore, view objects, function objects, program objects, window objects, and widget objects. Let's take business

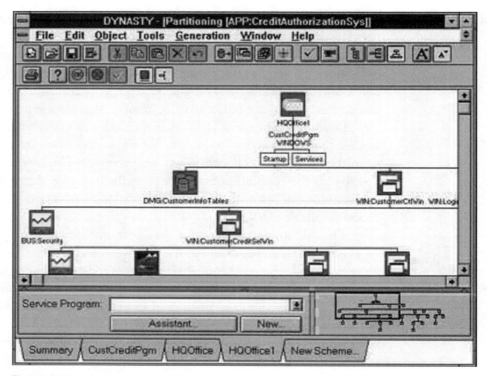

Figure 20-12 *Dynasty.*

objects as an example. Business objects define the various business processes, predefined so the developer does not have to do the defining. DataManager objects let developers link to supported databases as objects (similar to the relational wrapper feature of most Smalltalk tools, see Chapter 12). Developing Dynasty applications is just a matter of locating and extending the objects found in the repository to meet your exact requirements.

Dynasty is also repository-driven, and provides a shared repository (called the knowledge base) that contains prebuilt objects and new objects created by the local development team. The repository contains additional information about application-partitioning, platforms, and generation specifications.

When using Dynasty, you'll notice that there are shared knowledge bases and working knowledge bases. There are several shared knowledge bases associated with a single Dynasty development environment. Each developer on the development team uses his or her own working knowledge base that exists on the developer's own workstation. As developers access the shared knowledge base, they can move objects into their working Knowledge Base when building an application.

Dynasty provides developers with an object browser to surf through the object repository to locate classes and objects. The object browser represents the objects as a graphical hierarchy, making it easy for developers to locate an object, as well as figure out how that object fits into the repository. There is a graphical editor associated with each object type, and developers can extend the functionality of any object. The core of the Dynasty client development environment is not really a Dynasty product, but one based on Neuron Data's open interface elements.

For quick applications, Dynasty provides a tool known as quick layout. Quick layout automatically creates the application objects you need for database access, and the screens you'll need by simply reading the schema of the connected database. This is not very impressive when compared to other tools with similar facilities.

The process of creating a Dynasty application is described by Dynasty as a process of partitioning, targeting, and generating. Partitioning is actually a manual process where the developer splits up an application into clients and servers. Targeting means the developer supplies required information such as the target database, network, operating system, GUI, and middleware environment where each of the application partitions will exist. The generating process refers to the developer generating the source code for the application directly from the application objects already defined. The code generated is C. If you want to repartition, you'll have to run through this scenario again.

Dynasty provides transaction services through an interface with the Tuxedo TP monitor. Developers need not know the details of the Tuxedo API to use the TP monitor. Instead the developer works through a native Dynasty programming service. The presence of Tuxedo in the Dynasty environment makes me feel better about using proprietary application-partitioning tools. There is also support for DCE through Open Environment Corporation's Toolkit.

DYNASTY VERSUS FORTE

I know that Dynasty and Forte aren't the only application-partitioning game in town, but they are certainly the most popular of tools developed specifically for application-partitioning. Thus let's compare and contrast each tool before moving on to lighter-weight products.

Although Forte and Dynasty look very much the same, there are differences you need to consider. The biggest difference is support for the object-oriented development model. While both products support multiple inheritance, Forte will not allow classes to inherit conflicting methods or properties from different classes. Moreover, when using Forte, the smallest application partition a developer can create is a single object. Dynasty, in contrast, allows developers to assign individual methods of a single object to any number of partitions. Each tool supports a 4GL that resembles C++, and they both generate C code for native compilers.

These tools are going through a lot of evolution. I suspect some of the limitations that these tools have will disappear in future releases. Both Dynasty and Forte are aggressive with the innovation they put into their tools, and I expect big things from them.

Application Partitioning Does Intranet

So, how do application-partitioning tools fit in with the intranet? Forte, Dynasty, and Cactus all have mechanisms to deploy applications to the Web using traditional enabling technologies such as HTML and Java.

Like other client/server tools that have a Web development mechanism, application-partitioning tools are able to generate interfaces for Web browsers using the same development mechanisms. The same back-end architectures apply. Only the interface and platform are new.

You should know that these tools don't come cheap. Forte retails for over $75,000 for a five-developer license (including training). Dynasty is priced at $8,000 for each developer, and charges $12,000 to $22,000 for each platform you plan to deploy to. This is compared to the $2000-per-developer fee that organizations pay for traditional two-tier specialized client/server tools. The prices of application-partitioning tools are changing quickly, and seem to be moving downward.

You need to consider people cost as well. These environments are complex, and it will take extra time to get typical developers up and running. You also need to consider the risk. The proprietary nature of these tools means that you may be dependent on the success of very small companies.

When Application-Partitioning Is Overkill

One of the issues that I constantly face when working with organizations to develop and deploy client/server systems is the use of application-partitioning tools when there is no need. Application-partitioning tools cost more than traditional client/server tools, they are complex, and much more difficult to deploy. Therefore, they should only be used when a problem exists that can only be solved through the use of an application-partitioning tool.

The key problem that application-partitioning tools solve is scaling. These tools take a divide-and-conquer approach to client/server development. When there is an increase in the processing load, application developers can repartition the application across additional processors.

The problem is client/server architects who "manage by magazine" and use application-partitioning tools for the sake of using something that's state-of-the-art. They neglect the fact that they really don't need to support a large user and processing load, that the use of an application-partitioning tool is overkill.

Once again, don't make emotional decisions when selecting technology and tools. The latest and greatest is not always the right fit or the best fit.

COMPOSER

Composer (from Texas Instruments (TI)) is based on TI's IEF CASE tool, and provides another example of a proprietary ORB tool. Composer takes process diagrams and the data model created using IEF, and transforms them to applications deployable to various platforms as partitioned applications.

Once you've created the data model, developers can generate the physical database on any number of popular databases including Oracle, Sybase, and Informix. Composer uses a repository, and once created for an instance of an application database, developers can feed the repository information to a GUI painter. Composer provides a 4GL scripting language, a dialog painter, and an event-processing facility.

Similar to Forte and Dynasty, Composer generates 3GL code for its target platform directly from Composer objects. The packaging tool allows developers to partition the application between clients and server. The messaging mechanism is proprietary, but partitions may reside on mainframes, Unix servers, and PCs.

OBJECTSTAR

ObjectStar (from Antares Alliance Group) is a good application-partitioning tool if you're considering a move from mainframes to client/server. It's also another example of a proprietary ORB tool. ObjectStar supports incremental migration of the application from the legacy world, and can use mainframe tools such as COBOL. ObjectStar supports Windows and OS/2.

Developers partition ObjectStar applications through a virtual machine interface (VMI) that's consistent from platform to platform. Developers create ObjectStar objects using the ObjectStar development environment inside the VMI. The application is then partitioned and deployed using the local platform-specific execution mechanism at each remote server. ObjectStar can automatically resolve the location of an object (deciding where that object will run), but developers may embed location information to determine how the objects will communicate with one another.

VISION

VISION (from Unify) is a one of the first examples of a traditional two-tier client/server development tool that has migrated toward application-partitioning. As you may recall, VISION is a multi-platform development tool that now provides application-partitioning capabilities.

Once the VISION developer creates the application, he or she may divide the application by objects into partitions that reside on other servers and workstations. VISION client partitions contain user interface components (e.g., a data window), and server components are nonvisual (e.g., a data-sorting process). VISION allows partitioned applications to exchange information using a proprietary messaging mechanism.

POWERBUILDER

PowerBuilder (version 5) supports application-partitioning. Using a new subsystem known as Distributed PowerBuilder (DPB), developers can move nonvisual user objects (NVUOs) to remote servers.

For experienced PowerBuilder developers, application-partitioning is just a matter of creating NVUOs that contain application logic and executing them on a remote application server. Developers have to manually specify which object needs to exist on which remote server. Only a limited number of platforms are supported, including Windows 95 and Windows NT. The traditional PowerBuilder development environment is a part of DPB, thus developers don't have to learn a new set of tools. What's more, PowerBuilder hides the complexities of the underlying communications drivers from the developer. PowerBuilder's proprietary middleware layer does all the interprocess communications work for you.

PowerBuilder, however, can only communicate with remote processes synchronously. Like RPCs, this means that the calling process is halted while the remote process executes the request. This is a limitation since most application-partitioning tools use an asynchronous messaging system that I find to be a better fit for multi-tiered client/server computing.

When creating a distributed PowerBuilder application, you'll have to become familiar with some new concepts. For example, there are new Power-Builder object classes that are inherited from the nonvisual object and structure. PowerBuilder 5 also introduces the concept of PowerBuilder server applications, or an application that contains nonvisual user objects callable by one or several client applications. PowerBuilder calls these remote objects, which are accessible over a network or locally. You can create new distributed Power-Builder applications, or redeploy an existing PowerBuilder application as a distributed application with a little bit of work.

In addition to using native NVUOs as a means to partition PowerBuilder applications, developers may also partition applications through OLE automation and DCOM (by creating out-of-process OLE automation servers), as well as link to CORBA-compliant objects which are also supported by version 5. This means that PowerBuilder provides three ways to partition your application. Unfortunately, with this first release of PowerBuilder's partitioning power, they are a master of none.

VISUAL BASIC

Visual Basic's approach to application-partitioning, as you might expect, is purely Microsoft. The concept is simple. Since Visual Basic can create an out-of-process OLE automation server through DCOM, it can partition processing to other remote servers. Of course, this is only in Windows 95 and Windows NT environments.

When first released, Visual Basic was the first tool to offer a facility to place OLE automation servers on a remote server. This was before the release of DCOM as part of Windows NT version 4.

In addition to OLE-enabled application-partitioning capabilities, Visual Basic also provides several tools for the management of remote data access, including a remote data controller. This data controller works much like the Jet database engine. There is also a component manager that keeps track of OLE servers that exist on remote servers. And Visual Basic uses a pool manager to build pools of OLE objects and distribute them to clients. This will avoid the bottlenecks that are inevitable when managing many remote objects over a network.

DEVELOPER/2000

Oracle's Developer/2000 is our only example of a database-dependent application-partitioning tool. Unlike the other application-partitioning tools we're looking at in this chapter, Developer/2000 can only automate the partitioning of applications between clients and the server. That is, if the client runs Developer/2000 and the server runs the Oracle Database.

Developer/2000 contains a Windows version of Oracle Forms, which was one of the original database interface developers in the mainframe and mini-computer days. Forms for Windows, like other client/server GUI development tools, lets developers design, program, and deploy a client/server application. Developers can also create any number of Developer/2000 objects, which exist in a repository stored on the database server.

Developers can program Developer/2000 applications using Oracle's PL/SQL language. PL/SQL is really just SQL with proprietary Oracle extensions. PL/SQL is also the native language of Oracle database stored procedures and triggers. Therein lies the secret of Developer/2000's partitioning power.

Once the developer defines an application at the client, the developer may use Developer/2000's object navigator to partition the application between the client and the database server. This is just a process of dragging and dropping the object within the object navigator. Behind the scenes, Developer/2000 moves objects written in PL/SQL code from the client to the server where they run as stored procedures or triggers. Object navigator keeps track of where the objects are when executing an application. Since PL/SQL is an Oracle thing, this will only work with Oracle's database server. If you're running Sybase, Informix, or anything else, you're out of luck.

Developer/2000 is only automating what developers have been doing by hand, using stored procedures and any number of specialized client/server tools. What's more, since Developer/2000 is unable to partition applications to a true application server, the two-tier problem of scaling remains. Developer/2000 only makes sense for developers who are already bound to Oracle, and who are not looking to support a high user and processing load.

WHERE ARE THE STANDARDS?

As I use the word "proprietary" over and over in this chapter, you may be asking yourself: Where are the standards? The concept of distributed objects in both the DCOM and CORBA incarnations is not only supposed to create a tool-independent binary object standard, but provide a natural architecture for platform-independent object distribution, and thus an architecture for application partitioning.

Clearly, the most popular application-partitioning tools have not migrated toward standards, but things are slowly changing. For instance, both Forte and Dynasty are committed to support distributed objects. Specialized client/server development tools such as PowerBuilder, Delphi, and Visual Basic are counting on DCOM to provide them with application-partitioning capabilities and a migration path toward distributed objects.

It's going to take some time before key application-partitioning tools finally include distributed-object standards as part of their application architecture. (Currently, they only provide support through interfaces.) Once this happens, the whole application-partitioning tool market could become more of a market for commodity products.

Future of Application Partitioning

As I mentioned in the latest sidebar, you need to ask yourself if you really need application-partitioning before diving into the complex and costly world of application-partitioning tools. If you're in business to create small departmental applications, most two-tier client/server development tools will work just fine.

Application-partitioning tools are aligning for larger enterprise-wide applications. These are applications that need to go from 0 to 60 mph in just a few seconds, with the ability to scale to any number of users and processing loads. What's more, application-partitioning tools can provide fail-over redundancy, and leverage the best features of distributed development environments.

Application-partitioning continues to increase in popularity as developers seek new ways to make client/server scale. The tools available now are too complex, too primitive, and too expensive for casual client/server development, but as traditional specialized client/server tools begin to support partitioning, application-partitioning could be the next client/server revolution.

In the future, I see new features such as dynamic application-partitioning and distributed-object standards making their way into application-partitioning tools. I hope the Object Management Group (OMG) will finally get their act together, and propel CORBA as the standard platform for application distribution. Microsoft's DCOM may have a better shot at providing a standard ORB in terms of market share, and the fact that it owns the operating systems we chose to deploy to. Right now, the world of application-partitioning tools is very proprietary.

Implementing the Solution

Client/Server
Application Testing

Application testing is as old as application development. However, procedures applied to test procedural and batch-oriented legacy applications aren't applicable at all to client/server. For instance, event-driven front-end GUI applications provide users with the ability to do things in unpredictable sequences. What's more, the concept of client/server—spreading the processing loads across numerous processors and operating systems—makes testing all client/server components almost impossible.

Beyond the obvious differences in the front end, client/server brings a lot more complexity to computing. While the front end needs rigorous testing, so do the other client/server components (such as the database server and the application server). The developer needs the ability to test each client/server component in its own domain, or all components as one integrated system.

Fortunately, a few good testing tools dedicate themselves to the testing and troubleshooting needs of client/server applications. These tools can simulate user interaction, as well as spot problems, generate reports, and test the application's ability to handle all levels of processing loads.

As client/server becomes more complex, there is an even greater need for a rigorous approach to client/server testing. In 1995, the International Data Corporation Testing Report stated that, with prevalent use of specialized client/server development tools (such as Visual Basic and PowerBuilder), the time and effort required to test these applications increases. In this chapter, I'll tell you what you need to know about client/server testing, including client/server testing concepts, and tools available to make client/server testing quick and easy.

Lack of Testing

I'm always surprised at the number of client/server applications deployed without a rigorous testing cycle. Typically, untested client/server applications don't live up to the performance expectations of the users. They also tend to produce general protection faults (GPFs), or worse, produce erroneous results that become the basis of critical business decisions.

Why do developers and project managers neglect the testing cycle? There are many reasons. First, many managers and developers assume that RAD tools will protect them from many potential application development problems. Second, testing is the first task to go when the budget gets tight. Third, client/server applications are so complex (and thus difficult to test properly) that many developers just don't bother. Finally, testing always happens at the end of the project, and developers compress or reduce testing time to meet overly aggressive deadlines.

Testing always lands at the bottom of the list in development activities. In most of the client/server development projects I've worked on in the past, those who do the testing are people who have nothing better to do, or college students on summer break—hardly the types who know how to thoroughly test a system.

If you plan to deploy quality applications, you can't avoid a rigorous and sometimes expensive testing practice. You need a testing methodology, a test plan for each application, testing tools, and most importantly, the time required to test the client/server application properly.

Considering the Cost of Testing

So, if testing is such a good thing, why don't developers and application architects test as much as they should? If you ask most of them they tell you that testing costs too much.

But does it?

Consider a few similar systems I've worked on in the last few years. One system that I built for the government had only a rudimentary application test plan and no plan for testing the back-end servers (I yelled, believe me). While the government spent a mere $10,000 on testing, it spent more than $340,000 after deployment when you take into consideration the cost of pulling the application away from the user when the application failed to meet performance requirements. This does not include the invisible costs of the loss of user good will.

A similar system with a solid $100,000 testing budget (at least 20 percent of the overall development budget is about right, depending on the type of system) was deployed to the users, meeting all expectations right out of the gate. Now tell me which one is cheaper. Testing is cheap if you consider the cost of not testing.

Client/Server Testing Concepts

So you're sold on the fact that you need testing. Now what? The first step is to learn a few basic testing concepts that include regression testing, load testing, component testing, and integration testing. Let's also take a look at the new concept of object-oriented testing.

REGRESSION TESTING

If you ever snapped a new component or object into an application and watched the entire application collapse before your eyes, you already understand the need for regression testing. The purpose of regression testing is to ensure that certain changes to your client/server application don't cause it to regress, or become more unstable.

For example, when Windows 95 hit the streets, client/server developers quickly upgraded their desktops. While some existing client/server applications ran fine, others crashed due to incompatibilities with the new OS. Before deploying Windows 95 to the clients, it would have been helpful to perform some regression testing to determine how Windows 95 affects the existing client/server application. Same concept applies to upgrading development tools, object hierarchies, or databases.

When upgrading a C++ class hierarchy a few years ago, I found that the new classes to support the new GUI features made all my reports inoperable.

I traced the problem back to a bad base class—a problem quickly fixed by the C++ tool vendor. In this example, changes to objects (considering the object-oriented development model) have unpredictable effects on objects that inherit from them. Changes to any object require regression testing on all the objects that inherit from the changed object. This also leads to the concept of object-oriented testing (discussed later).

Compounding the testing problems of client/server applications, and making more of a case for regression testing, is the client/server process of application partitioning. Since we take a divide-and-conquer approach when we build client/server applications, each component should go through regression testing when we make changes to any other components. For instance, if you make changes to the database schema, you need to make sure the changes do not affect the front-end application. Often, a DBA makes changes to the database that cause front-end applications to fail when columns no longer exist, or if their names change.

Fortunately, some handy testing tools can help you meet many of your regression testing requirements. PreVue-X from Performance Awareness Corp., for instance, automates regression testing for the developer. Using PreVue-X, developers can execute several tests overnight, running the application through a number of predefined test cases. In addition, PreVue-X can verify that the test system returns correct responses, and that the test records all performance indicators. Developers can also check the new features of the application.

LOAD TESTING

Load testing means running a client/server application under an increasing user or processing load to determine how it will behave under high stress. To me, that means abusing the application to determine where it will break. All applications break under some load level. This testing practice determines the application's ability to scale, since scaling is just a matter of handling a larger and larger processing and user load (see Figure 21-1).

Usually I load-test a system by running an application continuously (overnight, typically) using a large number of varied testing procedures to simulate hundreds, sometimes thousands of users, depending on the requirements of the application. I then increase the load until I find a problem. The types of errors you should look for are saturation of the server or the client operating system, memory leaks on the front-end application (eating more and more memory as the application executes, usually resulting in a GPF), concurrency problems, processor and disk performance, or sudden, unexpected system crashes.

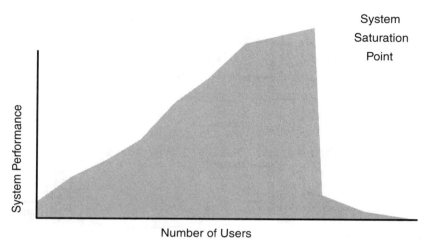

Figure 21-1 *Load testing.*

The problem with load testing is that it's fairly expensive to load-test even a two-tier client/server application, not to mention a more complex multi-tier client/server application that supports higher loads. The large number of clients required to simulate a high user load means a large number of PCs must participate in the test. For example, when doing some testing for a Web server article, we had to employ over one hundred PCs, all running Web browsers and testing software to place the appropriate load on the Web server during the test.

The friends of the load tester are the testing tools built to automate load-testing procedures. It's really a matter of recording a typical user session with your application and playing that session back over and over to simulate continuous user interaction. The number of clients running the testing software determines the load you want to place on the system (see Figure 21-2). However, there are better solutions available to simulate large user loads using a limited number of clients. Once again, you capture the user interaction with the application in test scripts, then use the testing software to run multiple instances of the test scripts. This means you can perform such tricks as simulating a thousand or so users with only a hundred or so clients (see Figure 21-3).

Typically, you want to monitor as many data points as possible when you do load testing. For instance, using the native performance management features of your database server, you can watch how the load testing affects cache, buffers, and disk performance. You can do the same thing with the network and client. It's a good idea to keep a log of the performance indicator, and most performance-monitoring tools will do this for you automatically.

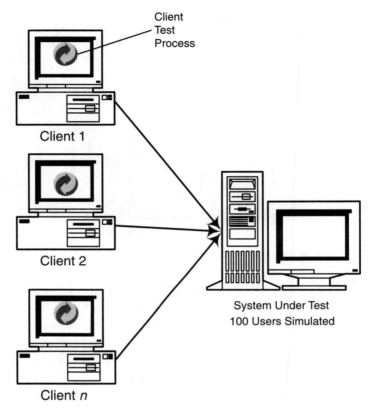

Figure 21-2 *Adding test clients.*

COMPONENT TESTING

While regression testing and load testing test the system as a complete unit, component testing is the process of testing each component of a client/server application separately (see Figure 21-4). This includes the front-end application, the database server, and the application server. Component testing can even include subcomponents like stored procedures and triggers on the database server, application services (e.g. transaction services on a TP monitor) on the application server, and objects on the client.

Component testing is really a quality control and software-engineering process to assure that the component has the ability to function as an independent unit before it's hooked up to the other components. I insist on component testing simply because it places the system in several domains, able to work apart, or to be connected together to form the system. This makes the system more valuable, since you should be able to mix and match components to form various applications. For example, you should be able to swap out database servers, application servers, and clients without much additional work. It also allows developers to component-test on more granular levels as well, and track down typical client/server application problems.

The advantage of using component testing is that you can test a component before you complete work on related components. In other words, you don't have to build your front end in order to test your database, or vice versa. Also, component testing allows you to isolate problems by allowing you to test each component independently (see Figure 21-5).

However, component testing requires a little extra work. Beyond building the application components, you need to create the "stubs" that allow the components to function on their own. For example, you test the front-end component of a client/server system by using a database server that runs on the client with the client application. In turn, you component-test the database server by using a number of SQL scripts that simulate a client connection.

Figure 21-3 *Simulating a large user load.*

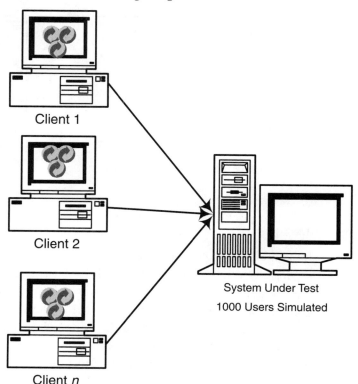

Client 1

Client 2

System Under Test
1000 Users Simulated

Client *n*

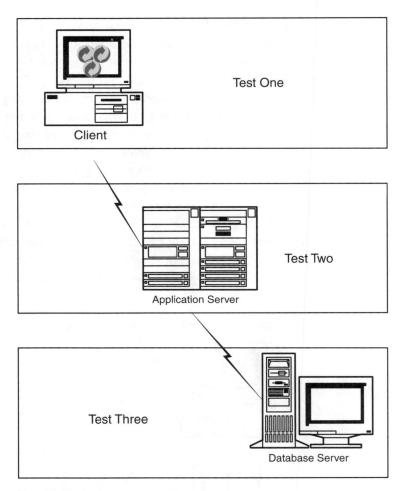

Figure 21-4 *Component testing.*

INTEGRATION TESTING

Integration testing is the next step in component testing. This is the process of linking all the components together to form the final system, and making sure all the components work and play well with others. For example, in a typical integration test, we hook the front end to the application server, and the application server to the database server, and the front end directly to the database server.

Problems that integration testing should find include middleware incompatibility issues, ODBC driver problems, network contentions, and problems

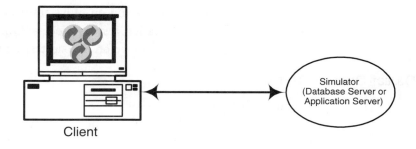

Client

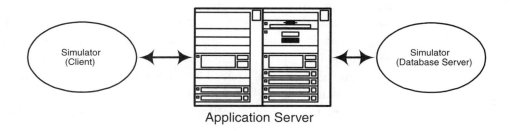

Application Server

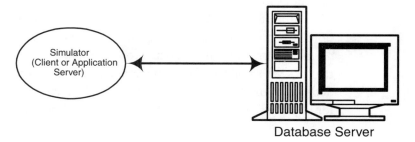

Database Server

Figure 21-5 *Testing each component independently.*

with the database, to name a few. For example, it took integration testing to find an incompatibility of two TCP/IP protocol stacks that ran on two clients for a client/server system I deployed a few years ago. While they would work by themselves, they did not get along on the same network. Once again a bug was found, fixed, and the system went through another integration test to prove that we solved the problem.

Typically, integration testing employs traditional client/server testing tools to automate the integration testing process. Once you know the components work together, you can move on to load testing (previously described).

OBJECT-ORIENTED TESTING

Of course, if there is object-oriented development which leads to object-oriented analysis and design, there must be object-oriented testing. Object-oriented testing means testing the system at the system, component (client, database and application server), object, and method level, factoring in the effects of inheritance and other object-oriented concepts. If this sounds a bit like the regression testing description, you're right. However, object-oriented testing digs a little deeper into the object-oriented development model, and has the potential of reducing your testing time by reusing tested objects.

For example, when I object-oriented-test a PowerBuilder application, I test all the high-level (ancestor) objects by themselves to prove that they can function independently (similar to component testing). Once tested, it's a safe bet that objects which inherit from the tested object (child objects) have been tested too. You only need to test what you change in that object, including the methods, and how the methods interact with the encapsulated data (see Figure 21-6). Once you test all the objects in the same manner, you do system-level testing to show how all the objects work and play together to form the application.

Object-oriented testing makes sense for some object-intensive applications that may become the basis for many other applications. However, this can be more work than it's worth. Moreover, object-oriented testing is a concept that has yet to materialize in the mainstream testing world, and there are many definitions of object-oriented testing. Right now it's mostly a hot-button topic for object-oriented technology magazines and books.

Testing Tools

Client/server testing tools perform a number of functions. They can:

- Simulate user interaction with the application, using a capture-and-playback mechanism.
- Record performance indicators over time.
- Test GUI event-driven applications.

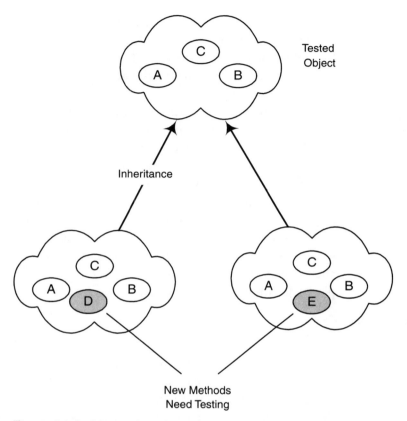

Figure 21-6 *Object-oriented testing.*

- Provide programming capabilities to create test scripts, or change captured test scripts.
- Generate reports and process a large amount of test data.
- Generate test data.

SIMULATING A USER INTERACTION

A fundamental feature of a client/server testing tool is its ability to capture the user interactions with the application, and then play them back over and over to simulate user interaction. This means the tool can record all key strokes, mouse movements, menu selections, and database interactions. The user drives the application for a certain amount of time while the recorder runs. When done, the tester can play back the test script and watch the application work as if it were driven by a ghost user.

Testing tools can go a bit further than simply recording and playing back events. They can also program the testing tools through a scripting language (described later) to recognize conditions where the user would normally pause, such as when data appears on the screen. This is an important feature: Sense responses from the database or application servers could vary. As the testing program plays back the user interaction, it documents differences in response, and records performance information in a central file or database. For instance, how long did it take the data to return from the database server, and how long did it take a report to display on the screen?

SQA Inc.'s SQA Robot is an example of a tool that can record user interaction with an application, and allow the tester to change the script for whatever reason, then play back the script to test the application. SQA Robot lets the tester insert test cases to capture a particular condition. Timers allow the tester and test script developer to record the duration of events (e.g., data returning to the client). Wait states allow the test script developer to synchronize test-procedure playback with the application under test. I find this tool powerful and easy to use.

PERFORMANCE MONITORING

Testing tools should record performance information while testing, including the duration of events, the interface I/O, and even the performance of external resources (such as database and application servers). Typically, the tool exports this performance data to a text file or database, so you can import the data into the spreadsheet or a database reporting tool, or process test data with the report features of the testing tool.

TESTING THE GRAPHICAL UNIVERSAL INTERFACE

As mentioned earlier in this chapter, testing tools should have the ability to capture events that occur in an unpredictable sequence. Testing tools need to process windows, data windows, menus, use of an ActiveX component, drop-down lists, buttons, and so on. Testing tools should also handle minor changes to applications, such as the repositioning of a GUI (graphical universal interface) control, or movement of a data window. SQA Robot, for example, can spot standard Windows objects such as buttons, check boxes, and list boxes. Robot can even process components such as ActiveX, or product-specific features such as native components found only in PowerBuilder or Visual Basic.

TEST SCRIPTS

Testing tools, like specialized client/server development tools, provide a scripting language to customize the testing process. These languages are typically proprietary to a particular tool, or, as in the case of SQA, they use the syntax from Visual Basic's VBA language. The Mercury line of products (including LoadRunner, described later) use a C-based language, and BenchWorks (also described later) uses an SQL-based language with structured programming capabilities.

TEST REPORTING

Aside from their ability to record performance data, testing tools should easily process the data. This means the testing tool's ability to depict your test data graphically, or as raw data. Typically, the tool stores test data in a database to make it easily accessible by either the reporting tools that come with the testing tool, or by third-party reporting tools (such as ReportSmith from Borland, and Crystal Reports from Seagate Software).

GENERATING TEST DATA

Finally, some tools have the ability to generate large amounts of realistic test data. The tool pumps this test data into the database to simulate how the database will perform after you transfer live data from a legacy system, or as the data accumulates over months and years.

Tools that support test data generation include BenchWorks, from INFOgy, Inc., which can generate data to populate tables from tester-defined criteria. For example, we can place numbers that look like phone numbers in the phone number column, and realistic-looking customer names in the columns that contain names. You can even create numerical data that uses random values, or an ordered sequence of unique elements (to simulate primary key).

TESTING-TOOL EXAMPLES

There are more testing tools than I can cover in a single chapter. A few companies that sell popular automated client/server testing tools are Mercury Interactive Corporation, Performance Awareness, Pure Software, SQA, Inc., and Segue Software, Inc. It's helpful to look at a few in detail to give you an idea of the state-of-the-technology, such as LoadRunner and WinRunner, both from Mercury Interactive.

LoadRunner. LoadRunner is an integrated client/server and Web (see sidebar) load-testing tool that can perform load testing for most client/server applications and systems. LoadRunner allows testers to monitor system behavior and performance during various simulated user and processing loads.

LoadRunner can load-test both the client and the server through the client load-testing (end-to-end) component, and the server load-testing component. Client load testing provides accuracy, speed and repeatability information in a multi-user, automated testing environment that gives us the ability to drive the test from a single client. LoadRunner can simulate many users across a network, each running an application. Using a single client as the sync point, LoadRunner can synchronize all the clients and collect the results for analysis. The clients are driven on the client by WinRunner (described next) or XRunner (for X-Windows) agents as GUI virtual users that run an application.

LoadRunner measures performance using the throughput model, from end to end, which provides meaningful performance measurements such as transaction response time as the user would see it. For instance, LoadRunner can press the OK button, wait for the results to appear, and record the time the system took to respond.

The server half of LoadRunner lets us load-test (stress-test) a server's capacity by simulating the processing load of many clients. LoadRunner simulates live application traffic through a multi-tasking database, "virtual users," and by simulating message traffic from the clients. The advantage is that a single machine can replicate application traffic under the load required for the test. You can simulate SQL calls to a server, such as those encountered with two-tier client/server, or through messages or transactional RPCs that occur with three-tier technology (such as TP monitors).

Testing Intranet Applications

The rise of intranet applications led to the rise of methods and tools to test these new applications based on Web technology. Until recently, there were few tools available to test intranet applications, but those days are behind us. Let's take a look at just one example of this new breed of tools.

Mercury Interactive Corp. now offers WebTest, a testing tool designed specifically for intranet Web-based applications. Just as we use client/server-based testing tools, WebTest can measure response time to a browser's HTTP request and find the largest number of hits a Web server can support before it crashes.

WebTest works in cahoots with LoadRunner (described in this chapter), and employs the same concept of the "virtual user," but now they become "virtual Web users." By simulating Web users, testers can determine how the Web server and intranet application will behave under increasing user loads. WebTest measures access response time, and makes sense of the test data using reports and graphs. Other client/server testing tool vendors are already working on their suite of Web-enabled test products.

WinRunner. As previously mentioned, WinRunner is the client-testing component of LoadRunner. The best feature of WinRunner is RapidTest, a mechanism that creates a full suite of GUI test cases for client/server applications. The idea is to get the testers up and running fast, and avoid the laborious process of creating tests by hand.

RapidTest uses a Wizard to create the test scripts after it learns the application automatically by navigating its way through the menus, menu items, and all available dialog boxes. RapidTest can generate scripts that provide full regression testing for your application, and Script Wizard creates a test script for every window and object that it finds in the client/server application.

I believe in the value of testing tools such as WinRunner, with its RapidTest subsystem. Quick and easy client/server testing makes it more likely that developers will test their applications. LoadRunner provides similar value, since developers don't have to arrange elaborate testing processes and architectures. They can simply simulate the user and processing loads they need. These tools have come a long way, and offer fair accuracy and reliability.

The Need for Testing

If you get anything out of this chapter, it's the need to test the client/server applications we build. The GUI and various complex client/server architectures are difficult to test, but with a few test tools, some common sense, and a basic test plan, you can ensure that your application will live up to user expectations.

As time goes on, client/server applications will become even more complex and more difficult to test. The answer is not to give up on testing, but to leverage technology to develop new test technology. If you set up an effective testing problem in your development organization, testing will become part of the application development infrastructure.

The key problem is not how to approach testing, but how to get development organizations to dedicate resources to testing. As budgets get tighter, and developers rely more on tools and less on process, testing is the task that falls by the wayside to save money or time. My advice: You can't afford to let that happen.

Putting Your
Application Together

Now that we've covered all the best tricks of client/server development, it's time to find out how you can turn your skills loose on a client/server development project. I'll talk about the client/server development issues you need to deal with, and make a few recommendations from a guy who made all the big mistakes (and learned from them). I'll finish up with a discussion of how you can avoid problems, or what to do when things go wrong. Finally, I'll tell you the seven deadly sins of client/server development, which you should copy down, put on your screen saver, or carve into your desk. A tattoo would work.

Developers, often, are only part of a team. They work with other developers to build applications. However, I find more and more client/server developers putting the projects together as well, including tasks such as estimating costs, creating project plans, and dealing with the business angle of the development project, as well as picking tools, talent, and technology (the three Ts of client/server).

The problem? Many developers don't acquire project management skills with technical skills, and thus they must learn by trial and error. For example, when I taught college, most of my computer science students were not required to take business courses that would teach them how to create a budget, or write a project plan. They entered the workplace ready to write the perfect C++ application, but unprepared to work through the problems the applications must solve.

However, with some rudimentary knowledge, you techie types (me included) will find that maneuvering your way through a client/server development project is as easy as finding your way around your next PowerBuilder application. I'll show you how.

Your Client/Server Project

It's 3:30. Your boss just called to inform you that you've been selected as the "lead developer" (that means you're a project manager, but they don't want to give you a raise). Your task is to build the new inventory control system, critical to the success of the company. You have a budget of a half a million dollars, and need to complete the project before the end of the fiscal year (in eight months). What you do next is the subject of this chapter.

There are many steps in developing a client/server system. I'll list them later. For now, let's talk about the first few steps required to get your project up and running. You need to create a work breakdown structure, create a budget, a project plan, and a plan to allocate resources. First, you determine what to do. Later, you determine how to do it using the information in the rest of the book.

Get a Methodology

Although we discussed some methodology issues related to object-oriented analysis and design in Chapter 7, we did not address the need for a methodology to drive your overall development process. First, let's get the semantics right.

I call object-oriented analysis and design, and database methodologies (e.g., Booch, OMT, Chin) "micro methodologies," or methodologies created to solve a particular problem of the life cycle. I call the overall process of working through the life cycle a "macro methodology." What's the difference? A macro methodology determines what must happen and when, while a micro methodology determines how it's done. For example, a macro methodology may define the basic activities of:

- Requirements
- Analysis
- Design
- Development
- Deployment

A micro methodology (also called a technique) will then define how to design an object-oriented system including the notation to use when creating an object model, the repository, and even the tool (see Figure 22-1).

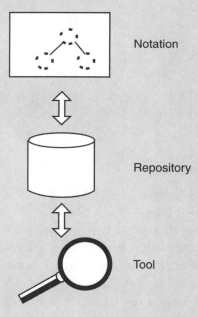

Notation

Repository

Tool

Figure 22-1 *A micro methodology.*

For instance, while the macro methodology tells you to work through the partitioning of the client/server application, it would not tell you the step-by-step process. That's where the micro methodologies come into play. Micro methodologies also include project management approaches, testing methodologies, database design methodologies, project estimating, and configuration management tools.

Of course, macro methodologies vary greatly from organization to organization, since they are most often custom-built. However, you'll find the same micro methodologies in many organizations (Booch, OMG, the

Unified Method, etc.). You can also build your own macro methodology, or buy one from a methodology vendor.

Project managers also use the macro methodology as a task checklist. The project manager can use the tasks defined in the macro methodology, at least as a starting point, to define the tasks that will make up the client/server development project.

Many methodology automation tools sell their own methodology content, or support macro methodologies you build from scratch (including LBMS's Process Engineer, and SHL System House's Transform). These tools help work through all the complex activities needed to build all types of distributed systems, including client/server. What's more, they can export information to popular project management and project estimating tools. However, they are not cheap.

If you do a lot of large-scale client/server development projects, I recommend that you look at tools such as these to drive their own content, or to drive your own.

WORK BREAKDOWN STRUCTURE

The first thing I do when I build a client/server application is create a work breakdown structure (WBS). A WBS is simply a list of the major tasks that must happen in order to build the systems. WBS also contains the name of the person responsible, an estimate of the time required to complete the tasks, and task dependencies (e.g., Task 2 must be finished before you can move to Task 3). Some organizations call this a "straw man," and some call it a work plan. As long as you list all the activities that must occur, it doesn't make much difference what you call it.

PROJECT PLANNING

After you create the WBS, it's time to create your project plan. Do yourself a favor and spend a few hundred dollars on a project management tool (such as Microsoft Project Manager). You can pump the WBS into the project management tool, which becomes a list of tasks for the project (see Figure 22-2).

Project management tools can represent tasks in many forms, including Pert (see Figure 22-3) and Gantt (see Figure 22-4) charts. In these charts, the project manager (that's you) can graphically map out the order of the tasks, the amount of time each task takes in reference to the project calendar, and the resources assigned to each task.

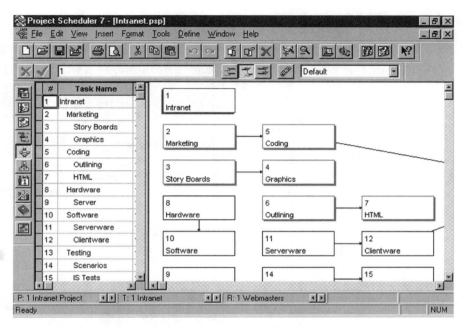

Figure 22-2 *You can pump the work breakdown schedule into the project management tool.*

Figure 22-3 *Pert chart.*

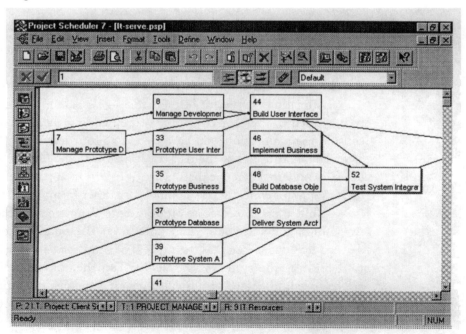

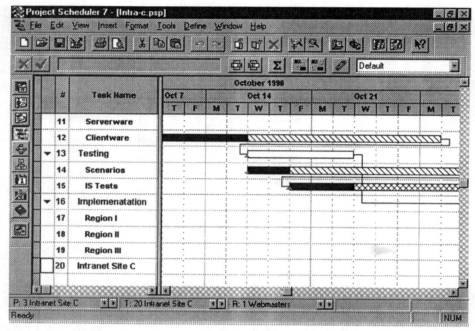

Figure 22-4 *Gantt chart.*

RESOURCES REQUIRED

Whenever you build an application, you need resources. Resources are office space, computers, software, and people. To figure out how much of each resource you need, you must learn the art of project estimation.

Estimating a project is just a matter of allocating time and money to each task defined in the project plan, and then adding them up. If you work for a consulting organization, you have to add a profit margin on top of your costs, as well as allocate cost to the risks associated with the project (e.g., the tool vendor goes under). There are many scientific ways to approach project estimation, such as lines of code, function points, and other forms of metrics.

While a detailed discussion of project estimation concepts is beyond the scope of this book, you should know that the function points concept (as defined by Casper Jones) is the process of counting certain aspects of a system to determine the system's complexity. You then assign weights to the data points based on degree of difficulty, which generates the estimated number of hours to build the system. It's simple mathematics, and there are many tools that can walk you through the process. These tools also allow you to access a database of experience, pulling out information on similar projects and adjusting the estimate for as much real-life experience as possible. Of course, you need to adjust the estimate based on your own experience.

When in Doubt, Aim High

I consistently see new project managers underestimate projects. Typically, they forget about certain necessary tasks (e.g., testing), or they don't build in vacations, holidays, or allow for the problems that always arise in a project.

My advice is to aim high. It's better to overestimate a project then to underestimate it. You'll look like a hero if you bring a project in under budget, but you'll look like a jerk if you don't. Aim high.

CREATING A BUDGET

From the WBS, project plan, and estimate, we can work out a budget for the project. In many instances, as with our previous example, someone gives you the budget, and you must try to estimate into the budget . . . somehow. This leads to the old "chicken or the egg" question, which becomes "the budget or the estimate."

Many times I'm asked to build a complex client/server system that will provide a business-critical service on an unrealistic budget. This is a time box problem. You can reduce the complexity of the system to meet the budget, or increase the budget. My advice is to stick to your guns, double-check your estimates, and don't start work on a client/server system that will fail to live up to expectations due to cutting corners, or run way over budget and thus lose money and credibility. These are common failures of client/server projects.

Client/Server Application Development Checklist

Although you must use common sense to adjust this to your own project, here is a high-level checklist of things you need to do when you build a typical client/server system:

- Define requirements
- Define the application
- Define the architecture
- Object-oriented analysis

- Define data
- Plan the deployment
- Design system tests (application test, system test, integration test, etc.)
- Select tools and technology
- Object-oriented design
- Database design
- Develop the system
- Deploy the physical database
- Deploy the system
- Establish operations procedures
- Train the users

Of course, these are not the only things to do. A complex client/server system may require 500 to 1000 separate tasks that are needed to ensure a healthy system, and there are dozens of subtasks that exist in these high-level tasks. All of this comes from your macro methodology (see sidebar).

What to Do When Things Go Wrong

So something goes wrong. Now what? First, don't panic. I've found that there are several common problems that afflict client/server development projects. They are:

- Underestimation
- Tool failure
- Architecture failure
- Desirement shift

UNDERESTIMATION

The most common problem I run into happens in projects that underestimate the time and resources required to build a client/server system (see Figure 22-5). I already preached about how to approach project estimation so you don't get into this mess, but some of you will still find yourselves facing the end of a budget without a working system despite what I say. Don't get me wrong; there are innocent victims here along with the guilty. A tool vendor could go under in mid-project, or you might lose key staff members before the project's completion. You just have to account for those risks when you do your project plan.

First thing, don't hide the problem. You need to gather information, including how far behind you are and the reasons why. Then, adjust your estimation taking the new information into account (this will be your last change

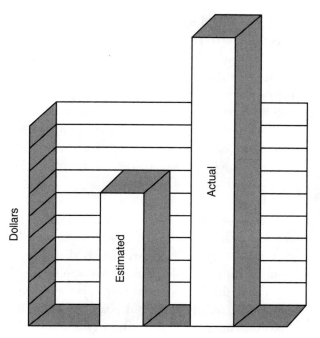

Figure 22-5 *Underestimating a project.*

to the system, by the way). Finally, you must confess the issues at hand to the powers-that-be, including how much more they need to spend to get the project up-and-running, and your plan to do it. While I can't guarantee what kind of reaction you'll get, it's always better to deal with these situations directly. In most cases, you'll find an understanding ear. Or fax me your résumé and I'll do what I can.

TOOL FAILURE

The second-biggest problem I encounter is tool failure, or the inability for your development tool(s) of choice to create the system you need. Most often, the tool can't meet the requirements of the application (such as performance, or the ability to create certain types of interfaces, or work on certain platforms). I see a lot of tool failure situations with the new set of intranet tools. The vendors rushed them out the door to latch onto a growing market, but, in many cases, they didn't fully test the tools, or admit to the limitations. For example, a tool I worked with could only generate HTML (version 1) code, and thus could not do frames, which was a requirement for the application. By the time this little fact came out, the developer was two months into the project.

As I mentioned in Chapter 8, you really have to test these tools before you select them. You'll spot the turkeys during this testing cycle. Don't rely on magazine reviews. They aren't reviewing the tool against your application requirements. You should also have an exit strategy that defines alternative tools in case the primary tool fails. The exit strategy should include how the replacement tool will work with your existing database, platform, and middleware layer.

When faced with tool failure, my advice is to dump the tool as soon as you can. Then, carefully select another tool to build the application. While this will delay the project a bit, you'll be better off in the long run.

ARCHITECTURE FAILURE

Sometimes tool failures aren't tool failures at all. Instead they are the result of the architecture's failure to solve the problem. Typically, this means using two-tier when the system clearly needs three-tier, or forcing a distributed-object solution into a simple client/server application. You name it, I've seen it.

Like the tool failure example, you need to identify the problem, create and test a new architecture, and head off in the new direction. You should know that the changes in going from two-tier to three-tier client/server are great, when you consider development time (see Figure 22-6). Count on doubling the development time as a rule of thumb (see Chapters 18 and 19).

DESIREMENT SHIFT

A frustrating problem is desirement shift, when the user changes the application requirements during application development. Ouch! While you can't eliminate desirement shift altogether, there are steps you can take to discourage it.

First of all, if you work for an outside consulting firm, and do the work for a firm, fixed price, make sure the contract's language states how the price will adjust during desirement shift. This means if they add, delete, or change functionality, you increase the price of the system accordingly. Even if your client deletes functionality, there will still be design work needed, as well as system modifications. That means more design and development time, not less.

Once again, it's a good idea to have a project estimation model in place (e.g., function points), where you can adjust the project cost as desirements change (see Figure 22-7). This is not only a way to determine the cost of a system, but it protects you from your clients, since you can always point to the metrics as the way you came up with your estimation. When clients question an estimation, I can refer to a stack of paper that defines the scope of the project, what each task entails, the resources needed to accomplish each task, and the cost of the resources.

Second, use a prototype when you design a system to depict what the system will look like, and how it will behave. Many users complain that they could not discern enough information from the design document, or even screen drawings, to determine if the system could meet their desirements. A prototype allows them to experience the system interface, and even some limited functionality. The prototype promotes discussion and interest as well, making the desirements-gathering task much easier. The only issue you have to deal with is

Figure 22-6 *The differences in two-tier and three-tier client/server.*

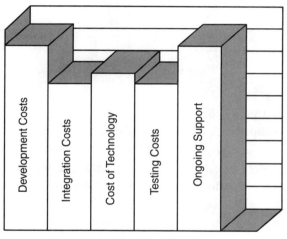

Three and *n*-Tier Client/Server
Development

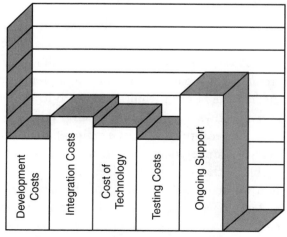

Two-Tier Client/Server Development

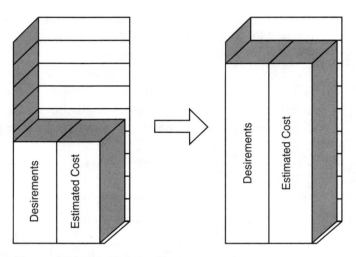

Figure 22-7 *Desirements change.*

setting an unrealistic expectation in the users' minds that the system is nearly complete, or worse, that it's ready for use.

Finally, and most fundamental, make sure you gather and account for all desirements. It's a process of crawling inside the business of your end-user, as well as performing some requirements activities like building a data dictionary and gathering use cases (see Chapter 7). Take enough time to gather desirements at the front end, and you reduce the risk of desirement shift.

Secrets of Client/Server Success

So how do you succeed at client/server development without really trying? There is one secret: Pay attention to the architecture, and everything else.

Although everyone agrees that all client/server systems require a sound architecture, today we are tool-rich and architecture-poor. Why? I'm sure the media hype has something to do with it. We seem to stress the new tools, and everyone always hopes for that "silver bullet."

The reality is not that exciting. Sound client/server systems demand that everyone understand the business requirements in detail, and the business problems that need to be solved. This means you have to cancel your subscription to the client/server-tool-of-the-month club, dust off the drawing board, and get to work. You have to do your homework, too. Take these steps and you ensure the success of your client/server development project.

SEVEN DEADLY SINS OF CLIENT/SERVER

Architectural mistakes are made in most client/server development projects—mistakes that I think are easily avoidable. I call the top seven mistakes the "Seven Deadly Sins of Client/Server." They are:

1. A fool with a tool is still a fool
2. Requirements attention deficit
3. No process, no problem
4. Bringing yourself to tiers
5. RAD on your way to success
6. Hype-driven architecture
7. Infrastructure avoidance

A Fool with a Tool Is Still a Fool. This deadly sin refers to developers and architects who believe that a silver bullet exists, that it's just a matter of time before "they" find it. These are the folks who believe all the hype—that the demonstration on the floor of the convention hall provides proof that the tool will magically solve their architectural issues.

Although selecting the right tool set of your client/server development project is always helpful, the tool should not drive the architecture. It should be the other way around. The requirements drive the architecture, and the architecture drives the tool.

Requirements Attention Deficit. This sin (RAD) refers to neglect of the requirements, and how to map them into an architecture. As technical professionals, we tend to focus on the technology and avoid the business issues at hand.

The fact is, if we neglect to understand the business problems we need to solve, there's little chance that we'll get the system right the first time. Information you need to acquire includes the business purpose of the system, the inputs and outputs, the type of system (transaction processing, occasional use, decision support, reporting, etc.), and all the legacy and new data sources that need to feed the application.

You also need to understand your user community in detail. Who they are, what do they do, and what interfaces will work for them? Get a user count as well. Not only the number of users, but the rate at which the user community will grow. While you can comfortably support a hundred users with the traditional two-tier client/server architecture, you have to do some quick rearchitecturing if you move to 500 or 1000. Good architects always have contingency plans to scale their architecture, and good architectures should scale. If you don't, there is a wall in your system that the user load could/will hit in the future.

No Process, No Problem. This sin means that developers and application architects avoid a rigorous and repeatable application development process. Fueled by a widely held belief that it's better to be a cowboy than an architect, developers build client/server systems without a consistent approach to the system design and development effort. Symptoms of this include actual costs that exceed the estimates, and poor-quality systems that are difficult to keep running.

Some client/server development organizations are moving to the strict SEI capability maturity model (CMM). The CMM uses five levels to reflect the development organization process maturity. You have to fill out a 100-point questionnaire to determine your level, which you should do to find out just where you are—kind of like a yearly physical.

At level 1 you'll find organizations with random or chaotic processes using ad hoc management of the application development effort. The vast majority of client/server systems are built in level 1 organizations. If you honestly assess your capabilities, chances are, you'll land at level 1. At level 2 the development process is considered repeatable, but the developers and architects keep the experience inside their heads. Level 3 is the nirvana of application development, where the process of client/server application development is well defined and built into the infrastructure of the organization. In level 3 organizations, developers focus on the development effort at the departmental level, and information is distributed across projects. Very few organizations can claim level 3.

I'm not saying that you need SEI to tell you how to build client/server systems, only that I see a consistent need to foster and promote some sort of repeatable process to create the right architectures and applications. Since this requires an initial investment in training and people, most organizations with a sound development process will save money in the long run.

Bringing Yourself to Tiers. This sin refers to over- or under-use of multi-tiered client/server architectures. Developers show up at the first system meeting with predefined architectures in their minds, no matter what business problem they need to solve. For example, there are those who promote three-tier architectures no matter how simple the problem. The end result is five users who run a simple client tracking application through a $100,000 TP monitor, or through a distributed-object architecture forced to fit the solution. This is better known as killing a fly with a sledgehammer. In contrast, there are those who use two-tier no matter what, then wonder why they run into scaling issues. I've talked about many of those issues already.

Rapid Application Development (RAD) on Your Way to Success. This sin refers to those who believe design is dead, that it's possible to RAD your way to a successful client/server development career. RAD (rapid application development) is not bad, but as many people have learned from one failed project after another, you can't RAD your way through most client/server development projects. You have to look upon RAD as one part of a means to an end, not the only part (see the sidebar in Chapter 7).

Hype-Driven Architecture. This sin refers to those who take a "management by magazine" approach to architecture. They let the hype drive the architecture. There is no better example than the use of Web technology to meet all client/server architectural requirements. While intranet and Internet development makes a good fit for some low-end client/server applications, the enabling technologies (e.g., Java, ActiveX, CGI) fall down quickly when they attempt to perform traditional high-speed transaction processing client/server applications. I'm sure we'll be there soon, but we are not there now.

Once again, the requirements drive the architecture, not the other way around. You need to decouple yourself from the architecture solution of the day, and select the proper architecture for your system. That is, unless your only goal is to upgrade your skills for that quick job change.

Infrastructure Avoidance. The last deadly sin refers to avoidance of the infrastructure. Slow networks mean slow applications, no matter how advanced your application. You'll also need system support, and the ability to deploy bug fixes and new applications to clients. Neglecting infrastructure is like building a city with no roads (see Chapter 3).

Sin No More

So how do you avoid the seven deadly sins? Sorry, there is no magic way to always build the right architecture—I have yet to find it. It's a rigorous, labor-intensive process.

My architectural rules of thumb may help. First, before developers and application architects make architectural decisions, they need to understand the requirements and define the business problem. If you make architectural choices too soon in the project, you increase the chance that the architecture will not solve the business problem.

Architecture Rules of Thumb

1. Understand the requirements and define the problem before considering the architecture
2. Consider architecture a part of the application design and development problem
3. Follow the hype, as long as the hype makes good architectural sense

Second, you need to consider architecture a part of the application design and development problem. It's not enough just to keep up with the state of the art, or attend a few conferences every year. You need to approach architecture as an engineering discipline. I like to separate client/server architectural issues into the categories of application design, network architecture, performance engineering, database architectures, and integration and testing. For example, an application architecture requires detailed object models that are easily mapped to your client/server development tool of choice. There are hundreds of other tasks that need to be carried out as well.

Finally, it's okay to follow the hype, as long as the hype makes good architectural sense. In many cases (i.e., Java), the hype leads the capabilities by about six months. Therefore, you could be caught building your architecture around technology that's not yet ready for prime-time computing. The vendors won't tell you. Even when the tools or technologies mature, they are simply another trick in your bag of tricks. Nothing more.

I think we are entering the next generation of client/server where architecture is everything. The systems will only get more complex, and end-users expect a higher degree of reliability and performance. Most of us have a long way to go before we can deliver on those requirements. Today, good client/server architects are hard to find.

Intranet Development
Technology and Tools

By now you know that the intranet is the most exciting thing to happen to client/server development in years, and thus it's such an important part of this book. The intranet pumped new life into the client/server development industry, and could very well become the standard mechanism to deploy client/server applications now and in the future.

This chapter brings together what we learned about intranet development throughout this book. It continues the discussion of enabling intranet technology that we began in Chapter 17 when we discussed intranet architecture, and extends the concepts to today's intranet tools and technology. See Chapter 24 for a look at the future of the intranet, and its place in the world of client/server computing.

In this chapter, I will discuss available intranet development tools, and teach you how to classify tools to make better sense of the hordes of products available today. The number of intranet development tools has just surpassed the number of client/server development tools, and the market shows no signs of slowing down. If you do client/server, you'll have to do intranet as well. There is no getting around that fact.

Same Tools, New Platform

The easiest way to look at the intranet in terms of client/server development is as a new platform. There are no significant differences in how we build intranet applications compared to client/server. In many cases, the tools are the same. Applications still access the same databases and application services. The only real difference is the interface and the architectures.

Intranet application development provides developers with the flexibility to employ widely available Web technology (browsers, servers, etc.) for use by business applications. This means we can deploy applications with fewer dollars, and thus reduce the overall cost of client/server development using the intranet. Many of the traditional problems of client/server integration simply go away. Don't let anyone tell you otherwise. We are running to the intranet because it makes good economic sense to be there.

Buyer Beware

The downside to intranet development is the number of standards that chase Web technology, and thus define and redefine the intranet quickly. Too quickly. For instance, while Java may seem the technology of choice today, ActiveX will likely take a significant bite into the Java market in the next year or so. The same can be said of HTTP and IIOP (see Chapter 19), and traditional Web-enabled protocols (such as CGI) with the advent of NSAPI and ISAPI. With change comes risk. The risk that you'll take depends on a solution that may simply go out of style.

What's more, Web technology does not meet all of our application development requirements. There are serious limitations to what intranet applications can do today. You need to understand these limitations before you write checks that the technology can't cash (see the "dog" sidebar in Chapter 17 for more information on the limitations of Web technology). You must test intranet technology yourself to see if it lives up to the hype.

Selecting Enabling Technologies

Before we begin our discussion of intranet development tools, let's finish our discussion of enabling technologies from Chapter 17. You need to understand the enabling technologies behind these intranet development tools to make an informed decision when you select a tool. You must pick a team, and the contenders are Java, ActiveX, and Netscape Plug-in, or Web server APIs such as CGI (really a protocol), NSAPI, and ISAPI.

Each of these intranet-enabling technologies brings dynamic behavior to the Web client, where once only static text and graphics appeared. Web clients can invoke applications by simply entering in a URL, and they then have all the features of traditional client/server applications (such as the ability to access data, generate reports, and access the processing power of remote application servers). However, each flavor of technology handles these applications in a different way.

HYPERTEXT MARKUP LANGUAGE

Before I get into the more sophisticated stuff, let's get HTML out of the way first. HTML (hypertext markup language) is the reason behind the Web explosion of the last few years. HTML is the native language of Web browsers, and allows browsers to display text, graphics, applets, and multimedia components to the end-user who runs a browser (see Figure 23-1). HTML also provides rudimentary application development capabilities (such as the ability to display forms for dialog with the user, and the ability to display data as tables and panels).

What developers need to know about HTML is the number of versions available, and how each version drives application development capabilities. For example, if all your end-users run Web browsers that only support version 2 of HTML, you can't exploit the capabilities of version 3 not to mention the

Figure 23-1 *HTML.*

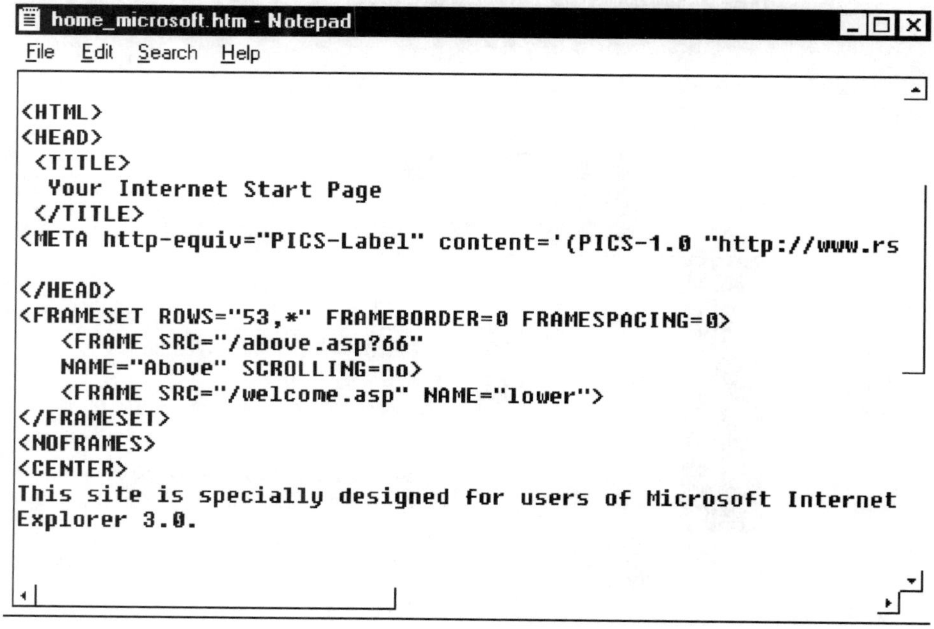
home_microsoft.htm - Notepad
File Edit Search Help
<HTML>
<HEAD>
<TITLE>
Your Internet Start Page
</TITLE>
<META http-equiv="PICS-Label" content='(PICS-1.0 "http://www.rs
</HEAD>
<FRAMESET ROWS="53,*" FRAMEBORDER=0 FRAMESPACING=0>
<FRAME SRC="/above.asp?66"
NAME="Above" SCROLLING=no>
<FRAME SRC="/welcome.asp" NAME="lower">
</FRAMESET>
<NOFRAMES>
<CENTER>
This site is specially designed for users of Microsoft Internet
Explorer 3.0.

Netscape extensions. While the application will run (if the intranet application can adjust to older browsers), the end-users won't be able to enjoy all the capabilities of the applications. I'm sure that many of you think it's just a simple matter of upgrading the browsers. While that's sometimes true, in many organizations, frequently upgrading a browser is cost-prohibitive, or the client operating system of choice does not support a browser that supports the state-of-the-art HTML version.

While HTML 1 only provided basic text capabilities, HTML 3 (in wide use today) provides more advanced features such as use of embedded graphics and the ability to create forms for the end-user. The big two web browser vendors (Netscape and Microsoft) have recently created their own set of extensions to HTML, including the ability to use frames and tables, and other features that make a Web page appear as a true application interface. For instance, frames and tables are useful for displaying and browsing through data (see Figure 23-2).

The moral of this story is to match the HTML of your intranet development tool with the HTML version supported by the clients. As a rule, I would not deploy an intranet application to anything less than a HTML 3-compliant browser, but there are many situations where you won't have that luxury. Also,

Figure 23-2 *Frames and tables.*

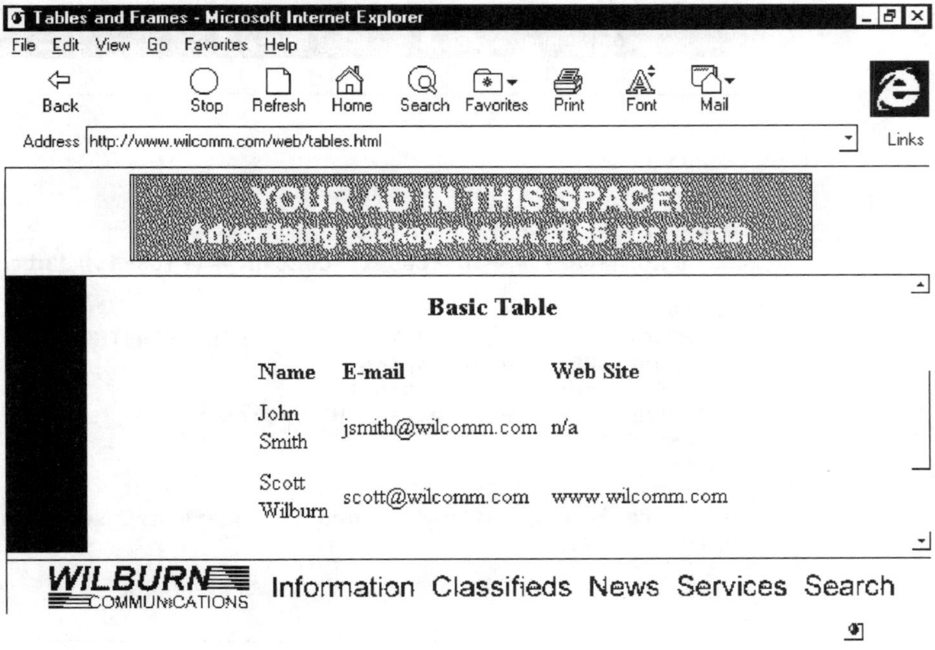

I would not build HTML features into an application that are only supported by a single browser vendor (e.g., Netscape and Microsoft).

COMMON GATEWAY INTERFACE

Continuing our three-tier and four-tier intranet discussion from Chapter 17, CGI (common gateway interface) is a Web-server API that lets developers send dynamic Web pages back to intranet clients who run a browser. The intranet client invokes a CGI application that runs in the native operating system on the Web server. The CGI process can do any number of things, but typically interacts with a database server to return information to the Web client as HTML. Also mentioned in Chapter 17, NSAPI and ISAPI solve many CGI problems, including performance and the ability to track states. However, ISAPI and NSAPI are proprietary to particular Web server vendors.

CGI is really a protocol, and not a programming language. CGI was the first attempt to offer dynamic application development for the intranet. Tool vendors, such as those who sell application development and database publishing solutions (see examples later in this chapter), exploit CGI as a means of deploying their applications to the intranet. They can automatically generate CGI code for the developer, and the developer no longer needs to code-in CGI directly. NeXT Software's WebObjects and ParcPlace-Digitalk's VisualWave are examples of intranet development tools that exploit CGI to deploy RAD applications.

Netscape API versus Internet Server API

If NSAPI and ISAPI are better than CGI, then what are they? NSAPI is really a framework that lets developers control Netscape Web servers from an application. In many respects, they are analogous to CGI. However, NSAPI provides a direct access to the features of the database server that runs inside the process space of Netscape. CGI applications are external to the Web server. NSAPI also provides functionality not available with CGI, such as error handling, authentication, and the ability to track states. What's more, NSAPI is several times as fast as CGI.

Like NSAPI, ISAPI is linked to Microsoft's Internet Information Server (IIS) and runs inside the process space of the Web server (as a DLL, of course). ISAPI provides many of the same benefits as NSAPI, including enhanced performance. ISAPI supports filtering during an HTTP request, and lets the server know about notifications that the server should watch out for.

JAVA

The basic idea behind Java is to bring dynamic application behavior to Internet and intranet applications. While Java was once limited to application development environments for Web site animation applets, it's now growing into first-rate client/server development technology with new features such as Java Beans and JDBC (described next). Like any other 3GL, Java can receive input from intranet clients, process the input, and even link and interact with database servers via C call-outs or JDBC.

While the Java language and HotJava architecture are great technology, Java did not really take off as a key client/server development environment until the Java RAD tools hit the market. Based on Sun's JDK 1.X, these tools, such as Symantec's Visual Café, Microsoft's Visual J++ (see Figure 23-3) and Borland's JBuilder, make Java-enabled intranet development quick and easy. They can also provide built-in database connectivity by using JDBC, or proprietary database middleware layers.

Java Beans. Java Beans is a new Java-enabled component software assembly paradigm that will bring the "assemble from parts" model to Java development

Figure 23-3 *Microsoft's Visual J++.*

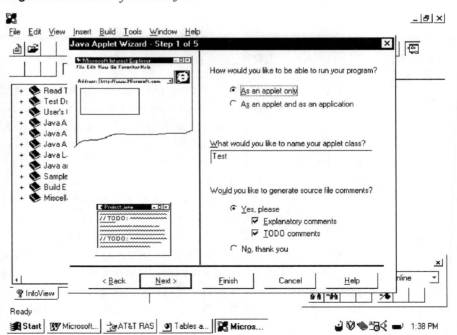

(see Chapter 19 for a discussion of components). At its core, Java Beans is an API that lets developers create dynamic Java components. The idea is to offer Java Beans with the current array of Java tools. I feel very certain that almost all Java tools will employ Java Beans in the near future. You should become acquainted with it now.

The Java Beans component model features a bridge to other non-Java component object models (including OLE/COM, OpenDoc, and Netscape's Live Connect). Since Java Beans is a part of the Java platform, developers don't need to send any extra libraries to get a Java Beans application up and running. Like Java, Java Beans is fully portable and developers can reuse Java Beans components across platforms. The idea is to "write once, use everywhere."

Java Beans is about APIs, and its APIs support event handling, properties, persistence, introspection, and an application builder API. The event-handling API allows one component to link to and send events to another component. The properties API lets developers set component attributes such as colors and fonts. With the persistence API, developer can store parts to the state of the parent container. The introspection API allows developers to learn about methods, interfaces, variables, and so on, for each Java class (introspection also supports design patterns). Finally, the application builder API uses editors (known as customizers) to provide developers with the means to customize components.

If you can't wait to begin programming in Java Beans, it's already part of version 1 (but not 1.0.1). Now that Java Beans is in the JDK, you can count on the Java vendors (such as Symantec, Borland, and Rouge Wave) to exploit its capabilities. Linked with JDBC, Java Beans could be the one-two punch that pushes Java into the traditional world of client/server.

Java Database Connectivity. JDBC, like ODBC, is a call-level interface (CLI) for Java. It is not a product, but a specification. JDBC provides Java the common API to most relational databases (such as Oracle, Sybase, and Informix). JDBC will drive two-tier Java-enabled intranets for applet-to-database connectivity. Since JDBC is really a bunch of native Java classes, there are no C call-outs or proprietary middleware APIs to deal with.

The strength of JDBC is not the API, but its ability to provide a consistent database connectivity standard for Java. Java tool vendors are already lining up to build JDBC into their development environments. I've used JDBC, and I'm impressed with both the API standard (one of the best in the business) and the performance. It will allow the two-tier intranet to take off, once it becomes widely available.

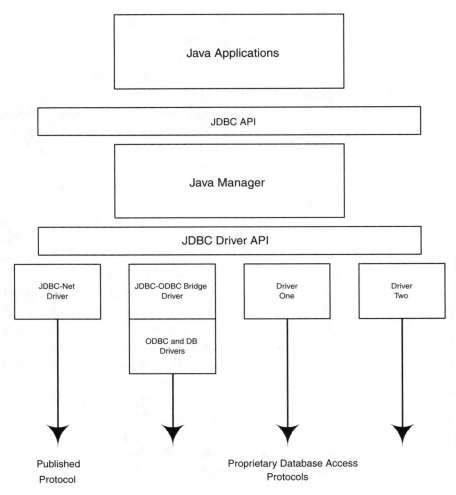

Figure 23-4 *JDBC features two API layers.*

JDBC features two layers: the JDBC API that provides application-to-JDBC manager connections, and the JDBC driver API that supports the JDBC manager-to-drive connection (see Figure 23-4). It's the job of the database vendor to provide the JDBC driver interface; or vendors may use a traditional ODBC connection. The drivers are really a group of Java classes (including java.sql.Connection, java.sql.Statement, java.sql.PreparedStatement, java.sql.CallableStatement, and java.sql.ResultSet). A developer who wants to access a database with JDBC uses these classes which can link to the database, sends a request, and processes the result set.

ACTIVEX

ActiveX is OCX rebuilt for the Web. ActiveX features an in-process OLE automation server with component capabilities, and Web features (such as use of security). Make no mistake. ActiveX was designed to compete with Sun's Java, and provides many of the same features. You can run ActiveX intranet applications from Microsoft Internet Explorer (see Figure 23-5), and you can create ActiveX applications with traditional client/server tools (such as Visual C++ and Visual Basic). Developers can connect to back-end databases using ODBC versus Java's JDBC (see earlier description).

While you don't need to understand the inner workings of Java or ActiveX for intranet development, as I mentioned in Chapter 17, you need to understand the architecture. Both Java and ActiveX support DORMAT (see Chapter 17 for the discussion of two-tier intranet), thus their applications truly run on the client within the Web browser (after their download from the Web server). They can operate disconnected from the Web server; therefore, they don't rely on Web server APIs (such as NSAPI or ISAPI). The applets sit in

Figure 23-5 *You can run ActiveX intranet applications directly from ActiveX-enabled Web browsers.*

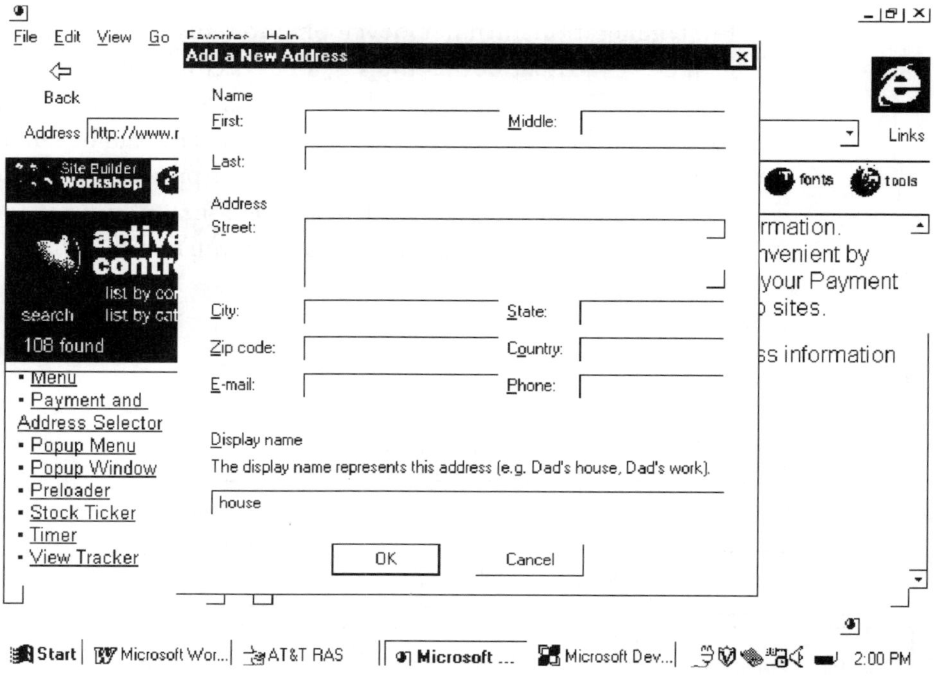

cache for use again, and as applet classes, change on the Web server as new classes are downloaded. This provides developers with the ability to distribute new versions of the software from a central location.

PLUG-INS

Plug-ins give developers the capability to take control of a Web browser that drives the intranet application. Plug-ins use a common interface that's functionally equivalent to a DLL in the world of Windows. Examples of Web browsers that support plug-ins are Navigator and Explorer.

Generations of Intranet Development

In truth, there are hundreds of intranet development tools. All take different approaches to intranet development, and all serve some specific purpose. To make sense of the chaos, I find it helpful to place them into categories (as we did with the traditional client/server tools). My categories for intranet development tools include first, second, third, and fourth generation (see Figure 23-6).

FIRST GENERATION

First-generation intranet development tools are the most primitive, and include HTML authoring tools. While Microsoft Front Page is a very sophisticated HTML authoring and Web server management tool, it's a very unsophisticated intranet development tool. The same can be said for other HTML authoring environments, even the ones that provide the ability to create data entry forms and integrate with search engines. You want to deal with first-generation intranet development tools if you're only delivering content, and not an application.

Figure 23-6 *Generations of intranet development tools.*

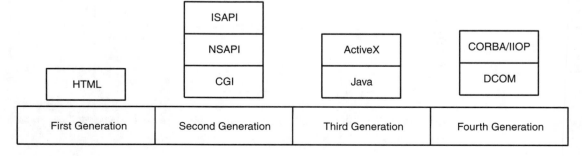

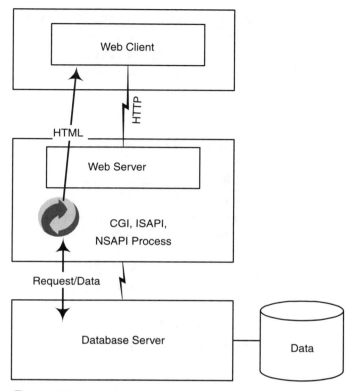

Figure 23-7 *Second-generation intranet development tools.*

SECOND GENERATION

Second-generation intranet development tools make up the majority of tools available today. Second-generation tools support the traditional Web server-centric or three-tier intranet development paradigm, and include enabling technologies such as advanced HTML (version 3 Netscape extensions), and Web server control technologies such as CGI, NSAPI, and ISAPI.

There are many examples of second-generation intranet development tools (such as VisualWave and Web Object, described in Chapter 12 and later in this chapter, respectively). These tools provide the ability to RAD your way through an intranet development project. Let the tool generate the CGI, NSAPI, or ISAPI programs required to deploy the application. All the processing occurs at the Web server, which dynamically sends HTML down to the Web clients (see Figure 23-7). Second-generation intranet development tools also include many database publishing tools, and most of the client/server report tools that now deploy to the Web (including ReportSmith and Crystal Reports).

Despite the interest in Java and ActiveX, these tools continue to be the backbone of intranet development. I suspect this will be true for the next year or so, especially considering the advent of CGI replacements such as NSAPI and ISAPI. Both provide the performance that CGI could not (see sidebar earlier in this chapter).

THIRD GENERATION

Third-generation tools are those that support two-tier intranet and DOR-MAT (see Figure 23-8). The enabling technologies include Java and ActiveX. While the technology that drives these tools is not very old, third-generation tools (such as J++, Jfactory, and Visual Café) are coming on strong. They now provide features you'd normally find in traditional client/server development tools, such as the use of components, and repository-driven database-centric development.

I see third-generation tools making up the majority of new tools that will hit the market in the next year or so. However, the tool vendors still have lots of improvements to make. They need to layer easy-to-use scripting languages on top of Java, provide better database support, integrate standards such as JDBC and Java Beans, and improve performance.

FOURTH GENERATION

Fourth-generation intranet development tools support both CORBA and DCOM-based distributed objects for intranet development (see Figure 23-9). Fourth-generation tools are more pie-in-the-sky, with few tools available today. Even the available tools don't offer general purpose C++ compilers that support these technologies. However, things are slowly changing. If IIOP becomes the HTTP of the Web, we'll see a boom in fourth-generation intranet development tools.

Figure 23-8 *Third-generation tools.*

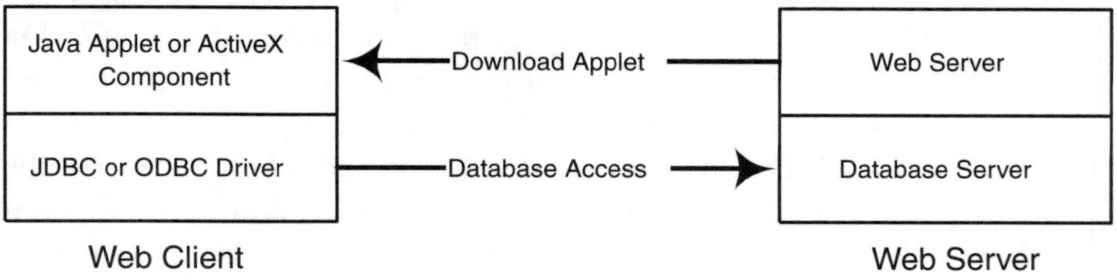

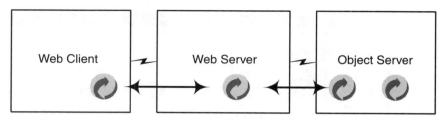

Figure 23-9 *Fourth-generation intranet development tools.*

Internet Development Tools

The number of intranet development tools may seem a bit overwhelming, so I'll just give you an overview of a few of my favorite tools. When you look at the intranet development tool vendors, you'll see the same client/server players such as Borland, Microsoft, Symantec, and Powersoft. These intranet development tools are a mixture of existing client/server development tools, redone for the intranet. You will also see new tools from traditional client/server vendors, or the dozens of start-up Internet companies.

VISUAL CAFÉ

Unlike Borland, Symantec will not intranet-enable their existing C++ compiler to Java. Instead, they offer Visual Café and Visual Café Pro, a mixture of Java and a specialized client/server tool. Café was one of the first visual development tools for Java. Café provides a development tool that can build two-tier client/server applications for the intranet, and links to remote database servers through JDBC, or through Symantec's proprietary database connection mechanism. Built for performance, Café includes a built-in just-in-time compiler, which allows applet processing to bypass the overhead of a byte-code interpreter and go directly to the processor.

VISUAL J++

Although Microsoft got into the Web game late, they provide some of the better tools. An example is Visual J++, a Java-based development environment that also supports ActiveX. Visual J++, as you may have guessed, is a cross between Visual C++ and Sun's JDK (see Figure 23-10). It provides all the capabilities of Visual C++, and I found it easy to use with typical Microsoft features (such as Wizards to guide the user through routine development operations, or to build portions of the application for the developer). While Visual J++ is an excellent Java development environment, you have to

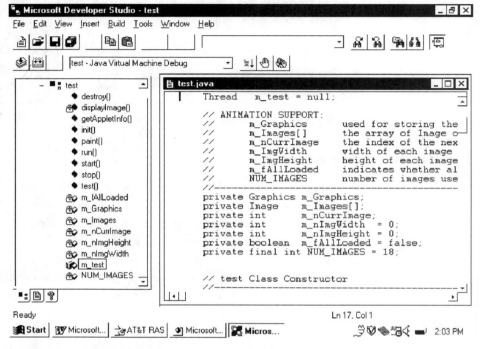

Figure 23-10 *Visual J++.*

expect that Microsoft won't support Java as its enabling technology of choice. If you want ActiveX development tools, Visual Basic and Visual C++ are better choices right now.

BORLAND C++

Borland C++, with version 5, became one of the few C++ compilers that also does Java. Like Café, Borland provides the intranet developer with a visual Java development environment, and a just-in-time compiler. This tool is a good fit for those who want to mix C++ development with Java. With Borland, developers can mix code.

JBUILDER

In addition to providing Borland C++, Borland will soon ship JBuilder. I saw JBuilder at the last Borland conference, and found it to be a Java-enabled version of Delphi, with the same RAD development features (including built-in database connectivity). I predict that this tool will take the Java development world by storm. That is, if Borland can ever get it out the door.

PowerBuilder

Despite its position as a client/server powerhouse, Powersoft opted to move to the intranet in baby steps. PowerBuilder, for example, provides plug-in capabilities for Web development, but plans to move toward an ActiveX-enabled architecture in the near future. The plug-in feature allows developers to migrate existing PowerBuilder applications to Web browsers (such as Navigator) through the use of the familiar PowerScript scripting language, and traditional PowerBuilder data windows.

Optima++

When you look at Optima++ (also from Powersoft), it's clear that PowerBuilder's plan is to hedge its bets by supporting both ActiveX and Java. Optima++ supports Web application development by supporting Java as well as a C++ native development language. Using Optima++, developers can create Java applications with the same visual development environment they use to create C++ Optima++ applications.

Uniface

One of the premier multi-platform tools, Uniface, from Compuware, can move applications to the intranet, or to a dozen or so platforms. The Uniface WebEnabler allows developers to move existing or new Uniface applications directly to the intranet without modifications. Web maintains all the features of the application, including the existing business rules and database connections. The basic idea is that WebEnabler translates an existing or new Uniface application into HTML, then sends the HTML to the Web browser. WebEnabler is an example of a second-generation intranet development environment that provides dynamic application behavior through CGI, NSAPI, or ISAPI.

VISION

Another multi-platform tool that's also turned to the Web is VISION, from Unify. VISION can generate Java code directly from native Unify applications, without forcing the developer to understand or code in Java. Just as I do, VISION looks upon the intranet as just another platform to support. Thus you can create a single VISION application for Unix, Windows, OS/2, the Macintosh, and the intranet. No code changes are required when you move the application from platform to platform.

JAM/WEB ENTERPRISE BUILDER

Yet another multi-platform tool that now does intranet is JAM from JYACC. JAM/WEB (Web Enterprise Builder) provides another means to RAD your way to intranet applications with JAM-like visual forms editors. The enabling technology is HTML and CGI, which can interact with any number of database servers by using the features of the JAM tool. Once again, JAM/WEB is a multi-platform tool that treats the Web as just another platform.

VISUALWAVE

While I described this product in much more detail in my Smalltalk chapter (Chapter 12), VisualWave, from ParcPlace-Digitalk, is a Web-enabled version of VisualWave. VisualWave uses CGI as the enabling technology, and provides session management capabilities to get around the state problem with CGI. If you're willing to learn Smalltalk, VisualWave is a good intranet development tool, and one of the first to hit the streets.

WEBOBJECTS

Similar to VisualWave, WebObjects, from NeXT Software, is an intranet version of the existing Enterprise Object Framework (EOF) client/server development tool. Like EOF, developers can visually create the application and then add behavior using Objective C. WebObjects generates the HTML and CGI code required to support the application and interface with the target database server. WebObjects supports NSAPI and ISAPI and Java. It's the most costly of the bunch, with a price tag of around $25,000 for a typical development environment.

JFACTORY

JFactory, from Rogue Wave Software, Inc., is another Visual Café- and Visual J++-like development environment to create Java applets and applications. There are several subsystems of JFactory, including a project manager, Windows and dialog designer, and menu design tool. It's just a matter of visually assembling the application using a set of prebuilt components (as in Visual Café and Visual J++), and then adding the Java code to give the application behavior.

CHANGING WORLD

Of course, this is only a cross-section of the intranet development tools available, and it's just an instant in time. For a current list you may want to check out www.dbmsmag.com, and through the "Internet Systems" portion of the *DBMS* Magazine home page, check out the buyer's guide for Internet development tools. The magazine does a good job of keeping it up to date, and things change weekly right now.

However, the tools won't undergo the rapid changes of months past. As tool vendors settle into their new world, they will do more refining than creating. What's more, many intranet development tool vendors will wait for the enabling technology to settle down—at least until there is a clear winner.

Intranet/Database Connections In-a-Box

Beyond full-blown intranet application development tools, there are tools specifically built for connecting databases to your intranet. They provide the plumbing and wiring, with little or no dynamic application development capabilities. I call these intranet tools WebBases, or connections in-a-box. Here are a few of the most popular.

Spider, from Spider Technologies, is an example of a database connectivity tool that can link directly to a database from HTML or Java applets. Cold Fusion, from Allaire, also provides database access from HTML. Sybase offers web.sql, which can link to Sybase System 10 databases from HTML. Web-DBC, from Nomad Development Corp., connects Web servers to databases using ISAPI and NSAPI.

For Java developers who can't wait for JDBC, there is JetConnect, from XDB System, Inc. JetConnect, like JDBC (see description earlier in this chapter) is a set of Java classes and drivers that can link to any relational database supported by ODBC.

Picking an Intranet Tool

So how do you pick an intranet development tool? First, you need to select the architecture required to solve the problem at hand. In Chapter 17 you'll find the available intranet architectures. Second, you need to select an enabling technology that fits your architecture. This is key, since you need to look at many features and a lot of tradeoffs. For example, while CGI works with any Web server, NSAPI and ISAPI provide better performance if you're willing to trade computability. There are tradeoffs with Java as well, and you can argue the Java versus ActiveX issue for days. Finally, you need to examine each tool on its own merits. Use the tool evaluation criteria as described in Chapter 8, and be sure to do your homework.

My experience with intranet development tools is frustrating. The hype that surrounds the technology, and the rapid change in the market, make it difficult to select the right tool. It was difficult enough just writing this chapter, since things were moving so fast.

A few final words of advice. Make sure you understand the problem you need to solve, and the type of application you want to develop for your intranet. Then dodge the hype and pick a few candidate tools. Use the requirements as a guideline, evaluate each tool, and don't forget to test.

Count on another few years before intranet development technology settles down. But who has time to wait for technology to settle down? I think you need to dive right in. The water is fine. Reading this chapter (and the book) is a great start.

The Future of Client/Server Development

Client/server development is still evolving. From year to year, project to project, I never do anything the same way twice. Today we are busy moving our client/server assets to the intranet. In a few years, who knows where we'll take client/server and distributed development. Will you be ready?

Spotting trends is not only a nice thing to do, it's a career skill. For instance, those who saw the rise of the intranet early on, and obtained the skills they needed to leverage the technology, were the same people who cashed in when the Web took off. Same can be said about three-tier client/server, and now the rise of distributed objects. We may also see the rise of user agents, or point-to-point networking.

In this, the final chapter, I'll discuss the bright future of client/server, including technology that you'll see in the near and distant future. I'll also let you know about some of the trends you can latch onto today, and where to catch the next wave of client/server technology. Then we'll call it a book.

Job Security

Client/server developers and application architects have a bright future. IDC (International Data Corporation) says that 33 percent of organizations are already committed to client/server computing, despite the long break-in period. The Strategic Focus reports that three-tier client/server applications will grow from 4.9 percent to 18.7 percent in just two years (see Figure 24-1). This growth will also fuel the rise of three-tier and *n*-tier client/server technology (such as TP monitors and distributed objects). Forrester Research estimates that the client/server marketplace will rise to $7.5 billion in 1996. Finally, the Gartner Group predicts that 65 percent of all applications created in the next five years will employ client/server technology.

Clearly, the growth of client/server is steady, and as time goes on, the vast majority of applications we build for businesses will employ client/server technology. We still have a ways to go, and many problems to solve, but you can bank on this certainty: The client/server development game will always have room for talented people.

Look around today's "corporate downsized" job market. Those in client/server development have little reason to worry. There are more job openings than candidates, and that's been a pretty steady trend for several years. For instance, my biggest challenge as a manager of a technology organization is to keep positions staffed with qualified people. That's why recruiters will beat down your door once you have a few years of experience in the business.

Figure 24-1 *Growth of Three-Tier Client/Server Applications.*

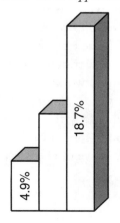

The Intranet-Client/Server Debate

Shortly before the publication of this book, I plan to participate in the "Great Debate" at the Database and Client/Server World Conference. The title of the debate: "Is the Intranet Killing Client/Server?" This debate just brings to light an argument that continues to rage in the client/server development community. The idea is that there is so much interest in the intranet that client/server will fall by the wayside. Actually, the opposite is true. As I mentioned at in the beginning of this book, the intranet and client/server complement rather than compete. In fact, the migration to the intranet simply deploys client/server technology using the commodity Web technology.

What the intranet brings to the table is a new platform, interface, and architectures. The intranet can employ existing client/server applications as true intranet applications, and integrate applications in the Web browser that would not normally work and play well together. The intranet also means that the vast amount of information on the Internet becomes available from the same application environment and the interface. That's the value.

The intranet also puts fat client developers on a diet. Since most intranet applications are driven from the Web server, the application processing is moving off the client and back onto the server. This means that maintenance and application deployment become much easier (see Figure 24-2), and developers

Figure 24-2 *Intranet applications are driven from the Web server.*

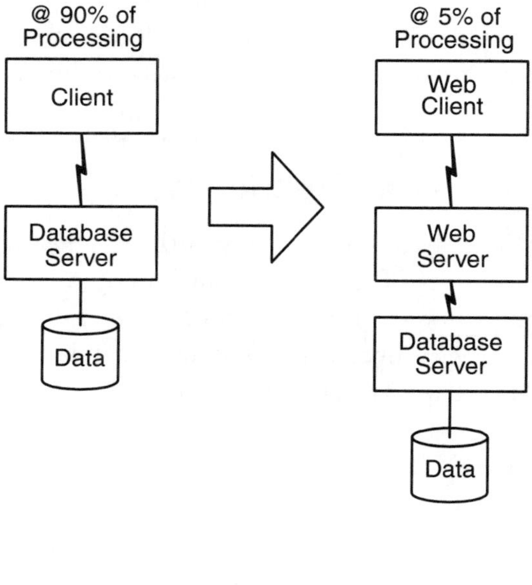

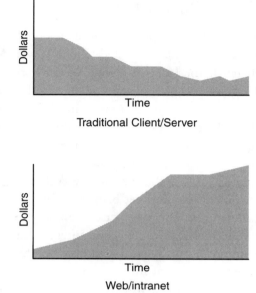

Figure 24-3 *Tool development dollars are shifting to the Web.*

don't have to deal with the integration hassles of traditional client/server (such as loading assorted middleware and protocol stacks).

There is a drawback to the intranet movement. The interest in the Web has taken most R&D dollars away from traditional client/server. In many respects, we put the evolution of traditional client/server technology (middleware, databases, and front-end development tools) on hold while the technology vendors moved their products to the Web (see Figure 24-3).

Moving to Proprietary Complexity

While the sheer simplicity of the intranet has driven its success, we are now in danger of driving this technology the same way we are driving client servers: to proprietary complexity. The signs are all over. Where HTML and CGI were once commonly held standards, we now have proprietary APIs such as NSAPI and ISAPI that are pushing CGI aside. Java was considered the only way to program dynamic Web applications, but now we have ActiveX hot on its heels. Even Netscape now touts the standard HTTP as "legacy technology."

It's difficult at this time to determine if this movement to proprietary technology is a good thing. One thing for sure is that the simple architecture of just a few years ago is gradually disappearing. In many respects, intranet development is becoming as complex as client/server development. The trend is going to continue. We could see even more complexity in the world of Web development than we ever saw with client/server.

As interest in the Web moves from getting intranet-enabled development tools out the door as quickly as possible to creating successful applications, we'll see more links between the intranet and traditional client/server. Right now, the tool vendors' fear that they will miss a large portion of the market puts them in a reactive rather than a proactive mode.

Technology to Come

Predicting technology is like predicting the weather. While it's safe to say that processors will be faster and disk space cheaper, it's much more difficult to predict the way we'll use and develop software. Developers don't create the trends, they follow them. For example, the interest in the intranet came from the millions of users who found a friendly home in their Web browser, and wanted a way to run their business applications with the Disney and CNN Home Pages. Same can be said about traditional client/server a few years ago. Users wanted to run business applications with their new GUI desktop applications.

Using the past as our guide, we can take an educated guess about the future of client/server. I like to break our predictions up into a few categories: networking, development tools, processors and servers, paradigms, and enabling technologies.

NETWORKING

The pipe between the client and server is still too narrow, and bandwidth has not kept up with development technology and modern architecture (see Figure 24-4). With the advent of ATM and switched networks, we can finally count on a pipe wide enough to push tons of data through. It will take a few years before we bring this wide pipe down to the desktop.

As I mentioned in Chapter 3, client/server developers must become networking gurus as well. The performance of the network dictates the performance of the client/server system. What's more, with the advent of application-partitioning

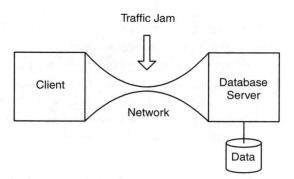

Figure 24-4 *The pipe between the client and server.*

technology (such as application-partitioning tools and distributed objects), the network not only links the client to the server, but links all the application objects together to form the virtual (partitioned) application (see Figure 24-5). Clearly, the network is the infrastructure of the distributed application.

In addition to upgrading the speed and reliability of enterprise network technology, we are looking for ways to upgrade the speed of WAN technology. Frame relay and other global networking solutions will create high-performance

Figure 24-5 *With the advent of application-partitioning technology, the network links all the application objects together to form the virtual application.*

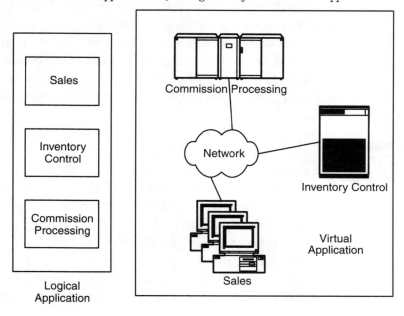

virtual systems, available throughout the world. Let us hope this technology will extend to the Internet. If you haven't noticed, it's creaking under the strain of thousands of additional users who start surfing every day.

DEVELOPMENT TOOLS

Client/server development tools are finally delivering on promises made five years ago, but there is a lot of room for improvement. Some of the areas I see where tools will do better include:

1. Use of true compilers
2. Native links to distributed objects and TP monitors
3. Better component development capabilities
4. Use of standards
5. Consistent language support
6. True application-partitioning capabilities
7. Consistent approach to the intranet

Use of True Compilers. With the advent of Delphi, developers saw the benefit of a specialized development tool that can not only do RAD, but create small, efficient, and speedy applications. The use of a true compiler allows developers to create native executables and avoid the overhead of dealing with an interpreter.

In the past, specialized client/server development tools counted on the fact that processors increased in speed every year to mask the inefficiencies of their deployment mechanisms. But users did notice, and they labeled PowerBuilder, Visual Basic, and other specialized development tool applications "dogs" on low-end PCs. Upgrading the hardware in the entire company to run a single application costs millions, and there is something to be said about efficient application development (such as is offered by most C++ development environments).

Today we see a trend in specialized client/server development tools that offers a true compiler. Besides Delphi, PowerBuilder runs close to native, and Visual Basic (version 5) will also provide a true compiler. Other specialized tool vendors are bound to head in that direction. Tool vendors should have done this from the start, and it's about time they got their act together.

Native Links to Distributed Objects and Transaction-Processing Monitors. Despite the fact that distributed objects and TP monitors are key enablers for multi-tier client/server development, few client/server tools exist that can easily use them. For instance, if we want to use a specialized client/server tool with a TP monitor, we have to load and invoke the services of a DLL (in most cases), or limit the selection of tools to those few that support TP monitors (e.g., Prolific, EncinaBuilder—see Chapter 18). The same can be said about distributed objects.

As mentioned above, the number of multi-tiered client/server applications keeps growing, and so will the need for client/server tools that can access the services of TP monitors and distributed objects. With demand comes innovation, and most tool vendors plan to provide links to distributed objects and TP monitors. With the advent of Transaction Server, for example, TP monitors come as close to a DCOM connection as any COM-enabled client/server development tools.

As IIOP (see Chapter 19) makes intranet development easier, we'll see a rise in the number of tools that support traditional client/server development *and* integration with distributed objects. Thus, as a byproduct of links to Web technology, we'll see the use of CORBA-compliant distributed objects as a part of most client/server development tools. Already, any Windows-based client/server development tool that does OLE automation can also link to DCOM, and thus, COM-enabled ORBs. The movement toward the use of distributed objects will continue.

Better Component Development Capabilities. The other side of distributed objects is the ability to assemble client/server applications from prebuilt components. While most client/server tools support the integration of components (e.g., ActiveX or Java), they don't support them well. Many components don't work and play well with others, and don't provide developers with enough granularity.

If component development is to work, tool vendors must provide consistent support for components that will allow developers to modify the interfaces, and easily link components together to create an application. What's more, the same tools should create components. We have many examples of tools today (such as Visual Basic and PowerBuilder) that can both create and use components. The future lies in tools that can easily create and share components, as well as mix and match tools to construct an application from a very low level (e.g., middleware) to a very high level (see Figure 24-6).

If current indicators continue to hold true, I believe ActiveX will provide the component standards we need for Windows, while OpenDoc will have limited success on non-Windows platforms. A lot will depend on Microsoft's ability to parlay ActiveX into a legitimate open standard. Right now, developers view ActiveX as a proprietary standard, still bound to Windows. They are right.

Use of Standards. Of course, the use of distributed objects, TP monitors, and components leads to a discussion of standards. While many standards and

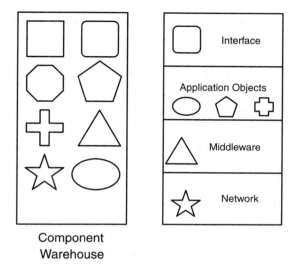

Component
Warehouse

Figure 24-6 *The future lies in tools that can easily create and share components.*

standards organizations exist today, standards are only as good as the number of developers who use them.

Key client/server standards include CORBA, COM, and SQL92, but many others run with the wolves. A common problem in the industry is our failure to use and enforce standards. The tradeoff is the exclusive advantage that vendors enjoy while they employ proprietary features versus the benefits they could reap if they would provide developers with standards they support in other tools. While many client/server technology vendors give lip service to the idea, standards are not yet a priority.

The movement toward standards really depends on the users/developers. If we demand that tool and technology vendors employ standards, and agree that interoperability is of great value, the vendors will respond. The standards organizations (such as OMG) also need to work harder to bring standards to the technology. It took five years before the OMG had a standard that actually spelled out a way for CORBA-based distributed objects to work together. That's just too long for this business.

Despite the slow movement, I think we'll continue to move toward a standard technology that will let everyone and everything work together. The trick now is to pick the standard(s) you think will win.

Consistent Language Support. Until recently, the mantra of client/server tool vendors was 'build a tool, build a proprietary language.' Fact is, we have more development languages today than ever before, with languages proprietary to particular tools. The reasons are the same as with our previous standards discussion.

To my delight, the most recent trend is for client/server tool vendors to employ nonproprietary languages in their tool, or to use the same language throughout a product line. For example, Delphi is based on Pascal, rather than a proprietary scripting language like PowerBuilder. Optima++ and VisualAge C++ use C++ as their native language. Visual Basic shares VBA with Access, Microsoft Office products, and even third-party tools such as Oracle's Power-Objects. VBA is licensed by Microsoft to over forty vendors. This trend will continue. While developers are happy to learn a new IDE, they aren't nearly as thrilled when they must learn a new programming language.

True Application-Partitioning Capabilities. Along with links to distributed objects, I believe that tools will continue to provide more sophisticated proprietary application-partitioning capabilities. Many traditional two-tier tools, such as PowerBuilder and Unify, are heading in this direction (albeit slowly), while Forte, Dynasty, and IBI's Cactus are learning to do a better job with their existing partitioning tools.

There is also a movement in the application-partitioning world toward the use of open technologies. For instance, distributed objects and TP monitors now work with the proprietary ORBs of application-partitioning tools. Proprietary ORBs are not a long-term solution, and the opening of these environments to nonproprietary technology will only increase their value to developers.

Consistent Approach to the Intranet. The enabling technology of the intranet must settle down to a few consistent approaches. For example, now we have HTML, SGML, VRML, CGI, NSAPI, ISAPI, Java, JavaScript, VBScript, ActiveX, Java, IIOP, and the list goes on. Although this provides developers with an arsenal of technologies and techniques, it's a few too many standards to follow, and confusing for developers.

Over the next year we'll see the list of intranet-enabling technologies shorten, as the market naturally removes the technologies that don't capture the hearts and minds of the developers and that offer redundant technologies. Redundant technologies include Java and ActiveX, JavaScript and VBScript. We'll also see a movement toward ISAPI and NSAPI, or back to CGI. Finally, we need to go with a single HTML standard, and move away from the proprietary extensions of Netscape and Microsoft.

PROCESSORS AND SERVERS

We can expect processing power to increase; I don't see any slowdown in that area. Today's servers were only a dream a few years ago, and I'm sure we'll say the same a few years from now. It's a safe bet that the power of servers will keep up with the requirements of your application, and we can now run mainframe class systems on commodity hardware (see Figure 24-7).

We'll also see the rise of symmetric multi-processing computers and operating systems for use as clients as well as servers. When Windows 95 and Windows NT merge, clients will have a powerful operating system that can make the most of this new hardware. Clients can once again become a location for application processing.

Servers will become more component-based. Architects will be better able to customize servers around particular application server and database server requirements, adjusting the cache, memory, processors, and disk size to the exact specifications of the application. The operating system that will run these servers will have to keep up. Advanced multi-processing operating systems (such as Windows NT and Unix) will provide better load balancing and fault-tolerant capabilities, including, for instance, the ability to better work through memory, disk, and processor failures without service interruptions.

Despite the religious implications of operating systems and an anti-Microsoft sentiment, Windows NT will take more market share away from the

Figure 24-7 *We can now run mainframe class systems on commodity hardware.*

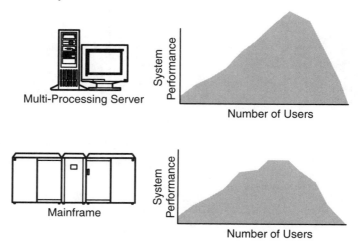

traditional server operating system for client/server: Unix. Windows NT is almost as powerful, supports multi-processing, and can run on a number of processors. What really drives the movement toward Windows NT is the ease of use it offers, as well as its ability to support the majority of off-the-shelf software. While Sun servers will run Oracle, they won't run Word for Windows as a native application. Web servers for use on intranets or the Internet will become the domain of NT as well. Microsoft is giving its Web server away with NT, and you can't have things more convenient than that.

PARADIGMS

Today we are well into the object-oriented development paradigm, and this will remain true. In fact, as we become better at using object client/server tools, we will dig deeper into their support for the object-oriented development model (see Figure 24-8).

The use of components will become more of an issue too. We really can't build an application by mixing and matching today's components. However, as component standards finally take off (see discussion earlier in this chapter), we'll be able to snap in many application components, and even mix and match components with the native objects of the tools.

Figure 24-8 *Digging deeper into their support for the object-oriented development model.*

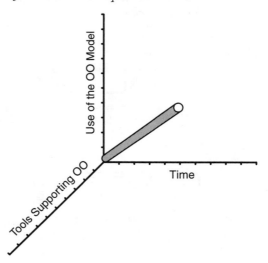

Enabling Technologies

We must consider the evolution of the enabling technologies of client/server. These technologies include distributed objects, TP monitors, the intranet, databases, and middleware.

Distributed Objects. As I already mentioned, the use of distributed objects will increase sharply and soon. Driven by the popularity of intranet development and the need for multi-tier client/server programming, we'll see the rise of CORBA and DCOM ORBs for use in general application programming. Tool support is critical, and that's in our future too.

Transaction-Processing Monitors. As we move headlong into large-scale, mission-critical distributed computing, we need an "ace in the hole." TP monitors are that ace. I had thought the TP monitor market was foundering, but it's now picking up steam as developers understand the benefits, and as other alternatives (such as proprietary application-partitioning tools) prove themselves to be a bit wet behind the ears. With the advent of Microsoft's Transaction Server, we now have a TP monitor that fits easily into commodity Windows environments, built from the ground up for ActiveX and the intranet. With the success of Transaction Server, I see more TP monitors heading into the market.

The Intranet. Due to sheer numbers, the intranet will continue to be the main area of interest for client/server development. As the hype settles down, we'll put the intranet into perspective and leverage its sex appeal and advantages to the bottom line.

Databases. Databases will continue to dazzle us with better performance and new features. I don't see the big three (Oracle, Sybase, and Informix) giving up much market share to other databases, and I don't see the relational database model going away. The concept of the universal server will enlarge the database market by allowing databases to be a "jack of all trades" for developers (object-oriented, relational, Web, binary, etc.). Databases vendors will find, as Oracle is finding now, that working with distributed objects provides a competitive advantage as the rest of the world moves there.

Middleware. Finally, middleware will evolve too. While middleware is powerful and necessary, it's difficult to use and deploy. In the next few years, we'll see a rise of middleware solutions—both message and RPC-based—that provide "snap-in" functionality and consistent interfaces. Microsoft's Falcon message-oriented middleware will once again prove that Microsoft can turn a high-end product into a consumer commodity, and other, more aggressive vendors will have to keep up.

Planning for the Future

Planning for the future is simply a matter of establishing the strategy and the tactics of our application development environment. From time to time you need to work with the powers-that-be to:

- Re-evaluate your business objectives
- Re-evaluate the current technology infrastructure
- Determine the differences (what's missing?)
- Adjust your technology infrastructure to meet your objectives

In most cases, this is a process of looking at new enabling technologies and paradigms that will better serve your needs. For example, if you need access to many applications for a single multi-platform user interface, then you may want to set a course for the intranet. Or, if you need to access a number of legacy resources as a single virtual system, then TP monitors and DCE are worth a look. Of course, you need to work out the tactics as well, including which enabling technology to employ, and then select the tools that support your enabling technology of choice.

Remember a few things when you work out your tactics. First, it's expensive to be innovative. If you want to lead technology, there should be a good business cause for doing so. Otherwise, you end up with failed project after failed project as new tools and technologies fail to deliver on promises. I always use the 80/20 rule. Vendors usually deliver 80 percent of their promises up front, and the other 20 percent shows up a few years later. For example, while Visual Basic and PowerBuilder offer proprietary application-partitioning mechanisms, they were so difficult to set up and so limited in what they could do that many development organizations abandoned them in their search for a quicker, easier way to move to *n*-tier. Visual Basic is fixing its limitations with DCOM and integration with Falcon and Transaction Server, but it took a few years.

Your best bang-for-the-buck in technology is to follow the technology curve. While distributed objects were new and unproven a few years ago, they are proven today. DCOM is not yet proven, and proprietary application-partitioning tools such as Forte or Dynasty are almost there.

Now What?

Now that you reached the end of the book, did you think I'd leave you without a way to get more information about what works with client/server technology? If you want to advance your career in the client/server marketplace, you should be constantly learning. Here are a few places that I go for information (See Figure 24-9).

First, make sure you read a few trade journals that are specific to client/server developer issues. *DBMS* Magazine is a great place for information (check out my column), as is *Database Programming and Design.* For those who want to dig into particular topic areas, you will find publications such as *Object* Magazine and *The C++ Report* helpful. There are also publications for particular client/server development tools such as Visual Basic, Power-Builder, and Delphi. If you live in those environments, their periodicals are must-reads.

Second, try to attend at least two client/server-related conferences each year. Watch out for conferences with a lot of marketing and product managers talking about technology. Make sure you hear from practitioners who are out there solving real problems, and are not trying to sell a product. Conferences

Figure 24-9 *Where to look for additional information.*

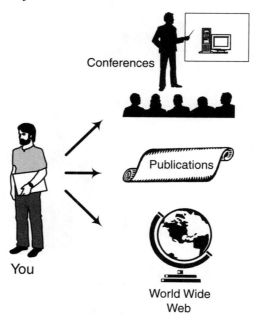

Conferences

Publications

You

World Wide Web

with expos are the best alternative since you can visit with tool vendors while you learn about the concepts.

Finally, learn to step out of your comfort zone. Learn concepts and technologies that you may not become exposed to in your day-to-day job. This means becoming a little more innovative, and a bit of a risk taker.

The world of client/server and intranet development remains one of the most exciting. It's in a constant state of change, and typically things change for the better. We have a lot of evolving to do, and we all need to learn to roll with the punches. Clearly, all roads lead to client/server and the intranet, and all journeys begin with a single step.

Further Reading

Berson, A. *Client/Server Architecture*. New York: McGraw-Hill, 1992.

Black, U.D. *Data Communications and Distributed Networks*, Second Edition. Englewood Cliffs, NJ: Yourdon Press, Prentice Hall, 1987.

Boar, B.H. *Implementing Client/Server Computing, A Strategic Approach*. New York: McGraw-Hill, 1993.

Booch, G. *Object-Oriented Analysis and Design With Applications*, Second Edition. Redwood City, CA: Benjamin/Cummings, 1994.

Booch, G. *Unified Method for Object-Oriented Development*, Version 0.8. Rational Software Corporation.

Chorafas, D.N. *Systems Architecture & Systems Design*. New York: McGraw-Hill, 1989.

Claybrook, B. *OLTP, Online Transaction Processing Systems*. New York: John Wiley & Sons, 1992.

Coad, P., Yourdon, E. *Object-Oriented Analysis*, Second Edition. Englewood Cliffs, NJ: Prentice Hall, 1991.

Date, C.J. *An Introduction to Database Systems, Volume I*, Fourth Edition. Reading, MA: Addison-Wesley, 1987.

Date, C.J. *An Introduction to Database Systems, Volume II.* Reading, MA: Addison-Wesley, 1985.

Firesmith, D.G. *Object-Oriented Requirements Analysis and Logical Design, A Software Engineering Approach.* New York: John Wiley & Sons, 1993.

Goldberg, A. *Object-Oriented Project Management.* Tutuorial TOOLS, Europe, Paris, 1991.

Goldberg, A., Robson, D. *Smalltalk-80: The Language and Its Implementation.* Reading, MA: Addison-Wesley, 1983.

Green, J.H. *Local Area Networks, A User's Guide for Business Professionals.* Glenview, Il: Scott, Foresman and Company, 1985.

Gray, J., Reuter, A. *Transaction Processing: Concepts and Techniques.* San Mateo, CA: Morgan Kaufmann, 1993.

Kerninghan, B.W., Ritchie, D.M. *The C Programming Language*, Second Edition covering ANSI-C. Englewood Cliffs, NJ: Prentice Hall, 1988.

Linthicum, D.S. "Client/Server Protocols: Choosing the Right Connection." *DBMS Magazine.* 7(1):60.

Linthicum, D.S. "Moving Away from the Network, Using Middleware." *DBMS Magazine.* 7(1): 66.

Linthicum, D.S. "Operating Systems for Database Servers." *DBMS Magazine.* 7(2):62.

Linthicum, D.S. "Client/Server Strategy." *DBMS Magazine.* 7(4): 46.

Linthicum, D.S. "4GLs: Productivity at What Cost?" *DBMS Magazine.* 7(5): 22.

Linthicum, D.S. "A Better PC?" *DBMS Magazine.* 7(7):24.

Linthicum, D.S. "Defending OOP with VisualAge." *DBMS Magazine.* 7(9): 22.

Linthicum, D.S. "CASE Does Powerbuilder." *DBMS Magazine.* 7(10):24.

Linthicum, D.S. "Lockhead Succeeds with C/S." *DBMS Magazine.* 7(13): 26.

Linthicum, D.S. "A Multiplatform Power Tool." *DBMS Magazine.* 8(1): 20.

Linthicum, D.S. "System Architect 3.0." *DBMS Magazine.* 8(1): 62.

Linthicum, D.S. "Reconsidering Message Middleware." *DBMS Magazine.* 8(3):24.

Linthicum, D.S. "EOF—a Next Step for C/S." *DBMS Magazine.* 8(4):26.

Linthicum, D.S. "Rethinking C++." *DBMS Magazine.* 8(5):23.

Linthicum, D.S. "Symantec Enterprise Developer 2.0." *DBMS Magazine.* 8(7): 22.

Linthicum, D.S. "Delphi 1.0." *DBMS Magazine.* 8(7): 28.

Linthicum, D.S. "Putting TP Monitors in Their Place." *DBMS Magazine.* 8(8): 22.

Linthicum, D.S. "Breaking Up is Easy to Do." *DBMS Magazine.* 8(9): 22.

Linthicum, D.S. "One-Stop Shopping with Oracle." *DBMS Magazine.* 8(10): 28.

Linthicum, D.S. "Travel Like A Native." *DBMS Magazine.* 8(11): 24.

Linthicum, D.S. "Keeping an Eye on Your Database Server." *DBMS Magazine.* 8(12):60.

Linthicum, D.S. "Banking on Delphi." *DBMS Magazine.* 8(13): 26.

Linthicum, D.S. "The Client/Server Internet." *DBMS Magazine.* 9(1): 26.

Linthicum, D.S. "Visual Basic 4.0: Ready for the Enterprise?" *DBMS Magazine.* 9(1): 44.

Linthicum, D.S. "ProtoGen+ Goes Virtual." *DBMS Magazine.* 9(2): 24.

Linthicum, D.S. "Moving Towards Remote Controlled OLE." *DBMS Magazine.* 9(3): 28.

Linthicum, D.S. "Cruising the Galaxy." *DBMS Magazine.* 9(4): 30.

Linthicum, D.S. "Battle of the Visual Masters." *DBMS Magazine.* 9(4): 91.

Linthicum, D.S. "Rise of the Intranet." *DBMS Magazine.* 9(5): 24.

Linthicum, D.S. "The Successes and Failures of Application Development Tools." *DBMS Magazine.* 9(5):71.

Linthicum, D.S. "DCE Lightens its Load." *DBMS Magazine.* 9(7): 24.

Linthicum, D.S. "Partitioning Power." *DBMS Magazine.* 9(8): 28.

Linthicum, D.S. "Selecting a Client/Server Application Development Tool." *DBMS Magazine.* 9(8): 41.

Linthicum, D.S. "Selecting a DBMS." *DBMS Magazine.* 9(8): 48.

Linthicum, D.S. "Here Comes the Java Tools." *DBMS Magazine.* (9)9: 24.

Linthicum, D.S. "C++ Tools for Client/Server Development." *DBMS Magazine.* 9(9): 89.

Linthicum, D.S. "The Staying Power of C++." *DBMS Magazine.* 9(10): 24.

Linthicum, D.S. "Objects Meet Data." *DBMS Magazine.* 9(10): 72.

Linthicum, D.S. "The ABCs of SAP R/3." *DBMS Magazine.* 9(11): 28.

Linthicum, D.S. "Tool Time." *DBMS Magazine.* 9(11): 15.

Linthicum, D.S. "The JDBC Connection." *DBMS Magazine.* 9(11): 21.

Hackathorn, R.D. *Enterprise Database Connectivity.* New York: John Wiley & Sons, 1993.

Hutchison, D. *Local Area Network Architectures.* Reading, MA: Addison-Wesley, 1988.

Krol, E. *The Whole Internet User's Guide and Catalog.* O'Reilly & Associates, Inc., 1992.

Object Management Group. *The Common Object Request Broker: Architecture and Specification.* OMG Document Number 91.12.1, Revision 1.1, 1992.

Object Management Group. *CORBAservices: Common Object Services Specification.* OMG Document Number 95-3-31, 1995.

Orfali, R., Harkey, D. *Client/Server Programming with OS/2 Extended Edition.* New York,:Van Nostrand Reinhold, 1991.

Orfali, R., Harkey, D., Edwards, J. *Essential Client/Server Survival Guide.* New York: Van Nostrand Reinhold, 1994.

Renaud, P. E. *Introduction to Client/Server Systems.* New York:John Wiley & Sons, 1993.

Rumbaugh, J, M Blaha, M., Premerlant, W., Eddy, F., Larensen, W. *Object-Oriented Modeling and Design.* Englewood Cliffs, NJ: Prentice Hall, 1991.

Salemi, J. *PC Magazine Guide to Client/Server Databases.* Emeryville, CA.:Ziff-Davis Press, 1993.

Shlaer, S., Mellor, S.J. *Object-Oriented Systems Analysis—Modeling the World in Data.* Englewood Cliffs, NJ: Yourdon Press, Prentice Hall, 1988.

Smith, J.D. *Reusability & Software Construction: C and C++.* New York: John Wiley & Sons, 1990.

Smith, P. *Client/Server Computing.* Carmel IN:Sams Publishing (A Division of Prentice Hall Computer Publishing), 1992.

Tannenbaum, A.S. *Distributed Operating Systems.* Englewood Cliffs, NJ: Prentice Hall, 1995.

Webster's New World. *Dictionary of Computer Terms.* New York, NY: Prentice-Hall, 1988.

Wirfs-Brock, R., Wilkerson, B., Wiener, L. *Designing Object-Oriented Software.* Englewood Cliffs, NJ: Prentice Hall, 1990.

Client/Server and Intranet
Tool and Technology

Product	Phone	Company	City	St.	URL
2D Spatial DataBlade and 3D Spatial DataBlade	800-331-1763	Informix Software Inc.	Menlo Park	CA	http://www.informix.com
4D Enterprise	408-252-4444	ACI US Inc.	Cupertino	CA	http://www.aci-4D.com
4D Server	408-252-4444	ACI US Inc.	Cupertino	CA	http://www.aci-4D.com
4S-Report 3.0	908-248-6667	Four Seasons Software	Edison	NJ	http://www.4seasons.com
4S-SuperNova 5.0	908-248-6667	Four Seasons Software	Edison	NJ	http://www.4seasons.com
4th Dimension	408-252-4444	ACI US Inc.	Cupertino	CA	http://www.aci-4D.com
Accell/SQL 2.5	916-928-6400	Unify Corp.	Sacramento	CA	http://www.unify.com
AccountMate Premiere	415-381-1011	SourceMate Information Systems Inc.	Mill Valley	CA	http://www.sourcemate.com
AccountMate Professional	415-381-1011	SourceMate Information Systems Inc.	Mill Valley	CA	http://www.sourcemate.com
AccountMate/400	415-381-1011	SourceMate Information Systems Inc.	Mill Valley	CA	http://www.sourcemate.com
ActionManager	801-645-2105	Park City Group	Park City	UT	
Active Web	415-254-0474	Active Software Inc.	Mountain View	CA	http://www.activesw.com
Actuate Reporting System	415-638-2000	Actuate Software Corp.	San Mateo	CA	http://www.actuate.com
Acumate Enterprise Solution (ES)	617-225-2200	Kenan Systems Corp.	Cambridge	MA	http://www.kenan.com
Acumate Web	617-225-2200	Kenan Systems Corp.	Cambridge	MA	http://www.kenan.com
AcuServer	619-689-7220	Acucobol Inc.	San Diego	CA	http://www.acucobol.com
Adabas/Natural Performance Pack	412-741-1677	Treehouse Software Inc.	Sewickley	PA	http://www.treehouse.com
Adabas/Natural Security Pack	412-741-1677	Treehouse Software Inc.	Sewickley	PA	http://www.treehouse.com
AdHawk	415-871-0189	Eventus Software Inc.	San Bruno	CA	http://www.eventus.com
AdHawk Spacer	415-871-0700	Eventus Software Inc.	San Bruno	CA	http://www.eventus.com
Advantage Database Server 4.0	208-322-7800	Extended Systems	Boise	ID	http://www.extendsys.com
AIO WIN 2.1	409-260-5274	Knowledge Based Systems Inc.	College Station	TX	http://www.kbsi.com
Aion Development System 6.4	800-442-6861	Platinum Technology Inc.	Oakbrook Terrace	IL	http://www.platinum.com

Product	Phone	Company	City	St.	URL
allClear III for Windows	617-965-6755	Clear Software Inc.	Newton	MA	http://www.clearsoft.com
Amzi! Prolog + Logic Server	508-897-7332	Amzi! Inc.	Stow	MA	http://www.amzi.com
Andyne GQL	613-548-4355	Andyne Computing Ltd.	Kingston, Ontario		http://www.andyne.on.ca
Apprise Financials 3.2	201-822-1551	Apprise Software (formerly Mycor Inc.)	Somerville	NJ	http://www.apprisesi.com
AppSync	813-226-2600	PowerCerv Corp.	Tampa	FL	http://www.powercerv.com
APTuser	617-221-1450	International Software Group	Burlington	MA	
AS-Expert Advisor	800-795-1993	Software Artistry Inc.	Indianapolis	IN	http://www.softart.com
askSam 5.1	904-584-6590	askSam Systems	Perry	FL	http://www.asksam.com
askSam Electronic Publisher	904-584-6590	askSam Systems	Perry	FL	http://www.asksam.com
askSam for Windows 3.0/ askSam Professional	904-584-6590	askSam Systems	Perry	FL	http://www.asksam.com
askSam Professional	800-800-1997	askSam Systems	Perry	FL	http://www.asksam.com
askSam Resume Tracking System	904-584-6590	askSam Systems	Perry	FL	http://www.asksam.com
Assembly Framework	513-662-2300	Cincom Systems Inc.	Cincinnati	OH	http://www.cincom.com
Async Professional for Delphi	719-260-9136	Turbopower Software Co.	Colorado Springs	CO	http://www.tpower.com
Auditre and AutoLoader	412-741-1677	Treehouse Software Inc.	Sewickley	PA	http://www.treehouse.com
Automated Test Facility (ATF)	617-576-2257	Softbridge Inc.	Cambridge	MA	
AutoTester Distributed Test Facility	214-368-1196	AutoTester Inc.	Dallas	TX	http://www.autotester.com
AutoTester for Windows and OS/2	214-368-1196	AutoTester Inc.	Dallas	TX	http://www.autotester.com
Axiant	617-229-6600	Cognos Inc.	Ottawa, Ontario	ON	http://www.cognos.com
B-Tree Filer	719-260-9136	Turbopower Software Co.	Colorado Springs	CO	http://www.tpower.com
BASIS Intranet Solution	800-328-2646	Information Dimensions Inc.	Dublin	OH	www.idi.oclc.org
BatchBuilder	813-226-2600	PowerCerv Corp.	Tampa	FL	http://www.powercerv.com
BBN/Cornerstone	617-873-2725	BBN Domain Corp.	Cambridge	MA	

Product	Phone	Company	City	St.	URL
BEA Connect	908-346-3100	BEA Systems Inc. (formerly IMC)	Edison	NJ	http://www.beasys.com
BEA Tuxedo	908-346-3100	BEA Systems Inc. (formerly IMC)	Edison	NJ	http://www.beasys.com
BenchWorks	818-564-2684	INFOgy Inc.	Pasadena	CA	http://www.infogy.com
Best Practice Objects (BPOs)	800-828-7660	Computron Software Inc.	Rutherford	NJ	http://www.ctronsoft.com
BONCase	805-685-1006	Interactive Software Engineering Inc.	Santa Barbara	CA	http://www.eiffel.com
Borland C++	800-233-2444	Borland International Inc.	Scotts Valley	CA	http://www.borland.com
BPwin	609-514-1177	Logic Works Inc.	Princeton	NJ	http://www.logicworks.com
brio.web.warehouse	415-856-8000	Brio Technology Inc.	Palo Alto	CA	http://www.brio.com
BrioQuery 3.5	415-856-8000	Brio Technology Inc.	Palo Alto	CA	http://www.brio.com
BrioQuery Enterprise	415-856-8000	Brio Technology Inc.	Palo Alto	CA	http://www.brio.com
BroadCast 1.0	610-865-3009	Softwell Development Corp.	Palmer	PA	
BRS/Search	617-621-0820	Dataware Technologies Inc.	Cambridge	MA	http://www.dataware.com
Btrieve 6	512-794-1719	Btrieve Technologies Inc.	Austin	TX	http://www.btrieve.com
Btrieve 6 Developer's Kit	512-794-1719	Btrieve Technologies Inc.	Austin	TX	http://www.btrieve.com
BusinessObjects	800-705-1515	Business Objects Inc.	Cupertino	CA	http://www.businessobjects.com
C-Index/II 4.2	818-584-9706	Trio Systems Inc.	Pasadena	CA	http://www.triosystems.com
c-tree Plus File Handler	573-445-6833	FairCom Corp.	Columbia	MO	http://www.faircom.com
C-Vision 4.0	610-584-4261	Gimpel Software	Collegeville	PA	
C/Database Toolchest	214-783-6001	Mix Software Inc.	Richardson	TX	
CA-OpenIngres	516-342-5224	Computer Associates International Inc.	Islandia	NY	http://www.cai.com
CA-OpenROAD	516-342-5224	Computer Associates International Inc.	Islandia	NY	http://www.cai.com
CA-Visual Express	516-342-5224	Computer Associates International Inc.	Islandia	NY	http://www.cai.com
CA-Visual Objects	516-342-5224	Computer Associates International Inc.	Islandia	NY	http://www.cai.com

Product	Phone	Company	City	St.	URL
CA–Visual Realia	516-342-5224	Computer Associates International Inc.	Islandia	NY	http://www.cai.com
Cafe	408-253-9600	Symantec Corp.	Cupertino	CA	http://www.symantec.com
Caffeine	415-286-1900	Visigenic Software Inc.	San Mateo	CA	http://www.visigenic.com
Cast Workbench 3.1	415-284-7970	Cast Software Inc.	San Francisco	CA	http://www.castsoftware.com
CDWeb	313-994-4800	Comshare Inc.	Ann Arbor	MI	http://www.comshare.com
Centura	415-321-9500	Centura Software Corp. (formerly Gupta Corp.)	Menlo Park	CA	http://www.centurasoft.com
Centura Application Server	800-444-8782	Centura Software Corp. (formerly Gupta Corp.)	Menlo Park	CA	http://www.centurasoft.com
Centura Ranger	415-321-9500	Centura Software Corp. (formerly Gupta Corp.)	Menlo Park	CA	http://www.centurasoft.com
Centura Team Developer	415-321-9500	Centura Software Corp. (formerly Gupta Corp.)	Menlo Park	CA	http://www.centurasoft.com
Centura Web Data Publisher	800-444-8782	Centura Software Corp. (formerly Gupta Corp.)	Menlo Park	CA	http://www.centurasoft.com
Choreo 2.0 for Visual Basic 4.0	415-266-7000	CenterView Software Inc.	S. San Francisco	CA	
ClassAssist	516-753-0985	Sheridan Software Systems Inc.	Melville	NY	http://www.shersoft.com
Clear Process for Windows 1.0	617-965-6755	Clear Software Inc.	Newton	MA	http://www.clearsoft.com
Clear:Access	515-472-7077	Sterling Software Data Access Division	Fairfield	IA	
Clear:Manage	515-472-7077	Sterling Software Data Access Division	Fairfield	IA	
ClientBuilder 4.0	914-631-5365	ClientSoft Inc.	Tarrytown	NY	
ClipSQL 3.0	310-312-8099	Stro-Ware Inc.	Los Angeles	CA	
CodeBase ++ 5.1	403-437-2410	Sequiter Software Inc.	Edmonton, Alberta		http://www.sequiter.com
CodeBase 5.1	403-437-2410	Sequiter Software Inc.	Edmonton, Alberta		http://www.sequiter.com
CodeBasic 5.1	403-437-2410	Sequiter Software Inc.	Edmonton, Alberta		http://www.sequiter.com
CodeServer 5.1	403-437-2410	Sequiter Software Inc.	Edmonton, Alberta		http://www.sequiter.com
CodeTranslator 2.1	403-437-2410	Sequiter Software Inc.	Edmonton, Alberta		http://www.sequiter.com

Product	Phone	Company	City	St.	URL
Cold Fusion Forums	612-831-1808	Allaire Corp.	Edina	MN	http://www.allaire.com
Cold Fusion Professional 2.0	612-831-1808	Allaire Corp.	Edina	MN	http://www.allaire.com
Collage Complete 1.1	603-465-3216	Inner Media Inc.	Hollis	NH	
Companion	800-661-9961	Cipher Systems Ltd.	Calgary, Alberta		
Computron Workflow	800-828-7660	Computron Software Inc.	Rutherford	NJ	http://www.ctronsoft.com
Condor 3	312-271-8759	Condor DBMS Services Inc.	Chicago	IL	
Connection for Java	415-598-1200	Open Horizon Inc.	Belmont	CA	http://www.openhorizon.com
Convert Series	415-543-1515	Forecross Corp.	San Francisco	CA	
CorVision	617-221-1450	International Software Group	Burlington	MA	
CorVu Enterprise Information Reporting System	612-944-7777	CorVu Corporation	Minneapolis	MN	www.corvu.com.au
CrossAccess Data Delivery System	708-954-0500	Cross Access Corp.	Oakbrook Terrace IL		
Crystal Info 4.5	604-681-3435	Seagate Software IMG	Vancouver, British Columbia		http://www.seagate.com/software/crystal/
Crystal Reports 4.5	604-681-3435	Seagate Software IMG	Vancouver, British Columbia		http://www.seagate.com/software/crystal/
Customer Accounts Activity System	516-253-0921	TalTech Corp.	Dix Hills	NY	
CW-Deploy	415-296-1300	Cast Software Inc.	San Francisco	CA	http://www.castsoftware.com
CW-Designer	415-296-1300	Cast Software Inc.	San Francisco	CA	http://www.castsoftware.com
CW-Doc	415-296-1300	Cast Software Inc.	San Francisco	CA	http://www.castsoftware.com
CW-Server	415-296-1300	Cast Software Inc.	San Francisco	CA	http://www.castsoftware.com
d-tree 3.5A	573-445-6833	FairCom Corp.	Columbia	MO	http://www.faircom.com
D3	714-261-7425	Pick Systems	Irvine	CA	http://www.picksys.com
Data Entry Workshop (DEW)	719-260-9136	Turbopower Software Co.	Colorado Springs	CO	http://www.tpower.com
Database Gateway for MVS 2.5	303-413-4000	Sybase Information Connect Division	Boulder	CO	http://www.sybase.com
Database Gateway for VSE and Access Server for VSE/CICS	303-413-4000	Sybase Information Connect Division	Boulder	CO	http://www.sybase.com

Product	Phone	Company	City	St.	URL
Database Xcessory	617-621-0060	Integrated Computer Solutions	Cambridge	MA	http://www.ics.com
DataFlex	305-238-0012	Data Access Corp.	Miami	FL	
DataFountain	617-229-9111	Dimensional Insight Inc.	Burlington	MA	http://www.dimins.com
DataGuide	520-574-4600	IBM Software Solutions	Somers	NY	http://www.software.ibm.com
DataHub	520-574-4600	IBM Software Solutions	Somers	NY	http://www.software.ibm.com
DataImport 4.0 for Windows	770-449-0594	Spalding Software Inc.	Norcross	GA	http://www.spaldingsoft.com
DataJoiner	520-574-4600	IBM Software Solutions	Somers	NY	http://www.software.ibm.com
DataLens Developer Toolkit	617-577-8500	Lotus Development Corp.	Cambridge	MA	
DataMgr VBX and Template Maker	914-354-8666	Bytech Business Systems Inc.	Pomona	NY	
DataPropagator Non-Relational	520-574-4600	IBM Software Solutions	Somers	NY	http://www.software.ibm.com
DataPropagator Relational	520-574-4600	IBM Software Solutions	Somers	NY	http://www.software.ibm.com
DataRamp	617-674-2669	Working Set Inc.	Lexington	MA	http://www.dataramp.com
DataRefresher	520-574-4600	IBM Software Solutions	Somers	NY	http://www.software.ibm.com
Datarun Methodology	201-391-6500	Computer Systems Advisers Inc.	Woodcliff Lake	NJ	http://www.silverrun.com
DataSync	617-497-1376	Syware Inc.	Cambridge	MA	http://www.syware.com
DataTable	609-655-5000	ProtoView Development Corp.	Cranbury	NJ	http://www.protoview.com
DataTools SQL-Backtrack for Sybase	415-617-9100	DataTools Inc.	Palo Alto	CA	http://www.datatools.com
DataTools-BackTrack for Oracle	415-617-9100	DataTools Inc.	Palo Alto	CA	http://www.datatools.com
DB-Examiner	703-847-9500	DBE Software Inc.	McLean	VA	http://www.dbesoftware.com
DB/Text WebServer	617-938-4442	Inmagic Inc.	Woburn	MA	
DB2 family	520-574-4600	IBM Software Solutions	Somers	NY	http://www.software.ibm.com
DB2 Performance Monitor	520-574-4600	IBM Software Solutions	Somers	NY	http://www.software.ibm.com
DB2 Visual Explain	520-574-4600	IBM Software Solutions	Somers	NY	http://www.software.ibm.com
DBArtisan	415-834-3131	Embarcadero Technologies Inc.	San Francisco	CA	http://www.embarcadero.com

Product	Phone	Company	City	St.	URL
DBench	415-903-9591	Stanford Management Group Inc.	Mountain View	CA	
DBGeneral Object Manager for Oracle	713-621-2808	Bradmark Technologies Inc.	Houston	TX	http://www.bradmark.com
DBGeneral Performance Monitor for Oracle & Sybase	713-621-2808	Bradmark Technologies Inc.	Houston	TX	http://www.bradmark.com
DBGeneral Tablespace Manager for Oracle	713-621-2808	Bradmark Technologies Inc.	Houston	TX	http://www.bradmark.com
DBProfiler JET Inspector 2.0 for MS Access and Visual Basic	818-345-2200	Mercury Interactive Corp.	Sunnyvale	CA	http://www.merc-int.com
DBProfiler SQL Inspector 2.0 for Oracle7	818-345-2200	Mercury Interactive Corp.	Sunnyvale	CA	http://www.merc-int.com
DBProfiler SQL Inspector for MS or Sybase SQL Server	818-345-2200	Mercury Interactive Corp.	Sunnyvale	CA	http://www.merc-int.com
DBtools.h++ 1.0	503-754-3010	Rogue Wave Software	Corvallis	OR	http://www.roguewave.com
DBView	818-564-2684	INFOgy Inc.	Pasadena	CA	http://www.infogy.com
dCryptr	707-829-5011	Hilco Software	Sebastopol	CA	
deFox 1.06	707-829-5011	Hilco Software	Sebastopol	CA	
Delphi	412-741-1677	Treehouse Software Inc.	Sewickley	PA	http://www.treehouse.com
Delphi Client/Server Suite 2.0	408-431-1000	Borland International Inc.	Scotts Valley	CA	http://www.borland.com
Designer/2000	415-506-7000	Oracle Corp.	Redwood Shores	CA	http://www.oracle.com
Developer/2000	415-506-7000	Oracle Corp.	Redwood Shores	CA	http://www.oracle.com
Dharma Integrator 1.2	603-886-1400	Dharma Systems Inc.	Nashua	NH	
Dharma SQLstore	603-886-1400	Dharma Systems Inc.	Nashua	NH	
Dharma/SQL Access	603-886-1400	Dharma Systems Inc.	Nashua	NH	
Dharma/SQL Gateway - Oracle version 4	603-886-1400	Dharma Systems Inc.	Nashua	NH	
Dharma/SQL ODBC Driver	603-886-1400	Dharma Systems Inc.	Nashua	NH	
Discover Development Information System	800-372-7273	Software Emancipation Technology Inc.	Lexington	MA	http://www.setech.com/setech

Product	Phone	Company	City	St.	URL
Distributed Database Connection Services (DDCS)	520-574-4600	IBM Software Solutions	Somers	NY	http://www.software.ibm.com
Distributed Object Management Environment (DOME)	714-938-8850	Suite Software Inc.	Anaheim	CA	http://www.suite.com
Distributed Relational Database Architecture (DRDA)	520-574-4600	IBM Software Solutions	Somers	NY	http://www.software.ibm.com
DOCS Open	800-933-3627	PC DOCS Inc.	Burlington	MA	http://www.pcdocs.com/
DOME Data Manager (DDM) 3.2	714-938-8850	Suite Software Inc.	Anaheim	CA	http://www.suite.com
DORS for Windows	403-237-7333	ObjectWorks Inc.	Calgary	AB	http://www.objectworks.com
Dr. DeeBee ODBC Driver Kit	617-497-1376	Syware Inc.	Cambridge	MA	http://www.syware.com
Dr. DeeBee Tools	617-497-1376	Syware Inc.	Cambridge	MA	http://www.syware.com
DSS Agent 3.0	302-427-8800	MicroStrategy Inc.	Vienna	VA	http://www.strategy.com
DSS Architect 3.0	703-848-8600	MicroStrategy Inc.	Vienna	VA	http://www.strategy.com
DSS Executive 3.0	703-848-8600	MicroStrategy Inc.	Vienna	VA	http://www.strategy.com
DSS Server 3.0	703-848-8600	MicroStrategy Inc.	Vienna	VA	http://www.strategy.com
DSS Web	800-927-1868	MicroStrategy Inc.	Vienna	VA	http://www.strategy.com
DynaDoc	412-741-1677	Treehouse Software Inc.	Sewickley	PA	http://www.treehouse.com
DynamiCube	614-895-3142	Data Dynamics Ltd.	Columbus	OH	http://www.datadynamics.com
Dynasty 2.0	708-769-8500	Dynasty Technologies Inc.	Lisle	IL	
DynaZip3.0	603-465-3216	Inner Media Inc.	Hollis	NH	
EasyCASE Database Engineer (DBE) 1.0 for Windows	800-929-5194	Evergreen Software Tools Inc.	Redmond	WA	http://www.esti.com
EasyCASE Database Engineer for PowerBuilder	206-881-5149	Evergreen Software Tools Inc.	Redmond	WA	http://www.esti.com
EasyCASE Professional 4.2 for Windows: Workgroup Edition	206-881-5149	Evergreen Software Tools Inc.	Redmond	WA	http://www.esti.com
EasyER 1.1	800-929-5194	Evergreen Software Tools Inc.	Redmond	WA	http://www.esti.com

Product	Phone	Company	City	St.	URL
EcoNet	810-737-7300	Compuware Corp.	Farmington Hills	MI	http://www.compuware.com
EcoTools	810-737-7300	Compuware Corp.	Farmington Hills	MI	http://www.compuware.com
EDA/SQL Product Family	212-736-4433	Information Builders Inc.	New York	NY	http://www.ibi.com
EDI Reference	310-230-2066	TradeRights (USA) Inc.	Malibu	CA	
Elements Environment	415-321-2238	Neuron Data Inc.	Mountain View	CA	http://www.neurondata.com
Empress 4GL/Empress GUI	301-220-1919	Empress Software Inc.	Greenbelt	MD	http://www.empress.com
Empress Connectivity	301-220-1919	Empress Software Inc.	Greenbelt	MD	http://www.empress.com
Empress Heterogeneous Database Server	301-220-1919	Empress Software Inc.	Greenbelt	MD	http://www.empress.com
Empress Hypermedia	301-220-1919	Empress Software Inc.	Greenbelt	MD	http://www.empress.com
Empress RDBMS	301-220-1919	Empress Software Inc.	Greenbelt	MD	http://www.empress.com
ENFIN Smalltalk 4.1	617-221-2100	Easel Corp.	Burlington	MA	
English Wizard	508-266-1818	Linguistic Technology Corp.	Acton	OH	http://www.world.std.com/~engwiz
Enterprise Developer 2.5	541-334-6054	Symantec Corp.	Cupertino	CA	http://www.symantec.com
Enterprise Manager	415-506-7000	Oracle Corp.	Redwood Shores	CA	http://www.oracle.com
Enterprise Series 6.0	407-351-3441	Data Code Inc.	Orlando	FL	
Enterprise Workbench	617-221-3000	Easel Corp.	Burlington	MA	
Enterprise/Access	612-828-0300	Apertus Technologies Inc.	Eden Prairie	MN	http://www.apertus.com
Enterprise/Integrator	612-828-0300	Apertus Technologies Inc.	Eden Prairie	MN	http://www.apertus.com
ER/1	415-834-3131	Embarcadero Technologies Inc.	San Francisco	CA	http://www.embarcadero.com
ERwin product family	800-783-7946	Logic Works Inc.	Princeton	NJ	http://www.logicworks.com
ERwin/ERX Family	609-514-1177	Logic Works Inc.	Princeton	NJ	http://www.logicworks.com
ERwin/Open	609-514-1177	Logic Works Inc.	Princeton	NJ	http://www.logicworks.com
Espia for FoxPro-DOS	206-643-7001	Espia Corp.	Bellevue	WA	
Espia Image Class for VFP 3.0	206-643-7001	Espia Corp.	Bellevue	WA	
Espia Multimedia Class	206-643-7001	Espia Corp.	Bellevue	WA	
Espia Twain Class	206-643-7001	Espia Corp.	Bellevue	WA	
Essbase Analysis Server	408-727-5800	Arbor Software Inc.	Sunnyvale	CA	http://www.arborsoft.com

Product	Phone	Company	City	St.	URL
Essbase Web Gateway	800-858-1666	Arbor Software Inc.	Sunnyvale	CA	http://www.arborsoft.com
ETI*Extract Tool Suite	512-327-6994	Evolutionary Technologies International	Austin	TX	http://www.evtech.com
Excalibur EFS, Excalibur EFS WebFile	800-441-6878	Excalibur Technologies Corp.	McLean	VA	http://www.excalib.com
Excalibur RetrievalWare	800-788-7758	Excalibur Technologies Corp.	McLean	VA	http://www.excalib.com
Executive Nomad 2.5	800-441-6878	Thomson Software Products Inc.	Norwalk	CT	http://www.thomsoft.com
Express	415-493-4122	Operations Control Systems	Palo Alto	CA	
Express Web Agent	800-672-2531	Oracle Corp. — OLAP Products Division	Waltham	MA	www.oracle.com/products/olap/html
Exsys Professional 5.0 Expert System Development Software	505-256-8356	Exsys Inc.	Albuquerque	NM	http://www.exsysinfo.com
Exsys RuleBook Expert System Development Software	505-256-8356	Exsys Inc.	Albuquerque	NM	http://www.exsysinfo.com
FairCom ODBC Driver	573-445-6833	FairCom Corp.	Columbia	MO	http://www.faircom.com
FairCom Server	573-445-6833	FairCom Corp.	Columbia	MO	http://www.faircom.com
Fault-XPert	810-737-7300	Compuware Corp.	Farmington Hills	MI	http://www.compuware.com
Financial Analysis	206-522-0055	FourGen Software Inc.	Seattle	WA	http://www.fourgen.com
firstcase 3.4 version 3	610-265-1550	AGS Management Systems Inc.	King of Prussia	PA	
FlexQL	305-238-0012	Data Access Corp.	Miami	FL	
FLEXX	604-538-4905	Databyte Corp.	Surrey	BC	http://www.databyte.com
FlowBuilder	813-226-2600	PowerCerv Corp.	Tampa	FL	http://www.powercerv.com
Focus	212-736-4433	Information Builders Inc.	New York	NY	http://www.ibi.com
Focus Six EIS Edition	212-736-4433	Information Builders Inc.	New York	NY	http://www.ibi.com
Focus Six for Windows Professional Developer's Kit	212-736-4433	Information Builders Inc.	New York	NY	http://www.ibi.com
Focus Six Report Server	212-736-4433	Information Builders Inc.	New York	NY	http://www.ibi.com
Focus/Database Server 6.2	212-736-4433	Information Builders Inc.	New York	NY	http://www.ibi.com

Product	Phone	Company	City	St.	URL
Foray PPP Server	517-333-2100	TechSmith Corp.	East Lansing	MI	http://www.TechSmith.com
Forte Application Environment	510-869-3400	Forte Software Inc.	Oakland	CA	http://www.forte.com
FourGen Enterprise Financials	206-522-0055	FourGen Software Inc.	Seattle	WA	http://www.fourgen.com
FourGen Supply Chain Management (SCM)	206-522-0055	FourGen Software Inc.	Seattle	WA	http://www.fourgen.com
FourGen Warehouse Manager	206-522-0055	FourGen Software Inc.	Seattle	WA	http://www.fourgen.com
Foxspell Checker	415-563-3755	Strategic Edge	San Francisco	CA	
FPNet 2.5	301-251-0497	Rory Data International	North Potomac	MD	
Front & Center for Reporting 1.1	800-441-6878	Thomson Software Products Inc.	Norwalk	CT	http://www.thomsoft.com
Frx2Prg 2.5	301-251-0497	Rory Data International	North Potomac	MD	
Fulcrum SearchServer	613-238-1761	Fulcrum Technologies Inc.	Ottawa, Ontario		http://www.fulcrum.com
FYI Planner	201-299-7177	Think Systems Corp.	Parsippany	NJ	
FYI Profitability	201-299-7177	Think Systems Corp.	Parsippany	NJ	
FYI Sales	201-299-7177	Think Systems Corp.	Parsippany	NJ	
FYI TradeManagement	201-299-7177	Think Systems Corp.	Parsippany	NJ	
Gain Momentum 3.0	510-596-3500	Sybase Inc.	Emeryville	CA	http://www.sybase.com
Gamelon	415-853-6450	Menai Corp.	Menlo Park	CA	
GemStone	503-629-8383	GemStone Systems Inc.	Beaverton	OR	http://www.gemstone.com
Genifer 5.02	510-527-1157	Bytel Corp.	Albany	CA	
Gentia Web Server	303-794-8701	Planning Sciences Inc.	Littleton	CO	http://www.gentia.com
GeoQuery 4.0	708-357-0535	GeoQuery Corp.	Naperville	IL	
GL Data Warehouse	617-672-8600	The Dodge Group Inc.	Waltham	MA	http://www.dodge.com
GraphBase 1.1	610-865-3009	Softwell Development Corp.	Palmer	PA	
GraphPalette	212-988-6268	Objective Technologies Inc.	New York	NY	http://www.object.com
GroundWorks	617-273-9003	Cayenne Software Inc. (a Bachman and Cadre Co.)	Burlington	MA	http://www.cayennesoft.com
HAHTSite	919-783-7803	HAHT Software Inc.	Raleigh	NC	http://www.haht.com
HAHTSite Application Server	800-996-3222	HAHT Software Inc.	Raleigh	NC	http://www.haht.com

Product	Phone	Company	City	St.	URL
Head Fix 1.14	707-829-5011	Hilco Software	Sebastopol	CA	http://www.objectspace.com
Help Designer	214-934-2496	ObjectSpace Inc.	Dallas	TX	
Heuristic Optimized Processing System (HOPS)	305-827-8600	HOPS International, Inc.	Miami Lakes	FL	http://www.hops.com
Holos	800-877-2340	Seagate Software IMG	Vancouver, British Columbia		http://www.seagate.com/software/crystal/
HotSockets ODBC Connectivity Software 2.1	612-641-8551	Ensodex Inc.	St. Paul	MN	http://www.ensodex.com
HS ODBC/400	408-369-7290	Hit Software Inc.	San Jose	CA	http://www.hit.com
HyBase 3.0	408-253-7515	Answer Software Corp.	Cupertino	CA	
HyperHelp 5.1	203-438-6969	Bristol Technology Inc.	Ridgefield	CT	http://www.bristol.com
HyperStar 2.2	508-366-3888	VMark Software Inc.	Westboro	MA	http://www.vmark.com
IconAuthor	603-883-0220	AimTech Corp.	Nashua	NH	http://www.aimtech.com
IDB Object Database 2.5	412-963-1843	Persistent Data Systems Inc.	Pittsburgh	PA	
Illustra Server 3.x	800-331-1763	Informix Software Inc.	Menlo Park	CA	http://www.informix.com
Image DataBlade	800-331-1763	Informix Software Inc.	Menlo Park	CA	http://www.informix.com
Impress	212-988-6268	Objective Technologies Inc.	New York	NY	http://www.object.com
Impromptu	617-229-6600	Cognos Inc.	Ottawa, Ontario	ON	http://www.cognos.com
Infinium:Financial Management	508-790-6848	Software 2000 Inc.	Hyannis	MA	http://www.s2k.com
Infinium:Human Resources/Payroll	508-790-6848	Software 2000 Inc.	Hyannis	MA	http://www.s2k.com
InfoAssistant 1.0	206-637-1504	Asymetrix Corp.	Bellevue	WA	http://www.asymetrix.com
InfoMaker 5.0	508-287-1994	Powersoft Corp. (a Sybase company)	Concord	MA	http://www.powersoft.com
InfoModeler 1.5	206-637-1504	Asymetrix Corp.	Bellevue	WA	http://www.asymetrix.com
Informix NewEra	800-331-1763	Informix Software Inc.	Menlo Park	CA	http://www.informix.com
Informix-Enterprise Gateway 7.1	800-331-1763	Informix Software Inc.	Menlo Park	CA	http://www.informix.com
Informix-Online Dynamic Server 6.0	800-331-1763	Informix Software Inc.	Menlo Park	CA	http://www.informix.com

Product	Phone	Company	City	St.	URL
Informix-SE	800-331-1763	Informix Software Inc.	Menlo Park	CA	http://www.informix.com
Inmagic DB/TextWorks	617-938-4442	Inmagic Inc.	Woburn	MA	
Integrity	617-338-0300	Vality Technology Inc.	Boston	MA	
Intelligent Query	770-446-8880	IQ Software Corp.	Norcross	GA	http://www.iqsc.com
InterBase 4.0	408-431-1000	Borland International Inc.	Scotts Valley	CA	http://www.borland.com
InterMart Toolkit	508-480-0877	NetScheme Solutions Inc.	Marlborough	MA	http://www.netscheme.com
Internet Explorer	800-426-9400	Microsoft Corp.	Redmond	WA	http://www.microsoft.com
Internet Information Server 3.0	800-426-9400	Microsoft Corp.	Redmond	WA	http://www.microsoft.com
Internet Studio	800-426-9400	Microsoft Corp.	Redmond	WA	http://www.microsoft.com
Intersolv DataDirect Developer's Toolkit v2.10	800-876-3101	Intersolv Inc.	Rockville	MD	http://www.intersolv.com
Intersolv DataDirect Explorer (Q+E 6.1)	800-876-3101	Intersolv Inc.	Rockville	MD	http://www.intersolv.com
Intersolv DataDirect Multi-Link/VB v2.04	800-876-3101	Intersolv Inc.	Rockville	MD	http://www.intersolv.com
Intersolv DataDirect ODBC Pack	800-876-3101	Intersolv Inc.	Rockville	MD	http://www.intersolv.com
InterViso IVBuild	310-313-9150	Data Integration Inc.	Los Angeles	CA	
InterViso IVQuery	310-313-9150	Data Integration Inc.	Los Angeles	CA	
IntraBuilder	800-233-2444	Borland International Inc.	Scotts Valley	CA	http://www.borland.com
IQ Access	770-446-8880	IQ Software Corp.	Norcross	GA	http://www.iqsc.com
IQ/LiveWeb	800-458-0386	IQ Software Corp.	Norcross	GA	http://www.iqsc.com
IQ/Objects	770-446-8880	IQ Software Corp.	Norcross	GA	http://www.iqsc.com
IQ/SmartServer	770-446-8880	IQ Software Corp.	Norcross	GA	http://www.iqsc.com
IQ/Vision	770-446-8880	IQ Software Corp.	Norcross	GA	http://www.iqsc.com
ISE Eiffel	805-685-1006	Interactive Software Engineering Inc.	Santa Barbara	CA	http://www.eiffel.com
ISYS Image	303-689-9998	ISYS/Odyssey Development Inc.	Englewood	CO	http://www.isysdev.com
JAGG	800-505-0105	BulletProof Corp.	Los Gatos	CA	http://www.bulletproof.com

Product	Phone	Company	City	St.	URL
JAM 7	212-267-7722	JYACC Inc.	New York	NY	http://www.jyacc.com
JAM Transaction Processing Interface (JAM/TPi) 7	212-267-7722	JYACC Inc.	New York	NY	http://www.jyacc.com
JAM/CASE Interface 2.0	212-267-7722	JYACC Inc.	New York	NY	http://www.jyacc.com
JAM/ReportWriter 7	212-267-7722	JYACC Inc.	New York	NY	http://www.jyacc.com
JAM/WEB	212-267-7722	JYACC Inc.	New York	NY	http://www.jyacc.com
Java Developers Kit (JDK)	415-960-1300	JavaSoft (subsidiary of Sun Microsystems Inc.	Mountain View	CA	http://www.javasoft.com
Java Relational Binding	415-842-7000	O2 Technology	Palo Alto	CA	http://www.02tech.com
Jbuilder	800-233-2444	Borland International Inc.	Scotts Valley	CA	http://www.borland.com
JDBC/ODBC Data-Direct Bridge	301-838-5065	Intersolv Inc.	Rockville	MD	http://www.intersolv.com
JDesignerPro	800-505-0105	BulletProof Corp.	Los Gatos	CA	http://www.bulletproof.com
JetAssist	410-312-9300	XDB Systems Inc.	Columbia	MD	http://www.xdb.com
JETConnect	410-312-9300	XDB Systems Inc.	Columbia	MD	http://www.xdb.com
JFactory	800-487-3217	Rogue Wave Software	Corvallis	OR	http://www.roguewave.com
Just Logic/SQL Client/Server	514-761-6887	Just Logic Technologies Inc.	Nun's Island	QC	http://www.pht.com/justlogic/
Just Logic/SQL Database Manager	514-761-6887	Just Logic Technologies Inc.	Nun's Island	QC	http://www.pht.com/justlogic/
KEY:Enterprise 4.1	404-231-8575	Sterling Software Inc.	Atlanta	GA	www.key.sterling.com
KEY:Workgroup	404-231-8575	Sterling Software Inc.	Atlanta	GA	www.key.sterling.com
Lake Avenue Accounting Series	818-445-9700	Lake Avenue Software	Arcadia	CA	
Lansa/AD	800-245-2672	Lansa USA Inc.	Oakbrook	IL	http://www.lansa.aspect.com.au
Lansa/Client	800-245-2672	Lansa USA Inc.	Oakbrook	IL	http://www.lansa.aspect.com.au
Lansa/CS400	800-245-2672	Lansa USA Inc.	Oakbrook	IL	http://www.lansa.aspect.com.au
Lansa/RUOM	800-245-2672	Lansa USA Inc.	Oakbrook	IL	http://www.lansa.aspect.com.au
Lansa/Server	800-245-2672	Lansa USA Inc.	Oakbrook	IL	http://www.lansa.aspect.com.au
Layout	800-424-6644	Objects Inc.	Danvers	MA	http://www.objectsinc.com
LBMS Systems Engineer (SE)	713-623-0414	LBMS Inc.	Houston	TX	
LegacyLink	800-338-8491	CEL Corp.	Edmonton, Alberta		http://www.celcorp.com

Product	Phone	Company	City	St.	URL
Level 5 Object Professional	212-736-4433	Information Builders Inc.	New York	NY	http://www.ibi.com
Liberty ODBC driver for PICK	800-898-6322	Liberty Software Corp.	Vancouver	BC	www.LibertyODBC.com
LicenseTrack	800-366-2374	CDSI (Central Design Systems Inc.)	Santa Clara	CA	
LiveConnect	415-254-1900	Netscape Communications Corp.	Mountain View	CA	http://home.netscape.com
LiveWire	415-254-1900	Netscape Communications Corp.	Mountain View	CA	http://home.netscape.com
LoadRunner	408-523-9900	Mercury Interactive Corp.	Sunnyvale	CA	http://www.merc-int.com
Logic Works AOS (Application Object Server)	609-514-1177	Logic Works Inc.	Princeton	NJ	http://www.logicworks.com
Lotus Approach 3.0 for Windows	415-335-2200	Lotus Development Corp.	Cambridge	MA	
Lotus Data Access Tools for Windows 2.0	617-577-8500	Lotus Development Corp.	Cambridge	MA	
Lotus Notes 3.30	617-577-8500	Lotus Development Corp.	Cambridge	MA	
Lotus Notes ODBC Drivers for Windows	617-577-8500	Lotus Development Corp.	Cambridge	MA	
Lotus Notes ViP for Windows	617-577-8500	Lotus Development Corp.	Cambridge	MA	
Mac A&D 5.0	515-752-5359	Excel Software	Marshalltown	IA	
MacAnalyst and MacAnalyst/ Expert 5.0	512-752-5359	Excel Software	Marshalltown	IA	
MacDesigner and MacDesigner/ Expert 5.0	515-752-5359	Excel Software	Marshalltown	IA	
Magic 6.0	714-250-1718	Magic Software Enterprises Inc.	Irvine	CA	http://www.magic-sw.com
MainWin Studio	408-774-3400	Mainsoft Corp.	Sunnyvale	CA	http://www.mainsoft.com
Manufacturing Software System (MSS)	612-851-1500	Fourth Shift Corp.	Minneapolis	MN	
Media	800-276-9950	Speedware Corporation Inc.	San Ramon	CA	http://www.speedware.com
MediaAssets	408-748-7400	MediaWay Inc.	Santa Clara	CA	http://www.mediaway.com
MediaDB	408-748-7400	MediaWay Inc.	Santa Clara	CA	http://www.mediaway.com

Product	Phone	Company	City	St.	URL
MediaDB Application Development Kit	408-748-7400	MediaWay Inc.	Santa Clara	CA	http://www.mediaway.com
MemoPlus 3.0	301-251-0497	Rory Data International	North Potomac	MD	
Metamorph 3.5	216-631-8544	Thunderstone Software - EPI Inc.	Cleveland	OH	http://www.thunderstone.com
Micro Focus Cobol/SQL Transparency System 1.2	415-856-4161	Micro Focus Inc.	Palo Alto	CA	http://www.microfocus.com
Micro Focus Correlate 1.0	415-856-4161	Micro Focus Inc.	Palo Alto	CA	http://www.microfocus.com
Micro Focus Embedded SQL Toolkit for Microsoft SQL Server 2.0	415-856-4161	Micro Focus Inc.	Palo Alto	CA	http://www.microfocus.com
Micro Focus Object Cobol 4.0	415-856-4161	Micro Focus Inc.	Palo Alto	CA	http://www.microfocus.com
Micro Focus Workbench 4.0	415-856-4161	Micro Focus Inc.	Palo Alto	CA	http://www.microfocus.com
Microsoft Access	800-426-9400	Microsoft Corp.	Redmond	WA	http://www.microsoft.com
Microsoft Access Up-Sizing Tools	800-426-9400	Microsoft Corp.	Redmond	WA	http://www.microsoft.com
Microsoft SQL Server	800-426-9400	Microsoft Corp.	Redmond	WA	http://www.microsoft.com
Microsoft SQL Server	800-426-9400	Microsoft Corp.	Redmond	WA	http://www.microsoft.com
Microsoft Visual Basic	800-426-9400	Microsoft Corp.	Redmond	WA	http://www.microsoft.com
Microsoft Visual FoxPro 3.0	800-426-9400	Microsoft Corp.	Redmond	WA	http://www.microsoft.com
MitemView	408-559-8801	Mitem Corp.	Menlo Park	CA	http://www.mitem.com
Mosaic Bridge	216-631-8544	Thunderstone Software - EPI Inc.	Cleveland	OH	http://www.thunderstone.com
Multimedia Objects	214-239-0623	Metasolv Software Inc.	Dallas	TX	http://www.metasolv.com
My Accountant Integrated Accounting	407-786-2160	Information Designs Corp.	Altamonte Springs	FL	
MyData Control	412-681-4343	Apex Software Corp.	Pittsburgh	PA	
Navigator	415-254-1900	Netscape Communications Corp.	Mountain View	CA	http://home.netscape.com
NEO (including Joe)	415-960-3200	SunSoft (subsidiary of Sun Microsystems Inc.)	Mountain View	CA	http://www.sun.com/sunsoft/

Product	Phone	Company	City	St.	URL
NeoAccess	510-524-5897	NeoLogic Systems	Berkeley	CA	http://www.neologic.com
NetAnswer	617-621-0820	Dataware Technologies Inc.	Cambridge	MA	http://www.dataware.com
NetCraft	800-462-5328	SourceCraft Inc.	Burlington	MA	http://www.sourcecraft.com
NetDynamics	415-462-7600	Spider Technologies Inc.	Menlo Park	CA	http://www.w3spider.com
NEWT SDK 5.0	408-973-7171	NetManage Inc.	Cupertino	CA	http://www.netmanage.com
Nimbus Report Writer for Paradox	503-520-0504	20/20 Software Inc.	Beaverton	OR	http://www.twenty.com
Nomad 6.0	800-441-6878	Thomson Software Products Inc.	Norwalk	CT	http://www.thomsoft.com
O2 ODMG Database System	415-842-7000	O2 Technology	Palo Alto	CA	http://www.o2tech.com
O2Web	415-842-7000	O2 Technology	Palo Alto	CA	http://www.o2tech.com
Object Analyzer Utility	214-239-0623	Metasolv Software Inc.	Dallas	TX	http://www.metasolv.com
Object Integration Server (OIS)	508-323-8372	Ontos, Inc.	Lowell	MA	
Object Master	408-252-4444	ACI US Inc.	Cupertino	CA	http://www.aci-4D.com
Object PSE Pro	800-962-9620	Object Design Inc.	Burlington	MA	http://www.odi.com
Object Studio	617-221-2100	Easel Corp.	Burlington	MA	
ObjectCatalog	214-934-2496	ObjectSpace Inc.	Dallas	TX	http://www.objectspace.com
ObjectForms	800-962-9620	Object Design Inc.	Burlington	MA	http://www.odi.com
ObjectFrame	403-237-7333	ObjectWorks Inc.	Calgary	AB	http://www.objectworks.com
ObjectIQ	212-751-6302	Hitachi America Ltd.	New York	NY	
Objectivity/DB 4.0	415-254-7100	Objectivity Inc.	Mountain View	CA	http://www.objectivity.com
ObjectMetrics	214-934-2496	ObjectSpace Inc.	Dallas	TX	http://www.objectspace.com
Objectory	408-496-3600	Rational Software Corp.	Santa Clara	CA	http://www.rational.com
ObjectPro 1.0	800-4426861	Platinum Technology Inc.	Oakbrook Terrace	IL	http://www.platinum.com
ObjectReuser 1.0	212-751-6302	Hitachi America Ltd.	New York	NY	
ObjectStart 4.0	708-706-4000	Greenbrier & Russel Inc.	Schaumburg	IL	http://www.gr.com
ObjectStore 4.0	617-674-5000	Object Design Inc.	Burlington	MA	http://www.odi.com
ObjectStore DBconnect	617-674-5000	Object Design Inc.	Burlington	MA	http://www.odi.com
Ocelot2 – The SQL! 2.16	403-421-4187	Ocelot Computer Services Inc.	Edmonton, Alberta		

Product	Phone	Company	City	St.	URL
ODB/Server 2.0	800-441-6878	Thomson Software Products Inc.	Norwalk	CT	http://www.thomsoft.com
ODBC Driver	800-331-1763	Informix Software Inc.	Menlo Park	CA	http://www.informix.com
ODBC SDK	603-886-1400	Dharma Systems Inc.	Nashua	NH	
OmniConnect (formerly OmniSQL Gateway)	303-413-4000	Sybase Information-Connect Division	Boulder	CO	http://www.sybase.com
OmniCopy	800-726-1234	Praxis International Inc.	Framingham	MA	www.praxisint.com
OmniLoader	800-726-1234	Praxis International Inc.	Framingham	MA	www.praxisint.com
Omnis	415-571-0222	Blyth Software	Foster City	CA	http://www.blyth.com
Onyx Customer Center	206-557-6715	Onyx Software Corp.	Bellevue	WA	http://www.onyxcorp.com
OOwin/CRC	609-514-1177	Logic Works Inc.	Princeton	NJ	http://www.logicworks.com
Open Client/C Developers Kit	510-596-3500	Sybase Inc.	Emeryville	CA	http://www.sybase.com
Open M	617-621-0600	InterSystems Corp.	Cambridge	MA	
Open Server version 10.0	510-596-3500	Sybase Inc.	Emeryville	CA	http://www.sybase.com
Open Workgroup Repository (OWR)	617-863-5800	Manager Software Products Inc.	Lexington	MA	
OpenAccess ODBC Driver	408-453-1099	Automation Technology Inc. Development Kit	San Jose	CA	http://www.atinet.com
OpenPath RDA/Clipper	818-854-6288	Trilogy Technology International	City of Industry	CA	http://www.openpath.com
OpenPath RDA/ODBC	818-854-6288	Trilogy Technology International	City of Industry	CA	http://www.openpath.com
OpenScape	617-923-6500	OneWave Inc.	Watertown	MA	http://www.busweb.com
Optima++	508-287-1994	Powersoft Corp. (a Sybase company)	Concord	MA	http://www.powersoft.com
Oracle Book	415-506-7000	Oracle Corp.	Redwood Shores	CA	http://www.oracle.com
Oracle Browser	415-506-7000	Oracle Corp.	Redwood Shores	CA	http://www.oracle.com
Oracle Call Interfaces, Oracle Precompilers, and Oracle SQL*Module	415-506-7000	Oracle Corp.	Redwood Shores	CA	http://www.oracle.com
Oracle Cooperative Applications	415-506-7000	Oracle Corp.	Redwood Shores	CA	http://www.oracle.com

Product	Phone	Company	City	St.	URL
Oracle Data Query	415-506-7000	Oracle Corp.	Redwood Shores	CA	http://www.oracle.com
Oracle Express Analyzer	800-672-2531	Oracle Corp. — OLAP Products Division	Waltham	MA	www.oracle.com/products/olap/html
Oracle Express Objects	800-672-2531	Oracle Corp. — OLAP Products Division	Waltham	MA	www.oracle.com/products/olap/html
Oracle Express Server	800-672-2531	Oracle Corp. — OLAP Products Division	Waltham	MA	www.oracle.com/products/olap/html
Oracle Glue	415-506-7000	Oracle Corp.	Redwood Shores	CA	http://www.oracle.com
Oracle Objects for OLE	415-506-7000	Oracle Corp.	Redwood Shores	CA	http://www.oracle.com
Oracle Power Objects	415-506-7000	Oracle Corp.	Redwood Shores	CA	http://www.oracle.com
Oracle7 Release 7.3	415-506-7000	Oracle Corp.	Redwood Shores	CA	http://www.oracle.com
Oracle7 Workgroup Server	415-506-7000	Oracle Corp.	Redwood Shores	CA	http://www.oracle.com
Orbix	508-640-6868	Iona Technologies Inc.	Marlborough	MA	http://www.iona.com
Orpheus	719-260-9136	Turbopower Software Co.	Colorado Springs	CO	http://www.tpower.com
OT String Kit	212-988-6268	Objective Technologies Inc.	New York	NY	http://www.object.com
OutFox 2.92 and OutFoxPro 1.30	707-829-5011	Hilco Software	Sebastopol	CA	
Outline Navigator Object	214-239-0623	Metasolv Software Inc.	Dallas	TX	http://www.metasolv.com
Pablo	613-548-4355	Andyne Computing Ltd.	Kingston, Ontario		http://www.andyne.on.ca
PADLock	813-226-2600	PowerCerv Corp.	Tampa	FL	http://www.powercerv.com
Paradox 7	800-233-2444	Borland International Inc.	Scotts Valley	CA	http://www.borland.com
Parts Wrapper for Relational Databases	408-481-9090	ParcPlace–Digitalk	Sunnyvale	CA	http://www.parcplace.com
Patrol	713-918-8800	BMC Software Inc.	Houston	TX	
PC-Install for DOS and Windows	503-520-0504	20/20 Software Inc.	Beaverton	OR	http://www.twenty.com
Persistence Framework	513-662-2300	Cincom Systems Inc.	Cincinnati	OH	http://www.cincom.com
Personal Oracle7	415-506-7000	Oracle Corp.	Redwood Shores	CA	http://www.oracle.com
Phyla	805-484-9400	Mainstay	Camarillo	CA	
Pilot Decision Support Suite	617-374-9400	Pilot Software Inc.	Cambridge	MA	http://www.pilotsw.com

Product	Company	City	St.	URL
Pilot Designer	Pilot Software Inc.	Cambridge	MA	http://www.pilotsw.com
Pilot Desktop	Pilot Software Inc.	Cambridge	MA	http://www.pilotsw.com
Pilot Internet Publisher	Pilot Software Inc.	Cambridge	MA	http://www.pilotsw.com
Platinum Apriori	Platinum Technology Inc.	Oakbrook Terrace	IL	http://www.platinum.com
Platinum AutoSys	Platinum Technology Inc.	Oakbrook Terrace	IL	http://www.platinum.com
Platinum DBVision	Platinum Technology Inc.	Oakbrook Terrace	IL	http://www.platinum.com
Platinum Desktop DBA	Platinum Technology Inc.	Oakbrook Terrace	IL	http://www.platinum.com
Platinum Fast Unload for Oracle	Platinum Technology Inc.	Oakbrook Terrace	IL	http://www.platinum.com
Platinum for DOS	Platinum Software Corp.	Irvine	CA	
Platinum for Windows	Platinum Software Corp.	Irvine	CA	
Platinum InfoBeacon	Platinum Technology Inc.	Oakbrook Terrace	IL	http://www.platinum.com
Platinum InfoReports	Platinum Technology Inc.	Oakbrook Terrace	IL	http://www.platinum.com
Platinum InfoSession	Platinum Technology Inc.	Oakbrook Terrace	IL	http://www.platinum.com
Platinum InfoTransport	Platinum Technology Inc.	Oakbrook Terrace	IL	http://www.platinum.com
Platinum Paradigm Plus	Platinum Technology Inc.	Oakbrook Terrace	IL	http://www.platinum.com
Platinum Plan Analyzer for Oracle	Platinum Technology Inc.	Oakbrook Terrace	IL	http://www.platinum.com
Platinum Plan Anlayzer for DB2	Platinum Technology Inc.	Oakbrook Terrace	IL	http://www.platinum.com
Platinum RuleServer	Platinum Technology Inc.	Oakbrook Terrace	IL	http://www.platinum.com
Platinum SQL NT	Platinum Software Corp.	Irvine	CA	http://www.platinum.com
Platinum TSreorg	Platinum Technology Inc.	Oakbrook Terrace	IL	http://www.platinum.com
Playback	Compuware Corp.	Farmington Hills	MI	http://www.compuware.com
POET 3.0	POET Software Corp.	San Mateo	CA	http://www.poet.com
Point.Man	Spectrum Associates, Inc.	Woburn	MA	
Polyhedra	Polyhedra PLC	Milton Keynes		
Power Expert	AJJA Information Technology Consultants Inc.	Ottawa	ON	

Product	Phone	Company	City	St.	URL
PowerBuilder Desktop 5.0	508-287-1994	Powersoft Corp. (a Sybase company)	Concord	MA	http://www.powersoft.com
PowerBuilder Enterprise 5.0	508-287-1500	Powersoft Corp. (a Sybase company)	Concord	MA	http://www.powersoft.com
PowerBuilder Professional 5.0	800-395-3525	Powersoft Corp. (a Sybase company)	Concord	MA	http://www.powersoft.com
PowerClass	206-803-0378	ServerLogic Corp.	Bellevue	WA	
PowerFrame Framework Library	214-239-0623	Metasolv Software Inc.	Dallas	TX	http://www.metasolv.com
PowerFrame Security Library	214-239-0623	Metasolv Software Inc.	Dallas	TX	http://www.metasolv.com
PowerHouse	617-229-6600	Cognos Inc.	Ottawa, Ontario	ON	http://www.cognos.com
PowerHouse Client	617-229-6600	Cognos Inc.	Ottawa, Ontario	ON	http://www.cognos.com
PowerLock	206-803-0378	ServerLogic Corp.	Bellevue	WA	
PowerObjects	206-803-0378	ServerLogic Corp.	Bellevue	WA	
PowerPlay	617-738-1338	Cognos Inc.	Ottawa, Ontario	ON	http://www.cognos.com
PowerTool	813-226-2600	PowerCerv Corp.	Tampa	FL	http://www.powercerv.com
preVue	919-870-8800	Performance Awareness Corp.	Raleigh	NC	http://www.PACorp.com
preVue-C/S	919-870-8800	Performance Awareness Corp.	Raleigh	NC	http://www.PACorp.com
preVue-X	919-870-8800	Performance Awareness Corp.	Raleigh	NC	http://www.PACorp.com
PrintWorks VBX	914-354-8666	Bytech Business Systems Inc.	Pomona	NY	
Prism Change Manager	408-752-1888	Prism Solutions Inc.	Sunnyvale	CA	
Prism Directory Manager 2.0	408-774-2649	Prism Solutions Inc.	Sunnyvale	CA	
Prism Warehouse Manager 4.3	408-752-1888	Prism Solutions Inc.	Sunnyvale	CA	
ProCap 2.1	409-260-5274	Knowledge Based Systems Inc.	College Station	TX	http://www.kbsi.com
Process Engineer (PE)	713-623-0414	LBMS Inc.	Houston	TX	
ProdeaBeacon	612-942-1000	Prodea Software Corp.	Eden Prairie	MN	
Professional IDL 1.4	412-963-1843	Persistent Data Systems Inc.	Pittsburgh	PA	

Product	Phone	Company	City	St.	URL
Progress RDBMS	617-280-4000	Progress Software Corp.	Bedford	MA	
Progress Results	617-280-4000	Progress Software Corp.	Bedford	MA	
Progress version 8	617-280-4000	Progress Software Corp.	Bedford	MA	
ProIndex	800-454-2690	InfoSphere LLC	Pleasant Grove	UT	http://www.fiber.net/infosphere/
Prolifics	800-458-3313	Prolifics (a JYACC company)	New York	NY	http://www.prolifics.com/
Promax	713-777-3282	Inter-Data Systems Inc.	Houston	TX	
ProSim 2.1	409-260-5274	Knowledge Based Systems Inc.	College Station	TX	http://www.kbsi.com
ProtoGen+ Client/Server Suite	609-655-5000	ProtoView Development Corp.	Cranbury	NJ	http://www.protoview.com
ProtoView Interactive Diagramming Object	609-655-5000	ProtoView Development Corp.	Cranbury	NJ	http://www.protoview.com
ProtoView Interface Component Set (PICS)	609-655-5000	ProtoView Development Corp.	Cranbury	NJ	http://www.protoview.com
ProtoView Visual Help Builder	609-655-5000	ProtoView Development Corp.	Cranbury	NJ	http://www.protoview.com
ProVision Workbench	810-443-0055	Proforma Corp.	Southfield	MA	http://www.proformacorp.com/pvwhome.html
Quadbase-SQL Server 4.0	408-738-6989	Quadbase Systems Inc.	Santa Clara	CA	http://www.quadbase.com
Quality Works	617-969-3771	Segue Software Inc.	Newton Centre	MA	
QualityTeam	510-597-5800	Scopus Technology Inc.	Emeryville	CA	http://www.scopus.com
Query Maker for Delphi	415-563-3755	Strategic Edge	San Francisco	CA	
Query Maker for FoxPro	415-563-3755	Strategic Edge	San Francisco	CA	
Quest and Quest Reporter 3.0	415-321-9500	Centura Software Corp.	Menlo Park	CA	http://www.centurasoft.com
Quest Server	407-729-6004	Level Five Research	Melbourne	FL	http://www.L5R.com
Quick-E	702-831-5595	Inclination Software Inc.	Incline Village	NV	http://www.isinc.com
QuickFix-2	707-829-5011	Hilco Software	Sebastopol	CA	
QuickServer	415-903-1720	Wayfarer Communications Inc.	Mountain View	CA	http://www.wayfarer.com

Product	Phone	Company	City	St.	URL	
R&R Report Writer Xbase Edition for DOS 6.0	508-366-1122	Concentric Data Systems Inc.		Westboro		MA
R&R Report Writer Xbase Edition for Windows 6.5	508-366-1122	Concentric Data Systems Inc.	Westboro	MA		
R&R Report Writer Xbase Edition for Windows 7.0	508-366-1122	Concentric Data Systems Inc.	Westboro	MA		
r-tree Report Generator	573-445-6833	FairCom Corp.	Columbia	MO	http://www.faircom.com	
R:Base 5.5 ++ for DOS	206-649-9500	Microrim Inc.	Bellevue	WA	http://www.microrim.com	
R:Base 5.5 for OS/2 PM	206-649-9500	Microrim Inc.	Bellevue	WA	http://www.microrim.com	
R:Base 5.5 for Windows	206-649-9500	Microrim Inc.	Bellevue	WA	http://www.microrim.com	
R:Base SQL Engine 2.0 for Windows	206-649-9500	Microrim Inc.	Bellevue	WA	http://www.microrim.com	
R:WEB 1.0	800-628-6990	Microrim Inc.	Bellevue	WA	http://www.microrim.com	
Raima Database Manager (RDM)	206-557-0200	Raima Corp.	Issaquah	WA	http://www.raima.com	
Raima Object Manager (ROM)	206-557-0200	Raima Corp.	Issaquah	WA	http://www.raima.com	
Ramco Marshal	510-494-2939	Ramco Systems Inc.	Fremont	CA		
Raosoft Ezreport 2.7	206-525-4025	Raosoft Inc.	Seattle	WA	http://www.raosoft.com/raosoft/	
Raosoft Survey 2.7	206-525-4025	Raosoft Inc.	Seattle	WA	http://www.raosoft.com/raosoft/	
Raosoft Uadmin	206-525-4025	Raosoft Inc.	Seattle	WA	http://www.raosoft.com/raosoft/	
Raosoft Ufill	206-525-4025	Raosoft Inc.	Seattle	WA	http://www.raosoft.com/raosoft/	
Raosoft USurvey	206-525-4025	Raosoft Inc.	Seattle	WA	http://www.raosoft.com/raosoft/	
Rapid SQL	415-834-3131	Embarcadero Technologies Inc.	San Francisco	CA	http://www.embarcadero.com	
Rational Apex	408-496-3600	Rational Software Corp.	Santa Clara	CA	http://www.rational.com	
Rational Rose Family	408-496-3600	Rational Software Corp.	Santa Clara	CA	http://www.rational.com	
RC/21 6.1	802-253-4437	Vermont Database Corp.	Stowe	VT	http://www.eats.com/vermont	
RDSecure 1.1	301-251-0497	Rory Data International	North Potomac	MD		
Recital 7.3	800-873-7443	Recital Corp.	Danvers	MA	http://www.recital.com	

Product	Phone	Company	City	St.	URL
Red Brick Warehouse Enterprise Control and Coordination	408-399-3200	Red Brick Systems Inc.	Los Gatos	CA	http://www.redbrick.com
Red Brick Warehouse for Workgroups	408-399-3200	Red Brick Systems Inc.	Los Gatos	CA	http://www.redbrick.com
Red Brick Warehouse VPT 4.0	408-399-3200	Red Brick Systems Inc.	Los Gatos	CA	http://www.redbrick.com
Red Brick Warehouse xPP	408-399-3200	Red Brick Systems Inc.	Los Gatos	CA	http://www.redbrick.com
Relational Financial Systems (RFS)	215-576-1001	Skylight Systems, Inc.	Wyncote	PA	
Replic-Action	510-736-7704	Casahl Technology Inc.	Danville	CA	
Replication Agent for DB2	303-413-4000	Sybase InformationConnect Division	Boulder	CO	http://www.sybase.com
Replication Server 10	510-596-3500	Sybase Inc.	Emeryville	CA	http://www.sybase.com
ReportSmith 3.0	800-233-2444	Borland International Inc.	Scotts Valley	CA	http://www.borland.com
RFFLow 3	970-663-5767	RFF Electronics	Loveland	CO	
Roaster Developer	800-999-4649	Natural Intelligence Inc.	Cambridge	MA	http://www.natural.com
RP/Server	800-441-6878	Thomson Software Products Inc.	Norwalk	CT	http://www.thomsoft.com
RPCpainter	708-706-4000	Greenbrier & Russel Inc.	Schaumburg	IL	http://www.gr.com
RSA Business Solutions	514-344-2390	Randy Soule & Associates Inc.	TMR	Quebec	
S-Designor	800-395-3525	Powersoft Corp. (a Sybase company)	Concord	MA	http://www.powersoft.com
S-Designor AppModeler 5.1	800-395-3525	Powersoft Corp. (a Sybase company)	Concord	MA	http://www.powersoft.com
S-Designor MetaWorks 5.1	800-395-3525	Powersoft Corp. (a Sybase company)	Concord	MA	http://www.powersoft.com
Sales Analysis	206-522-0055	FourGen Software Inc.	Seattle	WA	http://www.fourgen.com
Sales Vision Framework for PowerBuilder 2.0	704-549-0609	Sales Vision Inc.	Charlotte	NC	http://www.salesvision.com
SalesTeam	510-597-5800	Scopus Technology Inc.	Emeryville	CA	http://www.scopus.com
Salvo	800-267-9991	Simware Inc.	Ottawa, Ontario		http://www.simware.com

Product	Phone	Company	City	St.	URL
Sapphire/Web	609-727-4600	Bluestone Inc.	Mount Laurel	NJ	http://www.bluestone.com
SAS System, The	919-677-8000	SAS Institute Inc.	Cary	NC	http://www.sas.com
SBT Professional Series	415-331-9900	SBT Accounting Systems	San Rafael	CA	
SBT VisionPoint	415-331-9900	SBT Accounting Systems	San Rafael	CA	
Scalable SQL	512-794-1719	Btrieve Technologies Inc.	Austin	TX	http://www.btrieve.com
Scalable SQL Developer's Kit	512-794-1719	Btrieve Technologies Inc.	Austin	TX	http://www.btrieve.com
SCP-II	800-622-5020	Zitel Corp.	Fremont	CA	http://www.zitel.com
Screen Design Kit 1.0	510-256-8401	Butler Computer Systems	Walnut Creek	CA	
Search'97	408-541-1500	Verity Inc.	Sunnyvale	CA	http://www.verity.com
SearchBuilder for PowerBuilder	613-238-1761	Fulcrum Technologies Inc.	Ottawa, Ontario		http://www.fulcrum.com
SearchBuilder for Visual Basic	613-238-1761	Fulcrum Technologies Inc.	Ottawa, Ontario		http://www.fulcrum.com
Secure SQLBase	847-673-0900	Dunn Systems, Inc.	Lincolnwood	IL	http://www.dunnsys.com
Select Enterprise	714-825-1050	Select Software Tools Inc.	Santa Ana	CA	http://www.select-software.com
Select OMT Professional	714-825-1050	Select Software Tools Inc.	Santa Ana	CA	http://www.select-software.com
Serveyor	617-273-9003	Cayenne Software Inc. (a Bachman and Cadre Co.)	Burlington	MA	http://www.cayennesoft.com
Service Call Management (SCM) 3.0	800-888-9600	ProAmerica Systems Inc.	Richardson	TX	
ServiceTeam	510-597-5800	Scopus Technology Inc.	Emeryville	CA	http://www.scopus.com
SilverClip SPCS 4.12	214-247-0131	SilverWare Inc.	Dallas	TX	http://rampages.onramp.net/~silver
SilverComm 3.04	214-247-0131	SilverWare Inc.	Dallas	TX	http://rampages.onramp.net/~silver
SilverComm C Async Library (SPCS) 4.05	214-247-0131	SilverWare Inc.	Dallas	TX	http://rampages.onramp.net/~silver
SilverFox for Windows 4.10	214-247-0131	SilverWare Inc.	Dallas	TX	http://rampages.onramp.net/~silver
SilverFox SPCS 4.05	214-247-0131	SilverWare Inc.	Dallas	TX	http://rampages.onramp.net/~silver
Silverrun Professional Series	201-391-6500	Computer Systems Advisers Inc.	Woodcliff Lake	NJ	http://www.silverrun.com
Silverrun-Enterprise	201-391-6500	Computer Systems Advisers Inc.	Woodcliff Lake	NJ	http://www.silverrun.com

Product	Phone	Company	City	St.	URL
SilverWare Windows Communications Tool Kit 5.01	214-247-0131	SilverWare Inc.	Dallas	TX	http://rampages.onramp.net/~silver
SimbaExpress	206-441-0340	Simba Technologies Inc.	Seattle	WA	http://www.simbatech.com
SmartER 2.0	409-260-5274	Knowledge Based Systems Inc.	College Station	TX	http://www.kbsi.com
SmartFieldPalette	212-988-6268	Objective Technologies Inc.	New York	NY	http://www.object.com
SmartTabs	214-239-0623	Metasolv Software Inc.	Dallas	TX	http://www.metasolv.com
SnagIt Twin Pack	517-333-2100	TechSmith Corp.	East Lansing	MI	http://www.TechSmith.com
SoDA	408-496-3600	Rational Software Corp.	Santa Clara	CA	http://www.rational.com
SoftTest	415-924-9196	Bender & Associates Inc.	Larkspur	CA	
Solution Series/ST	312-454-1865	Cyborg Systems, Inc.	Chicago	IL	http://www.cyborg.com
Spatial Query Server (SQS)	703-658-4000	Vision Int'nl, a division of Autometric Inc.	Alexandria	VA	http://www.autometric.com/auto/html/vision.html
SpeedEdit A.07	702-831-5595	Inclination Software Inc.	Incline Village	NV	http://www.isinc.com
Spider-Man	800-286-8000	Hyperion Software	Stamford	CT	http://www.hysoft.com
SQA LoadTest	617-939-3000	SQA Inc.	Woburn	MA	http://www.sqa.com
SQA Manager	617-939-3000	SQA Inc.	Woburn	MA	http://www.sqa.com
SQA Process	617-939-3000	SQA Inc.	Woburn	MA	http://www.sqa.com
SQA Robot	617-939-3000	SQA Inc.	Woburn	MA	http://www.sqa.com
SQA Suite	617-939-3000	SQA Inc.	Woburn	MA	http://www.sqa.com
SQL Accounting for Windows	201-765-0583	SPFC	Madison	NJ	
SQL Director 2.1	310-312-8099	Stro-Ware Inc.	Los Angeles	CA	
SQL Enterprise Manager	800-426-9400	Microsoft Corp.	Redmond	WA	http://www.microsoft.com
SQL Monitor	510-596-3500	Sybase Inc.	Emeryville	CA	http://www.sybase.com
SQL Secure 3.1	617-982-0200	BrainTree Technology Inc.	Norwell	MA	http://www.sqlsecure.com
SQL*C++	310-424-4399	MITI	Menlo Park	CA	http://www.miti.com
SQL*Debug	510-596-3500	Sybase Inc.	Emeryville	CA	http://www.sybase.com
SQL*Net V2	415-506-7000	Oracle Corp.	Redwood Shores	CA	http://www.oracle.com
SQL*Operator	206-644-2121	ISA Corp.	Bellevue	WA	http://www.halcyon.com/isacorp

Product	Company	Phone	City	St.	URL
SQL*PAD	ObjectWorks Inc.	403-237-7333	Calgary	AB	http://www.objectworks.com
SQL*TextRetrieval 2.0	Oracle Corp.	415-506-7000	Redwood Shores	CA	http://www.oracle.com
SQL–Programmer for Windows	Sylvain Faust Inc.	819-778-5045	Hull, Quebec		http://www.sfi-software.com
SQL–Sombrero/OCX for CT-Library	Sylvain Faust Inc.	819-778-5045	Hull, Quebec		http://www.sfi-software.com
SQL–Sombrero/OCX for DB-Library	Sylvain Faust Inc.	819-778-5045	Hull, Quebec		http://www.sfi-software.com
SQL–Sombrero/OCX for Oracle Call Interface	Sylvain Faust Inc.	819-778-5045	Hull, Quebec		http://www.sfi-software.com
SQL–Sombrero/VBX	Sylvain Faust Inc.	819-778-5045	Hull, Quebec		http://www.sfi-software.com
SQLBase Desktop	Centura Software Corp. (formerly Gupta Corp.)	415-321-9500	Menlo Park	CA	http://www.centurasoft.com
SQLBase Server	Centura Software Corp. (formerly Gupta Corp.)	415-321-9500	Menlo Park	CA	http://www.centurasoft.com
SQLBuddy	Objective Technologies Inc.	212-988-6268	New York	NY	http://www.object.com
SQLWindows	ACI US Inc.	415-321-9500	Cupertino	CA	http://www.aci-4D.com
SQR Workbench	MITI	415-326-5000	Menlo Park	CA	http://www.miti.com
STAR:Flashpoint	Sterling Software Frontware Division	415-802-7100	Redwood City	CA	
StarTrieve	SelectStar Inc.	800-326-5516	New York	NY	http://www.selectstar.com
STL<ToolKit>	ObjectSpace Inc.	214-934-2496	Dallas	TX	http://www.objectspace.com
SupportAbility SDK	South Wind Design Inc.	800-897-9463	AnnArbor	MI	http://www.swdi.com/
Supportability/BTI	South Wind Design Inc.	800-897-9463	AnnArbor	MI	http://www.swdi.com/
SupportTeam	Scopus Technology Inc.	510-597-5800	Emeryville	CA	http://www.scopus.com
Surfboard	Fulcrum Technologies Inc.	613-238-1761	Ottawa, Ontario		http://www.fulcrum.com
Sybase APT Workbench	Sybase Inc.	510-596-3500	Emeryville	CA	http://www.sybase.com
Sybase Interactive Query Accelerator	Sybase Inc.	510-596-3500	Emeryville	CA	http://www.sybase.com
Sybase Navigation Server	Sybase Inc.	510-596-3500	Emeryville	CA	http://www.sybase.com

Product	Phone	Company	City	St.	URL
Sybase SQL Anywhere	800-265-4555	Sybase Inc., Workplace Database Products	Waterloo, Ontario		http://www.watcom.on.ca
Sybase SQL Server	510-596-3500	Sybase Inc.	Emeryville	CA	http://www.sybase.com
Sybase web.sql	800-685-8225	Sybase Inc.	Emeryville	CA	http://www.sybase.com
Synchronicity 2.1	617-221-2100	Easel Corp.	Burlington	MA	
System Architect 3.1	212-571-3434	Popkin Software & Systems Inc.	New York	NY	http://www.popkin.com
Systems<ToolKit>	214-934-2496	ObjectSpace Inc.	Dallas	TX	http://www.objectspace.com
T-Base (DOS version)	214-231-9200	Videotex Systems Inc.	Dallas	TX	
T-Base for Windows	214-231-9200	Videotex Systems Inc.	Dallas	TX	
Tabex/2	412-741-1677	Treehouse Software Inc.	Sewickley	PA	http://www.treehouse.com
TalentSoft Web+	612-338-8900	TalentSoft	Minneapolis	MN	http://www.talentsoft.com
Tango	905-819-1173	EveryWare Development Corp.	Mississauga, Ontario		http://www.everyware.com
Team SQL/Developer	415-834-3131	Embarcadero Technologies Inc.	San Francisco	CA	http://www.embarcadero.com
Team SQL/Project	415-834-3131	Embarcadero Technologies Inc.	San Francisco	CA	http://www.embarcadero.com
TeamBuilder 1.0	617-221-2100	Easel Corp.	Burlington	MA	
TeamConnection	520-574-4600	IBM Software Solutions	Somers	NY	http://www.software.ibm.com
TeleUSE/DB 2.0	800-833-0085	Thomson Software Products Inc.	Norwalk	CT	http://www.thomsoft.com
Terabytes!	708-441-2901	InfoStructures Inc.	Highland Park	IL	http://www.infostruct.com
Teradata Database System for Unix	800-447-1124	NCR Corp.	Dayton	OH	http://www.ncr.com
Terrain	617-273-9003	Cayenne Software Inc. (a Bachman and Cadre Co.)	Burlington	MA	http://www.cayennesoft.com
TestDirector	408-523-9900	Mercury Interactive Corp.	Sunnyvale	CA	http://www.merc-int.com
TestMate	408-496-3600	Rational Software Corp.	Santa Clara	CA	http://www.rational.com
Texis	216-631-8544	Thunderstone Software - EPI Inc.	Cleveland	OH	http://www.thunderstone.com

Product	Phone	Company	City	St.	URL
Text DataBlade	800-331-1763	Informix Software Inc.	Menlo Park	CA	http://www.informix.com
TextWare 4.1	801-645-9600	TextWare Corp.	Park City	UT	
The Dispatcher-Real Time Dispatching	516-253-0921	TalTech Corp.	Dix Hills	NY	
Time and Budget Project Management	516-253-0921	TalTech Corp.	Dix Hills	NY	
TimeSeries DataBlade	800-331-1763	Informix Software Inc.	Menlo Park	CA	http://www.informix.com
Titanium	317-463-7200	Micro Data Base Systems Inc. (mdbs)	West Lafayette	IN	
Tivoli Management	512-794-9070	Tivoli Systems Inc. Environment (TME) 2.0	Austin	TX	
TM1	800-822-1596	TM1 Software	Warren	NJ	
TM1 Server	800-822-1596	TM1 Software	Warren	NJ	
Total FrameWork	513-662-2300	Cincom Systems Inc.	Cincinnati	OH	http://www.cincom.com
Total Recall	617-621-0820	Dataware Technologies Inc.	Cambridge	MA	http://www.dataware.com
TPM 96	800-933-7668	The Database Solutions Company	Richmond	VA	http://www.dbsol.com
Track for Windows 2.2	408-263-2703	Soffront Software Inc.	Milpitas	CA	http://www.soffront.com
Translator 1.0	515-752-5359	Excel Software	Marshalltown	IA	
TransPortal Pro 4.2	914-428-7200	The Frustum Group Inc.	White Plains	NY	
tRelational/DPS	412-741-1677	Treehouse Software Inc.	Sewickley	PA	http://www.treehouse.com
True DBGrid 4.0	412-681-4343	Apex Software Corp.	Pittsburgh	PA	
Tun Plus	415-675-7777	Esker Inc.	San Francisco	CA	http://www.esker.com
Ultimedia Manager	520-574-4600	IBM Software Solutions	Somers	NY	http://www.software.ibm.com
UniData RDBMS and Application Development Environment	303-294-0800	Unidata Inc.	Denver	CO	
Uniface Six	810-737-7300	Compuware Corp.	Farmington Hills	MI	http://www.compuware.com
Uniface WebEnabler	810-737-7300	Compuware Corp.	Farmington Hills	MI	http://www.compuware.com
Unify Vision 2.0	916-928-6400	Unify Corp.	Sacramento	CA	http://www.unify.com

Product	Phone	Company	City	St.	URL
UniKix	602-862-4455	UniKix Technologies (Bull Information Sys.)	Phoenix	AZ	http://www.unikix.com
UniSQL/4GE Application Development Environment	512-343-7297	UniSQL Inc.	Austin	TX	
UniSQL/M Multidatabase System 3.0	512-343-7297	UniSQL Inc.	Austin	TX	
UniSQL/X Database Management System 3.0	512-343-7297	UniSQL Inc.	Austin	TX	
Unitrac Version 4.1.1	800-864-8722	Unitrac Software Corp	Kalamazoo	MI	
uniVerse 8.3.3	508-879-3311	VMark Software Inc.	Westboro	MA	http://www.vmark.com
V-Test 4	508-462-0737	Performance Software Inc.	Newburyport	MA	http://www.pstest/.com
VBA Companion	412-681-4343	Apex Software Corp.	Pittsburgh	PA	
Velocis Database Server	206-557-0200	Raima Corp.	Issaquah	WA	http://www.raima.com
Velocis Web Server Gateway	800-327-2462	Raima Corp.	Issaquah	WA	http://www.raima.com
Vermont HighTest 2.0	802-848-1248	Vermont Creative Software	Richford	VT	
Vermont Test 2.0	802-848-1248	Vermont Creative Software	Richford	VT	
Vermont Test/Terminal 2.0	802-848-1248	Vermont Creative Software	Richford	VT	
Versant Argos 1.0	415-329-7500	Versant Object Technology Corp.	Menlo Park	CA	http://www.versant.com
Versant Internet Adapter	800-837-7268	Versant Object Technology Corp.	Menlo Park	CA	http://www.versant.com
Versant ODBMS 4.0	415-329-7500	Versant Object Technology Corp.	Menlo Park	CA	http://www.versant.com
Versant/M 1.0	415-329-7500	Versant Object Technology Corp.	Menlo Park	CA	http://www.versant.com
Visible Analyst Workbench 6.0	617-890-2273	Visible Systems Corp.	Waltham	MA	http://www.visible.com
VisiBroker for Java	415-286-1900	Visigenic Software Inc.	San Mateo	CA	http://www.visigenic.com
Visigenic ODBC DriverSet	415-286-1900	Visigenic Software Inc.	San Mateo	CA	http://www.visigenic.com
Visigenic ODBC SDK	415-286-1900	Visigenic Software Inc.	San Mateo	CA	http://www.visigenic.com
Visigenic ODBC Test Suites	415-286-1900	Visigenic Software Inc.	San Mateo	CA	http://www.visigenic.com
Vision/Web	916-928-6400	Unify Corp.	Sacramento	CA	http://www.unify.com

Product	Phone	Company	City	St.	URL
Vision:Flashpoint	404-551-8300	Sterling Software Inc.	Atlanta	GA	www.key.sterling.com
Vision:Legacy 5.1	404-551-8300	Sterling Software Inc.	Atlanta	GA	www.key.sterling.com
Vision:Northstar 2.0	404-551-8300	Sterling Software Inc.	Atlanta	GA	www.key.sterling.com
Visual Cafe Pro	800-441-7234	Symantec Corp.	Cupertino	CA	http://www.symantec.com
Visual dBASE 5.5	800-233-2444	Borland International Inc.	Scotts Valley	CA	http://www.borland.com
Visual Fax 1.02	617-621-9545	Stylus Innovation Inc.	Cambridge	MA	http://www.stylus.com
Visual Information Retrieval (VIR) DataBlade and Image Viewer	800-331-1763	Informix Software Inc.	Menlo Park	CA	http://www.informix.com
Visual Smalltalk 3.1	408-481-9090	ParcPlace-Digitalk	Sunnyvale	CA	http://www.parcplace.com
Visual Smalltalk Enterprise 3.1	408-481-9090	ParcPlace-Digitalk	Sunnyvale	CA	http://www.parcplace.com
Visual Thought 2.1	415-586-8700	Confluent Inc.	San Francisco	CA	
Visual Voice 3.0	617-621-9545	Stylus Innovation Inc.	Cambridge	MA	http://www.stylus.com
Visual/Recital	800-873-7443	Recital Corp.	Danvers	MA	http://www.recital.com
VisualAge C++ for OS/2 version 3.0	520-574-4600	IBM Software Solutions	Somers	NY	http://www.software.ibm.com
VisualAge for Smalltalk	520-574-4600	IBM Software Solutions	Somers	NY	http://www.software.ibm.com
VisualGen version 2.0	520-574-4600	IBM Software Solutions	Somers	NY	http://www.software.ibm.com
Visualizer	520-574-4600	IBM Software Solutions	Somers	NY	http://www.software.ibm.com
VisualWave	408-481-9090	ParcPlace-Digitalk	Sunnyvale	CA	http://www.parcplace.com
VisualWorks 2.0	408-481-9090	ParcPlace-Digitalk	Sunnyvale	CA	http://www.parcplace.com
VoysAccess	510-252-1100	Voysys Corp.	Fremont	CA	
Wallop Build-IT	415-341-1177	Wallop Software Inc.	Foster City	CA	http://www.wallop.com
Watcom SQL for Windows	519-886-3700	Sybase Inc.	Emeryville	CA	http://www.sybase.com
Watcom SQL Network Servers 4.0	519-886-3700	Sybase Inc.	Emeryville	CA	http://www.sybase.com
Watcom VX REXX Client/Server version 2.1	519-886-3700	Sybase Inc.	Emeryville	CA	http://www.sybase.com
Web DataBlade	800-331-1763	Informix Software Inc.	Menlo Park	CA	http://www.informix.com
Web Publisher	800-800-1997	askSam Systems	Perry	FL	http://www.asksam.com

Product	Phone	Company	City	St.	URL
WebBase Pro	805-962-2558	ExperTelligence Inc.	Santa Barbara	CA	http://www.webbase.com
WebDBC Corp.	206-812-0177	StormCloud Development	Seattle	WA	http://www.stormcloud.com
WebObjects	415-366-0900	NeXT Software Inc.	Redwood City	CA	http://www.next.com
WebOLAP	612-820-0702	Information Advantage Inc.	Minneapolis	MN	http://www.infoadvan.com/
WebTest	408-523-9900	Mercury Interactive Corp.	Sunnyvale	CA	http://www.merc-int.com
WestLake Imager for dBASE/ FoxPro/Paradox	503-520-0504	20/20 Software Inc.	Beaverton	OR	http://www.twenty.com
Wind/U 2.0	203-438-6969	Bristol Technology Inc.	Ridgefield	CT	http://www.bristol.com
WinGIS	360-738-2449	Progis Corp.	Bellingham	WA	http://www.wji.com/progis/ homepage.html
WinMap	360-738-2449	Progis Corp.	Bellingham	WA	http://www.wji.com/progis/ homepage.html
WinMAP SDK	360-738-2449	Progis Corp.	Bellingham	WA	http://www.wji.com/progis/ homepage.html
WinQL	304-328-0012	Data Access Corp.	Miami	FL	
WinRunner	408-523-9900	Mercury Interactive Corp.	Sunnyvale	CA	http://www.merc-int.com
WinSock SDK for Macintosh 3.0	408-973-7171	NetManage Inc.	Cupertino	CA	http://www.netmanage.com
wIntegrate Release 2.4	303-294-0800	Unidata Inc.	Denver	CO	
winVue	919-870-8800	Performance Awareness Corp.	Raleigh	NC	http://www.PACorp.com
Workflow Framework	513-662-2300	Cincom Systems Inc.	Cincinnati	OH	http://www.cincom.com
XDB Link 5.0	410-312-9300	XDB Systems Inc.	Columbia	MD	http://www.xdb.com
XDB QMT 3.0	410-312-9300	XDB Systems Inc.	Columbia	MD	http://www.xdb.com
XDB Workbench 5.0	410-312-9300	XDB Systems Inc.	Columbia	MD	http://www.xdb.com
XDB-Server 5.0	410-312-9300	XDB Systems Inc.	Columbia	MD	http://www.xdb.com
XDB-SQL RDBMS 4.0	410-312-9300	XDB Systems Inc.	Columbia	MD	http://www.xdb.com
Xprinter 3.0	203-438-6969	Bristol Technology Inc.	Ridgefield	CT	http://www.bristol.com
XRT/3d 2.1	416-594-1026	KL Group Inc.	Toronto, Ontario		http://www.klg.com

Product	Phone	Company	City	St.	URL
XRT/field 1.0	416-594-1026	KL Group Inc.	Toronto, Ontario		http://www.klg.com
XRT/gear 1.0	416-594-1026	KL Group Inc.	Toronto, Ontario		http://www.klg.com
XRT/graph 2.4	416-594-1026	KL Group Inc.	Toronto, Ontario		http://www.klg.com
XRT/table 2.2	416-594-1026	KL Group Inc.	Toronto, Ontario		http://www.klg.com
XRunner	408-523-9900	Mercury Interactive Corp.	Sunnyvale	CA	http://www.merc-int.com
ZyImage for Internet	800-544-6339	ZyLab International Inc.	Gaithersburg	MD	http://www.zylab.com
ZyImage Web Server	800-544-6339	ZyLab International Inc.	Gaithersburg	MD	http://www.zylab.com
ZyIndex for Internet	800-544-6339	ZyLab International Inc.	Gaithersburg	MD	http://www.zylab.com

Client/Server and Intranet
Standards Organizations

Internet Engineering Task Force
c/o Corporation for National Research
  Initiatives
Suite 100
1895 Preston White Drive
Reston, VA 22091

ISO
1, rue de Varembé
Case postale 56
CH-1211 Genève 20
Switzerland

The Open Group
11 Cambridge Center
Cambridge, MA 02142

Object Database Management Group
14041 Burnhaven Drive, Suite 105
Burnsville, MN 55337

Object Management Group, Inc.
Framingham Corporate Center
492 Old Connecticut Path
Framingham, MA 01701

W3 Consortium
Massachusetts Institute of Technology
Laboratory for Computer Science
545 Technology Square
Cambridge, MA 02139

Index

Executive Publisher: Katherine Schowalter
Editor: Robert M. Elliott
Managing Editor: Erin Singletary
Text Design & Composition: V&M Graphics

Designations used by companies to distinguish their products are often claimed as trademarks. In all instances where John Wiley & Sons, Inc., is aware of a claim, the product names appear in initial capital or ALL CAPITAL LETTERS. Readers, however, should contact the appropriate companies for more complete information regarding trademarks and registration.

This text is printed on acid-free paper.

This publication is designed to provide accurate and authoritative information in regard to the subject matter covered. It is sold with the understanding that the publisher is not engaged in rendering legal, accounting, or other professional service. If legal advice or other expert assistance is required, the services of a competent professional person should be sought.

Library of Congress Cataloging-in-Publication Data:
Linthicum, David S., 1962–
      David Linthicum's guide to Client/Server and intranet development
   / David S. Linthicum.
         p.   cm.
      Includes index.
      ISBN 0-471-17467-X (pbk.   :   alk. paper)
         1. Client/server computing.   2. Intranets (Computer networks)
      3. Application software—Development.   I. Title.
      QA76.9.C55L56   1997
      004'.36—dc21   97-3995
                                                                                                    CIP

Printed in the United States of America
10 9 8 7 6 5 4 3 2 1

David Linthicum's
Guide to Client/Server and
Intranet Development

David S. Linthicum

WILEY COMPUTER PUBLISHING

John Wiley & Sons, Inc.
New York • Chichester • Weinheim • Brisbane • Singapore • Toronto